THE REIGN AND REJECTION OF KING SAUL

SOCIETY
OF BIBLICAL
LITERATURE

DISSERTATION SERIES

David L. Petersen, Old Testament Editor
Charles Talbert, New Testament Editor

Number 118

THE REIGN AND REJECTION OF KING SAUL
A Case for Literary and Theological Coherence

by
V. Philips Long

V. Philips Long

THE REIGN AND REJECTION OF KING SAUL
A Case for Literary and Theological Coherence

Scholars Press
Atlanta, Georgia

THE REIGN AND REJECTION
OF KING SAUL

V. Philips Long

Ph.D., 1987
Cambridge University

BS
1325.2
.L59
1989

Advisor:
Dr. Robert P. Gordon

Library of Congress Cataloging in Publication Data

Long, V. Philips.
 The reign and rejection of King Saul : a case for literary and
 theological coherence / V. Philips Long.
 p. cm. -- (Dissertation series / Society of Biblical
 Literature ; no. 118)
 Includes bibliographical references.
 ISBN 1-55540-391-3 (alk. paper). -- ISBN 1-55540-392-1 (pbk. :
 alk. paper)
 1. Bible. O.T. Samuel, 1st, XIII-XV--Criticism, interpretation,
etc. 2. Bible. O.T. Samuel, 1st, IX-XI--Criticism,
interpretation, etc. 3. Saul, King of Israel, I. Title.
II. Series: Dissertation series (Society of Biblical Literature) ;
no. 118.
BS1325.2.L59 1989
222'.4306--dc20   89-37526
                                              CIP

Printed in the United States of America
on acid-free paper

Contents

Preface

Of the "seemingly infinite number of scholars absorbed by the narrative of the books of Samuel",[1] many would trace their involvement to an initial interest in the story of King Saul. At the outset of the present study, which represents an only slightly revised version of my Cambridge Ph.D. dissertation, I would like to express my thanks to those who have preceded me in the study of this intriguing biblical character. As will be apparent in the following pages, I have learned much from them, and not least from those with whom I occasionally disagree.

I would also like to thank those whose generosity made possible my years of research in Cambridge. I am deeply grateful to Corpus Christi College for the John Edward Purvis Scholarship and to the Tyndale House Council for the Tyndale Research Grant. The support and encouragement that I received from these two bodies was far more than merely financial. Thanks are also due to the Committee of Vice-Chancellors and Principals of the Universities of the United Kingdom, through whom I received an Overseas Research Student Award, and to the trustees of the National Christian Charitable Foundation, who enabled me to pursue a fourth year of research in Cambridge. I would also like to express my appreciation to the University Library and to the Tyndale House Library in Cambridge, to the Ecole Biblique et Archéologique Française in Jerusalem and to the Concordia Seminary Library in St Louis for making their extensive resources available to me. Finally, I would like to thank the editors of the Society of Biblical Literature Dissertation Series for accepting this manuscript for publication.

As regards matters of form, the following require mentioning. In the interest of economy, I have followed recent precedent by citing books and articles by author's name and short title throughout the work. A full bibliography of works referred to is supplied on pages 243-73, to which has been appended for the present publication a brief, selected list

---

[1] So P. R. Davies, in a book notice, *JSOT* 35 (1986) 125.

of significant works that have appeared since late 1985, the essential *terminus ad quem* of my research for this volume. Also in the interest of economy, the abbreviations p. and pp. are generally omitted except when referring to the present work. The use of double and single quotation marks follows the guidelines provided in the British edition of Kate L. Turabian's *A Manual for Writers of Research Papers, Theses and Dissertations* (London: Heinemann, 1982): direct quotations other than block quotations receive double quotation marks, while quotations within a quotation receive single (§5:9); single quotation marks are also used to set off words and concepts being discussed which are neither direct quotations nor translations of other sources (§5:10).

Many friends and scholars have stimulated, encouraged and assisted me along the way. Preeminent among them is Dr R. P. Gordon, who supervised my research and whose kindnesses towards me and my family have far exceeded the call of duty. I am deeply grateful for what he has taught me, and the quality of his life and scholarship will remain an encouragement and a challenge to me in the years to come. I would also like to express thanks to Professor M. Weinfeld, who served as interim supervisor during my brief sojourn in Jerusalem (Michaelmas Term, 1983), and who offered many helpful suggestions relating to my work. A particular word of thanks goes to Drs John Barton of Oxford University and David J. A. Clines of the University of Sheffield who served as formal examiners for the present work and whose comments and questions were consistently stimulating and gracious. Thanks are also due to Dr T. Longmann, III, to Mr Lee Capper and to Dr G. W. Long, all of whom read portions of the manuscript, and to Mrs Eunice Lanz for her able assistance in the preparation of the camera-ready copy. While all the aforementioned have contributed in one way or another to the improvement of this work, I alone am responsible for the deficiencies that remain.

Finally, I would like to thank my wife, Polly, and my children, Philip, Taylor, Andrea and Duncan. The two latter were born while the present work was in process, but all have shared in the labour of bringing it to term. Polly has not only offered valuable assistance in proofreading English and German portions of the text, but has shouldered more than her share of family duties in order to allow me the necessary time to write. Without her loving sacrifice and that of our children, completion of this work might have been possible, but certainly not probable. To dedicate this work to them would be but to give them what they already own. I therefore dedicate it to my parents, Dr and

Mrs George W. Long, who first taught me to love and study the Bible, and to my parents-in-law, Mr and Mrs Andrew H. Trotter, who have consistently encouraged their daughter and me in our pursuit of God's vocation to us.

Abbreviations

In addition to abbreviations of periodicals, reference works, serials, etc., this list includes books, such as commentaries, that are cited by author's name alone.

AASF	Annales academiae scientiarum Fennicae.
AB	Anchor Bible.
ABC	Grayson, A. K. *Assyrian and Babylonian Chronicles.* Texts from Cuneiform Studies 5. Locust Valley, NY: J. J. Augustin, 1977.
Ackroyd	Ackroyd, P. R. *1 Samuel.* CBC. Cambridge: University Press, 1971.
AfO	*Archiv für Orientforschung.*
AHw	Soden, W. von. *Akkadisches Handwörterbuch.* 3 vols. Wiesbaden: Otto Harrassowitz, 1965-81.
AJBA	*Australian Journal of Biblical Archaeology.*
AJBI	*Annual of the Japanese Biblical Institute.*
AJSL	*American Journal of Semitic Languages and Literatures.* [Continued after 1941 as *Journal of Near Eastern Studies.*]
AnBib	Analecta Biblica.
ANET	Pritchard, J. B., ed. *Ancient Near Eastern Texts Relating to the Old Testament.* 3rd ed. Princeton: Princeton University Press, 1969.
AnOr	Analecta Orientalia.
Ant.	Josephus' *Jewish Antiquities.* [Cited from *Josephus,* trans. by H. St. J. Thackeray and R. Marcus. Vol. 3. The Loeb Classical Library. London: Heinemann, 1928.]
AO	Der Alte Orient.
APOT	Charles, R. H. *The Apocrypha and Pseudepigrapha of the Old Testament.* 2 vols. Oxford: Clarendon, 1913.
ARI	Grayson, A. K. *Assyrian Royal Inscriptions.* 2 vols. Wiesbaden: Otto Harrassowitz, 1972-76. [References are to volume and paragraph, e.g. 2:13.]
ARM	*Archives royales de Mari.*
ASTI	*Annual of the Swedish Theological Institute.*
ATD	Das Alte Testament Deutsch
BA	*Biblical Archaeologist.*
BAR	*Biblical Archaeology Review.*
BASOR	*Bulletin of the American Schools of Oriental Research.*
BAT	Die Botschaft des Alten Testaments.
BBB	Bonner Biblische Beiträge.
BC	Biblischer Commentar über das alte Testament.

BDB	Brown, F., Driver, S. R., and Briggs, C. A., eds. *A Hebrew and English Lexicon of the Old Testament.* Oxford: Clarendon, 1907.
BeO	*Bibbia e Oriente.*
BEvT	Beiträge zur evangelischen Theologie.
BHH	Reicke, B. and Rost, L., eds. *Biblisch-Historisches Handwörterbuch.* Göttingen: Vandenhoeck & Ruprecht, 1966.
BHS	Elliger, K. and Rudolph, W., eds. *Biblia Hebraica Stuttgartensia.* Stuttgart: Deutsche Bibelstiftung, 1977.
Bib	*Biblica.*
Bijdr	*Bijdragen. Tijdschrift voor philosophie en theologie.*
Blaikie	Blaikie, W. G. *The First Book of Samuel.* Expositor's Bible. London: Hodder and Stoughton, 1892.
Budde	Budde, K. D. *Die Bücher Samuel.* KHC VIII. Tübingen: J. C. B. Mohr, 1902.
BZ	*Biblische Zeitschrift.*
BZAW	Beihefte zur *Zeitschrift für die alttestamentliche Wissenschaft.*
CAD	Gelb, I. J. et al., eds. *The Assyrian Dictionary of the Oriental Institute of the University of Chicago.* Chicago: Oriental Institute, 1964-.
CB	The Cambridge Bible for Schools and Colleges.
CBC	Cambridge Bible Commentary.
CBOTS	Coniectanea Biblica: Old Testament Series.
CBQ	*Catholic Biblical Quarterly.*
CML	Gibson, J. C. L. *Canaanite Myths and Legends.* Edinburgh: T. & T. Clark, 1977.
CMHE	Cross, F. M. *Canaanite Myth and Hebrew Epic.* Cambridge, MA: Harvard University Press, 1973.
COT	Commentaar op het Oude Testament.
CQR	*Church Quarterly Review.*
CTM	Calwer Theologische Monographien.
DH	Deuteronomistic History.
Dhorme	Dhorme, E. P. *Les livres de Samuel.* EB. Paris: J. Gabalda, 1910.
Driver	Driver, S. R. *Notes on the Hebrew Text and the Topography of the Books of Samuel.* 2nd ed. Oxford: Clarendon, 1913.
EB	Encyclopaedia Biblica.
EH	Exegetisches Handbuch zum Alten Testament.
ET	English translation.
ETR	*Etudes Théologiques et Religieuses.*
EvT	*Evangelische Theologie.*
FRLANT	Forschungen zur Religion und Literatur des Alten und Neuen Testaments.

KHC	Kurzer Hand-Commentar zum Alten Testament.
Keil	Keil, C. F. *The Books of Samuel*. Trans. by J. Martin. Grand Rapids: Eerdmans, 1973 reprint.
Kiel	Kiel, Y. שמואל א (ספר שמואל). Jerusalem: Mosad Harav Kook, 1981.
Kirkpatrick	Kirkpatrick, A. F. *The First Book of Samuel*. CB. Cambridge: Cambridge University Press, 1881.
KJV	*The King James Version of the Holy Bible.*
KK	Kurzgefaßter Kommentar zu den heiligen Schriften Alten und Neuen Testaments.
Klein	Klein, R. W. *1 Samuel*. WBC 10. Waco: Word, 1983.
Klostermann	Klostermann, D. A. *Die Bücher Samuelis und Könige*. KK. Nördlingen: C. H. Beck, 1887.
KV	Korte verklaring der Heilige Schrift.
LXX	Septuagint.
LXX^A	Codex Alexandrinus.
LXX^B	Codex Vaticanus.
LXX^L	The Lucianic manuscripts (boc$_2$e$_2$).
Mauchline	Mauchline, J. *1 and 2 Samuel*. NCB. London: Oliphants, 1971.
McCarter	McCarter, P. K. *1 Samuel: A New Translation with Introduction, Notes & Commentary*. AB 8. Garden City: Doubleday, 1980.
McKane	McKane, W. *I & II Samuel*. TBC. London: SCM, 1963.
MT	Massoretic Text.
MUSJ	*Mélanges de la Faculté Orientale, Université Saint-Joseph Beyrouth (Syrie).*
NAB	*The New American Bible.*
NASB	*The New American Standard Bible.*
NCB	New Century Bible.
NEB	*The New English Bible.*
NERT	Beyerlin, W. *Near Eastern Religious Texts relating to the Old Testament*. Trans. by J. Bowden. London: SCM, 1978.
NES	Near Eastern Studies.
NIV	*New International Version of the Holy Bible.*
OBO	Orbis Biblicus et Orientalis.
OED	*The Oxford English Dictionary.*
Or	*Orientalia.*
OTL	The Old Testament Library.
OTWSA	*Die Ou-Testamentiese Werkgemeenskap in Suid-Afrika.*
Proof	*Prooftexts: A Journal of Jewish Literary History.*
QJS	*Quarterly Journal of Speech.*
RA	*Revue d'assyriologie et d'archéologie orientale.*
RB	*Revue biblique.*
RQ	*Restoration Quarterly.*

RSV	*The Revised Standard Version of the Holy Bible.*
SAT	Die Schriften des Alten Testaments.
SBFLA	*Studii Biblici Franciscani Liber Annuus.*
SBLDS	Society of Biblical Literature Dissertation Series.
SBLSP	Society of Biblical Literature Seminar Papers.
Schultz	Schultz, A. *Die Bücher Samuel.* EH 8, 1. Münster: Aschendorff, 1919 [First Samuel].
Smith	Smith, H. P. *A Critical and Exegetical Commentary on the Books of Samuel.* ICC. Edinburgh: T. & T. Clark, 1899.
SMM	*Student Map Manual: Historical Geography of the Bible Lands.* Jerusalem: Pictorial Archive, 1979.
SSI	Gibson, J. C. L. *Textbook of Syrian Semitic Inscriptions.* 3 vols. Oxford: Clarendon, 1971-82.
ST	*Studia Theologica.*
Stolz	Stolz, F. *Das erste und zweite Buch Samuel.* ZBK, AT 9. Zürich: Theologischer Verlag, 1981.
Stoebe	Stoebe, H. J. *Das erste Buch Samuelis.* KAT VIII/1. Gütersloh: Gert Mohn, 1973.
StudBT	*Studia Biblica et Theologica.*
SVT	Supplements to *Vetus Testamentum.*
Syr.	Syriac (Peshitta).
SWGGU	*Sitzungsberichte der wissenschaftlichen Gesellschaft an der Johann Wolfgang Goethe-Universität Frankfurt am Main.*
Targ.	Targum.
TBC	Torch Bible Commentary.
TDOT	Botterweck, G. J. and Ringgren, H., eds. *Theological Dictionary of the Old Testament.* Trans. by J. T. Willis et al. Grand Rapids: Eerdmans, 1974-.
THAT	Jenni, E. and Westermann, C., eds. *Theologisches Handwörterbuch zum Alten Testament.* 2 vols. München: Chr. Kaiser Verlag/Zürich: Theologischer Verlag, 1971-1976.
Thenius-Löhr	Thenius, O. *Die Bücher Samuelis.* KeH 4. 3rd ed. Revised by M. Löhr. Leipzig: S. Hirzel, 1898.
TRu	*Theologische Rundschau.*
TUSR	*Trinity University Studies in Religion.*
TynB	*Tyndale Bulletin.*
UF	*Ugarit-Forschungen.*
USQR	*Union Seminary Quarterly Review.*
ÜSt	Noth, M. *Überlieferungsgeschichtliche Studien: Die sammelnden und bearbeitenden Geschichtswerke im Alten Testament.* 2nd, unaltered edition. Tübingen: Max Niemeyer, 1957.

VAWA	Verhandelingen der koninklijke Akademie van Wetenschappen. Amsterdam.
VT	*Vetus Testamentum.*
Vulg.	Vulgate.
WBC	Word Biblical Commentary.
WMANT	Wissenschaftliche Monographien zum Alten und Neuen Testament.
WO	*Die Welt des Orients.*
WTJ	*Westminster Theological Journal.*
ZAW	*Zeitschrift für die alttestamentliche Wissenschaft.*
ZBK	Zürcher Bibelkommentar.
ZDMG	*Zeitschrift der deutschen morgenländischen Gesellschaft.*
ZDPV	*Zeitschrift des deutschen Palästina-Vereins.*
ZPEB	*Zondervan Pictorial Encyclopedia of the Bible.*

Introduction

Perhaps no other major figure in the Old Testament presents as many difficulties to the biblical interpreter and theologian as Saul, the first king of Israel. Theologically, historically and literarily, Saul's character and career are shrouded in uncertainty. The central theological enigma revolves around the two seemingly irreconcilable facts that Saul is first elected by Yahweh and thereafter rejected by him. The tension thus created might be relieved somewhat if the specific nature of Saul's failing were presented with crystal clarity in the narrative, but in this area as much as any biblical scholarship has experienced difficulty in coming to a consensus. Adding to the tension is the apparent imbalance between the crime and the punishment, between Saul's 'sin(s)' and the severity of the sentence handed down by Yahweh through the mouth of his servant Samuel. Indeed, Saul at times seems quite taken aback by Samuel's harsh reaction to what appear to be at most minor infractions, and his puzzlement, shared in no small measure by the reader, elicits a degree of sympathy for the ill-fated king. He appears to be less a villain than a victim, and, indeed, one of the most recent interpretations of the Saul traditions sees him as just that — a victim of the "dark side" of God.[1]

Historically, the picture is no less perplexing, and the verdict rendered by Cannon in 1932 is still representative: "The events by which he [Saul] came to the throne are and will remain a mystery."[2] The basis for such a verdict is the apparently uncertain testimony of the Saul narratives themselves. It is almost universally believed, for example, that the biblical account of Saul's rise to the throne is a composite of two, or perhaps three, originally independent and mutually contradictory accounts, and so is "rather unconvincing as a statement of fact."[3] But herein lies a further enigma, as Evans explains:

---

[1] Gunn, *Fate*, 131 and *passim*.

[2] "Reign of Saul", 326.

[3] Licht, "Biblical Historicism", 107.

1

> The material in 1 Samuel devoted to Saul's rise and fall
> and the rise of David tantalizes the reader: even though
> confronting him with doublets, the telescoping of
> events, the lack of a clear chronological order, and the
> differing attitudes toward Saul and the monarchy more
> generally, it creates a strong impression that he is see-
> ing some reflexion of what actually transpired.[4]

But even when this "strong impression" is buttressed by further evidence, such as Hauer's hypothesis that 1 Samuel 9:1-11:15 may reflect
the actual course of events by which Saul extended his dominions,[5]
attempts at historical reconstruction still founder on the apparent logical
and literary inconcinnities.

It would seem from even these brief introductory remarks that if
answers to the theological and historical questions are to be found, the
literary issues must be resolved first. That is to say, since the biblical
literature is virtually our only source of information about Saul, proper
interpretation of the literary deposit is fundamental to any theologizing
or historical reconstructing that we may attempt with respect to Israel's
first king. Within the limitations of the present study, it will not be
possible to conduct a thorough investigation of Saul's reign and rejection from all three perspectives — viz. the theological, historical and
literary. Therefore, the primary focus will be upon literary questions,
though, given the religious, theological *Tendenz* of the present form of
the Saul traditions, literary interpretation will inevitably entail
theological discussion. Historical issues will be touched upon only
occasionally, where, for example, the verisimilitude of an account may
be at stake, or where historical information may enlighten our literary
and theological analysis. But insofar as historical judgements are often
based, at least in part, on perceived doublets, tensions, contradictions
and the like within the Saul material, any new insights on these literary
phenomena may have implications for future historical studies.

Both the delimitation and the order of treatment of the texts which
form the basis of the present study are dictated by our main interest in
the question of Saul's rejection. Part One will serve as an extended
preface to the major exegetical treatment of 1 Sam 13-15 in Part Two.
Since our approach is in the first instance literary, Chapter 1 of Part
One will consider recent advances in literary method as applied to bibli-

---

[4] "Historical Reconstruction", 61.
[5] "Saul's Dominions", 310.

cal narrative, with special emphasis on the 'poetics' of Hebrew narrative.[6] As a practical exercise, and also as an important preliminary to the exegesis of 1 Sam 13-15, Chapter 2 of Part One will investigate the relationship of the much-contested Gilgal episode, 13:(4b)7b-15a, to its immediate and wider contexts.[7] Part Two will consist of an integrated reading of 1 Sam 13-15, since these are the chapters which most directly and fully treat the issue of Saul's rejection.[8] Conclusions drawn from the study of these chapters as regards the narrative portrayal of Saul and the cause(s) of his rejection will then be tested in Part Three against the wider context of the Saul traditions, specifically the account of his rise in 1 Sam 9-11.

---

[6] Meir Sternberg's *The Poetics of Biblical Narrative: Ideological Literature and the Drama of Reading* (Bloomington: Indiana University Press, 1985) came into my hands too late to be drawn upon in the present work.

[7] The prevailing view is that the account of Saul's initiation of hostilities with the Philistines in ch. 13 originally lacked any reference to a rejection by Samuel in Gilgal, i.e. that 13:(4b)7b-15a have been introduced secondarily into the account.

[8] Our selection of 1 Sam 13-15 as the unit of initial and primary interest is not, of course, meant to imply that these chapters constitute an original unity. Nevertheless, the narratives of 1 Samuel may be analysed in various ways other than according to putative original units of tradition. They may be grouped according to content, formal characteristics, style and so on. R. Knierim ("Messianic Concept", 25), for example, chose 1 Sam 9-31 as the unit of investigation in his 1968 study not because he regarded these chapters as an original unity but because he considered that a certain "messianic" concept ran through them. He cited a degree of "formal justification" for the limits of his investigation in the "mere fact of Saul's first entrance in I Sam., ch. 9, and of his death in I Sam., ch. 31." By the same token, but on a smaller scale, 1 Sam 13-15 form a balanced unit representing Saul's reign from its official inception (13:1) to its definitive rejection (15:35); cf. D. Jobling ("Saul's Fall", 367), who has observed that this unit is "sharply delimited" by the regnal formula of 13:1 on the one hand and the account of David's anointing (16:1-13) on the other. As Jobling further observes, the two rejection passages "form an *inclusio* and direct the reader's interpretation of the material between them."

Part One

Preliminary Considerations: Theoretical and Practical

1

RECENT ADVANCES IN LITERARY METHOD AS APPLIED TO BIBLICAL NARRATIVE

General Considerations

Reflecting upon his early reactions to Old Testament historical criticism as practised in Germany in the nineteenth and early twentieth centuries, Gerhard von Rad wrote in 1966,

> Viele der monumentalen Monographien und Kommentare dieser Forschergeneration beschäftigten sich viel weniger mit dem Text, der Erzählung, wie sie dastand, als mit ihrer Entstehung, ihren literarischen, sagengeschichtlichen oder mythologischen Vorstufen.[1]

Von Rad acknowledged the great erudition and acumen exhibited in the exegesis of, for example, the *Urgeschichte* and the *Vätergeschichte* in Genesis, but he nevertheless recalled an early uneasiness with the predominant approach:

> ... es beunruhigte mich schon früh, daß bei dieser Art von Lesen und Lehren etwas nicht stimmte, solange die Bemühung fehlte, den Text nun auch ebenso präzis in seiner Letztgestalt und im Rahmen seines Kontextes zu verstehen.[2]

The task, as von Rad saw it, was "den Weg ... wieder zum Text in seiner Ganzheit zurückzufinden und vor allem das Sinngebäude der

---

[1] "Gerhard von Rad", 659.

[2] "Gerhard von Rad", 659. As early as 1938 von Rad ("Problem des Hexateuch", 9) was disturbed by the scant attention paid to the "endgültigen Jetztgestalt des Textes" by the documentary analyses of his day.

7

großen literarischen Komposition zu verstehen, in die der jeweilige Text ein Baustein ja auch nicht zufällig geraten war."[3]

Like the older disciplines of source and form criticism, the traditio-historical approach advocated by von Rad took as its *starting point* the genetic question "how did the text come to be?"[4] Nevertheless, von Rad marked an advance over previous scholarship as he perceived it, in that he exhibited in his writings "a fine literary sense for the story"[5] and was "always anxious to move beyond the mere reconstruction of earlier stages in the growth of the biblical text and to begin to listen to the redactor, to ask how *he* meant us to read his finished text, and what he was trying to tell us."[6] Thus, von Rad moved beyond the 'how' of textual origin to the 'what' of textual meaning. In so doing, he heralded a change of direction in OT studies which has become increasingly apparent in recent years.

The Rise of Synchronic Literary Criticism

The two decades since von Rad wrote the words quoted above have witnessed a shift in Old Testament scholarship from an almost exclu-sive concern with the *pre-history* of biblical texts to a greater interest in the *texts as they stand.* In his treatise on method in the study of the Old Testament, John Barton observes that

> the last twenty years have seen a wholly new movement in biblical studies. This is the development of what is often called 'text-immanent' exegesis, which looks for the meaning of biblical texts as we now meet them in our Bibles instead of trying to get back behind the finished form of the text to earlier stages....[7]

The rise in popularity of so-called synchronic approaches to the Old Testament may in part be attributed to a growing sense of the limited

---

[3] "Gerhard von Rad", 659-60.

[4] This is indicated, for instance, by von Rad's reference to *finding one's way back* to the text in its entirety. Moreover, even von Rad's monograph on the Hexateuch, quoted in n. 2 above, was, as Nicholson (*Interpreting the Old Testament*, 20) has observed, "almost exclusively concerned with only one of the various literary strata which the Hexateuch comprises, the so-called Yahwist document."

[5] Barr, "Story and History", 10.

[6] Barton, *Reading*, 47.

[7] *Reading*, 2.

theological and aesthetic results achievable through historical-critical methods alone.[8] It would be disingenuous, however, to deny that trends in secular literary criticism have also played their part. For that matter, Barton makes the point that "biblical studies have in reality nearly always been more closely related to literary studies of other kinds than biblical scholars acknowledge or realize."[9] The sources of influence upon the various forms of 'text-immanent' exegesis are often apparent from the titles used for the approaches in question: for example, biblical *rhetorical criticism*,[10] *structuralism*,[11] *post-structuralism* or *deconstruction*[12] and so on. In other cases, the flow of influence may be less apparent,[13] but the biblical scholar is well-advised, before adopting a literary method that seems attractive, to familiarize himself with the philosophical assumptions that may underlie the newer literary approaches.[14] In other words, one must beware of embracing a *method*, whatever its apparent merits, without first inquiring as to the theoretical *model* that underlies it. L. Alonso Schökel describes a method as "a defined and controllable way of proceeding", while a model is either "a system of elements constructed to give a unified explanation to a set of observed data" or "a system already known and tested in one field which

---

[8] On the limitations of historical-critical methods see, for example, James Muilenburg's critique of form criticism in "Form Criticism", 5-6; cf. Barton, *Reading*, 77-78, 105-106.

[9] Barton, *Reading*, 141; cf. 106. A large portion of Barton's book is concerned with demonstrating the truth of this observation as it pertains to two prominent kinds of 'text-immanent' exegesis, namely biblical *structuralism* and Brevard Childs' *canon criticism*.

[10] A convenient review of the interplay between secular rhetorical criticism and biblical studies is provided by V. K. Robbins and J. H. Patton, "Rhetoric and Biblical Criticism", 327-37. The seminal theoretical discussion for Old Testament studies was Muilenburg's "Form Criticism"; for further literature up to 1977, see B. O. Long, "Trends", 64, n. 3. Subsequent treatments of methodological issues include Kikawada, "Some Proposals", 67-91; Melugin, "Muilenburg", 91-100; Kessler, "Introduction", 1-27.

[11] A summary bibliography is provided by Long, "Trends", 64-65, nn. 5-6. Theoretical discussions since 1977 include Jobling, "Structuralism", 135-47; Culley, ed., *Perspectives*.

[12] A recent work which draws upon the nomenclature and philosophy of deconstruction is Miscall's *Workings of Old Testament Narrative*.

[13] E.g., Barton (*Reading*, 153-54, 202-204 and *passim*) demonstrates several significant parallels between B. S. Childs' *canonical* approach and the New Criticism of the English-speaking world, though Childs himself (*Introduction*, 74) is at pains to distinguish the two approaches.

[14] Cf. Gunneweg, "Anmerkungen", 253.

is transferred to a new field of investigation." Once adopted, the model "becomes an *a priori* form of the research and its method. To the model we commit ourselves; of the method we make use."[15]

Barton also stresses the distinction between model and method, or as he puts it, between theory and approach. He argues that thorough-going structuralism, for example, involves basic philosophical assumptions that the historically-interested Old Testament scholar may find unacceptable, viz. "counter-intuitive" tendencies such as "its unreasonable hatred of authorial intention, referential meaning, and the possibility of paraphrase or restatement."[16] But while warning of the danger of uncritically imbibing the philosophies underlying some of the newer literary approaches, Barton nevertheless concludes that, even in the case of structuralism, as long as the biblical scholar remains cool towards its "claim to provide a universal theory of literature"[17] and "is prepared to sit lightly to its ideological commitment and illusions of grandeur",[18] he may have much to gain from a "text-centred approach".[19]

The common denominator among the various text-centred approaches, as the name implies, is a zeal to take more seriously the *Letztgestalt*, or, as von Rad also put it, the *Jetztgestalt* of the text. But this raises a difficult question for Old Testament studies today — how are the newer synchronic approaches to be related to their diachronic predecessors?

On the Interplay of Synchronic and Diachronic Concerns

In his presidential address to the 1983 meeting of the International Organization for the Study of the Old Testament (IOSOT), Alonso Schökel enumerated three possible but, as he sees it, undesirable relationships between the newer and the more traditional methods of exegesis. The first, an extreme position, is that of *mutual condemnation* in which the traditional biblical scholar accuses the modern literary critic of "analysing works which never existed", while the literary critic

---

[15] "Of Methods", 4-5.

[16] Barton, *Reading*, 191. For a discussion of these same tendencies in New Criticism (and hence in canon criticism), see *Reading*, 181-84.

[17] *Reading*, 180.

[18] *Reading*, 190.

[19] *Reading*, 193.

counters that the other is "reconstructing a process which never took place".[20] A second, and equally extreme, approach

> would be that of *courteous non-communication*, some-
> what like two neighbours who salute in passing but
> never stop to talk. Shyness, or exaggerated respect, a
> measure of fear, or perhaps a sense of self-sufficiency
> makes them keep at a polite distance from one another
> and avoid any sort of personal involvement.

The third possibility, quite similar to the second, is the "relatively peaceful one of *division of labour* according to different criteria" where we "resign ourselves to working in adjacent but sound-proof rooms". For his part, Alonso Schökel favours none of the above options, but rather calls for *dialogue*, "even if it should lead to open controversy".[21]

The point of Alonso Schökel's plea may be illustrated by likening the various critical disciplines to members of a family. Family members are not all alike; each has his own interests and abilities and his own way of looking at things. When confronted by a given set of circumstances, each will view it from his own perspective and approach it with his own set of expectations. Opinions will inevitably vary, but if the issue is an important one and if harmony within the family is to be maintained, some sort of consensus must be reached. Discussion and compromise will be necessary. Occasionally, one member may perceive the issue more clearly than the others, so that his opinion is ultimately vindicated. More often than not, however, the issue is complex and the clearest picture is attained when the insights of all the members are given due weight in arriving at a consensus. It never bodes well for a family when one member so dominates the others that his judgements are always unquestioningly accepted.

As our opening quotations from von Rad suggest, it has until recently been the diachronic members of the Old Testament family that have occupied positions of almost unquestioned dominance. Today, however, perhaps in reaction to this former imbalance, there appears to be a danger in some quarters of swinging to the opposite extreme. Some of today's literary critics are allowing literary interests so to eclipse all concern with historical questions that they appear to feel lit-

---

[20] Alonso Schökel, "Of Methods", 7.

[21] "Of Methods", 8. Similarly, G. W. Coats writes: "we cannot afford the handicap of compartmentalizing narrative research into various, competing schools" ("On Narrative", 138; cf. 141).

tle need for dialogue with the more traditional disciplines.[22] Fortunately, however, there are also scholars who are showing how insights derived from an increased sensitivity to literary aspects of the biblical text can be enlisted in the service of what remain essentially historically-oriented interpretations.[23] It is the view of this writer that it is neither necessary nor prudent to think of literary interpretation and historical-critical exegesis as unrelated or even antithetical approaches to the biblical text. This point has been given forceful expression recently by Charles Conroy:

> It is not a question, then, of "literary versus historical" in the sense of an either/or antagonism, but rather of working towards a responsible integration of the two areas of scholarly endeavour, while taking into account the particular nature of the text one happens to be studying. Just as historical criticism has been, and remains, essential for biblical study, so too a reasonable acquaintance with the theoretical and practical aspects of linguistics and literary study should be seen as indispensable in today's cultural situation. It will no longer do to regard such matters as harmless eccentricities or as subjective and non-scientific aberrations. Indeed, to persist in ignoring the possible literary dimension of a biblical text is profoundly contrary to the scholarly spirit, since it means closing one's eyes to an aspect of the reality one is studying. Certain biblical texts are narratives, not by a subjective decision of the interpreter but by their literary nature.[24]

Conroy's references to the *possible* literary dimension of biblical texts and to the narrative character of *certain* biblical texts brings up an important point requiring clarification. The contention that the Old Testament may be read as literature should not be understood to imply that the entire corpus is 'literary' in the same sense or to the same extent. Confusion has arisen in biblical studies precisely because the terms 'literature' and 'literary' are used in a number of different senses, and it is not always clear which is meant.[25] In a very general way, of

---

[22] Cf. the note of caution sounded by Nicholson in *Interpreting the Old Testament*, esp. 19-24.

[23] See, for example, our discussions of recent work by Loader (p. 16 n. 42 below) and Moberly (pp. 18-20).

[24] "Literary Analysis", 55.

[25] Cf. Ryken, *Literature*, 13: "There is perhaps no area of literature where careful definition is as important as in the study of biblical literature,

course, the entire Old Testament qualifies as literature simply by virtue of its being a written document. But this is not what one normally means when one speaks of a work of literature. David Robertson, in *The Old Testament and the Literary Critic*, draws a helpful distinction between 'pure' (imaginative, non-utilitarian) literature and 'applied' (utilitarian) literature. Robertson acknowledges that "the Bible was originally written as applied literature: as history, liturgy, laws, preaching, and the like" (3). Curiously, however, he adopts as his own "fundamental assumption, made at the outset as a self-conscious decision, ...that the Old Testament is to be viewed as 'pure' or imaginative literature".[26] Now, it may be proper and helpful, as a methodological *first step*, to approach a biblical narrative *as if it were* purely imaginative literature; such an approach encourages attentiveness to the texture and details of the text and to the possible coherence and significance of the selection, organization and presentation of the material. But this is a quite different thing from asserting that the Old Testament *is in fact* purely imaginative literature and, therefore, by definition non-referential.[27] Such an assertion may be true of some portions of the Old Testament,[28] but certainly not all. The error in such a procedure is that the *method* (or the first step of the method), viz. the literary analysis, is allowed to dictate the *theoretical model*, viz. the Old Testament as purely imaginative literature, rather than deriving the theoretical model from an inductive study of the text.

A less restrictive approach to the literary character of the Old Testament is advocated by A. Berlin in her article "On the Bible as Literature". According to Berlin, the concept of literature should not be limited to imaginative or non-referential works; literature cannot simply be equated with fiction or folklore. "Some histories, sermons, etc. may qualify as literature; others do not."[29] The point is that the question of

---

and a common failing in books and academic courses on the literature of the Bible is lack of precise definition. It is inaccurate to assume that everything in the Bible is literary in nature and intention."

[26] So G. M. Tucker, from the foreward to Robertson's book, p. vii.

[27] See, in this regard, Barton's critique (*Reading*, 160-67) of H. W. Frei's non-referential theory of biblical narrative texts.

[28] Licht (*Storytelling*, 123-28), for example, finds the 'historical' component lacking or minimal in Jonah, Ruth, Esther, etc., though some scholars would want to contest this judgement at various points. Cf. also Barton, *Reading*, 165.

[29] "Bible as Literature", 324. This is an important point and one that seems well-founded; the 15th edition of the *Encyclopædia Britannica*, for

literariness cannot "be decided on the basis of function, nor on how the work identifies itself."[30] Rather, it is the "artful verbal expression and compelling ideas" of the Bible that ultimately qualify it as literature.[31]

At the heart of this debate is the ontological question, What is the Old Testament? It is not only in the domain of historical criticism that the growing interest in literary approaches to the Bible has caused apprehension. Various scholars have expressed concern that a literary approach might obscure what is in their opinion the Old Testament's essential nature, namely its religious and theological character.[32] But again, an "either/or antagonism" seems unnecessary. As Robert Alter has observed, the point is simply that "in its abundant narrative and poetic portions" the Old Testament "uses manifestly literary means to serve chiefly religious — it might be more accurate to call them, covenantal — ends."[33] "Far from neglecting the Bible's religious character", critical discussion of the literary artistry of the biblical text "focuses attention on it in a more nuanced way",[34] so that to neglect the "artful devices" of Old Testament narrative may be to "condemn ourselves to reading the stories badly."[35] In short, an increased appreciation of the literary mechanisms of a text — *how* a story is told — often becomes the avenue of greater insight into the theological, religious and even historical significance[36] of the text — *what* the story means.[37]

---

example, includes an article entitled "literature, non-fictional prose" as well as one entitled "literature, art of".

[30] "Bible as Literature", 323-324.

[31] "Bible as Literature", 324. Cf. Ryken's "working definition of literature" as "an interpretive presentation of experience in an artistic form" (*Literature*, 13).

[32] See, for example, the debate between Kugel and Berlin in *Prooftexts* (i.e. Kugel, "Bible and Literary Criticism"; Berlin, "Bible as Literature"; Kugel, "Kugel Responds"). Cf. also M. Fishbane's evaluation of "Recent Work on Biblical Narrative".

[33] Alter, "How Convention Helps", 116.

[34] Alter, *Art*, 12.

[35] Alter, "How Convention Helps", 117.

[36] Though Alter's introduction of the term 'prose fiction' into discussions of biblical narrative is potentially confusing, it is apparent from his analysis of the story of Ehud's assassination of Eglon (Judg 3) that he does not regard the use of the technical resources of prose fiction as *necessarily* excluding a historical element: "In all this, as I have said, it is quite possible that the writer faithfully represents the historical data without addition or substantive embellishment. The organization of the narrative, however, its lexical and syntactic choices, its small shifts in point of view, its brief

Poetics and Interpretation

Of the various literary approaches that are finding advocates today, one of the more promising is that which concerns itself with the 'poetics' of Hebrew narrative. Many of Alter's observations, cited above, are of a poetic nature. Another recent contributor to this field of investigation, Adele Berlin, defines poetics as "an inductive science that seeks to abstract the general principles of literature from many different manifestations of those principles as they occur in actual literary texts." Its essential aim is not "to elicit meaning from a text" but rather "to find the building blocks of literature and the rules by which they are assembled." Thus, "poetics is to literature as linguistics is to language. That is, poetics describes the basic components of literature and the rules governing their use. Poetics strives to write a grammar, as it were, of literature."[38]

The goal of poetics is not, therefore, the interpretation of individual texts — that is more properly the task of rhetorical criticism. But poetics supports interpretation. Just as the student of a foreign language, lacking as he does the implicit grammatical sense of a native speaker, must learn the grammar and conventional modes of expression of his new language in order to comprehend individual sentences, so the student of 'foreign' literature — literature composed in a different cultural and/or temporal milieu — must learn what he can of the literary 'grammar' — the operative poetic conventions of the unfamiliar literature — in order properly to understand individual texts.

In the case of ancient Hebrew *poetry*, it has long been recognized that the operative poetic conventions differ markedly from those that

---

but strategic uses of dialogue, produce an imaginative reenactment of the historical event, conferring upon it a strong attitudinal definition and discovering in it a pattern of meaning. It is perhaps less historicized fiction than fictionalized history — history in which the feeling and the meaning of events are concretely realized through the technical resources of prose fiction" (*Art*, 41). On the relationship of history and fiction in Old Testament narrative, cf. also Lasine, "Fiction"; Oeming, "Fiktionen"; Fackre, "Narrative Theology"; Zakovitch, "Story"; Momigliano, "Biblical Studies"; Levenson, "1 Samuel 25".

[37] Alter speaks of "a complete interfusion of literary art with theological, moral, or historiosophical vision, the fullest perception of the latter dependent on the fullest grasp of the former" (*Art*, 19; cf. 179).

[38] *Poetics*, 15.

characterize modern, western poetry. It has taken rather longer for biblical scholars to come to the same conviction regarding Hebrew *prose*,
or narrative, perhaps because of the less obviously *literary* character of
prose as opposed to poetry. Thus, while considerable energy has been
expended in the interest of recovering some of the poetic conventions
governing ancient Hebrew prosody, the development of a poetics of
Hebrew narrative is still in its infancy.[39]

One way in which the study of narrative poetics distinguishes itself
from other modern literary approaches such as structuralism, which also
concerns itself with the *mechanisms* of literature, is in its decidedly
historical perspective. While recognizing that there are "elements of
continuity or at least close analogy in the literary modes of disparate
ages",[40] so that many of the insights and analytical procedures of modern literary and linguistic theory may profitably be applied to biblical
narratives, poetics concerns itself primarily with the particularities of a
specific literary corpus. Thus, a poetics of biblical Hebrew narrative
seeks to discover "the modes of literary communication that were shared
by Hebrew storyteller and audience" in biblical times.[41] Poetic criticism is more than a theory of reading. Its aim is not simply to *devise*
(or invent) conventions whereby Hebrew narrative texts can be read, but
rather to *discover* and *describe* those literary conventions which appear
to be actually operative in the biblical texts — viz., that "distinctive set
of narrative procedures which for readers of a later era has to be
learned."[42] In short, poetics seeks to provide the means of naturalizing

---

[39] Recent contributions to this field by Alter and Berlin include, in
addition to their major works already cited, Alter's "Sacred History and Prose
Fiction" and Berlin's "Characterization in Biblical Narrative: David's
Wives". Earlier book-length treatments of issues of poetic interest include
Licht's *Storytelling in the Bible* and Bar-Efrat's העיצוב האמנותי של הסיפור
במקרא (=*The Art of the Biblical Story*). An English abstract of Bar-Efrat's
Hebrew University dissertation, upon which his book is based, is available
in *idem*, "Literary Modes and Methods in the Biblical Narrative"; see also
idem, "Some Observations on the Analysis of Structure in Biblical
Narrative". Works treating literary aspects of both Old and New Testament
include Caird's *Language and Imagery of the Bible* and Ryken's *Literature of
the Bible*.

[40] Alter, "How Convention Helps", 117.

[41] Alter, "How Convention Helps", 117.

[42] Alter, *Art*, 188. A good example of a historically-oriented, literary approach is J. A. Loader's recent work on Ecclesiastes, *Polar Structures
in the Book of Qohelet*. Loader's thesis is summarized by Barton (*Reading*,
130) as follows: "None of Qoheleth's sayings can be properly understood,
unless it is seen that the book is so constructed that another, opposed say-

ancient texts according to historically appropriate criteria. Its goal is a historical one — the recovery, so far as possible, of an ancient literary competence.[43]

Such a task would, of course, be simpler and the results more certain if a much larger corpus of Hebrew narratives were available. But, barring some dramatic archaeological discovery, the quantity of evidence is not likely to change much.[44] Nevertheless, so long as we bear in mind the limited scope of the evidence and remain commensurately tentative about the results achieved, the quest to improve our understanding of the workings of ancient Hebrew narrative is a valid one.[45] To refuse even to make the effort, simply because of the risks involved, is to run an even greater risk of reading the narratives according to conventional understandings completely foreign to them.[46]

---

ing is to be read in antithesis to it." Although Loader employs some structuralist techniques and terminology, Barton points out that he is not a true structuralist; he "merely adds structuralist ideas to the historical-critical tool-box":

> Loader is plainly quite concerned with the intentions of Qoheleth, the author, and he is anxious to integrate his own work into the wider context of the study of ancient Near Eastern wisdom literature. We may say that, on his view, Qoheleth's intentions are manifested in the structure of his work as much as in any individual saying within it. The book can be understood only if its shape or structure is taken full account of, and precisely analysed. If this is true — as it may well be — then it is an adequate answer to a source-critical analysis, which would see contradictions between different sayings as evidence of more than one author. But (and this is the important point) it is essentially an answer on the same terms. Loader is saying, in fact, that Ecclesiastes has been misread because scholars have failed to see that the repertoire of techniques available to a wise man in post-exilic Israel included apparent self-contradiction in the interests of relativizing traditional dogmas. This is a historical suggestion, which if true undermines other historical suggestions,.... (pp. 130-31)

[43] On the notion of ancient literary competence, see esp. Berlin, "Bible as Literature", 326; cf. Kugel, "Bible and Literary Criticism", 220-21; Alter, *Art*, 185, 188.

[44] Comparative ancient Near Eastern literature, used with caution, can sometimes provide useful insights, as, for instance, in the case of the Ugaritic mythical texts *vis-à-vis* Hebrew poetry.

[45] Cf. Alter, "How Convention Helps", 118.

[46] Cf. Alter's criticism of this tendency in some structuralist interpretations: "As elsewhere in the academy, the manifest influence of the

To sum up our discussion so far: we have observed 1) that what is needed in response to the recent interest in various forms of text-immanent exegesis in Old Testament studies is not so much a paradigm shift, where one theoretical model is discarded to make room for another, but increased dialogue among the different members of the Old Testament critical family; 2) that literary and historical approaches to Old Testament narrative need not and should not be regarded as unrelated or even antithetical disciplines; and 3) that poetics, which concerns itself with discovering and describing literary conventions that were operative within a specific literary corpus, offers a promising means of combining literary and historical interests. In short, what we are advocating is a synthetic exegetical approach based on a more complex theoretical model and open to fresh intuitions on both the diachronic and synchronic levels of inquiry.

Moberly on Method

An exemplary demonstration of how literary, theological and historical concerns can be combined in a more holistic exegetical approach has been provided by R. W. L. Moberly in his book entitled *At the Mountain of God: Story and Theology in Exodus 32-34*.[47] In his programmatic first chapter, Moberly begins on a welcome note by rejecting any exegetical model that singles out either a literary or a historical-critical approach as "the correct method".[48] He warns, moreover, of the dangers involved in treating historical and literary study as wholly independent disciplines:

> One must not allow a kind of schizophrenia within the
> biblical exegete whereby he does his historical-critical
> research on the one hand and his literary and theological
> exegesis on the other, and either does not see how, or
> feels himself under no obligation, to bring together
> these two approaches to form a coherent understanding
> of the text. The phoenix of a conservatism which sim-

vogue of Structuralism on these Bible scholars [i.e. the younger generation of literary critics] has not been a very fruitful one; and one too often encounters in their work rather simple superimpositions of one or another modern literary theory on ancient texts that in fact have their own dynamics, their own distinctinve conventions and characteristic techniques" (*Art*, 15).

[47] The book is a revision of Moberly's 1981 Cambridge dissertation.

[48] *Mountain*, 22. Cf. Barton, *Reading*, 5, 204-207, and *passim*.

ply studies the final text and eschews any kind of historical criticism might swiftly arise from the ashes. The responsible interpreter must deal with every aspect and dimension of the the text he is seeking to interpret.[49]

The crucial issue, as Moberly sees it (and as we have suggested above),
is to discover "how to combine and hold together these two approaches".[50]

While "a diversity of texts will necessarily require a flexibility of
treatment",[51] Moberly proposes as a general rule that "a rigorous examination of the final text, treated in its own right as a literary and theological composition" should methodologically precede any attempt to
uncover the text's pre-history. The logic of this proposal becomes apparent when we consider that where independent sources of a given text
have not survived, as is most often the case in the Old Testament, the
"reconstruction of sources is ... entirely dependent upon unevennesses
and difficulties in the present text — doublets, contradictions, anachro-
nisms, variant linguistic usages, divergent theological emphases, etc."
The problem in such a situation, of course, "is to determine what constitutes a genuine unevenness."[52] We may illustrate this point by con-
trasting two divergent interpretations of Gen 7:17-20 recounted by
Moberly in his discussion of Hebrew narrative style.

Richard Simon, in his *Histoire critique du Vieux Testament*, cited
the repeated references to the rising of the waters in Gen 7:17, 18, 19,
and 20 as evidence that these verses of the flood account could not all
have come from a single author. He argued, "Is it not reasonable to
suppose that if one and the same writer had been describing that event,
he would have done so in far fewer words, especially in a history?" B.
W. Anderson, on the other hand, has maintained that the "repeated use
of the key words 'the waters prevailed'" functions as a literary device "to
create an ascending effect", an effect which Moberly describes as

---

[49] *Mountain*, 22. Cf. Barr, *Bible in the Modern World*, 65; *idem*,
"Childs' *Introduction to the Old Testament as Scripture* ", 15 (both cited by
Moberly, *Mountain*, 22).

[50] *Mountain*, 22.

[51] *Mountain*, 23.

[52] *Mountain*, 23.

"forceful and aesthetically satisfying".[53] Clearly, these disparate inter-pretations cannot both be valid, as Moberly explains:

> ...although the present literary unity is not incompatible with composite authorship, one cannot take this one factor in the text, that is the fourfold repetition, and argue that it shows both unity and disunity. If the literary assessment of the repetition as a unity is sound, then the fact of repetition in itself provides no evidence of composite authorship; that could only be argued on the basis of other criteria in the larger context.[54]

The validity of Moberly's deduction is obvious, but the objection lies close at hand that it is just as easy to find coherence and consistency, *when that is what one is looking for*, as it is to find tensions and inconsistencies. This objection has considerable force where the goal of a literary method is simply to *devise* ways of reading texts. Some structuralists and poststructuralists, for example, hold the view that reading should be creative, unconstrained "by the literary conventions and codes that went into the writing".[55] Given sufficient creative latitude, an imaginative literary critic could probably devise hypothetical conventions to account for even the most garbled of texts. It is precisely in response to this danger, that a study of the poetics of Hebrew narrative can provide some controls. Since its concern is to recover, as far as possible, an ancient literary competence, poetics offers a safeguard against reading texts according to arbitrary or anachronistic criteria. In the example cited above, what gives Anderson's analysis the edge is the poetic observation that repetition, of one form or another, is a literary convention of which Hebrew narrative makes considerable use.[56]

In the remainder of this chapter, we shall consider some of the distinctive characteristics of Hebrew narrative. Our aim is not to be comprehensive but rather to concentrate on those general and specific features of Hebrew narrative style that seem most pertinent to the body of text with which our investigation is chiefly concerned, namely the Saul narratives in 1 Samuel 9-15.

---

[53] *Mountain*, 29-30 (bibliographic information is provided by Moberly in nn. 51-52). N.B. also Moberly's improvement (30 n. 53) of Anderson's analysis.

[54] *Mountain*, 30.

[55] Abrams, *Glossary*, 199-200.

[56] On repetition, see below, pp. 34-39.

Selected Features of Hebrew Narrative Style

There are numerous ways in which a discussion of the poetics of biblical Hebrew narrative could be structured; we need only compare the works mentioned above by Licht, Bar-Efrat, Alter and Berlin to see the variety of possibilities.[57] For the sake of simplicity, our own discussion will be organized under three rubrics suggestive of basic traits of Hebrew narrative style: scenic narration, economy of means, and reticence and indirection.

Scenic Narration

To say that a given text is a 'narrative' is a very general assertion; it suggests that the text under consideration tells a story of some kind, probably in prose, but beyond this it reveals very little about how the story is told. It does not tell us *what kind of narrative* we are dealing with. To add precision to our discussion it is useful to consider how narrative in general can be classified. Drawing upon the work of secular literary critics such as W. Kayser and E. Laemmert, Jacob Licht has introduced into biblical studies a simple system of narrative classification according to four categories: "straight narrative, scenic narrative, description and comment."[58] Since these labels are largely self-explanatory, it may suffice simply to illustrate the distinctions between the various modes of narration by repeating Licht's "hypothetical episode", which he recounts in each of the four modes.

> *Straight narrative*: Richard rode through the woods for some hours until he reached the town. He dismounted at

---

[57] The elements featured by Licht (*Storytelling*) include scenes, repetitions, time, etc.; by Bar-Efrat (העיצוב האמנותי); cf. "Literary Modes and Methods") style, narrator, characterization by direct and indirect means, plot, time and space; by Alter (*Art*) prose-fictional techniques, type-scenes, dialogue, repetition, characterization, composite artistry, etc.; by Berlin (*Poetics*) characterization and point of view.

[58] Licht, *Storytelling*, 29. Bar-Efrat ("Literary Modes and Methods", 22) delineates only two modes of narration for conveying information, the scenic and the summary, but he recognizes that the narrator does occasionally interject evaluative comments or descriptions (21).

an inn, left his horse in the charge of the ostler, and strode to the market place, where he found Sir John. They quarreled, and after a while started fighting. *Scenic narrative*: "Here you are, you dog," cried Richard as he espied Sir John in the market place; "it took me hours of hard riding to find you!" "The honour is mine, I am sure," replied Sir John. "How dare you mock me, take that!" exclaimed Richard, striking Sir John in the breast. *Description*: The tall houses of the old town looked down on the market place, where a merry crowd milled among the stalls. In the corner by the handsome fountain a spot had been cleared around two men engaged in a fight. They were Richard and Sir John, who etc. *Comment*: There is no greater hatred than that between those who have been friends. Thus Richard, spurred on by bitter hate, thought nothing of riding for some hours to take his revenge on Sir John, nor was he ashamed to start a fight in public.[59]

In practice, of course, the various modes of narration usually occur in combination, but nevertheless one or the other narrative style will generally tend to dominate. If we try to imagine each of the above mini-episodes (apart from specific content of course) as occurring in the narrative portions of the Old Testament, it is readily apparent that the latter two styles do not seem to fit. This is not to say that the Old Testament is devoid of description and comment; some prose passages are comprised largely of these elements.[60] But when the Old Testament tells its stories, it is the scenic narrative mode that is nearly always preferred, with straight narrative being used primarily to introduce and close scenes and to recount action that cannot be presented scenically. Even where a biblical story contains a large amount of straight narrative, the highlights and the climax of the story are almost invariably scenic.[61]

But what do we mean when we say that a narrative is scenic? Although a narrative and a play are not the same thing, 'scenes' in both artistic media do share a number of common features, so that it is helpful in visualizing what is meant by a narrative scene to recall the chief characteristics of the more familiar theatrical scene. In a dramatic script, a scene normally begins with stage directions identifying and lo-

---

[59] Licht, *Storytelling*, 30.

[60] For a list of examples, see Licht, *Storytelling*, 33.

[61] Cf., for example, the story of Judah and Tamar in Genesis 38, cited by Licht, *Storytelling*, 31.

cating the players on the stage and 'setting the scene', viz. stating when, where, and under what circumstances the events of the scene are to be imagined as taking place. If specific props are singled out for attention, this is usually because they will have some mimetic or symbolic significance or will be required by the action of the scene. In some plays, a narrator stands on or just off stage, at any rate apart from the action, in order to provide the audience from time to time with necessary background information or commentary. The heart of the scene, however, is conveyed through the direct action and speech of the actors on stage. A scene normally portrays the development of a tension and/or its resolution.

In similar fashion, a 'narrative scene' comprises a fairly short account of a single event, situation, dialogue, etc., in which there is seldom a change of place or lapse in temporal continuity. Essential background information ('staging') may be conveyed by the narrator in straight narrative, but high points and the climax of the scene are almost invariably portrayed in direct speech and action. The effect of such narration is to give the reader a sense of immediacy; he feels that he is there watching the episode unfold rather than viewing it from a spatially and chronologically distant vantage point. Intrusions by the narrator for the purpose of commentary tend to lessen this sense of immediacy and are therefore kept to a minimum.[62]

Economy of Means

Whereas novels are written to be read at the reader's own pace, and hence may vary greatly in length, the scenes of a play are written to be experienced in one sitting and are therefore restricted in length. Each scene must economize and concentrate upon that which is essential to the development of its central theme or main point. Extensive digressions or lengthy commentary are rarely permissible.

---

[62] These general comments are not intended as a comprehensive or restrictive definition of what may constitute a scene. On the difficulties of finding an adequate definition of 'scene', note the following words by Fokkelman (*King David*, 9, n. 15; cf. n. 16): "A scene is a narrative text which to a high degree is understandable in itself and which is characterized by the initiation, building up and conclusion of an action (often a conflict), which usually demonstrates unity of place and time, and brings together one or two and sometimes three protagonists. This definition is already inadequate and may not be applied to the texts unamended."

A similar dynamic may be at work in many of the narratives of the Old Testament, as the following comment by E. L. Greenstein suggests:

> ...the Bible never quite "outgrew" its oral state. Many biblical episodes display traces of having evolved from orally told tales. Accordingly, biblical literature is geared toward the ear, and meant to be listened to at a sitting. In a 'live' setting the storyteller negotiates each phrase with his audience. A nuance, an allusion hangs on nearly every word.[63]

Regardless of whether or not the biblical narratives "derive from long-standing oral traditions" it is, at any rate, "altogether likely", as Alter has observed, "that they were written chiefly for oral presentation."[64] This being the case, the individual scenes of a biblical narrative, like the scenes of a play, tend to be brief.[65]

One effect of such brevity, as von Rad has pointed out, is to lend 'weight' and 'profile' to what is said. He writes:

> Sich recht zu bewegen in der Literatur eines antiken Volkes, das viel weniger schrieb und las, als das moderne Völker tun, das darum aber viel gesammelter schrieb, so daß dem einzelnen Wort in der Regel ein viel größeres Gewicht und ein markanteres Profil eigen ist — das ist eine Bemühung, in der keiner auslernt.[66]

The challenge which the laconic style of Old Testament narrative poses for the would-be interpreter is recognized also by Greenstein:

> Because the Bible's stories are so familiar, we are prone to underestimate the considerable differences in narrative style between biblical storytelling and that of most Western literature. For example — and at the risk of oversimplifying — the Western narrative in which we are steeped is meant to be read by leaps and bounds, passage after passage. The biblical text, by contrast, is intricate and intensive, demanding slow-paced attentiveness to detail.[67]

---

[63] Greenstein, "Narratology", 202.

[64] *Art*, 90.

[65] Even fairly long narrative sequences, such as the Joseph story, tend to progress episodically; cf. Licht, *Storytelling*, 121-43.

[66] "Gerhard von Rad", 659.

[67] "Narratology", 202.

In addition to the weight that accrues to individual words simply by virtue of their inclusion in sparsely-written narrative, the Old Testament writers had at their disposal various technical means of emphasizing, or *adding weight* to, certain words or phrases. Some of these will be considered below.

Leitwortstil

One of the most widely recognized of these techniques is the recurrence in narrative contexts of "key-words" or *Leitworte*. Martin Buber has defined a *Leitwort* as

> ein Wort oder ein Wortstamm ... der sich innerhalb eines Textes, einer Textfolge, eines Textzusammenhangs sinnreich wiederholt: wer diesen Wiederholungen folgt, dem erschließt oder verdeutlicht sich ein Sinn des Textes oder wird auch nur eindringlicher offenbar. Es braucht wie gesagt nicht dasselbe Wort sondern nur derselbe Wortstamm zu sein, der solcherweise wiederkehrt; durch die jeweiligen Verschiedenheiten wird sogar oft die dynamische Gesamtwirkung gefördert.[68]

Buber maintains that the repetition of key-words is probably the most effective of the *indirect modes* of communication — "das stärkste unter allen Mitteln, einen Sinncharakter kundzutun, ohne ihn vorzutragen".[69] Indeed, it is the capacity of *Leitwortstil* to make a point without recourse to didacticism, and thus without disrupting the flow of the narrative, that accounts for its "durch nichts zu ersetzenden *Äußerungswert* ".[70]

Buber illustrates his discussion with a number of instructive examples drawn from the Pentateuch. In Gen 11, for example, Buber identifies seven Leitworte: כל־הארץ "all the earth", שׂפה "tongue/language", הבה "come!", בנה "build", עיר ומגדל "city and tower", שׁם "name", פוץ "scatter". These seven, according to Buber, serve as a bridge between the *Aufstand* of vv. 1-4 and the *Überwindung* of vv. 5-9.[71] In another example, Num 16:1-17:5 contains several instances of *Leitwortstil*. Buber draws attention to the dominant *Leit-*

---

68 Buber, "Leitwortstil", 211.
69 "Leitwortstil", 211.
70 "Leitwortstil", 212.
71 "Leitwortstil", 214-17.

worte עדה "congregation" and מועד "assembly, etc.", both of which derive from the root יעד "appoint".[72] In addition, the episode is tied to its present context by references to "drawing near" (hi. of קרב)[73] since both Num 15 and 17:1-18:7 treat the issue of "Nahen und Nahung".[74] Finally, there is the mocking repetition in the mouth of both parties of key phrases such as רב־לכם ("You have gone too far/far enough!") in 16:3, 7 and המעט כי ("Isn't it enough ... that ...?") in 16:9, 13.[75] Yet other examples of *Leitwortstil* are found in the Joseph story of Gen 27ff. The themes of deception, birthright, blessing and name dominate and lend coherence to a fairly lengthy body of text. Though the narrator does not comment explicitly on Esau's anguished cry — "Is he not rightly named Jacob (יעקב), for he has deceived me (ויעקבני) these two times? My birthright (בְּכֹרָתִי) he took, and now he has taken my blessing (בִּרְכָתִי)" (27:36a) —, he does provide indirect, though pointed, commentary on the affair through Jacob's own misadventures with a relative, his uncle Laban:[76]

> When morning came, behold, it was Leah! So he [Jacob] said to Laban, "What is this that you have done to me? Was it not for Rachel that I served you? Why have you *deceived*[77] me?" Laban replied, "Such is not done in our place, to give the younger before the *first-born* (הַבְּכִירָה)." (Gen 29:25-26)

Finally, Buber concludes his essay with a selection of examples from the "weit über 40 distantielle Paronomasien" that can be found in the *Abrahamsgeschichte*.[78]

Though all of Buber's examples of *Leitwortstil* are taken from the Pentateuch, the technique can be similarly documented from other narrative portions of the Old Testament.[79] In another essay, "Die

---

[72] "Leitwortstil", 217-19.

[73] "Leitwortstil", 219-22.

[74] "Leitwortstil", 221.

[75] "Leitwortstil", 222.

[76] "Leitwortstil", 224-25.

[77] The word used here, pi. of רמה "to beguile, deal treacherously with", resembles in meaning that of the figurative usage of עקב to signify treachery or deception.

[78] "Leitwortstil", 226-38.

[79] Cf., for example, Crenshaw (*Samson*, 66-69), who shows how the verb נגד "tell" functions in the Samson narratives as a key-word in the development of the *Leitmotif* of "allegiance" and in "providing structural

Erzählung von Sauls Königswahl", Buber himself draws attention to several instances of *Leitwortstil* in the Saul narratives. One of the better known instances has to do with the way in which the narrator in 1 Sam 9:1-10:16, "ein Meister des Geheimstils", surrounds the important "Zentralwort *nagid* " with verbal forms of the same root.[80] Another well-known example of *Leitwortwstil* in the Saul narratives is found in 1 Sam 15, where the repeated use of the words שמע ("listen") and קול ("voice"), or in combination שמע בקול/לקול ("obey"), serves as a formal stylistic pointer to the passage's central issue, namely that of the king's obedience and who should command it.[81]

Given the natural limitations of vocabulary and the predilections of ancient Hebrew writers for repetitions of one sort or another, it would be mistaken to regard every set of repetitions in a given context as an instance of *Leitwortstil*.[82] But where a repetition seems to serve some thematic, structural or even aesthetic purpose, we may properly speak of these words or combinations of words as *Leitworte*.

Paronomasia

As with the use of *Leitworte*, *paronomasia* or word-play offers an effective and aesthetically pleasing means of *indirectly* drawing attention to particular words or phrases. Since the eighteenth century, literary paronomasia, especially punning, has been most closely associated with comedy.[83] But this has not always been the case. In the Old Testament, as in the ancient world generally, word-plays of various sorts were often put to serious use as rhetorical devices.[84]

By their very nature, puns are difficult to define and to classify. In his article entitled "Paronomasia in Biblical Literature", J. J. Glück has provided a helpful start.[85] Describing a pun as "based on ambiguity,

---

unity to the entire saga." The theme of telling is complemented by another key term, ידע "knowing", or more precisely "not knowing".

[80] "Sauls Königswahl", 126. The substantive occurs in 9:16; 10:1 and verbal forms in 9:6, 8, 18, 19.

[81] See Alter's brief description (*Art*, 93-94).

[82] Cf. Licht, *Storytelling*, 94-95.

[83] Cf. Abrams, *Glossary*, 149.

[84] Cf. Glück, "Paronomasia", 50-51.

[85] Glück's discussion has now been augmented, especially as regards "visual wordplay", by Sasson's "Wordplay". See also the discussion by Watson, *Classical Hebrew Poetry*, 237-50. Further literature on paronomasia in the Old Testament is listed by Segert, "Paronomasia", 460-61.

i.e. the use of a word in such a manner as to imply a meaning and draw an image other than the one expected in the context, or in addition to it as a secondary or tertiary idea",[86] Glück proceeds to offer a six-fold classification of biblical puns, which may be summarized as follows:[87]

> 1) An *Equivocal* pun, the simplest form of ambiguity, is a homonym in which "any one or more of the multiple meanings conveyed or implied by a word in the phrase may suit or change the context and/or create a doubt, shock and/or other sensation in the minds of the listeners or readers, confused, as they are likely to be, by the apparent lack of clarity in the diction."[88] 2) A *Metaphonic* or Patternal pun involves a "change in meaning ... introduced or suggested by vowel-mutation."[89] 3) A *Parasonantic* pun "involves the changing of consonants; in Hebrew and in the Semitic languages in general this amounts to substituting one word for another."[90] 4) A *Farragonic* pun (from farrago, meaning a confused mixture, hotchpotch)[91] involves an enigmatic or even "chaotic" word or combination of words which nevertheless "produce an atmosphere which in itself is not quite meaningless."[92] 5) An *Associative* pun has a metaphoric quality, where "the different words within a phrase are forced together to create an entirely new image, overshadowing the usual associations of the respective words of the phrase."[93] 6) An *Assonantic* pun involves assonance that is more than "mere decoration or ornament". Rather it "emphasizes the significant words" and "binds them together into a single figure-unit."[94]

Most of Glück's examples are taken from the prophetic books, especially Isaiah, but paronomasia is a fairly common feature of narrative texts as well. In the Saul narratives that form the focus of our study, for instance, the six occurrences in 1 Sam 14:24-29 of verbal

---

[86] "Paronomasia", 50. Because of the modern association of the term with humour, it is questionable whether 'pun' is the correct term for biblical paronomasia. Though he uses the term throughout his article, Glück concludes that "the biblical paronomasia is no pun but an integral part of the elevated diction of the Bible. ... an inseparable part of that word-magic, the subtle eloquence of the Bible" (78).

[87] Examples of the various classes are cited in Glück's article and will not be repeated here.

[88] "Paronomasia", 53.

[89] "Paronomasia", 61.

[90] "Paronomasia", 66.

[91] So *OED*.

[92] "Paronomasia", 70-71.

[93] "Paronomasia", 72.

[94] "Paronomasia", 75.

roots containing ר and א (viz. ארר 2x, אור 2x, ירא 1x, ראה 1x) may constitute an example of assonantic punning for rhetorical effect.[95] Here we see the basic distinction between punning and *Leitwortstil*. In the latter, the *same root* is represented in each case. A pun of some sort may also be involved in the enigmatic וַיִּאֶל of 1 Sam 14:24.[96]

In attempting to analyse the various techniques by which biblical narrators were able to achieve maximum expressive effect by the most economical of means, we must not lose sight of the fact that our analytical categories are descriptive and thus somewhat arbitrary. In practice, literary techniques often occur in combination, as, for example, in Gen 27:36 mentioned above. In Esau's outcry against Jacob, the emphasis upon the *Leitworte* "deception" and "birthright" is enhanced by the punning involved in the combinations ויעקבני/יעקב and בְּרָכָתִי/בְּכֹרָתִי. The effect of these word-plays, moreover, is not simply decorative. As Buber has suggested,

> Die Assonanz soll hier wie oft zur Einprägung des Verses als eines von zentraler Bedeutung, den man sich für das Weitere merken muß, beitragen.[97]

Poetry as Heightened Speech

Buber's recognition that literary style may signal the importance, as well as facilitate the retention, of what is said suggests yet another narrative technique which is characteristic of biblical narrative, namely poetry as heightened speech. To give an example: Arthur Weiser, in his essay on 1 Sam 15, drew attention to the *poetic form* of 1 Sam 15:22-23 as signalling that the account of Saul's second rejection had reached a "Höhepunkt" or climax.[98] In other words, the elevated diction of the verses is an indication of their *significance* or *weight*. Alter makes the more general observation that the inset of formal verse is "a common convention in the biblical narrative for direct speech that has some significantly summarizing or ceremonial function".[99] The casting of short segments of direct speech into poetic form creates what Alter

---

[95] See our discussion in Ch. 4, p. 120.

[96] See Ch. 4, p. 117.

[97] "Leitwortstil", 224, n.1.

[98] "1 Samuel 15", 10. For a full discussion of the significance of these verses, see Ch. 5, pp. 150-55.

[99] *Art*, 28.

calls "heightened speech".[100] Similarly, though he avoids the term poetry, Kugel recognizes the significance of "parallelism" ocurring

> in "unpoetic" places — in laws, cultic procedures, and so forth, and especially in *single lines* that come to punctuate, emphasize, or sum up less formally organized discourse.[101]

The implication of this poetic insight for the genetic study of biblical narratives is readily apparent. In studies attempting to reconstruct the history of a text's development, it is customary to cite shifts in style as indicating the incorporation of material from different sources. And, indeed, the Old Testament offers examples where this is explicitly the case. In Num 21:14-15, for instance, the 'poetical' section serves no apparent summarizing or climactic function, and its source is explicitly named, the "Book of the Wars of Yahweh" (ספר מלחמת יהוה; v. 14aβ).[102] It is therefore clear that in the matter of 'poetry' occurring in predominantly prose passages, both the synchronic and diachronic modes of explanation exist as options.[103] The point that we are making, however, is that since elevated diction is often employed in Hebrew narrative for rhetorical effect, the mere presence of 'poetical material' in a largely prose context is not sufficient evidence that disparate sources are involved. We must remain open to both possibilities and seek to establish our conclusions on other grounds.

In a study of 1 Sam 14, Blenkinsopp accepts the assumption "that much, if not all, of the heroic material which deals with the Holy War period existed originally in verse",[104] but he does not allow this diachronic presupposition to blind him to the rhetorical significance of the occurrence of poetic or semi-poetic sections in prose narrative contexts. In reference to 1 Sam 14:28-29, for example, he writes, "One of the army informs Jonathan of the oath, to which he makes an *important reply*, as seen by its careful *rhythmic composition*" (italics mine).[105] Blenkinsopp observes, moreover, that as a general rule, "the natural

---

[100] *Art*, 4.

[101] *Idea*, 70.

[102] Cf. also the attribution in 2 Sam 1:18ff of the "Song of the Bow" (in Hebrew simply קשת) to the "Book of Jashar".

[103] Cf. Alter, *Art*, 28.

[104] "Jonathan's Sacrilege", 437.

[105] "Jonathan's Sacrilege", 425-26.

rhythm of the language, whatever its primitive state, is intensified in dialogue especially when the protagonist speaks".[106] This tendency, we would argue, is quite in keeping with the scenic mode of narration in which the heart of the narrative is conveyed by means of direct speech and action.

<u>Reticence and Indirection</u>

In the above discussions of the scenic quality and economic style of much Old Testament narrative, we have occasionally made reference to the *indirect*, or *oblique*, modes of characterization and evaluation which seem typical of such narrative. Modern literary theory distinguishes two basic methods of characterization in narrative: *showing* and *telling*. M. H. Abrams has succinctly summarized the essential differences between the two as follows:

> In **showing** (also called "the dramatic method"), the author merely presents his characters talking and acting and leaves the reader to infer what motives and dispositions lie behind what they say and do. In **telling**, the author himself intervenes authoritatively in order to describe, and often to evaluate, the motives and dispositional qualities of his characters.[107]

While both modes of characterization have a place in biblical narrative, it is the former that tends to predominate.[108] As R. P. Gordon observes in his essay on 1 Sam 24-26:

> One of the outstanding features of biblical narrative, and perhaps the one which is most open to misinterpretation, is its tendency to laconicism, just at those points where the modern reader looks to the narrator to spell out his intention or, maybe, to moralize on the action of the story. Where the reader's sensibilities are of-

---

[106] "Jonathan's Sacrilege", 448, cf. 437, 442.

[107] *Glossary*, 21. These two modes correspond basically to Bar-Efrat's categories of "neutral omniscience" and "editorial omniscience" respectively ("Literary Modes", 21).

[108] Cf., for example, Gen 24:28ff., where it is Laban's actions when first we meet him, rather than any explicit narrative commentary, that suggest his calculating and self-interested character: "As soon as he saw the ring and the bracelets on his sister's wrists ... he went to the man ... and he said, Come in, blessed of Yahweh ...." (vss. 30-31). Explicit confirmation of Laban's character is delayed until chs. 29-31.

fended this taciturnity may be put down to moral
indifference on the part of the narrator, or simply — and
this has special relevance to 'David's Rise' — to undis-
guised hero-worship. But Hebrew narrative is much more
subtle than that, using a wide range of narrative techniques to perform the functions of the explicit commentaries in the more transparent narrative types.[109]

While our knowledge of the specifics of some of these techniques has
been advanced in recent years, the basic insight has a venerable history.
Hugo Greßmann, for example, writing on 1 Samuel 14 shortly after the
turn of this century, drew attention to what more recently has come to
be called the *reticence* of the biblical narrators:

> Die antiken Volkserzähler verschweigen die Gedanken
> und *Stimmungen*, die sie beherrschen, und reihen völlig
> objektiv die Tatsachen aneinander. Aber aus der Art, wie
> dies geschieht, können wir das Urteil des Verfassers
> deutlich entnehmen.[110]

What is true of 1 Sam 14 is true also of the Books of Samuel more
generally. Hertzberg has written:

> Der theologische Grundzug der Samuelbücher ist nicht so
> handgreiflich dargeboten wie in den anderen historischen
> Büchern; es wird dezenter vorgegangen, und manchmal
> steht mehr zwischen den Zeilen als in ihnen. Mitunter
> wird das, worauf es ankommt, wesentlich durch die Art der
> Anordnung deutlich, ist aber hinreichend erkennbar, und
> für den Leser dieser zum größten Teil ja meisterhaft
> erzählten Stoffe ist es immer wieder von besonderem
> Reiz zu sehen, wie die eigentliche theologische Linie
> innegehalten wird.[111]

---

[109] "David's Rise", 42.

[110] Greßmann, 44. On the reticence of biblical narrators, cf. von Rad
(*Theologie* 1:62): "Faszinierend ist ihre Darstellung, faszinierend ist aber
auch, so paradox es klingt, ihre Kunst des Schweigens, des Verschweigens
von dem, was sich der Leser selber sagen muß."; and cf. also Clines ("Story
and Poem", 122), who in his discussion of the book of Esther speaks of "a
consummate art in story-telling that broadcasts its fundamental world-views
by saying nothing, apparently, about them."

[111] Hertzberg, 11/ET 20. Cf. also more recently Smelik (*Saul*, 19):
"Men heeft de ideeën, die men de lezer duidelijk wilde maken, niet op een
beschouwelijke of polemische wijze uiteengezet".

In short: in the Books of Samuel, even more so than in the other historical books of the Old Testament, the favoured narrative mode is 'showing' rather than 'telling'. This is not to say that the implied narrator in Samuel abstains entirely from explicit commentary. Indeed, Levenson has the following to say about authorial editorializing:

> The author (or redactor) must editorialize, whether in his own voice or through the voice of his cast. If he only editorializes, he ends up with a sermon, not a narrative. The *desideratum*, then, is a story in which the author both defines his characters and lets the action and speeches prove his definition correct, in which the narrative bodies forth and bears out the author's moral vision.[112]

Editorial comments offering glimpses into the inner life of characters occur most often in the 'straight narrative' portions which introduce or conclude a scene.[113] Where these are evaluative in nature, they can be of great value in determining the ideological stance of the implied narrator. Only occasionally does the narrator 'break frame' in order to editorialize or provide background information within the main body of the scene.[114] By and large, however, the narrator's evaluation of characters and events is conveyed obliquely through a variety of indirect means.[115] Some of these we have already touched upon, but there re-

---

[112] "1 Samuel 25", 22. Levenson's observation refers specifically to 1 Samuel 25 but it is equally applicable to other portions of 1 and 2 Samuel.

[113] A few examples of explicit editorial comments in 1 Samuel are the following: "Eli's sons were worthless men; they did not acknowledge Yahweh" (1 Sam 2:12), "the boy Samuel continued to grow in stature and in favour both with Yahweh and with men" (2:26), "[Eli's] heart trembled for the ark of God" (4:13), "Saul was very angry, for the thing was evil in his eyes" (18:8), "Saul was afraid of David, because Yahweh was with David but had departed from Saul" (18:12), "Saul was David's enemy all his days" (18:29), "Jonathan knew that his father was determined to kill David. ... he was grieved for David, for his father had mistreated him" (20:33-34), "The woman was intelligent and beautiful, but her husband was hard and mean in his dealings" (25:3), "David was greatly distressed ..., but David found strength in Yahweh his God" (30:6), etc.

[114] On the concept of breaking frame, see Berlin, *Poetics*, 57-59, 99. Possible examples include 1 Sam 9:9; 14:18. Cf. also Berlin's comments on Ruth 4:1, 7 (*Poetics*, 99).

[115] Alter's (*Art*, 116-117) "scale of means ... for conveying information about the motives, the attitudes, the moral nature of characters" illustrates this point — all but the last-mentioned mode of characterization fall under the heading of indirect means: "Character can be revealed through the

main a couple of narrative techniques that are of particular interest for our study of the Saul narratives.

Repetition

The first of these, broadly defined, is repetition. In an article entitled "A Study in Hebrew Rhetoric: Repetition and Style", published in the first supplemental volume to *Vetus Testamentum*, James Muilenburg observed that the "iterative propensity of ancient Israel" is not limited to its poetry but is common in its prose as well. Indeed, "in narrative, the literary genre most characteristic of her life and thought, repetition appears as a *major stylistic feature* " (italics mine).[116]

Repetitions within Old Testament narrative occur on a number of different levels. We have already observed verbal repetition in our discussion of *Leitwortstil* and sonorous repetition in some varieties of paronomasia. Also common in Old Testament narratives, as indeed in other narrative traditions, is the repetition of motifs, themes and sequences of actions.[117] Beyond these fairly familiar conventions, Alter has suggested yet another form of repetition which he labels the biblical "type-scene". Borrowing and adapting this term from Homer studies,[118] Alter defines a "type-scene" as "an episode occurring at a portentous moment in the career of the hero which is composed of a fixed sequence of motifs."[119] A type-scene presupposes "a tacit understanding between the biblical authors and their audiences that in most cases, the portentous junctures in the life of the hero — conception and birth, initiatory trial, betrothal, deathbed — would be conveyed through a fixed sequence

---

report of actions; through appearance, gestures, posture, costume; through one character's comments on another; through direct speech by the character; through inward speech, either summarized or quoted as interior monologue; or through statements by the narrator about the attitudes and intentions of the personages, which may come either as flat assertions or motivated explanations."

[116] "Rhetoric", 100. As the bibliographic footnotes to his article adequately attest, Muilenburg was certainly not the first to recognize repetition as a characteristic feature of Hebrew writing. For more recent discussions of this phenomenon, see Licht, *Storytelling*, chaps. 3 and 4; Alter, *Art*, ch. 5; Berlin, *Poetics*, 71-82.

[117] On all these, see Alter, *Art*, 94-96.

[118] Cf. Alter, "How Convention Helps", 118.

[119] *Art*, 96. For Alter's major discussions of this convention, see, in addition to the article mentioned in the preceding note, the third chapter of *Art* (47-62).

of narrative motifs."[120] An awareness that such shared understandings existed can be significant for interpretations of biblical narrative, whether the type-scene develops in the expected manner or, as Alter puts it, is breached. Alter's theory of type-scenes is attractive in many respects, though the resulting interpretations are not always convincing.[121] At any rate, it should be balanced by Moberly's observation that parallel episodes in the lives of distinct biblical personalities may at times simply reflect "Olrik's ninth epic law, the Law of Patterning, according to which different people and situations are depicted in such a way as to show similarity between them".[122] Another term for such patterning is 'narrative analogy', to be discussed below.

Many of the above forms of repetition are familiar from our own literary tradition. We are accustomed to the repetition of key-words (though the convention is not usually exploited to the extent that it is in Hebrew narrative), motifs, themes and sequences of actions. And though we have nothing that corresponds exactly to Alter's notion of a type-scene, our concept of 'stock situations' has some points in common.[123]

More perplexing than these types of repetition, to modern sensibilities at least, is the rather surprising proportion of verbatim or near-verbatim repetition that some Hebrew narratives display. How are we to understand this phenomenon? The response of diachronic literary scholarship has characteristically been to assume that, except perhaps in

---

[120] Alter, "How Convention Helps", 118. Alter offers a more complete list in *Art*, 51: "Some of the most commonly repeated biblical type-scenes I have been able to identify are the following: the annunciation (and I take the term from Christian iconography precisely to underscore the elements of fixed convention) of the birth of the hero to his barren mother; the encounter with the future betrothed at a well; the epiphany in the field; the initiatory trial; danger in the desert and the discovery of a well or other source of sustenance; the testimony of the dying hero."

[121] A case in point, in the opinion of this writer, is Alter's classification of Saul's encounter with maidens at a well (1 Sam 9:11-12) as an aborted betrothal type-scene (*Art*, 60). As regards Alter's assertion that "the particular detail of an encounter on unfamiliar territory with maidens by a well would otherwise be gratuitous" (*Art*, 61), see Ch. 7, pp. 203-204.

[122] *Mountain*, 32.

[123] W. A. Bacon (*Art of Interpretation*, 496) defines 'stock situations' as "conventional, repeated situations readily recognized by readers or audiences as usual or trite, though they may be given fresh treatment. They are to situations what flat characters are to characterization. The rise of the poor boy from a log cabin to the White House is a stock situation in American lore."

the case of speeches, the recurrence of similar or identical material within a given literary context signals a conflation or juxtaposition of parallel or doublet traditions. And, of course, this may sometimes be the best explanation. But as knowledge of the poetics of Hebrew narrative has increased, it has become apparent that repetition is often more than a mere happenstance of the process of textual growth. The cumulative effect of recent studies of Hebrew narrative art has been to confirm Muilenburg's assessment of repetition as a "major stylistic feature".

Repetition may function resumptively, marking a return to the main narration after a digression or after the insertion of new material.[124] In oral literature, or literature written for oral presentation, where it is not possible to 'leaf back' in order to review something already stated, repetition may have provided a convenient means of "fixing a particular action or statement for special inspection".[125] Repetition can also signal the entrance of a new point of view into the narrative. And, more importantly, it offers an effective means of unobtrusively highlighting the differences between points of view — those of the characters as well as that of the 'omniscient narrator'. This can be done by having two or more characters talk about the same things in slightly different ways, or by juxtaposing a character's version of an action or event with that of the authoritative narrator. In such instances, it is the *variations* within the repeated matter, "the small but revealing differences in the seeming similarities,"[126] that are most significant. An addition or omission, a substitution of one term for another, a change in the order of terms, a change in syntax — these are but a few of the kinds of variation that take on semantic importance within a pattern of repetition. Thus, as Berlin has observed, repetition in the Old Testament represents more than a mere aesthetic device or an ancient tendency towards redundancy, "it is a key to perception, to

---

[124] C. Kuhl's influential article, "Die 'Wiederaufnahme' — ein literarkritisches Prinzip?", considers only the latter possibility, but cf. Berlin's more nuanced discussion (*Poetics*, 126-28), which offers numerous examples in which "the purpose of the second of the repeated phrases is to return the reader to the scene in which the first phrase occurred" (126). Cf. our discussion of 1 Sam 14:6 in Ch. 4, pp. 107-108.

[125] Alter, *Art*, 90.

[126] Alter, *Art*, 97.

interpretation; it calls attention to the similarity of two things or utterances, and may also be calling attention to their differences."[127]

We have already seen in our review of the competing interpretations of Gen 7:17-20 proposed by Simon and Anderson that greater sensitivity to repetition as a stylistic device not only enriches our synchronic reading of a text but may also call for a reassessment of some of our diachronic conclusions.[128] This point can be further illustrated from the Saul narratives by considering Saul's two confessions in 1 Sam 15:24-25 and 15:30. There is a widely-held opinion among interpreters of 1 Sam 15 that a section corresponding roughly to vv. 24-29 is secondary.[129] Even Weiser, who otherwise asserted the essential unity of 1 Sam 15, felt strongly that this section, in his view vv. 25-30aα, was intrusive.[130] He was led to this conviction by what he perceived as repetitions and contradictions between this section and its surrounding context. He cites three repetitions: Saul twice confesses his sin (vv. 24 & 30aα), he twice requests that Samuel return with him (vv. 25 & 30b), and twice Samuel pronounces judgement upon him (vv. 23b[131] & 26). To these he adds two major contradictions: 1) v. 29a (וגם נצח ישראל לא ישקר ולא ינחם כי לא אדם הוא <u>להנחם</u>) conflicts with v. 11aα (<u>נחמתי</u> כי־המלכתי את־שאול למלך) and v. 35b (<u>ויהוה נחם</u> כי־המלך את־שאול על־ישראל); and 2) Samuel's negative response in v. 26 to Saul's request that he return with him is reversed in v. 31.

Prima facie, this is an impressive array of arguments. But once we recognize the expressive potential of repetition as a distinctive feature of Hebrew narrative style and begin to look for the subtle (or, in this case, not so subtle) variations within the repeated elements, it becomes apparent that there is more involved in this passage than a mere juxtaposing of sources. In the crucial matter of Saul's two confessions, for example, the differences are striking. The first confession is rather full and ample-sounding: the initial admission, "I have sinned", is followed by thirteen words (in Hebrew) of elaboration and culminates in a plea

---

[127] *Poetics*, 136.

[128] See above, pp. 19-20.

[129] So, for example, McCarter (268) and Foresti (*Rejection*, 26-30). Seebass ("I Sam 15", 151-53) and Tosato ("La colpa", 258) limit the section to vv. 24-28.

[130] "I Samuel 15", 3-5.

[131] Weiser ("I Samuel 15", 4) cites v. 23a (mistakenly?).

that Samuel should "forgive my sin and return with me that I may prostrate myself before Yahweh" (vv. 24-25). By contrast, Saul's admission of guilt in the second confession (v. 30) is cut to a single word in Hebrew (חטאתי, "I have sinned"). Gone are the thirteen words of elaboration. Gone is even the request for forgiveness. In its place is a request that Samuel "honour me before the elders of *my* people and before Israel". The suggestive pronoun "my" of this phrase finds its counterpart in a small addition to the request that Samuel return — "that I may prostrate myself before Yahweh *your God* ".

The differences between the two confessions are not random, as one might expect in the case of doublets. The shift from "forgive me" to "honour me", along with the other, more subtle alterations, captures the spirit of Saul's machinations in a way that could hardly have been achieved through straight exposition.[132] In the light of these observations, Weiser's objection to the originality of vv. 25-30aα can no longer rest on the mere fact of the repetitions.[133] Moreover, it becomes apparent that Weiser's puzzlement at Samuel's reversal (v. 31) of his earlier refusal to return with Saul (v. 26) stems from the misperception that between the first and second confessions nothing has changed ("ohne daß sich an der Lage etwas geändert hätte").[134] With the failure of these its major elements, Weiser's case for regarding vv. 25-30aα as secondary collapses, for the remaining arguments, by themselves, are insufficient to support it.[135]

1 Sam 15 will be discussed in considerably more detail in Chapter 5, but enough has been said at this point to illustrate how, within a synthetic exegetical approach which encourages dialogue among the diachronic and synchronic Old Testament disciplines, literary insights may sometimes have a vital role to play in modifying certain historical-critical conclusions. Recognition of a greater degree of coherence and continuity in the section of 1 Sam 15 under consideration does not, of course, deny the possibility of a complex textual prehistory. It simply emphasizes the difficulty, in the present case, of reconstructing what this prehistory may have been; the problem of the 'disappearing redac-

---

[132] For further discussion of these matters, see Ch. 5, p. 164.

[133] As regards the third instance of repetition cited, it is not at all surprising, in view of Saul's confession in v. 24, that Samuel should reiterate in v. 26 the judgement first announced in v. 23b.

[134] "I Samuel 15", 4. Cf. Seebass, "I Sam 15", 151.

[135] On the tension between vv. 11, 35 and v. 29, see below, pp. 163-64.

tor' is well-known.[136] On the positive side, the resolution of what once
were perceived as unacceptable tensions within the text opens the door
to a fuller appreciation of the text in its present form. A fresh reading
is made possible, not on the basis of some arbitrary decision to treat the
text in its 'final form', but on the basis of a genuine resolution of perceived tensions through the application of generically appropriate literary criteria.

Analogy and Contrast

As our brief analysis of Saul's two confessions suggests, biblical
narrators were masters in the use of comparisons and contrasts as means
of characterization. This is true not only as regards a character's own
words and actions, but also in terms of comparisons and contrasts between two different characters or between a character's actions and an
expected norm.[137] One of the more prominent techniques by which
biblical narrators were able to provide implicit commentary was
through the use of 'narrative analogy'. R. P. Gordon describes the
technique as follows:

> Narrative analogy is a device whereby the narrator can
> provide an internal commentary on the action which he
> is describing, usually by means of cross-references to an
> earlier action or speech. Thus narratives are made to
> interact in ways which may not be immediately apparent;
> ironic parallelism abounds wherever this technique is
> applied.[138]

Although narrative analogy is by no means unique to the Old Testament, it appears to have been particularly favoured, perhaps because of
its potential for providing unobtrusive commentary. Alter writes:

---

[136] Cf. Barton (*Reading*, 57): "The more impressive the critic makes
the redactor's work, the more he succeeds in showing that the redactor has,
by subtle and delicate artistry, produced a simple and coherent text out of the
diverse materials before him; the more also he reduces the evidence on
which the existence of those sources was established in the first place."

[137] Cf. Berlin, *Poetics*, 40.

[138] "David's Rise", 42-43. Cf. Miscall ("Jacob and Joseph", 28-29)
who understands the phrase to refer to "texts which have enough in common
in terms of plot, characters, themes, etc. to be considered analogous and
which must therefore be analysed in conjunction to explicate more fully the
Biblical text under study." Cf. also Alter, *Art*, 21, 91-92, 180; Berlin,
Poetics, 136.

> The use of narrative analogy, where one part of the story provides a commentary on or a foil to another, should be familiar enough from later literature, as anyone who has ever followed the workings of a Shakespearian double plot may attest. In the Bible, however, such analogies often play an especially critical role because the writers tend to avoid more explicit modes of conveying evaluation of particular characters and acts. Thus, the *only* commentary made on Jacob's getting the firstborn's blessing from his blind father through deception occurs several chapters later in an analogy with a reversal — when he is deceived in the dark and given Leah instead of Rachel, then chided that it is not the law of the land to marry the younger sister before the firstborn.[139]

Recent studies have drawn attention to numerous examples of narrative analogy in the Old Testament text. While some of these seem assured, critical opinion will undoubtedly vary as to the validity of others; but, then, this is not at all surprising, given the oblique nature of the technique.

One fairly obvious example of narrative analogy in the Saul narratives, but one which seldom receives explicit comment, is the way in which Jonathan serves as a foil to Saul in 1 Sam 13-14.[140] In many respects, Saul and Jonathan, king and crown prince, are geminate. Both are in command of a contingent of troops (13:2). On the day of the battle of Michmash, only Saul and Jonathan are in possession of sword or spear (13:22). The two are frequently linked by relational epithets — "Saul and Jonathan, his son", etc. (13:16, 22 [2x]; 14:1, 21, 27, 28, 29, 39, 40, 41, 42). By placing Saul and Jonathan side by side in this way, the narrator creates an atmosphere in which the actions of the one will quite naturally be judged in the light of how the other acts in similar situations. An obvious case in point has to do with Saul's attempt to excuse his disobedience in the Gilgal affair, "because I saw the army scattering from me..." (13:11). The reticent narrator himself refrains from explicit commentary, but Samuel's initial negative reaction, "You have acted foolishly" (13:13), nevertheless receives unam-

---

[139] *Art*, 180.

[140] D. Jobling ("Saul's Fall") notes that in 1 Sam 14 "Saul's loss is at every point Jonathan's gain" (369), but he attributes this dynamic to the mere fact of Saul's rejectedness, not to some "sounder theology" on Jonathan's part (370). Moreover, he finds no meaning in Jonathan's exaltation in 1 Sam 14:1-46, but only in Jonathan's later mediatorial role in the transferral of authority to David (see *idem*, "Jonathan").

biguous vindication a chapter later in the mouth of Saul's own son, who appears throughout as the true hero of these chapters: "Nothing can hinder Yahweh from saving, whether by many or by few" (14:6).

There are many other, less obvious perhaps but nonetheless telling, contrasts between Saul and Jonathan. Saul's general passivity (cf. 14:2) contrasts with Jonathan's activity; Jonathan initiates the action (13:3; 14:1, 6, etc.), while Saul simply responds to it (13:3b; 14:16-18, etc.). Jonathan succeeds in discovering Yahweh's will, even without access to oracular devices (14:9-10), while Saul is singularly unsuccessful on three occasions, and his commitment to the divine inquiry seems to deteriorate as the narrative progresses — viz., in 13:8-9 Saul waits until the last minute before taking matters into his own hands, in 14:18-19 he calls for the oracle but breaks off the inquiry in mid-stream, and finally in 14:36 he must even be reminded that divine inquiry is necessary.

Conclusion

In scenic narrative, where economy of means and "showing" rather than "telling" are the rule, the task of literary interpretation is a challenging one, and the interpreter does well to heed Bar-Efrat's words of caution:

> Since themes or ideas are not stated overtly, but have to be extracted by means of interpretation, one should exercise a good deal of self-restraint and self-criticism before proceeding to the delineation of thematic or ideational structures.[141]

As in any form of analysis which seeks to move beyond what is obvious on the face of the text, the subjective element is never entirely absent from literary interpretation.[142] This fact should engender in the

---

[141] "Some Observations", 169.

[142] A degree of subjectivity is present not only when the critic is engaged in synchronic analysis but equally, or perhaps even more so, when his focus is upon the task of reconstructing a text's prehistory. The fact that synchronic literary interpretations depend, to some degree at least, upon drawing out inferences and reading between the lines in no wise invalidates the approach as such.

interpreter a proper humility and tentativeness towards the results he is able to achieve and encourage him to remain open to new insights, from whatever quarter they may come. The validity of any interpretation will be judged by its ability to account for all the evidence and by its compatibility with the wider literary context.

One of the aims of this chapter has been to illustrate how a study of the poetics of Hebrew narrative can lend historical depth to our literary judgements, which is to say, to the degree that poetic study is able to impart an 'ancient literary competence', the reader is in a better position to interpret the ancient text according to historically appropriate criteria. In what follows, our focus is not on poetics *per se* but rather on interpretation. Our exegetical approach to the narratives recounting Saul's reign and rejection will attempt to be more synthetic than this chapter, with its heavy emphasis on literary issues, might suggest. Dialogue between the various exegetical methods is seen as essential.

The textual history of 1 Sam 9-15 has been a matter of intense debate, and our own analysis focuses especially on those areas where some of the results of traditional literary criticism seem to be open to question. In some instances, as in the case of the disputed section in 1 Sam 15 discussed above, the impetus for revision comes from the new light which a 'poetic' insight sheds upon an old problem. In others, it is more a matter of reviewing and reevaluating the arguments by which certain viewpoints have gained the ascendancy.

In terms of procedure, Moberly is theoretically correct in asserting that a "rigorous examination of the final text" should be the first step in interpretation. In practice, of course, it is often difficult to approach the text without presuppositions. Critical conclusions pertaining to the text under consideration are often well-known, and we can hardly avoid testing these as our reading proceeds. Positively, we can frequently sharpen our own powers of observation by rehearsing the keen textual observations upon which previous critical conclusions have often been based.

In the next chapter, we shall investigate the relationship of the Gilgal episode (1 Sam 13:7b-15a) to its present context in 1 Sam 13. Not only will this provide opportunity to exemplify the synthetic exegetical approach that we have been advocating, but the results of this investigation will prove to be an important preliminary to our reading of 1 Sam 13-14 in Part Two.

2

A REASSESSMENT OF
THE GILGAL EPISODE
IN 1 SAM 13

The Current Consensus

At least since Wellhausen,[1] the vast majority of scholars have accepted as an 'assured result' the view that the account of Saul's first rejection in 13:7b-15a and the anticipatory reference in 10:8 belong only secondarily to their present contexts.[2] Typical of the confidence with which this view continues to be held are the words of T. Veijola:

> Daß die ganze aus dem Zusammenhang fallende Gilgal-Episode 1 Sam 13:7b-15a mitsamt ihrer ebenso isolierten Vorbereitung in 1 Sam 10:8 ein sekundärer Einschub ist, *bedarf keines Nachweises mehr*.[3] (emphasis added)

Before looking at the arguments adduced in support of this conclusion, it may be helpful to summarize briefly the sequence of events as recounted in the present form of 1 Sam 13:1-15.[4]

---

[1] E.g. *Prolegomena*, 266-68.

[2] E.g., Budde, 85; Schunck, *Benjamin*, 91, 108; Soggin, *Königtum*, 42 n.37; Stoebe, 207; Smelik, *Saul*, 120; McCarter, 228. For others, see the listing by Veijola, *Dynastie*, 55.

[3] *Dynastie*, 55. Cf. the comment of von Rad ("Zwei Überlieferungen," 203): "Daß der Passus 13,7b-15a als eine nachträgliche Interpolation zu verstehen ist, wird kaum bestritten".

[4] Issues only touched upon in the following summary are treated in greater detail in Chapter 3 below.

The Basic Biblical Story-line

Apart from the introductory regnal formula of v. 1, the chapter opens with the notice that Saul selected three thousand men,[5] retaining two thousand under his own command in Michmash and the hill country of Bethel and stationing one thousand with Jonathan in Gibeah (or Geba?) of Benjamin[6] (v. 2). V. 2b notes that the rest of the people were dismissed, "each man to his tent".[7] The text provides no information as to the purpose of this troop deployment, but the topographical details suggest that the forces were located on either side of a strategic pass traversing the Benjaminite hill country from the Jordan, near Jericho, in the east to Aijalon and the coastal plain in the west.[8]

The action begins dramatically in v. 3 with Jonathan's assassination of the Philistine governor (נציב),[9] an act of defiance which quickly becomes known to the rest of the Philistines. Saul responds to the crisis by having the trumpet blown throughout the land (v. 3b), and the report goes out that Saul has smitten the Philistine governor and that Israel is in a state of revolt (v. 4a).[10] The people (here the reference is probably to those who were dismissed in v. 2) are summoned to join

---

[5] Or military contingents; cf. Judg 6:15; 1 Sam 10:19; the comments of G. E. Mendenhall, "Census Lists", esp. 60-64; and McCarter, 107, 225.

[6] On the knotty problem of the variation in chs. 13-14 between Gibeah and Geba, see J. M. Miller's "Geba/Gibeah of Benjamin", in which Miller challenges Albright's identification of Gibeah with *tel el-fûl* and argues that Gibeah and Geba both refer to the same place, namely *jeba'*.

[7] The phrase appears to connote dismissal from military service; so McCarter, 107. Cf. Judg 20:8; 1 Sam 4:10; 2 Sam 20:1; 1 Kgs 12:16.

[8] G. A. Smith (*Historical Geography*, 246) describes this pass, the "Vale of Ajalon", as "a real pass across the [central] range. Not only did Israel by it first come up from the Jordan onto the tableland, and by it sweep down towards the sea, but it was in all ages a regular route for trade. ... In Saul's days the Philistines were naturally anxious to hold this route".

[9] The meaning of this term is debated (BDB, 662). One possibility is that it designates a 'stele' of some sort; cf. perhaps Old Phoenician נצב in *SSI*, 3:21.1; 3:22.1; and Old Aramaic נצבא (?) in *SSI*, 2:5.A.1; 2:7.iA.6. A second possibility is the meaning 'garrison' (for a defence of this view, see Joüon, "Notes"). The third and, in the present context, likeliest possibility is the meaning 'governor, prefect' (cf. Budde, 67; Blenkinsopp, "Quest", 97 n. 49). For a possible parallel to the semantic relationship between נצב hi. and נציב, cf. Akk. *šakānu* '(hin)stellen, (ein)setzen, anlegen; versehen mit' (*AHw*, 1134f.) with *šaknu* 'gestellt, gelegt, usw; Statthalter' (*AHw*, 1141).

[10] This seems to be the significance of the statement that Israel had become "odious" to the Philistines; see Ch. 3, p. 79.

Saul at Gilgal (v. 4b). The Philistines, meanwhile, mount a massive military response (v. 5), throwing the men of Israel into panic and sending many into hiding (v. 6). V. 7a records the flight of Hebrews across the Jordan, while v. 7b states that Saul is in Gilgal.

In v. 8 we learn that Saul is waiting for Samuel, in accordance with some pre-arranged appointment. When the prophet delays in coming, Saul orders that the burnt offerings and peace offerings be brought to him (v. 9), and by the time Samuel arrives, the sacrifices are well under way (v. 10). To Saul's apparent consternation, his act of personal initiative is interpreted by Samuel as a foolish breach of the command of Yahweh (v. 13). After announcing that Saul's kingdom will not endure and that his successor is already in the wings (v. 14), Samuel departs without further ado, and Saul, along with the faithful few who have not deserted, rejoins the fighting force in Gibeah/Geba (v. 15).[11]

This, in broad strokes, is the picture presented by 1 Sam 13:1-15. As we have already noted, however, the view that what we may call the Gilgal episode (i.e. 13:7b-15a) belongs only secondarily to its present context has since Wellhausen enjoyed the status of an 'assured result'. The major arguments in support of this conclusion can be found in some form already in Wellhausen's writings, and they can be summarized as follows.

Five Difficulties

First, it is held to be militarily unthinkable that Saul should have relinquished his position of strength in the hill country of Benjamin (cf. 13:2) to retreat to Gilgal.[12] Secondly, the sequence of events in ch. 13 after the removal of the Gilgal episode in vv. 7b-15a (and also possibly the reference to Gilgal in v. 4b) leaves "a rather straightforward account."[13] Thirdly, it is asserted that Saul's rejection is in no way pre-

---

[11] Following the longer reading of LXX; see our discussion of 13:15 in Ch. 3, pp. 94-95.

[12] Smith (93), for example, contends that "Saul's movement from Geba to Gilgal would be, from a military point of view an insane step." Similarly, Budde (85) writes, "Hier ist Gilgal vollends unmöglich, weil wir Sauls Aufenthalt aus v. 2 bereits kennen und die Jordanschlucht der denkbar ungünstigste Sammelplatz für ein kriegsbereites Heer wäre." Cf. Wellhausen, *Prolegomena*, 267.

[13] Birch, *Rise*, 78; cf. Smith, 94-95.

supposed in the subsequent narrative of chs. 13-14.[14] Fourthly, the fact that the Gilgal episode of ch. 13 clearly represents the fulfilment of Samuel's command to Saul in 10:8 strongly suggests a dislocation of traditions, for not only is there an apparently inexplicable gap of several chapters between the command (10:8) and the fulfilment (13:8), but there is also the embarrassing matter in 11:14 of an intervening encounter between Saul and Samuel at Gilgal, where no mention is made of the injunctions of 10:8![15] It is argued, moreover, that 10:8 also cannot be original to its present context, because it stands in direct contradiction of Samuel's authorization in 10:7 to "do what your hand finds to do".[16]

A final argument offered by Wellhausen[17] but largely neglected by subsequent scholars has been revived by B. C. Birch, who cites the syntax of 1 Sam 13:16 as virtual proof that Saul could not have been at Gilgal during the muster of Philistine forces at Michmash. He constructs his argument as follows:

> V. 16, however, presents a major difficulty when it states that Saul and his men had been camped at Gibeah of Benjamin when the Philistines had encamped opposite them at Michmash. Syntactically, there is no other way to read the verse. The first half of the verse uses a participial construction (יֹשְׁבִים) to indicate continuous action. This clearly contrasted with the second half of the verse which is a circumstantial clause (indicated by the placement of the subject before the verb) with a perfect verb (חָנוּ). In light of this contrast, one must read the verse to indicate that at the time the Philistines camped at Michmash, Saul and Jonathan continued to be camped at Gibeah. This would make any movement of Saul to

---

[14] Wellhausen (*Composition*, 248) writes: "In Kap. 14 verrät nicht die geringste Spur, dass das ominöse Ereignis auf Sauls, des Volkes und des Schriftstellers Seele lastet"; cf. *idem*, *Prolegomena*, 267; Budde, "Sauls Königswahl", 242; Smith, 93; Hertzberg, 82/ET 105; Schunck, *Benjamin*, 91.

[15] Wellhausen, *Prolegomena*, 267-68; *idem*, *Text*, 82; Budde, 85; Schunck, *Benjamin*, 91; McCarter, 228. Some, of course, would eliminate references to Samuel in ch. 11; but see our discussion in Ch. 7, pp. 224-28.

[16] Budde (69) writes: "Der Vers schlägt dem vorhergehenden ins Gesicht, indem jener schleuniges, unbedenkliches Handeln nach eigenstem Antrieb, dieser beschauliches Verhalten und Warten auf Samuels Weisungen vorschreibt." Cf. Wellhausen, *Prolegomena*, 268; R. J. Thompson, *Penitence*, 106; Stoebe, 210.

[17] See his remarks on 13:16 in *Prolegomena*, 267.

Gilgal impossible and thus stands in sharp contrast to the earlier portion of the chapter.[18]

A Preliminary Response

The above arguments have proved to be remarkably influential,[19] but it is the contention of this writer that neither singly nor in combination are they compelling. As regards the argument that a trip to Gilgal from Michmash would have been an insane step militarily, two comments can be made. First, the assumption that Saul's descent to Gilgal for a general muster would have entailed the relinquishing of the hill country seems unfounded. It would appear that Jonathan and the troops with him maintained their position in the hill country during the Gilgal interlude.[20] And it is a reasonable assumption that the two thousand soldiers originally under Saul's command were likewise intended to hold their positions north of the Aijalon Pass.[21] Yadin has described the troops deployed in 13:2 as "the first nucleus of a select and regular army which served both as a standing army and *as a striking and holding force while the whole militia was called up*"[22] (emphasis added). Secondly, far from being the "denkbar ungünstigste Sammelplatz",[23] Gilgal actually seems to commend itself in several respects as a site for a general muster. Noth has observed that Gilgal was centrally located,

---

[18] *Rise*, 76.

[19] Even Buber ("Sauls Königswahl", 137-39, 150), who otherwise has a rather high view of the coherence of the biblical account of Saul's rise (cf. 113-14), regards as "sicheres Ergebnis der Literarkritik" the view that 1 Sam 13:7b-15a and 10:8 are secondary insertions.

[20] There is no mention of Jonathan at Gilgal, and v. 15 in LXX explicitly describes Saul's return to the hill country to rejoin the fighting force (and Jonathan, as implied by v. 16). Hertzberg (83/ET 105) observes: "Offenbar ist es so vorgestellt, daß Jonathan mit seinen Leuten die Stellung bei Geba hält, während Saul in der Jordanaue Verstärkungen sammelt"; cf. also Garsiel, "קרב מכמש", 24.

[21] "Aijalon Pass" is the name used by B. Halpern ("Uneasy Compromise", 62) to designate the pass from Aijalon to Jericho which we mentioned above, p. 44.

[22] *Art of Warfare*, 264. Cf. Seebass ("I Sam 15", 158, n. 27): "Nach der gegenwärtigen Darstellung läßt Saul seine Truppen an Ort und Stelle und zieht allein nach Gilgal, um den Heerbann noch einmal aufzubieten. Während seiner Abwesenheit gerät die schlachtbereite Truppe in Angst und verkriecht sich (6. 7a). Dadurch ist Saul gezwungen, seine Position in Geba neu aufzubauen."

[23] So Budde, 85.

yet outside the area of direct Philistine control.[24]   Moreover, as Malamat has recently noted, Gilgal occupied a strategic position both as a link with Transjordan and as a springboard for operations into the hill country.[25]

As for the second argument — that ch. 13 yields a straightforward account when once the Gilgal material has been excised —, we can perhaps do no better than to cite W. A. Irwin:

> That these passages can be removed without leaving an apparent hiatus is probably true; but this is not the same thing as convicting them of spurious insertion, as any modern editor, of his own work or another's, will at once realize.[26]

The third argument — that the events of Saul's first rejection are nowhere reflected in the subsequent narrative — has been strongly challenged in recent studies, most notably by D. Jobling in his article entitled "Saul's Fall and Jonathan's Rise: Tradition and Redaction in 1 Sam 14:1-46".[27] Jobling has demonstrated convincingly that 1 Sam 14:1-46 "presents a skillful portrait of a rejected king, wholly coherent with the rejection oracles of chaps. 13 and 15. His character and fate bear out his rejection."[28] In short, "chap. 13 casts its shadow over all that follows".[29] Curiously, Jobling does not explore the possible implications of this conclusion for the standard view that the Gilgal episode in ch. 13 is secondary. Instead, he simply adopts without argument the "current theories about the passage's literary prehistory"[30] — viz., "that the traditions of these two chapters [13-14], with the exception of the first rejection pericope, are [or were originally] favorable to Saul" and

---

[24] *Geschichte*, 158. Cf. Hertzberg (82/ET 105): "An sich wäre gegen Sauls Gang nach dem Gilgal im Rahmen der anderen Ereignisse nichts einzuwenden. Ausdrücklich ist die Einberufung des Heerbannes in 4b zum Gilgal erfolgt, was vollauf begreiflich ist. Mizpa und Bethel wären bei der damaligen Lage als Sammlungsorte nicht in Betracht gekommen."

[25] "Inferior Israelite Forces", 31. Malamat's discussion focuses on the period of the 'conquest', but his observations regarding Gilgal remain valid for later periods as well.

[26] "Samuel", 123.

[27] Cf. also Gunn, *Fate*, 65-70; Wentz, *Monarchy*, 328; Smelik, *Saul*, 132.

[28] "Saul's Fall", 368.

[29] "Saul's Fall", 371.

[30] "Saul's Fall", 367.

that the insertion of 13:7b-15a "is the work of a redactor".[31] He is thus forced to conclude that the negative portrayal of Saul now evident in 1 Sam 13-14 *must be* purely redactional: "the pro-Saul traditions of 14:1-46 have been *radically recast* to tell an anti-Saul story, or, as we prefer to say, to draw a portrait of a rejected king"[32] (emphasis added). There is a degree of circularity in Jobling's argumentation; he begins by assuming an originally pro-Saul tradition in 1 Sam 13-14 and then proceeds to demonstrate its existence by attributing all negative elements in these chapters to a redactor. The crux of the issue remains the question of 13:7b-15a. If it can be demonstrated, on grounds other than the supposed pro-Saul stance of the surrounding materials in chs. 13-14, that these verses are secondary, then there is some force in Jobling's contention that their insertion brought about extensive "alteration and even reversal of traditions."[33] The point that we are making, however, is that chs. 13-14, as Jobling has demonstrated, *do now reflect the events of 13:7b-15a.* This being so, the argument under review, viz. that the Gilgal episode is secondary because it is nowhere reflected in the surrounding materials, is seen to be invalid.

Omitting the fourth point for the moment, we come to the fifth, where it must be admitted that Birch's reading of 13:16 is a possibility.[34] It is not the only way to read the verse, however. First, it should be noted that not only v. 16b but also v. 16a displays the subject + predicate word-order characteristic of circumstantial clauses. Secondly, although Birch seems to assume that v. 16b implies concomitant circumstance, R. J. Williams, whom Birch cites throughout in support of his syntactical argument, points out that the subject + verb word-order occurs in at least seven types of clauses, including those ex-

---

[31] "Saul's Fall", 371.

[32] "Saul's Fall", 371.

[33] "Saul's Fall", 375.

[34] 1 Sam 9:27, for example, displays the same basic syntactical structure as 13:16 (i.e. subject + participle + *waw* + subject + predicate) and can be read as follows: ...המה יורדים בקצה העיר ושמואל אמר אל־שאול , "As they were going down to the outskirts of the city, Samuel said to Saul ...". Cf. 1 Sam 9:11, but note that in both these examples, as Williams (*Hebrew Syntax*, §237) points out, the first subject is asyndetic. Likewise in the circumstantial clauses of 9:5, 14; Gen 29:9; 38:25; 44:3; and Judg 15:14; 18:3, all of which express simultaneous action, the subject of the circumstantial clause is without the *waw*, while the main clause has it; *this is not the case in 13:16.* See further Davidson, *Syntax*, §141 and Rem. 2; GK §156a.

pressive of "anterior time (equivalent to an English pluperfect; ...)."[35]
Williams notes further that whereas the predicate of a circumstantial
clause denoting concomitant circumstance may be a participle, an
adjective or a prepositional phrase,[36] "when the circumstances described
are past or future, a finite form of a verb is employed. For the past a
perfect aspect is used."[37] In the light of these considerations, it is
clearly possible to view both circumstantial clauses of v. 16 as introductory to the main action which follows. V. 16b, with its finite perfect tense, is expressive of action anterior to the main action, while v.
16a, with its participle, is concomitant with the main action. An
accurate, if somewhat wooden, English translation would be as follows:
"As Saul and his son Jonathan and the men with them were staying at
Geba of Benjamin (the Philistines having encamped at Michmash),
raiding parties went out from the Philistine camp...." Read in this
way, v. 16 in no way precludes a trip to Gilgal before or during the
convergence of Philistine forces upon Michmash.

Of the five difficulties raised in connection with the Gilgal episode
in 1 Sam 13, four have proved to be, at best, inconclusive. The remaining argument — that the link between the Gilgal episode of 1 Sam
13 and its obvious anticipation several chapters earlier in 10:8 is
indicative of a dislocation of traditions in one or both contexts —
requires more extensive treatment and will form a focal point of discussion in the present chapter and in Part Three below. So far, our attention has been directed primarily towards a reevaluation of the arguments
most commonly adduced to support the conclusion that vv. 7b-15a
cannot be original to ch. 13. It is now time to consider whether there
may be any positive indications that the Gilgal episode is integral to its
present context.

---

[35] *Hebrew Syntax*, §573.

[36] *Hebrew Syntax*, §494.

[37] *Hebrew Syntax*, §495; cf. GK §142b.

On the Relationship between 1 Sam 10:7-8
and the Gilgal Episode of 1 Sam 13

A Common Pattern

We may begin with two observations of fundamental importance: 1) of the link between 10:8 and the Gilgal episode in 1 Sam 13:7b-15a, recognized by virtually all interpreters of Samuel, there can be no reasonable doubt;[38] 2) less obvious, but nonetheless recognized by numerous scholars, is a similar link between the command of 10:7, to "do what your hand finds to do", and the assassination of the Philistine governor in 13:3. Stoebe, for example, writes:

> Die Tat, die hier [13:3] Jonathan zugeschrieben wird, erwartet man als Fortsetzung der Geistbegabung Sauls bei Gibea und der Aufforderung: "Tue, was dir vor die Hand kommt" (10,7).[39]

Halpern agrees:

> *Once the spirit has descended upon him, Saul is to 'do what comes to hand, for Elohim is with you' (10:7).* He is to reduce the garrison, taking the town (cf. Judg 9:33; note also Ps 21:9; 1 Sam 23:17; 1 Sam 10:14). That is the particular implication of the assurance of divine accompaniment (as, e.g., Judg 6:12). Again, *the continuation appears in chap. 13.* There, the notice occurs that Jonathan reduced the Philistine garrison, followed by the report that Saul's reduction of the garrison was noised abroad (vv 3-4). *The fulfillment of Samuel's instructions is in point.*[40] (emphasis added)

To be sure, many scholars, influenced by the present arrangement of the texts, seek the fulfilment of 10:7 in Saul's 'judge-like' deliverance of the Jabesh-gileadites from the Ammonites in ch. 11.[41] But several

---

[38] See Ch. 3, p. 88.

[39] Stoebe, 247; cf. 207.

[40] *Constitution*, 155-56. Cf. also Stolz, 85; Kittel, *Geschichte* 2: 82.

[41] E.g., Thompson, *Penitence*, 106; Blenkinsopp, "Quest", 84. Blenkinsopp recognizes that ch. 10 appears to be linked with ch. 13, but he dismisses this possibility on the basis of Saul's apparent youthfulness in ch. 10 and his accompaniment by a grown son in ch. 13. We shall later

factors militate against the acceptance of Saul's Ammonite victory as a *full and adequate fulfilment* of the command of 10:7.[42]

First and foremost is the fact that the account of Saul's anointing and commission in the section 9:1-10:16 focuses primarily (9:16), if not exclusively (cf. 10:1), upon the Philistines.[43] Thus, Richter has argued that Saul, like the pre-monarchic deliverers, was raised up to deal with a specific need and a specific enemy.[44] Yahweh's words to Samuel in 9:16, which represent the content of Saul's commission,[45] clearly identify that enemy.

> About this time tomorrow, I will send to you a man from the land of Benjamin. You shall anoint him nāgîd[46] over my people, and he shall deliver my people from the hand of the Philistines. For I have regarded my people, for their cry has come to me.

The focus of the commissioning scene upon the Philistines is reinforced in 10:5 by Samuel's mention of the Philistine governor at Gibeath-elohim, the site where the third and final sign confirming Saul's anointing will take place. Some scholars, rightly noting the correspondence of this reference to the mention in 13:3 of a Philistine governor at Gibeah,[47] but failing to see any further significance in the allusion in ch. 10 to the Philistine presence, eliminate 10:5a as a gloss. McCarter, for example, writes: "This notice is immaterial at this point

---

have occasion to query the notion that Saul was but a youth in chs. 9-10 (see Ch. 7, pp. 204-205).

[42] We shall argue in Ch. 6 (see p. 189) that the Ammonite victory does, in fact, function as the 'testing stage' in Saul's rise to power but, nevertheless, is not that which was originally envisaged in the account of his anointing.

[43] Cf. Lods, *Israel*, 353; Seebass, "I Sam 15", 155-56; Mayes, "Period of the Judges", 324, 326; Stolz, 85; Halpern, "Uneasy Compromise", 65; Whitelam, "Defence", 72.

[44] "Die *nāgîd*-Formel", 81.

[45] So Schmidt, *Menschlicher Erfolg*, 88.

[46] The precise connotations of this term are much debated. According to Westermann ("נגד", 34), at the time of Samuel and Saul it was used for "den designierten künftigen König". Richter ("Die *nāgîd*-Formel", 81-84) has argued that the title *nāgîd* was early used as a "Beinamen zum Retter", that the title-holder, as "die zeitgemäße Fortsetzung des Retters Israels", carried military responsibilities, and that he was "an den Propheten gebunden". For a summary of other views, see Ishida, "נגיד".

[47] See below, pp. 78-79 and n. 51.

and probably secondary, having been added along with the instructions in v 8 as preparation for c 13."[48] More plausible, however, is the view held by other scholars that the reference to a *Philistine* governor at the "hill of *God* " (גבעת האלהים) represents a broad hint by Samuel as to what Saul's hand should find to do, once all the signs have come to pass. Kittel, in discussing ch. 13, writes,

> Hier lag für Saul in Wahrheit, "was seine Hand finden sollte", wie ihm Samuel geheimnisvoll und doch wohlverständlich zugeraunt hatte.[49]

Similarly, Lods writes:

> According to this account it was the seer who gave Saul the idea of attacking the triumphal stele[50] of Gibeah by telling him that when he arrived at this spot he would meet the 'prophets', and would be possessed by the spirit of Jahweh: 'Do as occasion serve thee; for God is with thee.'[51]

Goslinga adds:

> Zo is ook vlg. Buber 'ה 'ג "kein Ortsname," maar een heuvel vlak bij Gibea, die door Samuël "Hügel Gottes" genoemd wordt om daartegenover te stellen de 'נציב פ ....
> De uitdrukking moet dus Saul stimuleren om straks de nationale vijand van Gods boden te verdrijven.[52]

Recognition that 10:5 contains a hint to Saul of what his role as deliverer should entail goes back at least as far as the Jewish commentator Kimchi, who notes that Samuel informs Saul of the "officers of the Philistines" (נציבי פלשתים), "hinting to him that he should remove

---

[48] McCarter, 182; cf. Ackroyd, 83.

[49] *Geschichte* 2: 82. Cf. Goslinga's (255) reference to the Philistine נציב in 13:3, "waarop Samuël reeds in 10:5 Saul gewezen had".

[50] This is Lods' understanding of נציב. On the various possibilities, see above, p. 44 n. 9.

[51] *Israel*, 353.

[52] Goslinga, 223. Cf. Smelik (*Saul*, 107): "Door de Filistijnse bezetting aldaar te vermelden, onderstreept Samuël Sauls taak om Israël te verlossen."

them from there and save Israel out of their hands" (רמז לו כי הוא
יסירם משם ויושיע ישראל מידם).[53]

A second factor militating against acceptance of ch. 11 as a fully
adequate fulfilment of 10:7 is the problem of the time lapse between
Saul's anointing and commission in ch. 10 and the victory of ch. 11.
If, as is often asserted, Saul stood, in some respects at least, in
continuity with the hero-deliverers of the pre-monarchic period,[54] it is
surprising that the bestowal of the divine spirit, predicted in 10:6 and
accomplished in 10:10, did not immediately propel him into an act of
deliverance. Again, Stoebe makes the point:

> Handelt es sich um die Geistbegabung, wie sie von den
> charismatischen Führern bekannt ist, müßte sie nun zu
> einer konkreten Tat führen. Diese Tat scheint im ur-
> sprünglichen Überlieferungsbestand wirklich 13,3 en-
> thalten zu sein.[55]

Of course, if delay is a problem when ch. 11 is viewed as the sequel to
10:7, the problem is even more acute if ch. 13 is assumed to fulfil that
role. But we shall return to this point later.[56]

In view of these factors, especially the focus of Saul's commission
upon the Philistines (9:16) and the clear link between the references to
the Philistine governor in 10:5a and 13:3, the common view that ch.
11 provides an adequate fulfilment of 10:7 must be rejected. Rather, the
primary 'command-fulfilment' relationships are 10:7 fulfilled in 13:3
and 10:8 fulfilled in the Gilgal episode of 13:7b-15a. Recognition of
these relationships leads to the further observation that both ch. 10 and
ch. 13 exhibit a common pattern or sequence involving 1) an individual

---

[53] From Kimchi's commentary on 1 Samuel available in Rosenberg,
Samuel I.

[54] See below, p. 60.

[55] Stoebe, 207. Cf. Von Rad's comment on the pattern of charismatic leadership (*Theologie*, 1: 329): "Der Berufung folgt alsbald der öf-
fentliche Erweis des Charismas in einem Sieg über die Feinde". Beyerlin
("Königscharisma", 188) has sought to resolve the difficulty by arguing
that Saul's charisma was *nebiistic* — of a different order from that of the
judges. While there may be some validity in this observation, Beyerlin almost certainly goes too far in asserting that Saul's charisma "hat [nicht] das
Geringste zu tun mit der Geistbegabung, wie sie den Großen Richtern zuteil
wurde." At any rate, whatever the precise significance of the bestowal of the
spirit, the command of 10:7 removes all doubt that as soon as the signs are
fulfilled, Saul is to *do something*.

[56] See p. 65 below and, especially, Part Three.

action against the Philistine governor (10:5-7; 13:3) followed by 2) a move to Gilgal in order to rendezvous with Samuel for sacrifice and further instructions (10:8; 13:7b-15a). For the sake of convenience, we may refer to this pattern in terms of provocation-convocation, and our results so far may be presented diagrammatically.

	Provocation	Convocation
Command	10:7	10:8
	ǀ	ǀ
	ǀ	ǀ
Fulfilment	13:3	13:7b-15a

The question which now presents itself is how the pattern in each context may best be explained. Is it merely the result of redactional activity[57] or are there indications that it may be original to one or both contexts?

The Pattern in Ch. 13: Integral or Redactional?

With respect to ch. 13, the first thing we notice is that the Gilgal episode (vv. 7b-15a) presupposes precisely such a setting as is described in the rest of 1 Sam 13-14, namely a Philistine battle in the area of Michmash. Saul's complaint in v. 11, for example, that "the Philistines were assembling at Michmash" recalls the information of v. 5 that "the Philistines assembled to fight with Israel, ... and they came up and camped at Michmash". Similarly, the notice in v. 7b that Saul is in Gilgal with all the army (כל העם) trembling after him presupposes the summons to the army (העם) to come out after him in v. 4b.[58] One way to deal with such evidence, of course, is to label one or

---

[57] E.g., Schunck (*Benjamin*, 107-108) attributes the insertion of both 10:8 and 13:7b-15a to a Deuteronomistic redactor. Stoebe (210-11) recognizes that the similarity in content between chs. 10 and 13 makes it unlikely that 10:8 is simply a linking gloss and contends rather that both 10:8 and 13:7bff. are the result of "eine[r] gemeinsame[n] Überarbeitung, die allerdings nicht sekundär deuteronomistisch zu sein braucht". Budde (85), on the other hand, regards both as representing an "innerjahwistischen Zuwachs".

[58] That כל העם does not always connote 'all the army' in an absolute sense is demonstrated by Judg 7:7: "And Yahweh said to Gideon, 'With the 300 men who lapped I will deliver you, and I will give Midian into your

both members of the linked pairs as secondary. It is quite common, for example, to treat v. 4b as a redactional expansion,[59] though often for no other reason than that it clearly anticipates the Gilgal episode (vv. 7b-15a), which itself is believed to be secondary.[60] In fact, however, there is evidence that v. 4b may not be divorced from the verse that precedes it without disrupting an important structure inherent in the two verses.

This point is argued by H. Madl in his Bonn dissertation entitled *Literarkritische und Formanalytische Untersuchungen zu 1 Sam 14*. In a comparative analysis of 1 Sam 13:3-4 with Judg 3 (Ehud vs Moab), Judg 6 (Gideon vs Midian), and 2 Sam 20 (the Sheba revolt), Madl detects a "viergliedriges Schema" — comprising "Situationsangabe, Blasen des Schofarhornes, Aufruf und Versammlung zur Aktion" — common to all four passages.[61] Adopting Madl's schema as our starting point, we may display the comparable features of the four passages as follows:

---

hands, so let all the army (כל העם) go, each to his own place'." In the present context the sense is 'all the army apart from the troops previously deployed', viz. in v. 2.

[59] So, for example, Budde, 85; Schunck, *Benjamin*, 91 n. 67; Stoebe, 244; Stolz, 85. Vv. 5 and 11, both of which mention a Philistine assembly in Michmash, are seldom queried.

[60] So, for example, de Vries, "Temporal Terms", 98.

[61] *Untersuchungen*, 182.

	Ehud vs Moab	Gideon vs Midian	Saul/Jonathan vs Philitia	Sheba vs Judah
Critical Situation[62]	Judg 3:15-25	Judg 6:33	1 Sam 13:3a	2 Sam 19:40-20:1a
Trumpet Blast	Judg 3:27a	Judg 6:34b	1 Sam 13:3bα	2 Sam 20:1bα
Address[63]	Judg 3:28a	(implied v. 35)	1 Sam 13:3bβ-4a	2 Sam 20:1bβ
Assembly for Action[64]	Judg 3:27b, 28b	Judg 6:34b-35	1 Sam 13:4b	2 Sam 20:2a

Though, not unexpectedly, the various episodes show diversity in details,[65] they do attest a basic sequence of crisis, trumpet blast, appeal and assembly for action (or at least a reference to "going up after ..."). Thus, Madl's conclusion that any possibility of regarding v. 4b alone as secondary is precluded by the fixed *Schematik* of vv. 3b-4 seems well founded.[66] Ironically, Madl omits v. 3a in the above summation

---

[62] The first element in Madl's schema is too general, leading Madl to cite Judg 3:27aα ("And it came about when he arrived") and 2 Sam 20:1a ("And a worthless fellow happened to be there whose name was Sheba, the son of Bichri, a Benjaminite") as the *Situationsangaben* which preceded the trumpet blasts in the two relevant passages. We prefer to label the first element the 'description of a critical situation', for it is the *critical* situation in each passage (i.e. the assassination of Eglon in Judg 3:15-25 and the bitter exchange in 2 Sam 19:40-20:1a between the men of Israel and the men of Judah as to who had more claim on David) that provides the necessary background to the trumpet blast and summons to revolt.

[63] Madl labels the third member the "Aufruf" (182) or the "Ansprache" (183). If we accept for the time being MT of 1 Sam 13:3 (but see our discussion in Ch. 3, pp. 79-80), we may observe that in three of the four passages under consideration this third member takes the form of a direct address, while in Judg 6:35 the address is implied by the sending of messengers.

[64] Typical of this element, the "Versammlung des Kriegvolkes", are verbs such as ירד, עלה or niphal of צעק/זעק, and the "Ausdruck des Folgens" employing אחר/אחרי (*Untersuchungen*, 184).

[65] Madl (*Untersuchungen*, 182) recognizes from the outset that his four-part schema is one which "natürlich teilweise variieren kann."

[66] *Untersuchungen*, 185. As against Budde (85), who argues that v. 4b must be secondary since נצעק and זועק are nowhere directly coupled with the place-name "wohin das Aufgebot berufen wird", Madl (184) points out that "Ri 3,28bβ und 2 Sam 20,14 eine feste Ortsangabe bieten und glggl [*sic*] daher nicht ohne weiteres gestrichen werden darf." Also protective of the Gilgal reference is Smith, 95.

(apparently in the interest of a source-critical theory he is pursuing),[67] but in so doing he robs his fixed schema of precisely that element that he had earlier named as its first member![68] Despite this curious inconsistency in his concluding statement, Madl has successfully shown that 1 Sam 13:3-4 represents a well-structured unit that would be destroyed were v. 4b to be removed as a secondary expansion.

The organic link between v. 3 and v. 4, along with the fact that v. 4b clearly sets the stage for the Gilgal episode in vv. 7b-15a, provides significant evidence for the integrity of the provocation/convocation pattern in 1 Sam 13. So far, the following links have been established:

	Provocation	Convocation
Command	10:7	10:8
	|	|
	|	|
Fulfilment	13:3————13:4b, 5——13:7b-15a	

The Pattern in Ch. 10: Integral or Redactional?

As noted earlier, the major argument against the originality of 10:8 is that it flatly contradicts the preceding verse.[69] While v. 7 seems to license Saul to act on his own initiative, v. 8 immediately places him back in a position of subordination to the prophet.[70] Not surprisingly in view of this seeming contradiction, J. Kegler, like many others before him, regards 10:8 as a "theologische Korrektur" intended to safeguard the prophetic claim to unconditional obedience.[71] The conviction that 10:8 is but a tendentious correction of a text which seemed to give Saul too much freedom is further reinforced by the frequently expressed opinion that Samuel was in reality little more than an obscure village

---

[67] *Untersuchungen*, 184-85.

[68] *Untersuchungen*, 182.

[69] See p. 46 above.

[70] For a rebuttal of Keil's attempt to ease the tension by construing v. 8aα as a conditional clause, see Driver, 81-82.

[71] *Politisches Geschehen*, 264; according to Kegler (ibid.), the correction is "'geschichtlich' verifiziert" in 13:4b + 7b-15. If some such dynamic were at work, however, one wonders why the 'prophetic revisionists' did not simply expunge the objectionable 10:7.

seer whose image and role have been greatly exaggerated by later prophetic schools.[72] Against this view, however, there is a considerable body of opinion which says that Samuel must have played an important part in the foundation of the monarchy, whatever may be the difficulties involved in discovering his precise role in the matter. Grønbæk, for example, envisages Samuel's role as a multi-faceted one brought about by the critical times in which he lived:

> Obgleich seine Hauptfunktion offentsichlich die des 'Kleinen Richters' gewesen ist, hat die nationale und religiöse Notsituation, in der Israel stand, *fraglos eine Erweiterung seiner Befugnisse zur Folge gehabt.*[73] (Italics added.)

Moreover, as Buss observes in his article on "Prophecy in Ancient Israel", it is not unlikely that "the combination of functions is older than their separation since societal development has generally been in the direction of increasing specialization."[74] Blenkinsopp exhibits no hesitancy in assigning to Samuel a diversity of functions — prophetic, political and military:

> One of the most historically trustworthy of the traditions about Samuel [i.e. 1 Sam 19:18-24][75] presents him as leader of a band of ecstatic prophets, and there can be no doubt that both he and they were involved in the political and military events of that critical period in the consolidation of the tribes.[76]

In short, as Greßmann observed three-quarters of a century ago, the biblical traditions are explicable only...

> wenn Samuel wirklich groß war. Das dankbare Volk pflegt seine Helden noch heldenhafter, seine Könige noch königlicher darzustellen, als sie in der Geschichte

---

[72] For an articulation of this view, see Mayes, "Period of the Judges", 324-25, 330.

[73] *Geschichte*, 68. For a list of others who consider Samuel's various roles to be compatible, see R. K. Gnuse, *Dream Theophany*, 217 n. 4.

[74] "Prophecy", 694.

[75] See *History of Prophecy*, 65.

[76] *History of Prophecy*, 67. See also Ishida, *Royal Dynasties*, 32-35; Evans, "Historical Reconstruction", 67.

gewesen sind, aber es verschwendet seine Liebe im
Allgemeinen nicht an Unwürdige.[77]

It is not unreasonable, therefore, to assume that Samuel was significantly involved in the introduction of monarchy to Israel. What then
can be surmised regarding the nature of that involvement?

There is wide-spread agreement among students of the early monarchy period that Saul "stands firmly in line with pre-monarchic forms of
Israelite leadership".[78] The truth of this assertion is attested both by the
literary shape of the traditions — Saul's rise to power falls within the
'judges period'[79] — and by the way in which Saul gains public support.[80] It would be a mistake, however, to underplay the differences
between pre-monarchic and monarchic leadership. After all, monarchy
was viewed as *something new* in Israel.

One basic distinction between Saul and his pre-monarchic
predecessors is the manner in which their 'charisma', as it were, is ad-
ministered.   It has often been observed that the account of Saul's
anointing and commission (1 Sam 9:1-10:16) exhibits the main elements of the 'call narrative' schema as represented, for example, in Exod
3 and Judg 6, *but in a modified form*.[81] More than anything else, the

---

[77] Greßmann, 27.

[78] So Mayes, "Period of the Judges", 325; cf. Soggin, "Charisma und
Institution"; Halpern, "Uneasy Compromise", 65, 72; Blenkinsopp, *History of Prophecy*, 66-67; Bright, *History*, 188-90; Weisman, "Anointing",
395; Schulte, *Geschichtsschreibung*, 111. Cross also recognizes "the
continuities between the institutions of the covenanted tribes in the era of
the league and the early monarchy in Israel" (*CMHE*, 219), and he notes that
even David "moved slowly in the matter of innovation and stressed
continuities between his kingship and the constitution or covenant of the
league" (232). For a discussion of some differences between Saul and the
'judges', see Beyerlin, "Königscharisma", esp. 188-90.

[79] Mayes, for example, remarks that the story of the period of the
judges "begins in [Judg] 2.6, which follows directly on Joshua 23, and continues beyond the book of Judges to 1 Sam 12, where Samuel's speech marks
the end of the era and the beginning of the period of the monarchy" ("Period
of the Judges", 287; following Noth, *ÜSt*, 5).

[80] "Saul was accepted primarily because, in his victory over Ammon
(ch. 11), he exhibited charismatic gifts as had the judges before him"
(Bright, *History*, 188).

[81] For discussions of the formal characteristics of call narratives, see
Habel, "Call Narrative"; Schmidt, *Menschlicher Erfolg*, 88-89; Richter,
Berufungsberichte; Birch, *Rise*, 35-40; March, "Prophecy", 170-72;
Halpern, *Constitution*, 116 and n. 19.

modifications to the standard form seem to stem from the fact that Saul's call is *mediated* by a human agent. Schmidt explains:

> Die Veränderungen des Schemas hängen wohl mit der anderen Situation zusammen. Erteilt sonst Gott bzw. Jahwe dem militärischen Führer direkt den Auftrag, so erfolgt die Berufung Sauls durch einen Mittler. Dadurch wird der Auftrag aufgegliedert. Der Mittler führt eine *Berufungshandlung* durch, die Salbung. *Der Wortlaut*, die Bedeutung des Auftrages, wird in eine Botschaft Jahwes [i.e. 9:16] an den Mittler über die Wirksamkeit der Person umgesetzt.[82]

Although not entirely without precedent in the pre-monarchic period,[83] prophetic mediation of the divine initiative became especially prominent with the institution of monarchy.[84] Talmon describes the change in terms of "a 'bifurcation' of the divine presence":

> In pre-monarchic Israel, the divine spirit revealed itself exclusively in the person of the leader, like Moses, or the inspired saviour. ...With the establishment of the monarchy a 'bifurcation' of the divine presence in the nation set in. God revealed his spirit in two types of leaders: the charismatic king (II Sm 7, especially vv. 12-17), and the messenger-prophet. The latter claimed precedence over the former in giving direction to the *res publica* in accordance with the divine will. The prophet became, in fact, the intermediator between God and the leader-king.[85]

The mediatorial role of the messenger-prophets is particularly evident in three areas: in the divine election of kings, in their rejection when this

---

[82] *Menschlicher Erfolg*, 88. Cf. Birch (*Rise*, 36-37) on "the two-character modification of the form"; and Z. Weisman, "Anointing", 395.

[83] Seebass ("Vorgeschichte", 164) notes, for example, that the manner in which Saul in 10:8 "an die Anordnungen des kriegführenden Gottes gebunden [wird]" finds a parallel in the relationship of Barak to Deborah in Judg 4.

[84] Cf. Cross's generalization (*CMHE*, 223): "the institution of prophecy appeared simultaneously with kingship in Israel and fell with kingship." Similarly, Westermann (*Grundformen*, 70) observes that "die Epoche der Prophetie mit der Epoche des Königtums in Israel zusammenfällt". Cf. also Tsevat, "Samuel", 781.

[85] Talmon, "Biblical Idea", 244.

became necessary, and in the conduct of war.[86] As regards the latter area of activity, R. Bach has argued that "die Prophetie schon vor dem 9. Jahrhundert begonnen habe, eine Rolle im Kriege zu spielen und vor allem in die Aufforderung zum Kampf zu sprechen."[87] The early monarchy period experienced a "Spaltung der Funktion des alten Charismatikers" whereby the king became the executor of the "'militärische' Funktion", while the "'charismatische' Funktion" — viz., the reception and communication of divine initiative — fell to the prophet.[88]

The 'divine initiative' plays a central role in warfare not only in the Old Testament but in the ancient Near East generally. Tadmor notes, for example, that

> every war of Assyria, led by her monarch — and in theory the high priest of Ashur — was on a theological as well as on a practical-cultic level a "holy war", ordered by Ashur and approved by oracles, celestial and terrestial.[89]

---

[86] See F. M. Cross's discussion of *royal oracles, oracles of judgement*, and *war oracles* (*CMHE*, 223-229); Cross emphasizes the point that these three activities are characteristic not only of the northern prophets of the tenth and ninth centuries but of the classical, eighth and seventh century prophets in Judah as well.

[87] *Aufforderung*, 111.

[88] *Aufforderung*, 111-112. Similarly, Weiser ("I Samuel 15", 22) contends that the Israelite monarchy, *from its very beginning*, exhibited a characteristic structure ("eigene Struktur") in which the king was to act as "Vollstrecker des Gotteswillens" while the prophet (Weiser names Samuel) served as "Künder und Hüter dieses Willens."

[89] "Autobiographical Apology", 42. Babylonian and Assyrian historical texts from the time of Hammurabi to the siege of Jerusalem by Sennacherib make frequent reference to (trust-inspiring) oracles of the deity/deities prior to battle (e.g., *ANET*, 270, line 31; 275 §a; 277 §§a,b; 281 §5; 287 §8; cf. 279, 285). Mediation of the oracle through prophets or priests is not explicitly mentioned in these passages, though the king sometimes assumes the title of high priest (e.g., *ANET*, 277, 281, 289). An inscription from the reign of Ashur-nasir-apli II, however, distinguishes "king" and "diviner" among the conquered forces of Karduniash, and it is particularly noteworthy that the diviner is also described as a "commanding officer", suggesting a combined religious and military role (*ARI*, 2:577.iii 20f.). Mesha, king of Moab, is commanded by Chemosh to attack Nebo in Israel (*SSI*, 1:76 line 14), but again the means by which this message was delivered is not described. Of special interest is the eighth century Zakir inscription written in Old Aramaic, in which king Zakir of Hamat and Lu'ath, under threat from Barhadad of Aram and an alliance of seventeen kings, receives an 'oracle of salvation' through the mediation of "seers" and

In the Old Testament it is customary to 'consecrate' (pi. of קדשׁ) war[90] and to speak of warriors as 'consecrated'.[91] An attempt to consult the deity, through priest[92] or prophet[93] or otherwise,[94] generally preceded battle[95] and was sometimes accompanied by sacrifice and/or prayer.[96] There can be little doubt, as W. D. Stacy has noted, that "there was a pre-battle rite, or rather a number of different pre-battle performances, in ancient Israel".[97] In these, prophets often figured prominently, and, indeed, prophetic involvement in warfare often extended beyond the ritual aspect to the advisory and supervisory. As E. W. Nicholson has observed:

> They [i.e. prophets] appear often on the battle-field beside the armies of Israel advising the king and demanding that the wars be carried out according to the sacral principles of the Holy War (cf. 1 Kings 20:13-14, 22, 28, 35f.; 2 Kings 3:11f.; 13:14f.). It is not surprising therefore to find Elijah and Elisha referred to as "the chariots of Israel and its horsemen" (2 Kings 2:12; 13:14).[98]

In view of these various considerations, the supposed contradiction between 1 Sam 10:7 and 10:8 can be resolved. 10:7 does not represent a *carte blanche* whereby the inheritor of the political/military functions of the charismatic tradition is freed from any further responsibility to

---

"messengers" (*NERT*, 231; *ANET*, 655). It is in the Mari letters, however, that prophetic involvement in military affairs is most apparent (*NERT*, 122-28; *ANET*, 623-32). A brief summary of ancient Near Eastern prophecy outside Israel is provided by Blenkinsopp, *History of Prophecy*, 54-58.

[90] Jer 6:4; Joel 3:9; Mic 3:5.

[91] Is 13:3; cf. Jer 22:7; 51:27.

[92] Deut 20:2-4; 1 Sam 14:18-19, 36f.; 23:1-12; 30:7-8; cf. Judg 18:5.

[93] 1 Sam 28:6; 1 Kgs 22:4-28; 2 Kgs 3:11.

[94] Judg 6:36-40; 1 Sam 14:8-12.

[95] In addition to the references listed in the three preceding notes, cf. Judg 20:17-28; 2 Sam 5:19, 22-24, where the method of inquiry is not specified.

[96] Judg 20:26-28; 1 Sam 7:5-12; 13:8-12; 1 Kgs 8:44. The Ugaritic "prayer-song of El" (*NERT*, 222) provides a parallel example of prayer and sacrifices in a crisis situation.

[97] "Pre-Battle Rite", 471.

[98] *Deuteronomy*, 69. Cf. Birch, *Rise*, 146.

the guardian of its religious/ideological centre. Rather, Samuel, as co-inheritor of the charismatic tradition and as mediator of Saul's call, commissions Saul to challenge Philistine domination by an initial act of defiance, assuring him of divine assistance in the accomplishment of this feat. As we have argued, not only the Philistine focus of Saul's commission, but also the reference to the Philistine governor at the site of the third and final sign confirming Saul's appointment, strongly suggest that Saul's first action should be against the said governor. The effect of such an action would, of course, be mainly provocative, flinging down the gauntlet to the Philistines and placing the Israelites in a state of revolt. The major conflict would remain to be fought. And since it must not commence independently of Yahweh's spokesman, Saul is commanded in 10:8 to follow-up his first action by repairing to Gilgal to await the arrival of Samuel, who will come not only to consecrate the battle but also to *instruct* the new appointee as to what he should do.

In 1 Sam 10:7-8, therefore, Saul is given two orders, the execution of the second being contingent upon the fulfilment of the first.[99] The picture that emerges, of a circumscribed military leadership subordinate to the prophetic spokesman of Yahweh, accords well with the ideology of warfare as consistently portrayed in Israel's historiographical traditions.[100] There is, therefore, no compelling reason to question, on ideo-

---

[99] Seebass ("Vorgeschichte", 161) exhibits a sound intuition regarding the contingency of the command in 10:8 when he writes: "Abschließend erhält er [Saul] den Auftrag, *nach dem ersten Akt der Befreiung von den Philistern* Gilgal aufzusuchen, um dort weitere Weisungen in Empfang zu nehmen 10₈" (italics added). Curiously, however, Seebass fails to recognize the connection between the "first act of liberation" and the command of 10:7, to "do what your hand finds to do". The only explanation for this oversight seems to lie in the fact that Seebass wishes to assign 10:7 and 10:8 to originally distinct narratives, 10:7 to his "Jugendidylle Sauls" (162) and 10:8 to his "Salbung Sauls" (161). But in so doing, he leaves 10:7 without a sequel ("Hier bricht die Erzählung ab" [163]) and 10:8 without antecedent (the "first act of liberation from the Philistines" is left unspecified). In another place ("I Sam 15", 155), however, Seebass explicitly identifies this first act with the elimination of the Philistine post in Gibeah.

[100] The ideological appropriateness of the picture does not, of course, prove its historicity. Even Blenkinsopp (*History of Prophecy*), who feels himself on "firmer historical ground" in recognizing the intimate association of prophecy with the monarchy, beginning with Saul, and with "times of political crisis, such as then existed with the struggle against the Philistines" (60), expresses reservations as to our ability to discover much about "Samuel as a historical figure" (65). These reservations stem primar-

logical grounds, the integrality of 10:8 in its present context. Our overall conclusions may once more be summarized with a diagram:

<pre>
                    Provocation   Convocation

    Command   10:7———————————————10:8
                      | |
                      | |
    Fulfilment   13:3————13:4b, 5————13:7b-15a
</pre>

Conclusion

In this chapter we have argued that 10:7 and 10:8 are not in conflict but represent a two-part commission that is fulfilled, in a qualified sense, in the events of 1 Sam 13:3-15.[101] Moreover, we have attempted to show that both passages are integrally tied to their present contexts. If this is so, they should be taken into consideration in our reading of the larger context. But this leaves us with a problem. What are we to make of the large gap, in terms of narrative time and sequence, between the commission in ch. 10 and its fulfilment in ch. 13? In Part Three below we shall develop the thesis that the gap may be explained as resulting from a failure on Saul's part to fulfil the first stage of his commission, a failure remedied only in ch. 13 through the initiative of his son Jonathan. For the present, as we turn to consider in the next

---

ily from 1) the fact that so many roles are assigned to Samuel — judge, sacrificing priest, man of God, paradigm of prophetic opposition to kingship (65); and 2) the common view that in 1 Sam 9:1-10:16 an originally anonymous 'man of God' or seer has "only at a later stage of editing" been "identified with Samuel the kingmaker" (66). Blenkinsopp apparently regards seers and ecstatics as distinct, and he is sceptical that Samuel could have functioned both as a seer and as a leader of a band of "ecstatic dervishes" (66; cf. 1 Sam 19:18-24). He acknowledges, however, that Samuel's preceptorship over an ecstatic brotherhood "did not exclude a wide range of other activities" (73), including possibly involvement in warfare and in "designating and anointing leaders and kings" (66; cf. *idem*, "Quest", 93). On Samuel's multi-faceted role, see above, pp. 59-60. And for an alternative interpretation of 1 Sam 9:1-10:16, see Ch. 7, pp. 196-99.

[101] The necessity of qualification arises, first, from the fact that in 13:3 it is Jonathan, not Saul, who strikes the first blow against the Philistines and, secondly, from the fact that the second stage, the rendezvous in Gilgal, goes badly awry and so is not really fulfilled at all.

chapter the matter of Saul's first rejection, it will suffice to bear in mind the very direct link between the events of 13:3-15 and Saul's initial commission in 10:7-8.

Part Two

The Reign and Rejection of King Saul: An Integrated Reading of 1 Sam 13-15

3

SAUL VERSUS THE PHILISTINES:
A KING REJECTED (1 SAM 13)

For reasons of convenience and manageability, we shall follow biblical precedent in presenting our exposition of 1 Sam 13-14 in two chapters. This should not, however, obscure the fact that the biblical account of Saul's initial Philistine encounter presents itself as a connected and sequential narrative.[1] The continuity between chs. 13 and 14 is suggested by various points of contact between the two chapters, including 1) the correspondence of characters and of setting, 2) various verbal and material links,[2] 3) a high degree of thematic continuity and 4) a logical overarching structure.[3] Moreover, the narrative is formally delimited by the framing verses 13:1 and 14:47-51(52). J. M. Miller offers some suggestive observations with respect to the setting and significance of 1 Sam 13-14:

> 1 Sam 12 concludes the period of the Judges in the deuteronomistic survey of Israel's history, and the judgeship of Samuel in particular. The focus of interest begins to shift in chapters 15-16, on the other hand, from Saul to David. Chapters 13-14 were apparently intended, therefore, to represent Saul's reign in the deuteronomistic scheme, although in fact these two chapters consist primarily of a narrative complex which focuses

---

[1] The narrative may, of course, comprise material drawn from various sources, but we are less confident than, for example, Birch (*Rise*, 90-91) as to the possibility of distinguishing these sources in the present text.

[2] E.g., links can be discerned between 13:5, 11, 16, 17 and 14:15 (references to Philistine camp at Michmash); 13:6-7 and 14:11, 22 (references to hiding and to Hebrews); 13:15-16 and 14:2 (references to Saul in Gibeah with six hundred men); 13:17 and 14:15 (references to the raiders [המשחית]); 13:(22),23 and 14:1, 6, 15 (references to the outpost [מצב]).

[3] These various points will be developed in the course of the exegesis.

on Saul's struggles with the Philistines. 1 Sam 13:1 is a fragmented deuteronomistic introduction to Saul's reign. And 1 Sam 14:47-52 are the sort of notes which the deuteronomistic redactor often provided for the kings of Israel and Judah.[4]

It is obvious from the broader context of 1 Samuel that Saul's reign was not limited to the events of chs. 13-14, but these chapters are nevertheless set forth as particularly representative of his reign — as characterizing and exemplifying its essence. That the Philistine wars should be highlighted in this way is understandable, however, when we recall the centrality of the Philistine problem in Saul's original commission.[5]

It is not simply the link with that commission, however, and certainly not a purely historical interest in military history, that ultimately accounts for the preservation of this material. As McCarter has remarked, "this is finally a story about Saul and Jonathan, and an interest in them is the reason it has come down to us at all."[6] If, as was argued in the preceding chapter, the Gilgal episode is integral to its present context, then we would contend that it is the rejection of Saul in ch. 13 and the elucidation and justification of this rejection in ch. 14 — accomplished by means of a contrastive characterization of Saul and Jonathan — that form the gravitational centre of the story.[7] But here we are anticipating conclusions that arise out of our exegesis, so it is to this task that we must now turn.

Our exegetical discussion will be organized according to narrative scenes.[8] In an integrated narrative complex such as 1 Sam 13-14 any division into scenes will, of course, entail a subjective element and risk

---

[4] "Saul's Rise", 161.

[5] See our discussion in the preceding chapter (especially pp. 52-54, 63-64); and cf. also Driver, *Introduction*, 175; Birch, *Rise*, 91.

[6] McCarter, 241.

[7] Israel was not unique in the aNE in displaying a 'religious' interest in the recounting of military events. E.g., J. A. Brinkman (*Political History*, 316) observes that in post-Kassite Babylonia "Babylonian official records — such as royal inscriptions and chronicles — exhibit a profound disinterest in most military or political events. Instead, their orientation is largely religious; and, when Babylonian military exploits are recorded in detail, as in the case of Nebuchadnezzar's feats against Elam, it is principally because of the religious significance of these events (i.e. the recovery of the Marduk statue)".

[8] On the nature of a narrative scene, see above, pp. 21-23.

appearing somewhat arbitrary. In our analysis of ch. 13, for example, vv. 2-7a are treated as a scene, displaying not only straight exposition[9] but also action and speech (though without dialogue). This section does not, however, include a resolution of tension, but describes, rather, the mounting military pressure which provides the backdrop for the events of 13:7bff. Similarly, the second scene (13:7b-15), though it reaches an important climax in the rejection of Saul by Samuel (vv. 13-14) and exhibits typical scenic closure (v. 15), also leaves the military tension unresolved. An expositional interlude, 13:16-23, further heightens this tension by detailing the military imbalance. And so the whole of ch. 13 sets the stage for the events of ch. 14. Thus, while division of the narrative into scenic units is exegetically helpful and in keeping with the nature of Hebrew narrative artistry, it is clear that the scenes within the broader narrative sequence are neither more nor less independent than, for example, the scenes of a play.

In view of the above considerations, our reading of chs. 13-14 shall pay attention not only to the inner development of each scene but also to the contribution of each to the larger story. But before we take up each scene in turn, some comments on the controversial opening frame verse are in order.

The Opening Frame
(1 Sam 13:1)

Few verses in 1 Samuel have excited such diverse explanations as the first verse of ch. 13. In purporting to record the monarch's age at accession and the length of his reign, this verse bears a formal similarity to introductory regnal formulae elsewhere in Samuel and Kings.[10] Yet a straightforward reading of MT 13:1 yields an apparently impossible sense: "Saul was a year old[11] when he began to reign, and he reigned two years[12] over Israel." The difficulties are self-evident, and attempts

---

[9] On this designation, see above, pp. 21-22.

[10] E.g., 2 Sam 2:10; 5:4; 1 Kgs 14:21; 22:42.

[11] For בֶּן־שָׁנָה meaning "one year old", cf. Exod 12:5.

[12] For defences of MT's שְׁתֵּי שָׁנִים, as opposed to the more common שָׁנֹתִים (cf. 1 Kgs 15:25; 16:8; 22:52; 2 Kgs 15:23), see Noth, *ÜSt*, 25 n. 1; Stoebe, 243; Birch, *Rise*, 78; Smelik, *Saul*, 71; Althann, "1 Sm 13,1", 242. Cf. also 2 Sam 2:10 (שְׁתַּיִם שָׁנִים), in the light of GK §134a,b.

to make sense of the text as it stands have been few. The Targum re-sorts to a rather fanciful, interpretative rendering: "As a one year old in whom is no guilt was Saul when he began to reign, and he reigned two years over Israel". Many modern scholars, assuming the verse to be corrupt, have proposed emendations of one sort or another.[13] A basic difficulty for hypotheses assuming textual corruption, however, is the fact that one must assume two instances of corruption within the same line, with both affecting *only the numerals*.

Perhaps the most popular current theory, based on comparative aNE material, is that the numerals were lacking from the start, either because the information was simply unavailable to the narrator or be-cause of conflicting data in the traditions. In 1963 G. Buccellati drew attention to several examples of what appear to be intentional lacunae in aNE sources. The sources cited included two economic texts from Ur (c. 2000 B.C.), a list of personal names from the Old Babylonian pe-riod, and the Sumerian King List.[14] In the same year, A. K. Grayson added another example from a Babylonian text in the British Museum[15] and more recently he has pointed out two more cases of apparently in-tentional lacunae.[16] One other possible example may be found in the Assyrian King List where the regnal years of six kings in succession appear to be missing.[17] However, each of the three surviving copies of the list[18] shows severe damage where the numerals would normally be

---

[13] As regards v. 1a, these include inserting שלשים on the basis of τριακοντα in a few MSS of LXX (i.e. MSS oe₂ ; other witnesses to the Lucianic recension reflect MT; LXX[B] omits 13:1 entirely); emending בן to כן and assuming the derivation of שנה from the verb "to repeat"; assigning nu-merical value to certain consonants (e.g., בן = 52, נה = 55); or assuming that a marginal note (שנה "ב = 2nd year) has crept into the text (on all these, see Stoebe, 242-43). As for the second half of the verse, though a two year reign has had a few distinguished defenders (e.g., Noth, *USt*, 24; *idem*, *Geschichte*, 163; Smelik, *Saul*, 71), it is generally agreed that the events of Saul's reign (cf. 1 Sam 14:47-48) require more than just two years (see be-low, p. 74 n. 28). Again scholars have posited textual corruptions of one sort or another to explain the apparently defective numeral, but no theory has yet been able to gain wide acceptance (cf. Stoebe, 243).

[14] Buccellati, "1 Sam 13:1", 29.

[15] Grayson, "1 Sam 13:1", 86, 110.

[16] I.e. *ABC*, 72 (1.i.25); 107 (7.ii.9); cf. his remarks ad loc.

[17] Cf. *ANET*, 564.

[18] The oldest of the three was published by E. Nassouki ("Grande Liste") and the other two, the so-called Khorsabad and SDAS lists, by I. J. Gelb ("King Lists").

placed, so that the supposition that the numerals were *originally* missing must rest solely on a phrase which precedes the list of six kings: *ša li-ma-*-ni-šú-nu la-ú*-ṭu-ni*.[19] Gelb suggests translating, "whose eponymies are destroyed". But uncertainty regarding the meaning of *lâṭu* leaves the value of this example in doubt.[20] As regards the other examples, however, both Buccellati and Grayson relate their findings to 1 Sam 13:1 and thereby buttress the view that the numerals are simply missing. The strengths of this explanation are that it 1) acknowledges the formulaic character of 13:1 and 2) rests upon an observable textual phenomenon in aNE literature. It is, however, open to several objections: 1) it cannot be denied that בן שנה is a grammatically acceptable construction and can be read "one year old",[21] 2) if 13:1 was without numerals from the beginning, one must somehow explain how שתי found its way into v. 1b, and 3) parallel examples of intentional lacunae are, to the best of this writer's knowledge, lacking in the Old Testament.

A different approach to the problem of 13:1 has been proposed recently by R. Althann,[22] who suggests that 1 Sam 13:1 is not a regnal formula at all, but a poetic couplet. Althann asserts that "the progress of Northwest Semitic studies suggests a new line of approach" to the problem of בן שנה in v. 1a. Noting, first, the occasional use of afformative *nun* with various Northwest Semitic prepositions and, secondly, the occurrence in Ugaritic of the prepositions *b* and *l* with the meaning "from", Althann conjectures that בן of 1 Sam 13:1a should be read as comparative *b* (similar to Hebrew comparative *min*), written with afformative *nun* and detached from its object. Thus, he translates: "More than a year had Saul been reigning, even two years had he been reigning over Israel." Weaknesses of Althann's theory include 1) the fact that examples of the preposition *b* with afformative *nun* are not clearly attested in Northwest Semitic,[23] 2) the necessity of rendering במלכו (v. 1a) as "had been reigning" instead of "when he began to reign" as elsewhere in the DH,[24] and 3) the fact that this theory does not do

---

[19] Khorsabad, i.26; cf. SDAS, i.25, which varies slightly.

[20] *AHw* suggests "überdeckt sind (??)", while *CAD* states simply that the meaning is unknown.

[21] So Driver, 97; and see n. 11 above.

[22] "1 Sam 13,1", 241-46.

[23] "1 Sam 13,1", 243.

[24] "1 Sam 13,1", 244.

justice to the resemblance of this verse to accession formulae found elsewhere in the DH.

As noted earlier, there have been few attempts to make sense of MT of 13:1 as it stands. Probably the most able defender of a two-year reign for Saul was Martin Noth. He maintains that from a chronological perspective, at least, the notion of a two year reign is "unanfechtbar",[25] inasmuch as it fits nicely into the Deuteronomist's overall chronological scheme of 480 years from the Exodus to the fourth year of Solomon's reign (1 Kgs 6:1).[26] There is something to be said for this observation, but when Noth goes on to defend a two-year reign as plausible also from the historical perspective[27] his case begins to weaken.[28] Not only does the text of Samuel give no indication that the battle of Gilboa was launched in retaliation for the events of 1 Sam 13-14, but 14:52 indicates, in fact, that Saul's reign was characterized by a period of protracted struggle with the Philistines. Moreover, the summary of Saul's reign in 14:47-51, possibly a deuteronomistic construct, also seems to require a longer reign. Another weakness of Noth's scheme is that it does not offer a satisfactory explanation of בן שנה in the first phrase of 13:1. He remarks only that the Deuteronomist must have lacked information on Saul's age at accession and, therefore, left the formula blank.[29] But perhaps MT's statement that Saul was "a year old" at accession points in another direction. If we are to make any sense at all of this statement as it stands, then we must assume that it is not to be taken literally. Might not the same also be true of the "two-year" reign? It seems apparent that the deuteronomistic historian(s) of 1 and 2 Kings would have assumed a general correlation between the righteousness of a king and the length of his reign. We note, for example, that, while both the Northern and Southern kingdoms experienced a succession of about twenty kings, in Israel their combined reigns lasted only about 210 years, whereas in the

---

[25] *Geschichte*, 163.

[26] *ÜSt*, 24-25.

[27] Ibid., 24 n. 5; *Geschichte*, 163.

[28] See esp. Schunck's extended treatment (*Benjamin*, 110-120) in which he argues on the basis of 1) the events recounted in the biblical tradition, 2) the archaeological evidence from Tell el-Ful, and 3) certain chronological considerations, that a longer reign is required. The arguments adduced under the first category (110-115) are the more weighty. Cf. also Seebass, "Vorgeschichte", 168 n. 49.

[29] *ÜSt*, 24 n. 3.

Judah the same number of kings reigned for around 345 years. Could it be that the reduction of Saul's reign to only two years represents an implicit judgement by the historian who inserted the formula?[30] If such an interpretation could be accepted, then even 13:1 might be seen as contributing to an unfavourable depiction of Saul, adumbrating his rejection only a couple of chapters later. The difficulty with this explanation, of course, is that a non-literal interpretation of a regnal formula is without parallel in the Old Testament (regnal formulae occurring elsewhere in the Deuteronomistic History always refer to the monarch's physical age and actual length of reign). But then, as we have already seen, the other suggested explanations of 13:1, such as the intentional omission theory or the poetic couplet theory, also lack biblical precedent.

Scene One: Provocation of the Philistines (1 Sam 13:2-7a)

13:2, Mise en scène

The first scene opens typically with the identification and location of its principal characters — Saul is in command of two military contingents deployed north of the *wadi suweiniṭ* near Michmash and Bethel, while Jonathan is over one contingent deployed south of the wadi.[31]

A slightly curious feature of v. 2 is that Jonathan, who appears here for the first time in the Old Testament, is introduced simply by name, without further qualification or even a hint of his relationship to Saul. Several explanations of this peculiarity have been proposed: 1)

---

[30] He may well have found some justification for this reduction in the circumstance that, in a sense, Saul's reign was over *de jure* (1 Sam 15) some time before it was over *de facto* (1 Sam 31). The problem of Saul's age at accession would still remain a problem. A solution to both problems was suggested by the medieval Jewish commentator Isaac Abrabanel (פרוש, 234) and subsequently overlooked. According to Abrabanel, Saul's yearling status would refer to the time which elapsed between Saul's secret anointing (1 Sam 10) and the renewal of the kingdom (11:14-15), while the two-year reign would be reckoned from his official inauguration (13:1) to the anointing of David (ch. 16).

[31] In Gibeah or Geba; on the difficulties involved in the occurrences of these names in 1 Sam 13-14, see above, p. 44 n. 6.

that an original בנו has dropped out of the series יונתן[בנו]בגבע;[32] 2) that
chs. 13-14 have been extracted from an independent source recounting
Saul's battles, in which, presumably, Jonathan was properly introduced;[33] 3) that 13:2 represents an anachronistic anticipation of the results of the Philistine battle and thus presupposes knowledge of
Jonathan.[34]

None of these explanations, however, is fully convincing. The
versional support for the first is minimal, since the Syr. reading may
simply represent a correction of what was perceived as a deficiency in
the text. The plausibility of this explanation is further diminished by
A. Millard's conclusion that "*scriptio continua* was not a practice of
early Hebrew scribes".[35] As regards the second proposed explanation, it
is difficult to imagine why a compiler deriving material from another
source would not have incorporated a fuller introduction of Jonathan,
had such existed in his source. The third theory also fails to resolve the
tension, for Jonathan appears without introduction not only in v. 2 but
in v. 3 as well.

One other possible explanation is suggested by the fact that, for
example, both Joshua (Exod 17:9) and Eli (1 Sam 1:3), when they first
appear in the OT, are also introduced by name only. Perhaps full
introductions were considered unnecessary for personages sufficiently
well-known in Israelite tradition. Nevertheless, in view of the stress
laid upon the familial relationship between Jonathan and Saul elsewhere
in 1 Sam 13-14,[36] the lack of an epithet in 13:2 remains noteworthy.
In view of the semantic potential of epithets in Old Testament narrative
as described, for example, by Clines[37] and Alter[38], it seems a fair question whether the omission might not mark an attempt by the narrator to
distance Saul from Jonathan at this particular juncture of the narrative,
where Jonathan is about to distinguish himself (13:3a) as "der, von dem
der Anstoß zu den Philisterkämpfen ausgeht"?[39] In answer to the pos-

---

[32] So Budde, 84; cf. Smith, 93. בנו is attested by Syr.
[33] So Goslinga, 254.
[34] So Stoebe, 247; cf. *idem*, "Zur Topographie", 278; McCarter, 227;
Miller, "Saul's Rise", 161. This hypothesis will be discussed below, pp.
77f.
[35] "*Scriptio continua*", 14.
[36] I. e. 13:16, 22; 14:1, 27, 28, 29, 39, 40, 42.
[37] "X, X ben Y".
[38] "Literary Approach", 73.
[39] Hertzberg, 81/ET 104.

sible objection that, by the same token, 14:1 should also suppress Jonathan's status as "son of Saul", we would point out that the impact of the explicit association of Saul and Jonathan in v. 1a is turned in a negative direction in v. 1b by the notice that Jonathan "did not tell his father" what he was about to do.[40]

Another debatable point with respect to 13:2 is whether the verse provides a suitable introduction to what follows, or whether it represents an anticipatory summary of the results of the battle. The position of 13:2 at the beginning of the account of Saul's reign would seem to imply that it is introductory to what follows — i.e. a description of the deployment of Saul's forces *prior* to his first Philistine encounter. Scholars have noted, however, that such an understanding of v. 2 entails certain difficulties. Dhorme, for example, points out that whereas v. 2 places Saul in Michmash, v. 5 has the Philistines occupying the same locality, with no notice that combat has been joined. V. 4, on the other hand, finds Saul in Gilgal, where he assembles his forces. In v. 2 Jonathan is in Geba,[41] but in v. 3 the site is occupied by the Philistine 'governor'[42] who must first be eliminated by Jonathan. Finally, Dhorme notes that the end of v. 2 is more suggestive of the conclusion of an account than of its beginning.[43]

Solutions to these difficulties have traditionally been sought along source-critical lines, and Dhorme is again representative. He identifies v. 2 as the conclusion to 12:25 and attaches it ultimately to the putative source that places the enthronement at Mizpah. V. 3 he regards as the continuation of 11:15, where Saul is at Gilgal.[44] More recently, scholars such as Stoebe, McCarter and Miller have offered an entirely different explanation — viz., that v. 2 functions as an anticipatory summary of the outcome of the Philistine battle.[45] Stoebe, for example, labels v. 2 "einen kleinen Anachronismus, nämlich eine zusammenfassende Vorwegnahme der Ergebnisse der Schlacht von Michmash und des Sieges von Kap. 14."[46] Miller adds that Isa 7:1 offers an in-

---

[40] Cf. Chapter 4, pp. 101-103.

[41] Here Dhorme (108) emends MT "Gibeah" on the basis of LXX and in the light of the proximity of Geba to Michmash.

[42] Dhorme renders נציב 'garrison', but see above, p. 44 n. 9.

[43] Dhorme, 108.

[44] Dhorme, 108. On the latter point, see also McCarter, 227.

[45] Cf. above, p. 76 n. 34.

[46] "Zur Topographie", 278.

stance of the "same sort of literary technique".[47] This suggested parallel, however, is not entirely apposite, inasmuch as Isa 7:1 represents a true *summary* of events, while 13:2, according to the theory, records only the *outcome* of the battle.

Before going any further in either of the directions mentioned in the preceding paragraph, we should observe that, given the interpretation of 10:7-8 proposed in Chapter 2 — viz., that Saul received a two-part commission entailing, first, a provocation of the Philistines (10:5a, 7), to be followed by a rendezvous with Samuel in Gilgal for the purpose of consecrating the battle which would inevitably ensue (10:8) — the objections raised against the most natural reading of 13:2 as introductory to what follows disappear. The reader is not, as McCarter supposes, "shunted unceremoniously from the vicinity of Gibeah (v 3) to Gilgal (v 7b, cf. 4b) and then back to Gibeah (v 15)." Rather, the action progresses logically according to the pre-determined pattern — the provocation of 13:3a triggering Saul's immediate movement to Gilgal for the above-stated purpose (13:3b ff.).

In sum, therefore, there is nothing to prevent us from reading 13:2 as describing the situation prior to Saul's first Philistine encounter. This is not to deny, of course, that the verse may serve a transitional as well as an introductory function. Saul's selection of 3,000 soldiers "from Israel" and his dismissal of "the rest" does appear to presuppose the context of a general gathering of some sort, such as the Gilgal celebration of 11:14-15,[48] but as explicit reference to such is lacking in v. 2, firm conclusions are unattainable.

13:3-4, The First Strike

Whatever may have been the strategy behind Saul's initial troop deployment in v. 2,[49] Jonathan's assassination of the Philistine governor in v. 3 determines irrevocably the course that subsequent events will take. Whether the Philistine governor had his headquarters at Geba, as in MT, or at Gibeah, or whether both names refer to the same

---

[47] "Saul's Rise", 161.

[48] So, for example, Budde, 83; Hertzberg, 81/ET 104. Goslinga (254) links 13:2 with ch. 12, which he sees as a continuation of 11:14ff. For a full defence of the thesis that 1 Sam 11:14-12:25 comprise a composite unit describing a covenant renewal ceremony in Gilgal, see J. R. Vannoy, *Covenant Renewal*.

[49] For a few conjectures, see below, pp. 82-83.

place,[50] there can be little doubt that the same site as in 10:5-7 is in view.[51] That the intent of Jonathan's action is to precipitate an Israelite insurrection by provoking the Philistines seems obvious. First of all, the assassination of a foreign official was a "time-honoured way of starting a revolt."[52] This point is well illustrated by an inscription from the reign of Ashur-nasir-apli II:

> While I was in the land of Kadmuhu this report was brought to me: "The city Suru which belongs to Bit-Halupe has rebelled. They have killed Hamataya, their governor, (and) appointed Ahi-yababa, son of a nobody, whom they brought from Bit-Adini, as their king." With the assistance of Ashur (and) the god Adad, ..., I mustered my chariotry and troops .... I approached the city Suru which belongs to Bit-Halupe. Awe of the radiance of Ashur my lord overwhelmed them. The nobles (and) elders of the city came out to me to save their lives.[53]

Secondly, the sounding of the trumpet (v. 3b) often served as a call to arms, to revolt, to flight, or to assembly in times of crisis.[54] Thirdly, the use of בָּאַשׁ ni. (v. 4aγ) seems to connote a political challenge or provocation. M. Tsevat has argued that in all four occurrences of the root בָּאַשׁ in Samuel,[55] and probably also in Exod 5:21, the verb בָּאַשׁ "epitomizes an act of political challenge, mostly by insubordination".[56] Finally, LXX contains an explicit reference to revolt — i.e. LXX 13:3bβ reads ἠθετήκασιν οἱ δοῦλοι, "the slaves have revolted". The reading "slaves", equivalent to Hebrew עֲבָדִים, may have arisen through a misreading of ר as ד in an original עֲבָרִים. Moreover, since ἀθετέω

---

[50] See p. 44 n. 6.

[51] So Driver, 98; Schunck, *Benjamin*, 111; Goslinga, 255; Stoebe, 243; Birch, *Rise*, 79; McCarter, 227. Hertzberg (79/ET 101) even substitutes "'Hügel' (Gottes)" (cf. 10:5a) for Geba in 13:3. For a dissenting view, see Dhorme, 109.

[52] Blenkinsopp, "Quest", 87 n. 49, citing Judg 3:15-30.

[53] *ARI*, 2:547.

[54] E.g., Judg 3:27-28; 6:34-35; 2 Sam 20:1-2; Jer 4:5, 19, 21; 6:1; Hos 5:8; 8:1; Neh 4:20, etc.

[55] I.e. 1 Sam 13:4; 27:12; 2 Sam 10:6; 16:21. These include the only three attestations of בָּאַשׁ ni. in the OT.

[56] "Marriage", 242-43. He compares the consistent practice of the Targum to Samuel of rendering the verb by אַתְגְּרִי, "to provoke, challenge". For a different view, see Ackroyd, "Hebrew Root בָּאַשׁ", 31-32.

is often used in LXX to render Hebrew פשׁע, "to rebel",[57] it may be that
ישׁמעו of MT 13:3bβ should read פשׁעו. In the light of these two observations, numerous scholars have reconstructed 13:3bβ to read
פשׁעו העברים, "the Hebrews have revolted"[58] and have transposed the
clause to a position between 13:3a and 13:3ba,[59] arguing that 1) ישׁמעו
requires a direct object and 2) a reference to "Hebrews" is hardly likely
in the mouth of Saul. Neither of these latter arguments is conclusive,
however,[60] and MT's reading continues to find favour with various
scholars.[61]   In the light of D. T. Tsumura's recent discussion of
"Literary Insertions (AXB Pattern) in Biblical Hebrew",[62] a further option may be possible, one which would preserve MT's word order,
while at the same time adopting the sense of the reconstruction based
on LXX:

A	13:3aβ	וישׁמעו פלשׁים	And the Philistines heard
X	13:3b(a)	ושׁאול תקע בשׁופר בכל־הארץ	(while Saul blew the trumpet throughout the land):
B	13:3b(β)	לאמר פשׁעו העברים	"The Hebrews have revolted."

A more expansive example of this same pattern is attested in Deut 5:4-
6:

---

[57] 1 Kgs (=III Kingdoms) 8:50; 12:19; 2 Kgs (=IV Kingdoms) 1:1;
3:5, 7; 8:20, 22; etc.

[58] Cf. Smith, 92-93; Budde, 84; Driver, 98; Hertzberg, 79/ET 101;
Ackroyd, 105; Mauchline, 112; McCarter, 225.

[59] This transposition is without versional support.

[60] As K. Koch ("Hebräer", 46 n. 1) has noted, שׁמע is frequently used
absolutely (e.g., Jos 11:1; Ps 30:11; 34:3) and may be so used in 1 Sam
13:3aβ. The "Hebrews" criterion likewise seems no longer as certain as was
once thought. Gottwald (*Tribes*, 423) explains that Saul is appealing to a
"third force" of *'apiru* warriors. Similarly, Stolz (84) writes: "'Israel' zählt
zu den 'Hebräern' — aber nicht alle 'Hebräern' gehören zu 'Israel'; .... Sauls
Aufruf wendet sich an alle Hebräer, an alle Gruppen, die sich in einer
ethnisch-kulturell-sozial vergleichbaren Lage finden."

[61] E.g., Gottwald, *Tribes*, 423; Blenkinsopp, "Quest", 89 n. 56;
Stoebe, 243, 249-50; Goslinga, 255.

[62] Tsumura (469) defines the AXB Pattern as follows: "A and B stand
for two words, phrases, clauses, or even discourses which constitute grammatically and/or semantically either a composite unit [AB] or a compound
unit [A & B]; X is an affix, word, phrase, clause, or discourse which is inserted between A and B and yet limits the complex A-B *as a whole*
grammatically or semantically."

A ^{Vs. 4} "Face to face Yahweh spoke to you at the mountain from the midst of the fire
X ^{Vs. 5} (while I was standing between Yahweh and you at that time to declare to you the word of Yahweh, for you were afraid of the fire and did not go up the mountain):
B ^{Vs. 6} 'I am Yahweh your God, who brought you out of the land of Egypt, out of the house of slavery'."

It is clear, in any case, that the effect of Jonathan's provocative action is to launch a rebellion. As we attempted to show in Chapter 2, just such an act of provocation seems to be implied in 10:5-7 as the first stage of Saul's two-part commission. It comes as no surprise, therefore, that in 13:4b ff. the second stage — viz., the rendezvous between Saul and Samuel in Gilgal to prepare war — is immediately initiated. What *is* surprising, however, in view of these considerations, is the fact that Jonathan, not Saul, emerges as the deliverer through whom 'Stage One' of Saul's commission is accomplished. There is a disjunction between expectation and realization, and this is felt all the more keenly as the report goes out in v. 4a that *Saul* has smitten the Philistine governor. Of the various explanations put forward to account for this dual ascription of the deed, first to Jonathan and then to Saul, the most common is simply that, as king, Saul was automatically credited with the accomplishments of his subordinates.[63] While a few *possible* examples of such a practice in the Old Testament can be cited,[64] it seems quite clear, particularly in Samuel, that there existed in the popular consciousness a sharp distinction between successes

---

[63] Cf. Budde, 85; Dhorme, 109; Halpern, *Constitution*, 156 n. 56; *idem*, "Uneasy Compromise", 62 n. 16. For an opposing view, see Stoebe, "Zur Topographie", 279.

[64] E.g., 2 Sam 8:13 speaks of David's defeat of 18,000 Edomites (so LXX, Syr.; MT has Arameans) in the Valley of Salt, whereas the victory is ascribed to Abishai in 1 Chr 18:12 and to Joab in the superscription to Ps 60. Textual difficulties, however, make it uncertain whether the same victory is in view in all these; see the "comprehensive solution" suggested by McCarter, *II Samuel*, 246; for a different view, see Goslinga, *Tweede boek Samuël*, 175-77. 1 Kgs 15:20 reports that Ben-Hadad "sent the commanders of his forces against the towns of Israel." Then it states, "*He* conquered Ijon, Dan," etc. In LXX^B, Syr., Vulg. and the parallel verse 2 Chr 16:4, however, the plural pronoun is used. 2 Sam 5:7, which states that David captured Jerusalem, though apparently Joab led the way (cf. 1 Chr 11:6), is not analogous to 1 Sam 13:3-4, because in 2 Sam 5:7 the actions of David and Joab are distinct.

accomplished under the personal leadership of the king and those ef-
fected by subordinates. This is apparently the case in the women's
song: "Saul has slain his thousands, but David his ten thousands".[65]
Also noteworthy is Joab's urgent message to David (2 Sam 12:26-28)
that he should gather the people and personally participate in the capture
of Rabbah "lest I capture the city myself and it be named after me."

Other attempts to resolve the problem of the dual ascription at-
tribute the inconsistency either to a change of author between vv. 3 and
4[66] or to the redactional fusing of accounts of two similar feats, one by
Saul and the other by Jonathan,[67] or of two parallel versions of the one
incident.[68] Given the evidence available, however, such hypotheses remain highly speculative and, at any rate, do little to elucidate the text as
it stands. More pertinent, perhaps, is Jobling's remark that these verses
"suggest Saul's getting credit for deeds not his own". Of course, this
interpretation might also appear highly speculative, were it not for the
"strong confirmation of it in chap. 14".[69]

It would be helpful in assessing the import of 13:3-4 if we knew
what military strategy is to be assumed behind Saul's selection and deployment of troops in 13:2. About all that we may deduce from the
minimal data of that verse, however, is that, while Saul apparently anticipated some sort of military activity, an all-out military engagement
was not immediately in view. The former deduction is based on the selection and split deployment of the three contingents of soldiers.[70] The
latter derives logically from the dismissal of "the rest of the people".
Suggestions as to the type of limited operation Saul may have had in
mind are generally quite vague.[71] From a purely military perspective,
the notion of a protracted resistance movement would make perhaps the

---

[65] 1 Sam 18:7; cf. 21:11; 29:5.

[66] So Smith, 95.

[67] So Stoebe, 243, 247; *idem*, "Zur Topographie", 279.

[68] So Miller, "Saul's Rise", 162-64.

[69] So Jobling, "Saul's Fall", 369.

[70] On tripartite troop deployment as a standard military procedure at
the time of Saul, cf. 1 Sam 11:11; Yadin, *Art of Warfare*, 263-64; Hauer,
"Shape", 154 n. 5.

[71] Hauer ("Shape", 154 n. 5) notes that "the purpose of the patrol is
not clear. It may have been a training exercise, or a sweep directed against
irregular raiders". Similarly, Mauchline (112; cf. Goslinga, 254) speaks of
"maintaining order and peace in the hill country of Ephraim and Judah in
which the Philistines must have been always watchful and sporadically
active."

best sense, both in view of the inferiority of Saul's troops in terms of experience and equipment, and in view of the advantages to be gained by inferior troops in mountainous terrain.[72] If such was Saul's strategy, then he may have been almost as surprised by Jonathan's precipitate attack as was the Philistine governor. Our text leaves the matter undetermined, however, and we must therefore allow at least the possibility that Saul ordered the attack. But whether Jonathan's feat in 13:3a is meant to suggest an *Alleingang* by Jonathan (in the manner of his independent action in 1 Sam 14) or a stratagem devised by Saul and executed by Jonathan, the mere fact that the first blow against the Philistines was delivered by someone *other than Saul* rests uneasily on the mind of the reader aware of the close connection between the Philistine problem and Saul's appointment as *nāgîd* .[73]

13:5-7a, *The Philistine Reaction and Its Effects*

Whether solo performance or part of a larger strategy, Jonathan's deed provokes a massive Philistine reaction. The phraseology of v. 5 — viz., the notice that the Philistines first assembled for battle (נאספו להלחם v. 5aα), presumably in "safe" (Philistine?) territory,[74] and then advanced (ויעלו) to take up battle positions in Michmash, east of Beth Aven[75] (v. 5b) — suggests a procedure similar to that which Saul followed in mustering troops in Gilgal (v. 4b), away from the scene of the impending conflict. The Philistine muster, however, is reported as markedly more successful than Saul's (v. 5).[76]

---

[72] These advantages include the ability of an inferior force to elude direct confrontations while engaging in guerrilla warfare, and to do so in territory where superior equipment, such as chariots, is least effective. On the ancient Israelites' use of "indirect approaches" in overcoming superior foes, see Malamat, *Early Israelite Warfare*, 10-23; *idem*, "Inferior Israelite Forces", esp. 31f. Cf. also I. Eph'al, "On Warfare".

[73] See above, pp. 51-54.

[74] Cf. 1 Sam 29:1-2, 11, where the Philistines gather their forces in Aphek before advancing to do battle with Israel in Jezreel.

[75] In the present context, Beth-Aven does not represent a disparaging transformation of the name Bethel (as in Hos 10:5; cf. 1 Kgs 12:28-29) but a different site, possibly to be identified with *burqa*, south of *beitîn* (Bethel). The site is mentioned in order to clarify the location not of Michmash, but of the Philistine encampment (so Stoebe, 244; Goslinga, 256-57; Hertzberg, 82 n. 2/ET 105 n. a).

[76] MT refers to 30,000 chariots, while LXX[L] and Syr. attest the number 3,000. Even this lower figure seems high by aNE standards: e.g., Sisera had 900 (Judg 4:3); David killed 700 Aramean charioteers (2 Sam 10:18);

The reference to chariots in v. 5 is often discounted on the assumption that chariots would have been useless in mountainous terrain.[77] But this assumption overlooks the fact that one function of chariotry was to terrorize the enemy.[78] Moreover, we have the explicit witness of numerous Assyrian royal inscriptions that chariots were indeed sometimes transported into "unsuitable/impassable" terrain.[79] This is not to imply that geographic features never necessitated the abandonment of chariotry,[80] but even in "impassable" regions, a way was

---

Solomon had 1,400 chariots (1 Kgs 10:26); Tukulti-Ninurta II had "2,702 horses in teams [and chariots], more than ever before" (*ARI*, 2:477). In view of the fairly late introduction of cavalry in Canaan (cf. J. Wiesner, *Fahren und Reiten*, 44-90; Albright, *Archaeology*, 135-36, n. 25; Yadin, *Art of Warfare*, 5, and the reliefs on pp. 484-85 [403]) and the pictorial evidence of travelling bands of Philistines comprising "three main elements: chariots, infantry, and noncombatants" (ibid., 249-50), the rendering of פרשים in 1 Sam 13:5 as "cavalry" or "horsemen" (so many modern translations) is not to be preferred. פרשים may also denote charioteers or teams of chariot horses (so *HAL*, 919; Ficker, "רכב", 778). If the Philistines, like the Hittites, employed 3-man chariot crews (cf. Yadin, *Art of Warfare*, 250; Sandars, *Sea Peoples*, 120, and illustrations on pp. 28-29, 30-31), the number 6,000 would best refer to the chariot horses, though some variation of the chariot *Besatzung* is not impossible; cf. the 2-, 3- and 4-man Assyrian crews (Galling, *Biblisches Reallexikon*, 1:424) and the possible evidence of 2-man Mycenaean chariots (Sandars, *Sea Peoples*, 188-89). For the view that פרשים in the OT consistently refers to chariot horses, not horsemen, see Arnold, "The Word פרש", 43ff.; Montgomery and Gehman, *Kings*, 82-83; and the comprehensive treatment by Mowinckel, "Drive", 289-95.

[77] Smith, 95; Budde, 85; Stoebe, 244.

[78] Cf. Wiesner, *Fahren und Reiten*, 71; Hertzberg, 82/ET 105; Hauer, "Shape", 155 n. 8. And cf. also Sandars' comments (*Sea Peoples*, 72) regarding the importance of Mycenaean chariotry as "symbol". For discussion of various other deployments of chariotry, e.g. in protecting advancing infantry, in pursuing an enemy in flight, or in providing a mobile firing platform, see Malamat, "Inferior Israelite Forces", 28; Yadin, *Art of Warfare*, 4-5. On the latter deployment, cf. perhaps the references to Philistine archers (31:3) and chariots (2 Sam 1:6) in the accounts of Saul's last battle. For a description of the type of chariot employed by the Philistines, see ibid., 250; also Spanuth (*Philister*, 17-18), who includes a photograph of such a chariot from the grave of Ramses III.

[79] In an inscription of Tiglath-pileser I (*ARI*, 2:13), for example, we read: "Taking my chariots and warriors I hacked through the rough mountain range and difficult paths with copper picks and made a good way for the passage of my chariots and troops." Cf. also *ARI*, 2:216 (Ashur-bel-kala), 430 (Adad-nerari II), 544, 565, 635 (Ashur-nasir-apli II).

[80] E.g., in the inscription mentioned in the preceding note, we read: "Riding in my chariot when the way was smooth and going by foot when the way was rough, I passed through the rough terrain of mighty mountains.

sometimes found![81] While allowing for the hyperbolic nature of the Assyrian reports, we are still left with the impression that the Assyrians could be very persistent in overcoming obstacles in order to get their chariotry to the scene of battle. We probably underestimate the Philistines if we imagine that they were less so. But be that as it may, the literary function, at least, of v. 5 is clear: it is to dramatize the odds facing the Israelites. As Scene One draws to a close, Israelites on whom the military imbalance is not lost can be seen exhausting every avenue of escape or concealment (vv. 6-7a). The situation looks dire. But it is not yet hopeless, for Saul has gone to Gilgal to gather reinforcements (v. 4b), apparently intending also to rendezvous with Samuel (13:8) in accordance with the command of 10:8.

Scene Two: Convocation and Rejection
(1 Sam 13:7b-15)

Formally, the second scene, which recounts Saul's sojourn in Gilgal and his first rejection by Samuel, reflects the major elements of a "prophetic judgement speech to an individual".[82] According to Westermann, whose *Grundformen prophetischer Rede* represents the seminal analysis of this *Gattung*,[83] "das prophetische Gerichtswort an Einzelne" had its floruit in the period of the monarchy, before the so-called writing prophets.[84] Although all examples from this period are

---

In Mount Aruma, a difficult area which was impassable for my chariots, I abandoned my chariotry" (*ARI*, 2:16). Cf. also *ARI*, 2:222 (Ashur-bel-kala), 468 (Tukulti-Ninurta II).

[81] Again from the Tiglath-pileser I inscription (*ARI*, 2:21): "In the high mountains, which *cut* like the blade of a dagger and which were impassable for my chariots, I put the chariots on (the soldiers') necks (and thereby) passed through the difficult mountain range."

[82] For the view that the rejections of Saul in 13:7b-15a and 15:1-34 "are not to be considered doublets but serve two quite distinct purposes", see Birch, *Rise*, 105-108; so also McCarter, 270-71 n. 4. On the integrality of this scene to 1 Sam 13, see Ch. 2 above.

[83] But cf. also the modification of Westermann's treatment by Koch, *Formgeschichte*, 258-270/ET 210-220. For brief summaries of the state of scholarship on this genre, see March, "Prophecy", 141-77; Tucker, *Form Criticism*, 54-65; Wilson, *Prophecy*, 141-43; *idem*, "Form-critical Investigation", 100-127.

[84] *Grundformen*, 99/ET 138.

embedded in narrative contexts, Westermann believes that he is able to discern a basic two-part structure for the genre, consisting of an accusation (*Anklage*) and an announcement (*Ankündigung*).[85] The accusation may be expressed through an accusing question (*anklagende Frage*) or a simple assertion (*Aussagesatz*), and its function is to emphasize the offence or abuse requiring judgement. The second part of the judgement speech, the announcement, is often introduced by a messenger formula (*Botenformel*), although a messenger formula may also stand before the accusation.[86] In many cases, the judgement speech is accompanied by a sign, which relates in every instance to the announcement of judgement.[87] Another common feature is the contrast motif (*Kontrastmotiv*), which generally contrasts the offence of the accused with the favoured status he has previously enjoyed (or could have enjoyed) as the recipient of Yahweh's special blessing.[88] Finally, the judgement speech is characterized by a correspondence of announcement and accusation (*Entsprechung von Ankündigung und Anklage*), a clear example of this feature being 1 Sam 15:23b: "Because you have rejected the word of Yahweh, he has rejected you as king". Westermann confesses that he is not yet able to explain the "Herkunft und Sinn dieses Motivs der Entsprechung",[89] but, as Birch observes, "there seems to be a conscious attempt to show the punishment as appropriate to the transgression".[90]

---

[85] A third element mentioned by Westermann, the introduction (*Einleitung*), appears less consistently. The introduction, which characteristically includes the commissioning of a messenger (*Botenauftrag*) and sometimes also a summons to hear (*Aufforderung zum Hören*), is normally formulated by the narrator, sometimes being completely transformed into narrative (*Grundformen*, 102/ET 142).

[86] *Grundformen*, 102-115/ET 142-161. The *Botenformel* is expressed most frequently in the words לכן כה אמר יהוה, but the texts display considerable freedom of formulation: כי may take the place of לכן; כה אמר יהוה may stand alone, as may לכן; or a simple ו may introduce the announcement. In other examples, הנה or הנה לכן takes the place of the *Botenformel*. For biblical references, see *Grundformen*, 107/ET 149.

[87] *Grundformen*, 113-114/ET 158-160.

[88] *Grundformen*, 111-113/ET 155-158.

[89] *Grundformen*, 114-115/ET 160-161.

[90] *Rise*, 101; cf. Tucker (*Form Criticism*, 64): "Within the prophetic view of history, God's judgment is not capricious or irrational, but reasonable."

13:7b-9, Saul's 'Sin'

Bearing in mind these general features of the 'prophetic judgement speech', and especially the expected correspondence between offence and punishment, we may readily see why the confrontation between Saul and Samuel at Gilgal marks one of the most perplexing episodes in the Old Testament. On the one hand, given the dire military situation, Saul's decision to proceed with pre-battle sacrifices in the absence of the tardy prophet (13:8) impresses many readers as entirely justified.[91] The severity of Samuel's rebuke, on the other hand, seems inexplicable. Efforts to understand Samuel's reaction by pinpointing some failure on Saul's part encounter difficulty in discovering what exactly Saul's "sin" was.[92] No consensus has been reached, but in the history of interpretation two views have tended to dominate: 1) that by offering sacrifices himself, Saul is guilty of overstepping his bounds as king, arrogating to himself priestly prerogative;[93] and 2) that by failing to await Samuel's arrival, Saul is guilty of disobeying the command of 1 Sam 10:8.[94]

Looking ahead to 1 Sam 13:13ba we learn that, as far as Samuel is concerned, the essence of Saul's transgression lies in his failure to keep the 'charge' (מצוה)[95] of Yahweh: "You have not kept[96] the charge (מצוה) of Yahweh your God which he laid upon you (צוך)". The per-

---

[91] Mauchline (115), for example, commends Saul's conduct as "sincere, legitimate, justifiable and necessary in terms of the critical situation in which Saul had to take urgent action."

[92] Gunn (*Fate*, 33-40) provides an insightful analysis of the problems involved and draws attention to the "sympathetic depiction of Saul and the problem of the hard-to-find fault" (38).

[93] Cf. Noth, *Geschichte*, 162; Soggin, *Introduction*, 190; Blenkinsopp, "Quest", 81; Hayes, "Unsung Hero", 39; Jobling, "Saul's Fall", 367.

[94] Cf. Beyerlin, "Königscharisma", 198.

[95] This rendering is preferable to 'command' in the present context. צוה and its derivatives encompass both notions; BDB (845) gives as the basic meanings of צוה to 'lay charge [upon], give charge [to], charge, command, order'. The sense 'charge' or 'commission' is attested, for example, in Num 27:19, 23; Deut 3:28; 31:14, 23 (all with reference to Joshua) and in Deut 1:16 (with reference to the judges commissioned by Moses).

[96] Or perhaps, "If you had kept ..." or "Would that you had kept...", following a suggestion by Wellhausen and many others that MT לא should be read לא (or לוא); so, e.g., McCarter, 226; Klein, 122-123. Stoebe (245) defends MT on the basis of the wide versional support and the fact that "die Bedingung auch aus der vorhergehenden Aussage ergänzt werden kann"; cf. Keil, 129. Whichever reading we adopt, the sense is much the same.

sonal tone of this indictment, "*you* have not kept the charge ... which he [Yahweh] laid upon *you* ", rules against the notion that Saul's sin was simply disregard for some *general prohibition* against laity officiating at sacrifices. Rather, Saul has failed to keep a *specific charge*. What charge? In 13:8 we learn that Saul has *waited seven days for Samuel to come to Gilgal* in accordance with the *appointment* (מועד)[97] set by Samuel. In 13:9 we see Saul calling for the *burnt offering and fellowship offerings* and commencing with the sacrifices in the absence of the prophet. All of these elements point unequivocally to Samuel's instructions in 10:8. In addition to these links between ch. 13 and 10:8, there are firm grounds for linking 13:3 to 10:7, as we attempted to show in Chapter 2.[98] Moreover, it is worth noting that in both ch. 10 and ch. 13 Saul's *nāgîd* status is at issue — it being bestowed in the former and removed in the latter (cf. 9:16; 10:1; 13:14). In the light of these considerations and of our analysis of 10:7-8 in Chapter 2, we would conclude that Saul's primary failure, according to the text before us, is not to be understood as a breach of cultic protocol, though a cultic infraction may be secondarily involved, but rather as a violation of the specific "charge" associated with his *nāgîd* appointment. The nature of this violation will be discussed in more detail in the following two sections.

13:10-12, Accusation and Defence

When Samuel finally arrives and is greeted by Saul (13:10), he responds immediately with an accusing question: "What have you done?" (13:11).[99] Saul's response is two-fold: 1) *you*, Samuel, did not come within the appointed number of days, and 2) troop desertions and the mounting military threat at Michmash precluded further delay (13:11). The text, in fact, leaves open the question whether the seven days had actually elapsed when Samuel arrived, or whether he arrived sometime on the seventh day. But even if we assume the former, it can still be argued that, in proceeding with the sacrifices, Saul adopted an inappropriately narrow interpretation of the command of 10:8. For the com-

---

97 As in the English word 'appointment', Hebrew מועד may include connotations of both time and place (cf. 1 Sam 20:35; BDB, 417, 'appointed time, place, meeting'; *IIAL*, 528-29) and, as Rost (*Vorstufen*, 6) adds, may also be linked to a given situation ("gegebene Lage").

98 See pp. 51-55.

99 Cf. Gen 3:13; Josh 7:19; 1 Sam 14:43.

mand in 10:8 was not only that Saul should wait seven days, but that he should wait *until Samuel arrived.*[100]

Against this view, Gunn contends that 10:8 is essentially ambiguous and can legitimately be read either way, so that "on Saul's understanding no sin has been committed". Thus, Gunn suggests that the true cause of Saul's rejection is to be sought not in any failing on Saul's part but in the less than benevolent motives of Yahweh and his prophet, who arbitrarily require of Saul "this" rather than "that" interpretation of the command to wait.[101] *Prima facie*, Gunn's vindication of Saul appears to conflict with Saul's own admission in 13:12, as he brings his defence to a close: "So I said (to myself), 'Now the Philistines will come down against me in Gilgal, and I have not appeased Yahweh.[102] So I *forced myself*[103] and offered the burnt offering". The issue is clouded, however, by difficulties in determining the precise meaning of וָאֶתְאַפַּק. Of the seven occurrences of אפק hithp. in the Old Testament, six have the sense of "restraining oneself, refraining",[104] and only in 1 Sam 13:12 has the idea of forcing or compelling oneself been suggested.[105] Extra-biblical support for this latter sense has been sought in 1 QH 14:4, 9, but even in these Qumran references, the more common definition of the verb seems preferable; in fact, Lohse renders both occurrences with "sich zusammennehmen".[106] If, then, we adopt the usual significance of אפק hithp. in 1 Sam 13:12, we might paraphrase Saul's defence as follows: "Though the situation was falling apart around me, I *restrained myself* (i.e. *pulled myself together when the temptation was to flee*) and offered the burnt offering." According to this reading, Saul would not be admitting to a breach of conscience, as commonly assumed, but, on the contrary,

---

[100] So Greenstein, "Narratology", 207.

[101] *Fate*, 39-40.

[102] Saul's use of the phrase חלה פנים 'mollify, appease', etc. makes a slightly negative impression, as if "Brand- und Heilsopfer ... an sich und für sich schon — ohne das Gebet — ex opere operato Jahwe günstig stimmen könn[t]en" (so Seybold, "Reverenz und Gebet", 15). On the expression, cf. also Ap-Thomas, "Notes", 239-40.

[103] וָאֶתְאַפַּק is so translated, for example, by *RSV, NAB*, etc. *NEB, NIV* translate, "I felt compelled". Even Gunn (*Fate,* 34) observes that Saul offered the sacrifices "reluctantly" (but cf. also his note 1, p. 34).

[104] So BDB, 67; cf. *HAL*, 77, 'sich zusammennehmen, an sich halten'.

[105] *HAL*, 77, 'sich ermannen, wagen'.

[106] *Texte aus Qumran*, 163.

would be claiming to have acted in a self-controlled and even heroic manner.

If this is the sense of Saul's claim in 13:12, it may be, of course, that he is prevaricating. But even if we again give him the benefit of the doubt and assume that he is *sincerely* unaware of wrongdoing — that he has acted only in good faith — this still does not vindicate him at the expense of Yahweh and Samuel. In view of prophetic participation in warfare in general and Samuel's mediation of Saul's commission in particular,[107] Samuel's insistence upon "this" rather than "that" interpretation of 10:8 is far from arbitrary. As we saw in the preceding chapter,[108] a division of labour between king and prophet was fundamental to the establishment of Israel's theocratic monarchy — the king bearing responsibility for the execution of military affairs, but only as directed by the prophet whose responsibility it was to receive and communicate the divine initiative. Ideologically, monarchy in Israel was acceptable only insofar as it was *not* "like [that of] all the other nations", that is, only insofar as the king was willing to acknowledge his subordination to the Great King and his designated spokesman. The command of 10:8, that Saul should await Samuel's arrival in order to consecrate battle and receive instructions, was designed to safeguard this theocratic authority structure, and Saul's failure, or refusal, to recognize that point formed the basis for the announcement of judgement, to which we now turn.

13:13-15, Announcement of Judgement

Samuel's first word to Saul, after hearing his defence (vv. 11-12), tends to confirm the above analysis: נסכלת, "You have acted foolishly!" (v. 13a). Roth, in his study of the Hebrew root סכל, concludes that "the basic notion of the verb in the Old Testament is that of intellectual inability or failure."[109] Similarly, Stoebe, while recognizing that a moral aspect is not lacking, observes that the dominant notion is that of a "wahnhafte Verkennung der Wirklichkeit".[110] What reality is it that Saul has misperceived if not the subordinate nature of his own kingship? To be sure, in appealing to the military crisis as forbidding delay, Saul shows himself also to be out of accord with the 'Yahweh

---

107 See above, pp. 58-64.
108 Pp. 60-62.
109 "Study", 77.
110 Stoebe, 252-53.

war' ideology that informs 1 Sam 13-14,[111] but, more importantly, it is his attempt to justify himself *vis-à-vis* the command of 10:8 that earns explicit refutation from Samuel: "You have not kept the charge (מצות) of Yahweh your God with which he charged you (צוך)" (v. 13b*a*).[112] Repetition of the root צוה twice more in v. 14 suggests a causal relationship between Saul's failure to keep his "charge" and his failure to establish an enduring kingdom. One way to view the structure of vv. 13-14 is as follows:

v. 13		Samuel said to Saul,
Saul	A	"You have acted foolishly,
Charge	B	you have not kept the **charge** (מצות) of Yahweh your God with which he **charged you** (צוך);
Kingdom	C	for then (כי עתה)[113] Yahweh would have established your *kingdom* over Israel forever.
v. 14		
Kingdom	C'	But now (ועתה) your *kingdom* will not endure;
Saul's replacement	A'	Yahweh has sought out a man after his own heart,
Charge	B'	and Yahweh has **charged him** (ויצוהו) to be *nāgîd* over his people, because you have not kept that which Yahweh **charged you** (צוך).

As this overview indicates, vv. 13-14 set up a contrast between the "foolishness" of Saul and the "man after Yahweh's own heart" (A and A'). A similar opposition is found in 2 Chr 16, where Hanani accuses King Asa of disloyalty to Yahweh in making an alliance with Aram (16:7), despite Yahweh's proven ability to bring victory even against

---

[111] On which, see below, pp. 109-110.

[112] The rendering of צוה as "charge" and מצוה as the corresponding noun, in the sense of "commission" has already been discussed above (p. 87 n. 95). In our discussion of vv. 13-14, this rendering is preferred to McCarter's (228) suggestion, "appointment", which, although it allows a more pleasing English translation, can be misleading, since the temporal connotation in English of "keeping an appointment" tends to focus attention on the time reference in 10:8 in a way that is not justified by the Hebrew terminology. On the identification of this charge with 10:8, see our discussion of 13:8 above (pp. 87-88).

[113] I.e., "had you done so, then ...".

great numbers of chariots and horses (16:8).[114] Hanani concludes in v. 9:

> For the eyes of Yahweh move to and fro throughout the earth to strengthen those whose *hearts* are loyal to him (עם־לבבם שלם אליו). You have *acted foolishly* (נסכלת) in this; indeed from now on, you will have wars.

It is apparent from the references to 'hearts' and 'foolishness' that 2 Chr 16:9 echoes not only 1 Sam 13:13[115] but v. 14 as well.

As regards the familiar rendering of איש כלבבו in 1 Sam 13:14b*a* by "a man after his own heart", McCarter (229) has argued that the phrase is more properly translated "a man of his own choosing". In support of McCarter's position, we note a similar phrase in the Babylonian "Chronicle Concerning the Early Years of Nebuchadnezzar II":

> The seventh year: In the month Kislev the king of Akkad mustered his army and marched to Hattu. He encamped against the city of Judah and on the second day of the month Adar he captured the city (and) seized (its) king. A king of his own choice (*šarra šá libbi-šu*) he appointed in the city (and) taking the vast tribute he brought it into Babylon.[116]

This text clearly implies vassal kingship, and if such is the connotation of כלבבו in 13:14b, this accords well with the prophetic view of circumscribed kingship reflected elsewhere in Samuel. While divine choice seems to be the major import of כלבבו in 13:14b, the more traditional understanding of the phrase as implying something about the character of the chosen one *vis-à-vis* the chooser is not ruled out entirely, for implicit in the selection of a vassal is an expectation that the new appointee will act in harmony with the suzerain's will and purpose, viz. 'in accord with his heart'. On this latter sense, we might compare 1 Sam 14:7, where the response of Jonathan's armour-bearer — "I am with you according to your heart (כלבבך)" — may imply 'chosenness' but certainly also implies 'unity of purpose' and a willingness to act in

---

[114] We note the similarity of this reference to the pressures facing Saul in 1 Sam 13.

[115] Cf. Williamson, *Chronicles*, 275.

[116] *ABC*, 5.Rev.11-13 (A. K. Grayson's translation).

concert.[117] In the light of these considerations, McCarter (229) perhaps overstates his case in asserting that 1 Sam 13:14b "has nothing to do with any great fondness of Yahweh's for David or any special quality of David, to whom it patently refers." While it is stated of both Saul and David that they were chosen by Yahweh,[118] a comparison of 8:22a, שמע בקולם והמלכת להם מלך כי-ראיתי בבניו לי, with 16:1bβ, מלך,[119] suggests that David was Yahweh's choice in a way that Saul, given in response to the people's request,[120] was not. At the time of David's anointing, an indication of the basis of Yahweh's preference is given: "man looks on the (outward) appearance, but Yahweh looks at the heart" (16:7b).[121]

The allusion to David in 1 Sam 13:14, though obvious in the light of later episodes, is only anticipatory in the present context, so that the emphasis falls not so much upon the sufficiency of David as upon the deficiency of Saul. Like King Asa after him, Saul proves by his 'foolish action' that he is not 'of a mind with' Yahweh. It is this state of affairs that Samuel finds intolerable and that leads to Saul's first rejection. As soon as Samuel has completed his business, though clearly not the business originally envisaged in 10:8, he departs, thus marking the end of the scene.[122]

---

[117] For discussion of this verse, see Ch. 4, p. 110. Cf. also the dual implication of כלבי in Jer 3:15; the shepherds whom Yahweh will appoint will be of his 'own choosing' and will also act 'according to his heart', viz., "they will shepherd you with knowledge and understanding." Veijola (*Dynastie*, 56) likens the designation איש כלבבו of 13:14 to the description in 1 Sam 2:35 of the "faithful priest, who will act according to what is in my [God's] heart and mind" (כהן נאמן כאשר בלבבי ובנפשי יעשה).

[118] 1 Sam 10:24 (Saul); 2 Sam 6:21 (David); cf. 1 Sam 16:12.

[119] Cf. also 16:3bβ, ומשחת לי את אשר-אמר אליך.

[120] 1 Sam 8:5, 19-20; 12:13.

[121] The terminology employed in the first half of this verse — viz., the reference to Eliab's "height" (גבה קומתו) and the notice that Yahweh has rejected (מאס) him — is reminiscent of the election (9:2; 10:23) and rejection (15:23, 26; 16:1) of Saul. In this light, Eliab's castigation of David in 17:28 — "I know your insolence and the wickedness of your heart" — is more than a little ironic. References in the DH to David's wholehearted loyalty to Yahweh include, e.g., 1 Kgs 3:6; 9:4; 11:4; 14:8; 15:3.

[122] On departure as a closure device, see Bar-Efrat, העיצוב האמנותי, 142-43; Alter, *Art*, 65; Wilcoxen, "Narrative", 91. And cf., for example, 1 Sam 8:22; 14:46; 15:34; 16:13; 21:1; 24:23; 26:25; 28:25; 29:11.

Excursus on 1 Sam 13:15

MT v. 15 raises several material difficulties, in that, for example, Samuel is sent to Gibeah Benjamin, though he plays no part in the subsequent events there, while Saul's departure is not mentioned, though he appears in v. 16 alongside Jonathan at Geba Benjamin.[123] In view of these difficulties, most scholars have appealed for help to the longer text of LXX v. 15, which reads as follows:

Καὶ ἀνέστη Σαμουὴλ καὶ ἀπῆλθεν ἐκ Γαλγάλων <u>εἰς</u>
<u>ὁδὸν αὐτοῦ· καὶ τὸ κατάλιμμα τοῦ λαοῦ ἀνέβη</u>
<u>ὀπίσω Σαοὺλ εἰς ἀπάντησιν ὀπίσω τοῦ λαοῦ τοῦ</u>
<u>πολεμιστοῦ.</u> αὐτῶν παραγενομένων ἐκ Γαλγάλων
εἰς Γαβαὰ Βενιαμείν, ...

The underlined portion is lacking in MT, and it is easy to see how homoioteleuton could account for the inadvertent omission of the intervening material. The LXX reading, however, is itself not without difficulties, as Driver explains:

(1) לדרכו following, as it would do ויעל, would give rise to a phrase not in use (וילך לדרכו is always said). (2) εἰς ἀπάντησιν ὀπίσω represents a non-Hebraic combination .... (3) αὐτῶν παραγ., if it represents, as it seems to do, הם בָּאִים must be followed by ושאול פקד, not as MT. by ויפקד שאול ....[124]

Driver's third point need not detain us, as it is by no means certain that the Greek participle would indicate a participle in Hebrew.[125] As regards the second, cited by Stoebe as proof that the LXX reading cannot be original,[126] it may be observed that not only the combination לקראת אחרי but also the corresponding εἰς ἀπάντησιν ὀπίσω are grammatically anomalous. Since εἰς ἀπάντησιν, like לקראת, requires a nominal or pronominal form as its complement, the word ὀπίσω after ἀπάντησιν in LXX 13:15 is

---

[123] In what can only be regarded as a *Verlegenheitslösung*, rabbinic commentators such as David Kimchi and Levi ben Gershon have assumed that Saul must have followed Samuel to Gibeah in order to receive instructions (cf. 10:8).

[124] Driver, 101-102 (his punctuation).

[125] Thenius-Löhr, 56.

[126] Stoebe, 245.

almost certainly corrupt.[127]   As such, its evidential value for
deciding between LXX and MT of 13:15 is nil.

Driver is therefore correct in omitting the objectionable word
from his Hebrew reconstruction, which reads as follows:

ויקם שמואל ויעל מן־הגלגל [וַיֵּלֶךְ לְדַרְכּוֹ: וְיֶתֶר הָעָם

עָלָה אַחֲרֵי שָׁאוּל לִקְרַאת עַם [or אַנְשֵׁי] הַמִּלְחָמָה וַיָּבֹאוּ

מִן הַגִּלְגָּל] גבעת בנימ'ן וג'

In keeping with his objection to the combination ויעל ... לדרכו
(see his first point), Driver inserts וילך, though unattested in LXX,
into his Hebrew reconstruction. Budde offers a simpler solution,
citing ἀπῆλθεν in LXX as evidence for an original וילך where ויעל
now stands in MT.[128]   Budde's reconstruction, ויקם שמואל וילך
... מן־הגלגל לדרכו, is preferable to that of Driver inasmuch as it
corresponds to the *number* of words represented in LXX, but an
even simpler solution may be possible. Although it is true that
the preferred partner of לדרך is a form of הלך, the Old Testament
contains several instances of לדרך with a verb of motion other
than הלך,[129] and this suggests that the combination ויעל ... לדרכו
is at least a theoretical possibility.[130]   Moreover, it is by no
means certain that ἀπῆλθεν must imply וילך, since LXX several
times renders a form of עלה in MT by a form of ἀπέρχομαι (i.e.
Josh 10:36; Jer 21:2; 2 Chr 16:3). Thus, we would read: ויקם
שמואל ויעל מן־הגלגל לדרכו ...

Whatever specific Hebrew reconstruction one adopts, and
there is clearly room for debate about details, the predominant
preference for the longer text of LXX in 1 Sam 13:15 seems justified.[131]   Thus, in our reconstructed v. 15, Samuel simply goes on
his way, while Saul returns to the hill country to join Jonathan and
the remnant of troops left there.

---

[127] Whether it represents an inner-Greek corruption (e.g., a belated
dittography of the first occurrence of ὀπίσω four words earlier) or a corrupt
variant within or arising out of a Hebrew Vorlage (e.g., a misreading of אנשי
as אחרי or of עם as עֵ; for ὀπίσω rendering עָם, see 1 Kgs 1:8) can only
be a matter for speculation. According to the Cambridge Septuagint (ad
loc.), the problematic word is not attested in the Armenian or Ethiopic versions, nor in the Latin MSS that reflect the longer reading.

[128] Budde, 87-88; cf. McCarter, 227; anticipated by Smith, 99.

[129] Gen 33:16 (שׁוב); 1 Sam 25:12 (הפך); 1 Kgs 19:15 (שׁוב); Isa 56:11
(פנה) [?].

[130] Cf. Driver's defence (125) of וישכם ... לקראת in MT 15:12 on the
basis of its being "in thorough analogy with Hebrew usage".

[131] But for a more tentative approach, see Pisano, *Additions*, 175-83.

Expositional Interlude: Israel's Plight
(13:16-23)

The section 13:16-23 does not appear to constitute a scene in its own right. It describes, for the most part, in straight narrative,[132] the events following Saul's abortive attempt to gather reinforcements at Gilgal. At the same time, it sets the stage for the battle of Michmash which will follow in ch. 14. Thus, the chief function of 13:16-23 is to provide a transition between the Gilgal episode of ch. 13 and the first scene of ch. 14. In addition, as we shall see, this transitional section adds to the overall development of the narrative in two ways: by heightening the tension created by Israel's military predicament, and by adumbrating the central roles that Saul and Jonathan will play in Israel's deliverance.

13:16-18, Battle Positions

In v. 16 we learn that Saul, Jonathan (here for the first time receiving the epithet "his son") and the army that is with them are together in Geba Benjamin. The Philistines, meanwhile, have encamped in Michmash, not more than 2.5 kilometres from Geba across the winding *wadi suweiniṭ*. After the words "Geba Benjamin" of the first clause, LXX appends καὶ ἔκλαιον, "and they wept", suggesting Hebrew ובכים (after...ישבים). This variant has generally received short shrift from commentators, who have dismissed it on the grounds that it is "tout à fait en opposition avec le reste du récit".[133] Textual considerations are inconclusive in this case, but in view of the graphic similarity between ובכים and בנימן[134] it is a fair question whether an original reference to weeping may not have dropped out of MT through haplography.[135] The material objections levelled against the LXX reading —

---

[132] On the term 'straight narrative', see above, pp. 21-23.

[133] So Dhorme, 112; cf. Stoebe, 245; Smith, 100; Budde, 88.

[134] The consonants ב and כ are easily confused in both the square and old Hebrew scripts; so Würthwein, *Text*, 104-105.

[135] So Klostermann, 43. Haplography, of course, is not the only possible explanation. It is also possible that בכם represents a corruption of an original בנימן, or vice versa; and if so, the LXX reading could have arisen when a marginal correction found its way into the text. Alterna-

for example, that "it is hardly likely that the little band of soldiers would so give way to grief before they had tried conclusions with the enemy"[136] — seem ill-founded. Weeping is not infrequent in 1-2 Samuel,[137] and, given our interpretation of the course of events up to this point in the narrative, weeping would not seem out of place here — the general muster has proved singularly unsuccessful, the six hundred soldiers remaining are without arms,[138] and, perhaps worst of all, Samuel has departed without consecrating the battle and without making known to Saul what he is to do next (cf. 10:8bβ).[139]

With their base of operations established in Michmash, the Philistines send out raiding parties to, broadly speaking, the north, west and east. The precise function of these bands is not stated, but their designation as המשחית, possibly a technical military term,[140] suggests that their duties included plundering and ravaging the land. The commonly held view that the raiding parties were part of the Philistine response to the action described in 13:3 has been challenged by Stoebe on the grounds that a frontal attack on Geba would have been more to the point.[141] Stoebe's observation has validity, however, only if we assume that the raiding bands had no strategic function. It is quite possible, however, as Garsiel has argued,[142] that attack and plunder were only part of the assignment of the raiding parties and that their primary task was, in fact, a strategic one. Garsiel's theory runs as follows. One of the raiding parties moved westward toward Beth Horon in order to secure access to Philistine territory. Another moved northward towards

---

tively, the mention of Saul and Jonathan "sitting down" (ישבים) might have triggered the addition of "weeping" on the analogy of references elsewhere to "sitting down and weeping" (e.g. Ps 137:1; Ezra 8:14; Neh 1:4).

[136] Smith, 100.

[137] Forms of בכה occur in the following passages (underlining indicates references to soldiers, or the people, weeping): 1 Sam 1:7, 8, 10; 11:4, 5; 20:41; 24:17; 30:4; 2 Sam 1:12, 24; 3:16, 32, 34; 12:21, 22; 13:36; 15:23, 30; 19:1, 2.

[138] See below, at 13:19-22.

[139] For a similar interpretation, see Graetz, *Geschichte*, 1:175. De Boer (*Research*, 60) also recognizes the reference to weeping in LXX as "alluding to Samuel's words and going away".

[140] So Houtsma, "Textkritisches", 59.

[141] Stoebe, 253. Goslinga's explanation (262) that the unfavourable terrain made a frontal attack inexpedient is unconvincing, and, at any rate, it remains rather curious that the deployment of the raiding parties does not seem to focus on Geba.

[142] "קרב מכמש", 25-27.

Ophrah,[143] where it turned east/south-eastward along a route leading down into the Jordan Valley near Jericho.[144] The third travelled east-ward along the "border road" (דרך הגבול) which overlooked the "Valley of the Hyenas" (גי הצבעים).[145] Assuming that the Philistines must have learned that Saul was centralizing his forces in Gilgal, Garsiel concludes that the strategic aim of the two eastward-bound parties may have been to create a "pincer movement" (תנועת מלגחיים) against Saul's camp in Gilgal. Here we would qualify Garsiel's theory with the observation that, since it seems unlikely that the Philistines would have recognized the meagre force of six hundred with Saul and Jonathan in Geba as all the *Kampffähige* of Israel, the strategic aim of the east-ward-bound units may have been simply to prevent a flanking action by Israelite forces coming up from the Jordan Valley by controlling two major passes into the hill country from the Jericho region.[146] At any rate, the Philistines' obvious freedom of movement in 13:16-18 signi-fies their military superiority in the area and contributes to the impres-sion that the diminutive Israelite forces at Geba are in an almost hope-less situation — an impression which is only intensified by the verses that follow.

13:19-21, Israel Disarmed

Though not explicitly stated, it may be inferred from the digression in vv. 19-21 that the Philistines had by some means deprived the Israelites of the means of producing and maintaining swords, spears, and even farm implements, either by deporting key personnel, as was the common practice of conquering forces in the ancient Near East,[147] or, as

---

[143] Ophrah is probably to be identified with modern *et-taiyibeh* (ca. 9 air-kilometres north of Michmash).

[144] The Jordanian-built road from Ramallah via *et-taiyibeh* to Jericho seems to follow an ancient route; Garsiel ("קרב מכמש", 25-26) calls atten-tion to the still observable remains of an old Roman road. Garsiel's specu-lation that the Philistine band turned to follow this route into the valley is plausible but difficult to demonstrate from the text, especially in view of the persistent difficulties in identifying "the land of Shual" (v. 17bβ).

[145] For summaries of attempts to identify this valley, see esp. Stoebe, 246, and Driver, 103.

[146] Cf. Stolz, 87.

[147] Cf., for example, 2 Kgs 24:14-16; Jer 24:1; 29:2; and the extra-biblical examples mentioned by Budde, 89. As Stoebe (256) has noted, however, mass deportations generally presuppose considerable geographi-cal distance and are not particularly suited to neighbouring states.

seems more likely, by simply depriving Israel of the more advanced
Philistine technology.[148] That a general state of affairs is being described is indicated by the initial imperfect of v. 19: "Now no smith
(חרש)[149] was to be found in all the land of Israel, for the Philistines
said, 'Lest the Hebrews make swords and spears'." Given its position
between this frequentative imperfect of v. 19 and the equivalent w-pf. of
v. 21, וַיִּרְדוּ of MT v. 20 should be repointed as a w-pf., וְיָרְדוּ, likewise with frequentative force:[150] "And all Israel would go down to the
Philistines to sharpen[151] each man his ploughshare, his mattock, his
axe and his sickle."[152]

13:22-23, Israel's Hope

After the brief digression of vv. 19-21, v. 22 returns to the specific
situation facing Israel prior to the battle of Michmash. Mention of the
army with Saul and Jonathan recalls 13:16, and the enigmatic מלחמת,
which appears to have suffered corruption,[153] may suggest an original
reference to Michmash.[154] והיה of v. 22 should read ויהי, as is indicated
not only by the above considerations but also by the subsequent verbal

---

[148] On which, see the following footnote. The presence of this
parenthesis within the main narrative is not necessarily indicative of secondary insertion (contra Greßmann, 39; Smith, 100; Budde, 89), for the information provided appears to be ancient and entirely appropriate to the
present context (so Dhorme, 112; cf. Hertzberg, 84/ET 107; Blenkinsopp,
"Quest", 87; McCarter, 238).

[149] The Hebrew term means simply "craftsman, artificer" (cf. Ackroyd,
"Note", 19), and it is impossible, therefore, to deduce from MT alone that
iron smiths are in view. It is clear from the archaeological evidence now
available, however, that the Philistines led their neighbours in the technology of iron-working (see esp. Dothan, *Philistines*, 91-93), and a true recol-
lection may be contained in LXX's τέκτων σιδήρου (cf. Stoebe, 254).

[150] LXX employs an imperfect tense here.

[151] Since the verb לטש means "to hammer" as well as "to sharpen,
whet" (BDB, 538; cf. *HAL*, 502), the notion of an initial forging of implements should not be excluded from v. 20 (cf. Stoebe, 255) — especially in
the light of the words of the preceding verse: "Lest the Hebrews make (יעשׂו)
swords and spears".

[152] "Sickle" follows LXX; on which, see McCarter, 234.

[153] Stoebe's suggestions (255) of an unusual *status absolutus* or a plural form מלחמות (so also Klein, 123) are not very convincing.

[154] Either מכמש has dropped out after מלחמת (cf. LXX) or מלחמת itself
should read מכמש. For the former suggestion, see Smith, 103; Thenius-
Löhr, 57; Dhorme, 113; Driver, 105; McCarter, 235; and for the latter, see
Toy (cited by Smith, 103), and cf. Budde, 90.

forms, נִמְצָא[155] and וַתִּמָּצֵא.[156] All these factors combine to return the reader's attention to the immediate situation prior to ch. 14. "So on the day of the battle [of Michmash] sword and spear were not found in the possession of any of the army with Saul and Jonathan, but Saul and his son Jonathan had them" (13:22). The effect of v. 22 is not only to highlight Israel's extreme military vulnerability, but also to single out Saul and Jonathan as the ones upon whom all Israel's hope of deliverance must rest. It will be for ch. 14 to develop this theme.

As a final preparation for ch. 14, 13:23 reports that the Philistines stationed an outpost (מצב) at the "pass of Michmash" (מעבר מכמש). Whether the reference is to the pass running from the hill country to the Jordan valley[157] or to a "pass" across the *wadi suweinit* itself,[158] the *strategic intent* of posting troops at the pass may well have been to monitor or forestall enemy troop movements[159] and to provide early warning in case of attack. Ironically, however, as we shall see in ch. 14, the *strategic effect* of the outpost was to be quite the opposite.

---

[155] Contrast the ipf. יִמָּצֵא in v. 19 and w-pf. והיתה in v. 21.

[156] For other instances in 1 Samuel of confusion of והיה and ויהי, see 1:12 and 10:9.

[157] Cf. Budde, 89; Smith, 103; Keil, 135.

[158] Driver, 105; Kiel, 123.

[159] In the course of Sargon's eighth campaign, Metatti of Zikirtu is said to have positioned outposts in the passes in order to slow the advance of Sargon's troops; see Saggs, "Assyrian Warfare", 152.

4

SAUL VERSUS THE PHILISTINES:
A REJECTED KING (1 SAM 14)[1]

Scene Three: Jonathan in Action Again
(1 Sam 14:1-15)

14:1-5, On the Day of Battle

To the reader already familiar with Jonathan's intrepid attack upon the Philistine governor in Geba (13:3), it comes as no great surprise that "on the day"[2] it is again Jonathan who distinguishes himself by his initiative: "One day Jonathan son of Saul said to his armour-bearer, 'Come, let us cross over to the Philistine outpost on the other side'" (14:1a). More unexpected, however, is the notice that immediately follows: "but his father he did not tell".[3] In a manner typical of the reticent narrative style of the books of Samuel, it is left to the reader to draw out the implications of this information. At a basic level, the notice seems to suggest some tension between father and son,[4] but to assume that this tension is rooted in a desire on Jonathan's part to usurp authority from his father or to indulge in self-glorification would be to ignore the overall depiction of Jonathan in 1 Samuel. A desire to safe-

---

[1] Since 1 Sam 13-14 are treated here as a continuous narrative, introductory comments on ch. 14 were included already at the beginning of the preceding chapter.

[2] MT ויהי היום. This idiomatic expression, which occurs in 1 Sam 1:4; 2 Kgs 4:8, 11, 18; Job 1:6, 13; 2:1, generally functions proleptically to introduce a day which is then defined in the subsequent narrative (cf. Smith, 104; GK §126s; Schneider, *Grammatik*, §52.5.7.4.; Blenkinsopp, "Jonathan's Sacrilege", 429). It is difficult to find an equivalent expression in English, and the most frequent translation is simply "one day".

[3] This English rendering reflects the emphatic word order of the Hebrew.

[4] Cf. Whitelam (*Just King*, 78): "Here we have brief indications [Whitelam refers to 14:1 and 14:27] that a certain tension existed between father and son, whether on the historical or redactional level".

guard the element of surprise may partially explain Jonathan's secrecy, but the effect of the notice in its present literary context is to suggest a certain apprehensiveness in Jonathan with respect to his father's leadership — something not wholly unexpected after the events of ch. 13. Saul's misguided behaviour in ch. 13 caused Samuel to depart (v. 15) without telling him what to do (cf. 10:8), and now Jonathan also declines to tell his father what he is about to do.

In a structural study of 1 Samuel, Jobling observes that "the theme of <u>knowledge</u>, of who knows what is going on in the narrative, is a very important and also a very problematic one".[5] The significance of 'knowledge' in the Saul narratives is noted also by Gunn, who suggests that Saul's lack of knowledge may even explain (excuse?) his failure "to surrender his kingdom gracefully".[6] In the Old Testament, however, ignorance is seldom, if ever, neutral. Indeed, O. A. Piper contends that "in the field of religion, 'knowledge' is the principal term used to describe man's right relation to God".[7] "In the OT the person who does not act in accordance with what God has done or plans to do has but a fragmentary knowledge, which, if not coupled with the fear of God, will eventually result in moral disintegration".[8] In this light, Soggin seems justified in linking Saul's incomprehension with "spiritual insensitivity".[9] Saul's ignorance is neither neutral nor excusable, as Jobling explains: "Saul does not learn who his successor is, but he does learn of the rejection of his house, so that ignorance of this on his part is <u>refusal to know</u>".[10]

Looking elsewhere in 1 Samuel, we find another instance of a 'refusal to know' in the Nabal episode of 1 Samuel 25. The significance of this episode within the Saul-David narratives is highlighted by Gordon in his discussion of narrative analogy in 1 Sam 24-26. Specifically, he proposes "the simple equation: Nabal = Saul. Saul does not vanish from view in 1 Samuel 25; he is Nabal's *alter ego*".[11] It is not Nabal, however, but his wife Abigail, who, like Jonathan in 1

---

[5] "Jonathan", 20.

[6] *Fate*, 121.

[7] "Knowledge", 43.

[8] "Knowledge", 44.

[9] *Introduction*, 195.

[10] "Jonathan", 21.

[11] "David's Rise", 43; see esp. pp. 43-51 for a defence of this equation.

Sam 13-14, occupies centre stage in the episode. Abigail is praised as an intelligent, beautiful and discerning woman (25:3, 33). Most importantly, she shows herself to be receptive to (cf. vv. 14-18) and knowledgeable of Yahweh's grand design for David (vv. 28-31). Nabal, by contrast, refuses knowledge (vv. 10-11), so that even his own servants despair of communicating with him: והוא בן־בליעל מדבר אליו, "He is such a good-for-nothing that it is no good talking to him" (v. 17b; *NEB*). Abigail, who recognizes the divine plan for David, has an equally clear perception of her husband: "Fool is his name, and folly goes with him." Is it any wonder that she declines to share her plans with "that worthless man" (איש הבליעל הזה) (v. 25)?[12] Her refusal to tell Nabal of her intention to intercept David is recounted in terms almost identical with 14:1b.

1 Sam 25:19b	ולאישה נבל לא הגידה
1 Sam 14:1b	ולאביו לא הגיד

Abigail's words and actions clearly imply a profound lack of confidence in her husband Nabal, and there appears to be at least a hint of the same in Jonathan's attitude towards his father at the beginning of 1 Sam 14.

Thus, the first verse of ch. 14 touches upon two themes initiated in ch. 13, namely, 1) the *military threat,* arousing hope that Jonathan may be able to do something about it (though it remains unclear what can be done) and 2) the *comparison and contrast of Saul and Jonathan,*[13] introducing a disconcerting sign of disunity into the relationship of father and son, who at the conclusion of ch. 13 stood side by side as those upon whom Israel's hope rested.

With the basic tenor of the scene thus established, vv. 2-5 digress in order to provide further staging before the action is resumed in v. 6.[14] V. 2 describes Saul's position "on the outskirts of Gibeah, beneath the

---

[12] Knowledge does eventually force itself upon Nabal, but when it comes, it proves fatal (vv. 36-38).

[13] On this see, in addition to the exegesis of 1 Sam 13 in the preceding chapter, our comments under the heading "Analogy and Contrast" in Ch. 1, pp.40-41.

[14] The preponderance of nominal sentences in vv. 2-5 is commensurate with their focus upon the "Hintergrund des Erzählens" (see Schneider, *Lehrbuch,* §44.2).

pomegranate tree, which was on the threshing floor."[15] V. 2b, recalling 13:15b, notes that Saul was accompanied by an army of about 600 men, while v. 3 makes a point of the circumstance that Ahijah, of the house of Eli, was included in Saul's entourage and was bearing (or wearing[16]) an ephod. V. 3b adds that the army was also unaware of Jonathan's departure.

The originality of vv. 2-3 in their present context has been challenged by Schicklberger[17] on four grounds: 1) neither Saul nor Ahijah has an important part to play in the immediate context; 2) the distinctly retarding character of vv. 2-3 is out of place so soon after the initiation of the narrative; 3) vv. 2-3 themselves arouse a sense of expectation (Schicklberger does not elaborate) which remains unfulfilled in the surrounding context; and 4) the sudden transition from appeal (*Appellfunktion*) in v. 1 to static representation (*ruhenden Darstellungsfunktion*) in v. 2 is awkward. Thus, according to Schicklberger, despite certain superficial correlations with their immediate context, vv. 2-3 interrupt the thematic progression of the narrative and belong only secondarily with vv. 1 and 4ff.

These observations show keen insight, but they do not necessarily lead to Schicklberger's negative verdict. As regards his second and fourth observations, which are similar in import and can be treated together, we note that Schicklberger is not alone in recognizing a tonal contrast between the first and second verses of ch. 14. Smelik, for example, writes, "Sauls passiviteit staat in een duidelijk contrast tot Jonathans activiteit."[18] We have already seen that in ch. 13 Saul and Jonathan, king and crown-prince, are placed side by side in such a way as to stress their similarity in role and station. We have suggested,

---

[15] MT's במגרון is difficult and should probably be read not as a place name (cf. Isa 10:28) but as a corruption of במו גרן (so McCarter, 235; cf. Stoebe ["Zur Topographie", 277] who also supports the view that the reference is to a threshing floor). For a survey of other suggested interpretations, see Stoebe's commentary, 258. Seebass (*David*, 88 n. 103) relates that, as of the summer of 1978, the threshing floor could still be seen quite well. See esp. the map provided on p. 161 of his earlier article, "1 Sam 15", in which he locates the threshing floor south of the "Passweg" midway between *jeba'* and *ḥirbet el-miqṭara* (on the location of the latter, see below, pp. 106-107).

[16] For a defence of the former rendering, which seems preferable in view of the basic meaning of נשא, see Klein, 135; Smith, 105; contrast McCarter, 232, 239.

[17] "Jonathans Heldentat", 327-38.

[18] *Saul*, 124; cf. already Gutbrod, 105.

moreover, that the first overt indication of disunity between the two is introduced in 14:1b. In the light of these earlier observations, we would argue that the activity vs passivity contrast in 14:1-2, far from disrupting the "thematische Progression"[19] of the narrative, contributes significantly to it, as the simple juxtaposing and comparing of Saul and Jonathan in ch. 13 evolves in ch. 14 into a rivalry and progressive alienation between them.

In view of the foregoing, Schicklberger's first point — viz., that neither Saul nor Ahijah plays an important role in the immediate context — is seen to be without force, at least as regards the reference to Saul; he is mentioned for the sake of the contrast with Jonathan. But what of the reference to Ahijah? Why do he and his family pedigree feature here? And why is his genealogy so curiously formulated, diverging from the line of direct descent to mention an uncle, Ichabod (v. 3a)? The eccentricity of this genealogical notice is sometimes cited as proof that v. 3a is a gloss.[20] But this is a moot point, for there is no reason to suppose that a glossator would have been less capable of composing a 'normal' genealogy than would an original 'author'.[21] Perhaps the question is best approached from a different angle, bearing in mind Alter's observation regarding the significance of "epithets and relational designations" in biblical narrative: "the narrator is generally telling us something substantive without recourse to explicit commentary".[22] In this regard, Jobling's reading of the Ahijah genealogy is instructive:

> Saul is accompanied by Ahijah, a member of the house of Eli (14:3), and this first mention of an Elide after the disasters which befell Eli's family in chap. 4 triggers the response "rejected by Yhwh." Lest the point be missed, it is reinforced by the odd and needless genealogical ref-

---

[19] Schicklberger, "Jonathans Heldentat", 328.

[20] E.g., Corney ("Eli", 85) writes: "But vs. 3 seems spurious, for the genealogical clause is without syntax, and the mention of a brother's name in a genealogy is unusual. Nor does the genealogy serve any purpose in the ensuing account."

[21] For a review and rebuttal of arguments brought against the originality of v. 3a, see Tsevat's excursus on 14:3a in his article "1 Sam. 2:27-36", 209-214. While Tsevat succeeds in showing the deficiency of the challenges to the half verse, he leaves largely unanswered the more positive question of its *function* in the context of ch. 14, stating only that "it serves the Eli-Abiathar genealogy" (214).

[22] *Art*, 20, 180.

erence to Ichabod, Ahijah's uncle, picking up on 4:21-
22, and reminding the reader that "the glory has departed." His own glory gone, where else would we expect
Saul to be than with a relative of "Glory gone"?[23]

Despite the disconcerting undertones noted thus far, the early verses
of ch. 14 retain a certain ambiguity. Since there is reason to believe
that threshing floors were sometimes regarded as appropriate places for
theophanies, "Schauplätze von Gotteserscheinungen",[24] Saul's location
at the threshing floor may encourage a modicum of hope that, despite
his forfeiting of Samuel's guidance in ch. 13, he may yet succeed in
discovering Yahweh's will for the impending battle. Such a hope
would be augmented by the presence of a priest bearing an ephod.
Nevertheless, this hope is not realized as the narrative continues, and if
something like this is what Schicklberger has in mind in his third observation, viz. that vv. 2-3 arouse an expectation that remains unfulfilled in the immediate context, then we would concur.[25] But again,
this need not imply that the verses are secondary, for the fact that an
expectation remains unfulfilled may be precisely the point.[26] In sum:
none of Schicklberger's observations necessarily leads to his conclusion
that vv. 2-3 are intrusive in ch. 14.

Vv. 4-5 round off the introductory section with a description of the
terrain lying between Jonathan and the Philistine outpost. The precise
locations of the "pass(es) of Michmash" and the "teeth of rock" (14:4)

---

[23] "Saul's Fall", 368.

[24] So Stoebe, "Tenne", 1952. McCarter (238-39) also notes the association of threshing floors with theophany and divine consultation, citing 1 Kgs 22:10 and especially Aqhat 17.5.4-8, in which the Ugaritic hero
Daniel, just prior to his visitation by the deity Kothar-and-Khasis (lines
9ff.), is described in terms strikingly similar to 1 Sam 14:2a — viz., seated
"before the gate under the mighty tree which is on the threshing floor".
Since the 1917 study by A. J. Wensinck, "Some Semitic Rites of Mourning
and Religion", the view that threshing floors in the aNE had sacral associa-
tions has been widely held. Among recent scholars, cf. Stacy, "Pre-Battle
Rite", 472; Porter, "Ancient Israel", 198; Ahlström, "Prophet Nathan",
115. For a different view, see Münderlein ("גרן", 64-65), who queries the
cultic interpretations.

[25] It is, in fact, doubtful that such is the expectation envisaged by
Schicklberger (as noted already he does not specify), but his general observation remains valid nonetheless.

[26] On two subsequent occasions in ch. 14, Saul will fail to obtain divine guidance (see our discussion of vv. 18, 37).

continue to be debated,[27] but this much, at least, can be said with certainty: the topography of the area around Jeba and Michmash, especially in the vicinity of *ḫirbet el-miqṭara* where the wadi *suweiniṭ* begins to develop the steep sides of a gorge, is well suited to the kind of exploit described in 1 Sam 14.[28] As to its literary function, the descriptive material not only adds to the verisimilitude of the account, but, more importantly, stresses the magnitude of the challenge facing Jonathan. If Dalman is correct in his etymological analysis of Bozez as "der Schlupfrige" and Seneh as "der Stachliche",[29] then even the names of the rock outcroppings serve the same end.[30]

14:6-15, Jonathan as 'Holy Warrior'

After the brief digression of vv. 2-5, the action is resumed in v. 6a, which repeats, in slightly modified form, the hortative challenge of v. 1a. Because of the striking similarity between the two clauses, v. 6a has been regarded by some as a doublet of v. 1a.[31]

---

[27] A helpful survey of the debate is provided by Madl (*Untersuchungen*, 510-13, n. 9), though his attempt to revive the minority view that Bozez and Seneh are to be sought south of *tel miryam* at *jebel abu ziad* is, as Seebass (*David*, 88 n. 103) observes, "mit der Wirklichkeit kaum in Übereinstimmung zu bringen".

[28] Cf. Dalman, "Der Paß von Michmas"; *idem*, "Das Wādi eṣ-ṣwēnīṭ"; Seebass, "1 Sam 15", 161-68; *idem*, *David*, 88 n. 103. The present writer made two brief visits to the area in the autumn of 1983 and was able to confirm that the rimose rock formations in the area of *ḫirbet el-miqṭara* make it possible to climb undetected to a position on a level with and slightly to the southeast of that site.

[29] "Der Paß von Michmas", 169. Dalman is followed by the majority of commentators; see Stoebe, 258-59.

[30] For a different view, see Lombardi ("Alcune questioni", 281-82), who suggests that Seneh of the biblical account should be identified with *qala'at ed-dāmūsiyeh* (apparently the same as *qala'at abu dāmūs* on Dalman's 1905 map), the largest of the outcroppings on the southern side of the wadi in the vicinity of *ḫirbet el-miqṭara*. He admits that the Arabic name bears no resemblance to the name Seneh, but notes that, since it seems to connote something like "la roccia delle caverne", the identification would correspond nicely to the mention of "Hebrews coming out of the holes" in 1 Sam 14:11. He also reports that the opposing outcropping of rock, unmarked on Dalman's map, apparently bears the Arabic name *baṣṣah* (meaning "brillare"), a name which he believes to be both ancient and philologically equivalent to Hebrew *boṣeṣ*.

[31] E.g., Madl, *Untersuchungen*, 22-24; Seebass, "1 Sam 15", 160.

v. 1 וַיֹּאמֶר יוֹנָתָן בֶּן־שָׁאוּל אֶל־הַנַּעַר נֹשֵׂא כֵלָיו לְכָה וְנַעְבְּרָה אֶל־מַצַּב פְּלִשְׁתִּים אֲשֶׁר מֵעֵבֶר הַלָּז

v. 6 וַיֹּאמֶר יוֹנָתָן אֶל־הַנַּעַר נֹשֵׂא כֵלָיו לְכָה וְנַעְבְּרָה אֶל־מַצַּב הָעֲרֵלִים הָאֵלֶּה

As the above comparison shows, however, the two clauses are not identical. The anaphoric reference to "these uncircumcised" in v. 6, which clearly presupposes v. 1, is ample indication that v. 6 is not a doublet but, rather, a resumptive repetition[32] or, to borrow Schicklberger's term, a "Pro-Form".[33]

Jonathan's derisive reference to the Philistines as "these uncircumcised", together with his assertion of Yahweh's ability to save regardless of the odds (v. 6b), invites comparison with David's confident utterances prior to his defeat of Goliath in 1 Sam 17 — for example, "Who is this uncircumcised Philistine, that he should defy the armies of the living God?" (17:26; cf. vv. 36-37). In both contexts, it is the *words* of the young heroes even more than their *deeds* that mark the high points of the respective scenes. In ch. 17, David steps on to the stage as the "confessor of Yahweh",[34] boldly proclaiming Yahweh's ability to save his people, despite the denials of this not only in the slanderous challenges of the Philistine champion (vv. 10, 16, 23, 25) but also, and less excusably, in the obvious trepidation of Saul and his troops (vv. 11, 24, 32). In ch. 14 it is Jonathan who first assumes the role of "confessor of Yahweh". It is he who proclaims Yahweh's ability to save "whether by many or by few" (v. 6b)[35] and, ultimately, it is he, not Saul, who emerges as the "representative of true Yahwistic piety".[36]

---

[32] See above, p. 36 n. 124.

[33] Schicklberger ("Jonathans Heldentat", 329) defines a "Pro-Form" as "eine Variable, die für eine andere Form anaphorisch, kataphorisch oder deiktisch eintritt". This device, according to Schicklberger, is a common stylistic feature in Hebrew narrative and is employed when the writer "ganz betont zum Hyperthema zurückführen und das zwischen den Hauptreferenzträgern stehende als Rahmenprogression kennzeichnen [will]."

[34] So Knierim, "Messianic Concept", 35-36.

[35] We have already noted the literary impact of this verse as oblique commentary on Saul's excuse in 13:11 (see pp. 40-41).

[36] So Stoebe, 263: "Vertreter wahrer Jahwefrömmigkeit".

Even from what we have seen thus far, it is apparent that Jonathan's bold initiative is to be understood as motivated not so much by personal bravado or derring-do as by the ideology of 'holy war'.

Excursus on 'holy war'

A summary and evaluation of research on the subject of holy war is provided by A. de Pury in his recent article entitled "La guerre sainte israélite: réalité historique ou fiction littéraire?"[37] After a brief introduction listing the relevant biblical texts and outlining some of the difficulties inherent in the topic, de Pury traces the history of research, beginning with antecedents to von Rad's influential work, which he succinctly recapitulates, and then discussing in some depth the subsequent contributions of Smend, Stolz, Weippert and Weimar. Accepting Stolz's view that holy war in Israel was more theory (ideology) than practice (institution), de Pury nevertheless queries Stolz's contention that the theory first arose within the deuteronomistic school, noting that even Stolz "est obligé d'admettre que les origines de la théorie sont plus anciennes que l'époque de Josias et remontent au moins aux cercles d'opposition prophétiques du royaume du Nord" (29). Weippert's study places holy war in its broader aNE context, while Weimar argues that holy war ideology in Israel found its earliest literary expression in the Davidic period, among circles opposed to David.

Reluctant to close his discussion without asking the question whether and to what extent "la nostalgie de nos narrateurs se réfère à un modèle historique réel", de Pury concludes by aligning himself with von Rad on an essential point: "c'est à la période pré-monarchique que se constitue le répertoire d'expériences normatives qui donnera naissance à une tradition de la 'guerre de YHWH' et qui permettra plus tard l'élaboration d'une *théorie* de la guerre sainte" (35). While von Rad's theory of an "institution" of holy war from the Judges period "est trop massive" (especially when viewed as a uniquely Israelite phenomenon and linked with a hypothetical amphictyony of twelve tribes), von Rad's opponents "sont allés trop loin lorsqu'ils ont tenté de présenter l'idéologie de la guerre sainte comme une invention de la théologie

---

[37] This article appeared along with several others pertinent to the subject of holy war (including a fairly comprehensive bibliography of twentieth century works to 1979 compiled by J. G. Heintz) in the 1981 issue of *Etudes Théologiques et Religieuses*. See also the seminal treatise by von Rad, *Der heilige Krieg im alten Israel* (esp. pp. 6-14). A briefer summary of the basic features is available in Toombs, "War", 796-801; on challenges to von Rad's view, see Gottwald, "Holy War", 942-44. Advocates of 'Yahweh war' as a more appropriate designation for 'holy war' in Israel include, *inter alios,* Richter (*Untersuchungen*, 186), Jones ("'Holy War' or 'Yahweh War'?") and Mayes ("Period of the Judges", 319-20).

deutéronomique, voire de l'historiographie deutéronomiste." Rather, "lorsque les cercles prophétiques, au Nord comme au Sud, se font les porteurs de l'idéologie de la 'guerre de YHWH', ils se situent dans la ligne des traditions israélites archaïque bien plus que dans celle de la liturgie du Temple de Jérusalem" (36).

Returning to 1 Sam 14, we observe that Jonathan's hopeful outlook, "Perhaps Yahweh will act[38] on our behalf" (v. 6aβ), finds ready response from his armour-bearer: "Do all that is in your heart (בלבבך); go ahead,[39] I am with you *according to your heart* (כלבבך)"[40] (v. 7). Yet battle is not to be joined without first consulting Yahweh, so Jonathan proposes a sign (vv. 8-10). That the primary purpose of the sign is oracular and not merely to discover the psychological state of the Philistines (though this may be a secondary effect)[41] is amply indicated by the presence of an *Übereignungsformel*, כי־נתנם יהוה בידנו (v. 10).[42]

Upon receiving a favourable sign (vv. 11-12), Jonathan "goes up on his hands and feet" with his armour-bearer close behind (v. 13a). MT's description of the suprise attack — the Philistines "fell before Jonathan", whereupon his armour-bearer was "dispatching" (מְמוֹתֵת) them (v. 13b; cf. 17:51) — highlights "das Wunderbare"[43] in its success, and thus yields a sense appropriate to a holy war context.[44] Suc-

---

[38] MT יעשה. McCarter (235) suggests emending to יושיע ("will give us victory") on the basis of להושיע in the subsequent clause (v. 6b; cf. v. 23), but this emendation is without textual support, and cf. v. 45 (עשה הישועה).

[39] Rendering MT's difficult נסה לך. Stoebe (259) defends the imperatival sense of MT; cf. Goslinga, 268. Others (e.g., McCarter, 235-36; Driver, 107) follow LXX: Ποίει πᾶν ὃ ἐάν ἡ καρδία σου ἐκκλίνῃ (lit. "Do all to which your heart inclines").

[40] LXX makes the sense explicit: ὡς ἡ καρδία σού καρδία μού. Whether this reflects a Hebrew original, כלבבך לבבי, remains doubtful; כלבבך כלבבי would be more idiomatic. MT's reading, though unusual, may be compared with 13:14, כלבבו, where, as we have argued, the expression implies unity of will and purpose, a sense entirely appropriate to 14:7.

[41] Cf. Goslinga, 269; Blaikie, 223.

[42] Cf. v. 12: כי־נתנם יהוה ביד ישראל; cf. also v. 37. On this typical holy-war formula, see Birch, *Rise*, 89; Richter, *Untersuchungen*, 21-25.

[43] So Stoebe, 259.

[44] Emendation of MT on the basis of LXX's καὶ ἐπέβλεψαν κατὰ πρόσωπον Ἰωναθὰν, καὶ ἐπάταξεν αὐτούς ("and they looked upon the face of Jonathan, and he smote them") is, therefore, unnecessary, though McCarter's (236) suggested reconstruction ויפנו לפני יונתן ויכם ("and when

cess in this case includes not only enemy casualties but, more importantly, the demoralizing of the remaining Philistine forces. "Panic", according to v. 15, engulfs them all — those in the camp, the field, the outpost, the raiding parties, etc. The ultimate attribution of this "panic" to divine agency ("it became a trembling of God [חרדת אלהים]!")[45] is consistent with Jonathan's own perspective that Yahweh alone gives victory (vv. 6, 10, 12), and in no wise diminishes the illustrious portrait of Jonathan in the episode. Indeed, at the end of the day all the people acknowledge that it is Jonathan "who has brought about this great deliverance in Israel ... for with God he did [this thing] this day" (v. 45).

Scene Four: Saul in Action Again
(1 Sam 14:16-23)

As we have already seen, 1 Sam 13-14 display a common scheme, in which Jonathan initiates the action and Saul responds. So far in ch. 14, Jonathan has been the active agent (vv. 1-15). Now in a short but significant scene (vv. 16-23) we learn of Saul's response. Not surprisingly, in view of the depiction of Saul elsewhere in chs. 13-14, the scene before us is presented in such a way as to reflect unfavourably upon Saul or, at least, to minimize any impression that he contributes significantly to the defeat of the Philistines.

14:16-19, Preparing to Enter the Fray
It is apparent from Saul's response to the news of the Philistines' "melting away"[46] in all directions that he suspects Israelite involvement in the disturbance across the wadi, for he does not ask "if" but "who" has departed from his ranks (v. 17). It is equally apparent, however, by

---

the Philistines] turned toward Jonathan, he struck them down") is not unreasonable, since LXX often uses ἐπιβλέπειν to render פנה in MT.

[45] This interpretation of the phrase חרדת אלהים is suggested by the broader context with its many reflections of holy war ideology (cf. Klein, 137), but the alternative which regards אלהים as an intensifier — thus, "a very great panic" — is also possible. In fact, the two notions of magnitude and divine agency are not mutually exclusive, as McCarter (240) seems to recognize.

[46] Cf. BDB, 556. On Wellhausen's attempt to link נמג with an Arabic root meaning 'surge', see Driver, 110 n. 1.

virtue of the fact that an inquiry is necessary, that Saul is unaware of Jonathan's latest initiative. Thus, as the scene opens, we are reminded of Jonathan's decision, back in 14:1b, not to take his father into his confidence.

Upon learning that Jonathan and his armour-bearer have absented themselves, Saul immediately orders Ahijah to "bring the ark of God (ארון האלהים)" (MT v. 18). Reference to the ark at this point in 1 Samuel is surprising for several reasons: 1) it is explicitly stated in 14:3 that Ahijah was in possession of an "ephod", and there is no mention of the ark; 2) the implication of 1 Sam 7:1 and 2 Sam 6 is that the ark remained at Kiriath-jearim[47] during the reign of Saul[48]; 3) נגש hi. ("bring near") seems appropriate with reference to an ephod (and is so used in 23:9 and 30:7) but not with reference to the ark; 4) Saul's command in v. 19 to "withdraw your hand" hardly fits any known use of the ark but accords well with the manipulation of the Urim and Thummim frequently associated with an ephod.[49] Not surprisingly, a majority of scholars have followed LXX (cf. also Josephus, *Ant.* 6:115) in reading "ephod" in 14:18,[50] though the question of how the reading "ark" may have arisen in MT remains a difficult one.[51]

---

[47] On the identity of Baal-Judah (2 Sam 6:2) with Kiriath-jearim, see Josh 15:9, 60 and 1 Chr 13:6.

[48] A view apparently shared by the Chronicler, who states (1 Chr 13:3) that the ark was not sought (דרש) during the reign of Saul.

[49] Cf. de Vaux, *Ancient Israel*, 2: 351. Perhaps it was the unacceptability of the idea that Ahijah would have had his hand on or even in (!) the ark that caused the Targum, which follows MT in reading "ark", to substitute קריב אפודא in v. 19 for MT's אסף ידך; cf. Stoebe, 260.

[50] For an instance of confusion of ארון and אפוד outside the Old Testament, see 2 Baruch 6:7 (cf. the note ad loc. in *APOT*).

[51] Stoebe (260, 264) retains "ark" in v. 18 as *lectio difficilior,* though he denies the inferences sometimes drawn that there were duplicate arks or that the ark was ever used as an oracular device (but cf. Judg 20:27[?]). P. R. Davies ("Ark or Ephod"; cf. *idem,* "History of the Ark") has postulated that the reference to the "ark" in v. 18 is an "accidental" survivor of a systematic suppression and replacement with "ephod" of original references to the ark in the Samuel narratives. The exchange was made necessary when an editor inserted a story of the ark's capture in 1 Sam 4-6 and of its eventual restoration in 2 Sam 6. Davies' theory rests on several assumptions: 1) that "the historicity of the capture of the ark as recorded in 1 Sam. IV-VI is dubious", 2) that "the point at which the capture has been inserted in the total narrative depended on the decision of the editor who almost certainly had no knowledge of the correct historical juncture (if there was one) at which to insert the story" and 3) that references to Eli or his sons in 1 Sam 4 are secondary (since these would otherwise form a point of contact

Whatever we make of the "ark" or "ephod" issue in 14:18, it seems apparent that Saul's intention in addressing Ahijah is to initiate a divine inquiry as to how he should respond to the growing tumult across the wadi. Whether or not this inquiry is necessary, Saul's discontinuance of the procedure once it has begun (v. 19) can hardly reflect favourably upon him.[52] His failure to wait for an answer recalls his failure to wait for Samuel's instructions in ch. 13 and raises the question whether Saul is not again 'acting foolishly' (cf. 13:13a).[53]

14:20-23, Yahweh's Victory

The wording of v. 20 — "Saul and all the troops with him assembled (וַיִּזָּעֵק) and came to battle" — is unusual, but it is confirmed by Judg 18:22-23. Smelik remarks that the niphal form "versterkt de indruk, dat men Saul zo min mogelijk eigen initiatief will toeschrijven."[54] Certainly v. 20b indicates that the victory was virtually assured by the time Saul and his followers arrived on the scene: "Behold, every man's sword was against his fellow — a very great confusion", a confusion which may be partially accounted for by the shifting allegiances in the midst of battle (vv. 21-22). The lack of any explicit reference to Saul's joining in the fight may be a further reflection of the tendency in the narrative to diminish Saul's part in the victory.[55] Ultimately it is Yahweh who rescues Israel (v. 23a), yet it will be said of Jonathan, not Saul, that "he has been at work with God today" (v. 45; *NEB*).

---

with the earlier chapters of 1 Samuel). Ahlström ("Travels of the Ark", 145) finds Davies' theory convincing, but for those, like the present writer, who query one or more of Davies' assumptions, the theory does not offer a final answer.

[52] Stoebe (264) regards the inquiry as unnecessary but remarks, "auf jeden Fall war plötzliches Abbrechen auffallender als der Verzicht."

[53] Cf. Kirkpatrick, 133; Smelik, 125; McCarter, 240.

[54] *Saul*, 126.

[55] Cf. Smelik, *Saul*, 126.

Scene Five: The Troubler of Israel
(1 Sam 14:24-46)

14:24, Saul's Adjuration of the Army

The interpretation of v. 24, which provides the necessary background for the rest of the chapter as far as v. 46, is a matter of some debate. Not only does LXX present a longer and significantly different reading for vv. 23b-24a (see below), but there are also apparent difficulties in MT. Chief among these is the reference to the men of Israel being "in distress (נגשׂ) on that day" (v. 24a). This notice has been regarded as entirely inappropriate in the light of the deliverance described in the immediately preceding context (vv. 20b-23).[56] The difficulty is sometimes obviated in translation by making the distress the result of the oath of abstinence imposed by Saul. *RSV*, for example, translates the first two clauses of v. 24 as follows: "And the men of Israel were distressed that day; for Saul laid an oath on the people...".[57] But this rendering of the w-ipf. in the second clause as introducing a causal sentence is contrary to Hebrew syntax, inasmuch as the imperfect consecutive normally expresses "actions, events, or states, which are to be regarded as the temporal or logical sequel of actions, events, or states mentioned immediately before."[58] Syntactically, therefore, v. 24 suggests that the distress of the men of Israel may have *prompted* rather than resulted from Saul's oath.[59]

This, of course, raises the question of what, if not Saul's oath, might have occasioned the army's distress. Perhaps the place to begin in seeking an answer to this question is to note that the only other reference in 1 Sam 13-14 to the "distress" (נגשׂ) of the army is found in 13:6, in the aftermath of Jonathan's provocative attack upon the Philistine governor.[60] We should also recall that as ch. 14 opened, the

---

[56] Cf. Thenius-Löhr, 61; Smith, 117; Budde, 96; Dhorme, 119.

[57] Similarly, *KJV, NIV, NASB*.

[58] So GK §111a. On the construction of causal sentences, see GK §106f and esp. §158. *NEB* 's resistance to the causal rendering in v. 24 marks an improvement over previous translations but nevertheless falls short of the sense of consequence basic to the w-ipf.: "Now the Israelites on that day had been driven to exhaustion. Saul had adjured the people in these words...".

[59] Cf. Stoebe, 265, 271.

[60] Stoebe (271) points out that נגשׂ "eine Notlage [schildert], die Verwandschaft mit 13,6 zeigt"; cf. also Driver, 112; Jobling, "Saul's Fall", 374; Pisano, *Additions*, 39-40. Some have suggested that 13:6 may be

cause of distress in 13:6, viz. the threatening Philistine military presence, had by no means diminished. The ill-equipped remnant force under Saul and Jonathan had every reason to be fearful, especially after the signal failure of the muster in Gilgal. The discovery in 14:17 that Jonathan had absented himself and, by all appearances, was engaged in yet another *Alleingang* against the Philistines would have done little to allay the fears of troops still experiencing the effects of his first initiative. While troop morale might have been bolstered by a favourable oracle, Saul's aborting of the procedure (14:18-19) could only have had the opposite effect. In view of these considerations, the suggestion that Saul's adjuration of the army was issued as a substitute for the omitted oracle[61] has more cogency than is sometimes allowed.[62]

If the above observations are in the main correct, then v. 24 should be read as a 'flashback' or retrospective description of events which took place just prior to Saul's advance on Michmash.[63] Taking both verbal forms (pf., w-ipf.) as pluperfects, which is fully in accord with Hebrew grammar,[64] we may render v. 24 as follows: "Now the men of Israel had been in distress on that day, so that Saul had placed them under an oath...." The reason this information is introduced retrospectively at this particular juncture in the narrative is that it provides the necessary background to the account of Jonathan's inadvertence which follows immediately in vv. 25ff.

As to whether Saul's adjuration of the people was wise or foolish, opinions vary. The former view, represented, for example, by Hertzberg, rests on the assumption that Saul's omission of the oracle

---

conflate (e.g. Hertzberg, 79/ET 101; Stoebe, 244, 251; McCarter, 226), but there is little evidence to support this view.

[61] So Budde, 94; Hertzberg, 90/ET 114; cf. Greßmann, 43.

[62] This view seems preferable to that of Pisano (*Additions*, 39), who also defends MT's בוצ but attributes the "distress" to the pressures of the battle in progress. For while v. 23a, "so Yahweh delivered Israel that day", might be taken as a proleptic summary of the day's events, the total picture created by vv. 20-23 leaves little room for assuming that the battle itself brought distress upon the men of Israel; the Philistines, in a state of utter confusion, were literally destroying themselves (v. 20), the "Hebrews" formerly allied with them had changed sides (v. 21), and Israel's army had been further reinforced by the return of its own former deserters (v. 22).

[63] On time manipulation as a narrative device, see Licht, *Storytelling*, 109-111; Bar-Efrat, "Some Observations", 160.

[64] On the use of a w-ipf. to continue the sense of a preceding perfect, see GK §111q; Davidson, *Syntax*, §48c. Examples involving a change of subject include Gen 26:18; Num 14:36; 1 Sam 28:3.

was necessitated ("notgedrungen") by the situation heating up across the wadi, and that his adjuration of the people evidences "wie ernst Saul die Sache mit Gott nimmt".[65] There can be little doubt that Saul took the battle seriously, but the words with which he concludes his adjuration arouse suspicion regarding the propriety of his motivation: "until *I* have avenged *myself* on *my* enemies". This phrase need not imply that Saul is motivated simply by a desire for personal vengeance,[66] but it cannot be denied that it "tamelijk profaan klinkt",[67] especially when compared with Jonathan's earlier reference to Yahweh giving the Philistines "into the hand of Israel" (14:12).[68] As we have already seen in our analysis so far, it is Jonathan, not Saul, who appears in chs. 13-14 as the true instrument of Yahweh's initiative. This role will later be assumed by David, who alone in 1 Samuel will be credited with "fighting the battles of Yahweh".[69]

In view of the foregoing, it seems reasonable to view the setting and significance of Saul's oath as follows. Prior to his advance upon Michmash in ch. 14, Saul, scenting victory but sensing also the trepidation of his troops, took matters into his own hands, as he had done once before (13:9), and, in the absence of a favourable oracle, imposed an oath upon his troops designed to insure their full engagement in the ensuing conflict. The implication, of course, is that in this instance, as in the former, Saul's action was foolish. Indeed, the longer reading of LXX makes this point explicitly: καὶ Σαοὺλ ἠγνόησεν ἄγνοιαν μεγάλην ἐν τῇ ἡμέρᾳ ἐκείνῃ, καὶ ἀρᾶται τῷ λαῷ λέγων, ... For the first phrase, Wellhausen[70] suggested the following Hebrew retroversion: וְשָׁאוּל שָׁגָה שְׁגָנָה גְדֹלָה בַּיּוֹם הַהוּא. In an article which concerned itself with "the more precise definition of the technical term שגגה", J. Milgrom defined שגגה as an "inadvertence" which "may result from 2 causes: negligence or ignorance". In either case the performer of the inadvertence is "conscious of his act ... but not of its consequences."[71] In his commentary on 1 Samuel, McCarter follows Wellhausen's reconstruction and cites Milgrom's definition as support

[65] So Hertzberg, 90/ET 114.
[66] Contra Goslinga, *I Samuël*, 177; Keil, 142.
[67] So Smelik, *Saul*, 127.
[68] Cf. Jobling, "Saul's Fall", 369.
[69] 1 Sam 25:28; cf. 17:45; 18:17; 30:26; etc.
[70] *Text*, 90.
[71] "Cultic שגגה", 117-118.

for his translation: "Saul made a great blunder that day."[72] Though McCarter does not pursue the matter further, it is worth noting that, from a literary perspective, this reading would provide a striking irony. In the account that follows, it is Jonathan who inadvertently breaks the vow of abstinence, yet in the narrative framework it is Saul, not Jonathan, who is charged with committing a great blunder — an inadvertent sin.

As attractive as this reading is from a literary perspective, it is questionable whether the longer reading supplied by LXX should be preferred to MT.[73] If the understanding of נגש in MT suggested above is in the main correct, then the basic reason for preferring LXX is removed. Nevertheless, there may still be a hint of the idea of foolishness in MT's enigmatic וַיֹּאֶל. It is generally assumed that this is a form of the verbal root אלה II, which in the hiphil means to 'adjure, put under oath'.[74] But if this is the case, then the vocalization of the form in v. 24 is anomalous.[75] While some scholars seek to resolve the problem by simply emending the text,[76] others see in this enigmatic form a possible *double entendre*.[77] We may recall Glück's description of what he terms metaphonic or patternal puns involving a "change in meaning ... introduced or suggested by vowel mutation".[78] Lending support to the notion of a *double entendre* is König's observation that the only conceivable explanation for MT's וַיֹּאֶל is that it arose through "äusserlichen Gleichmachung" with a root יאל.[79] The most likely candidate would seem to be יאל I, 'to be foolish'.[80] Given LXX's penchant for "Auflösungen prägnanter Darstellungen",[81] the suggestion that the longer reading of LXX represents a double translation of וַיֹּאֶל is an attractive one.[82]

---

[72] McCarter, 243.

[73] See, most recently, Pisano, *Additions*, 37-41.

[74] BDB, 46.

[75] Gesenius' attempt to explain the anomaly (see GK §79d) is effectively contested by König, *Lehrgebäude*, 2: 578-79.

[76] E.g. Smith, 118; Budde, 96; Stoebe, 267.

[77] So Jobling, "Saul's Fall", 374.

[78] "Paronomasia", 61; see Ch. 1, p. 28.

[79] *Lehrgebäude*, 2: 578-79.

[80] BDB, 383.

[81] Thenius-Löhr, LXXXVII.

[82] Cf. Stoebe, 267. This would not explain, however, the other differences between LXX and MT, so that the matter of which text may reflect

14:25-31, Jonathan's Inadvertence

Despite the doubtful wisdom of Saul's oath, the army complies. Even a fortuitous find of honey cannot deter them from their dogged obedience, for they "fear the oath" (vv. 25-26). Jonathan, however, has heard nothing of the oath (v. 27a) and so does not hesitate to refresh himself with a little honey.[83] The tantalizingly slow and unusually detailed description of his movements in v. 27aβ-b not only dramatizes the action but makes the point that Jonathan's refreshment was taken 'on the march'.[84] But no sooner have Jonathan's eyes "brightened",[85] than one of the soldiers, in apparent dismay,[86] informs him of Saul's injunction. Whether the phrase that follows, ויעף העם[87] (v. 28b), comes from Jonathan's informant or, as seems more likely in view of ויעף העם מאד (v. 31b), is commentary by our narrator, the two phrases form an *inclusio* which frames and highlights Jonathan's reaction to what he has just heard.[88]

---

the earlier reading remains unresolved. For an attempt to explain how MT's shorter reading may have arisen from a haplographic reading of LXX, see Seebass, "Zum Text", 74-82. The major weakness in Seebass' theory is that it requires that radical surgery first be done to LXX.

[83] On the textual difficulties in MT of vv. 25-26, see Wellhausen, *Text*, 91-92; McCarter, 245.

[84] I.e. "ohne sich aufzuhalten" (so Stoebe, 273).

[85] Reading the Qᵉrê וַתָּאֹרְנָה with the ancient versions (see Stoebe, 267) and most commentators; supported also by כִּי־אֹרוּ עֵינָי (v. 29bα).

[86] Perhaps indicated by the emphatic construction הַשְׁבֵּעַ הִשְׁבִּיעַ (v. 28).

[87] On the anomalous vocalization וַיָּעַף here and in v. 31, Judg 4:21 and 2 Sam 21:15, see GK §72t.

[88] McCarter's objection to v. 28b as "disruptive at this point" is counterbalanced by his own recognition that it is "explanatory of Jonathan's remarks in vv 29-30" (246).

A	Army tired	ויעף העם	v. 28b<u>And the troops (were) tired.</u>
B	First cause of fatigue: Saul's adjuration		v. 29And Jonathan said, "My father has troubled the land.
C	What eating achieved for Jonathan	ראו־נא כי־ארו ...	Look how my eyes have brightened,
D	Jonathan's eating	כי...	because I ate a little of this honey.
D'	Army's not eating	אף כי...	v. 30How much more,[89] had the troops only eaten today from their enemy's spoil which they found,
C'	What eating could have achieved for the army	כי־עתה ...	for then the defeat of the Philistines would have been greater."[90]
B'	Second cause of fatigue: the long pursuit		v. 31And they smote the Philistines that day from Michmash to Aijalon.
A'	Army very tired	ויעף העם מאד	<u>And the troops (were) very tired.</u>[91]

In an unequivocal condemnation of his father's actions, Jonathan proclaims, עכר אבי את־הארץ (v. 29). The charge of 'troubling' (עכר) is but one of several parallels between the present context and the Achan episode of Josh 6-7.[92] In both contexts lot-casting is the means of discovering the offender. And in both, the respective interrogations are couched in almost identical terms:

Josh 7:19	הגד־נא לי מה עשׂיתה
1 Sam 14:43	הגדה לי מה עשׂיתה

In the Achan episode it is the one upon whom the lot falls who is charged with troubling Israel. In the present context, however, the situation is reversed. Ultimately the lot will fall upon Jonathan (14:42), but already in v. 29, almost it seems in anticipation of the later lot-casting, Jonathan lays the charge of 'troubling the land' at his

---

[89] The sense seems to be, "how much more (would the refreshment have been)"; on לוא followed by a perfect, see BDB, 65; *HAL*, 495-96.

[90] For a defence of this reading, see Driver, 115; McCarter, 246.

[91] V. 31 is often construed as a temporal clause, linked to v. 32 and introducing the account of the army's cultic infraction (e.g. Budde, 98; Stoebe, 265, 268; McCarter, 243, 249). The lack of an explicit subject in v. 31a, however, seems to presuppose the subject of v. 30 as its antecedent, while v. 32 has an expressed subject and so may open a new paragraph. Thus, we take v. 31 as a summary comment by the narrator, reiterating an important theme of the preceding verses, namely the exhaustion of the troops, and thereby preparing for the events of the succeeding paragraph.

[92] Cf. Blenkinsopp, "Jonathan's Sacrilege", 428-29.

father's feet.[93]   A similar ironic reversal may be involved in the circumstance that although in v. 27 Jonathan becomes technically guilty of an inadvertence, we have learned already from v. 24 (explicitly in LXX and implicitly in MT) that the real blunder of the day was Saul's.

The sense of inversion — that things are not as they at first seem — is supported also on the linguistic level.   Blenkinsopp has drawn attention to the assonance achieved in v. 29 through the reversal of consonants, noting in particular ארת/ראו and מעם/טעם.[94]   We would suggest that the root-play involving א and ר takes on added significance when viewed in the context of vv. 24-29. According to Saul's oath, the man who tasted food before evening would be accursed (ארור; vv. 24, 28). Because they feared (ירא) the oath, the people ate nothing (v. 26), in spite of their extreme fatigue (vv. 28-31).   Yet the result of Jonathan's eating was not *curse* (root ארר) but *brightening* of the eyes (root אור; v. 27). When informed of the curse (v. 28), Jonathan is quick to point out that he has experienced just the opposite: "Look (ראו־נא)! My eyes have brightened (ארו)" (v. 29). Thus, in the space of six verses, verbal roots containing א and ר appear six times (ארר twice, אור twice, ירא once, and ראה once). Jonathan's root-play, converting curse to brightening, adds to the developing contrast between himself and his father.   As Jobling has noted, "Jonathan implicitly contrasts himself with his father as he compares his own refreshed condition ... with the troops' debilitation; he, not his father, has correctly interpreted Yhwh's will."[95]

14:32-35, The Army's Infraction and Saul's Reaction

If our interpretation of vv. 24-31 is basically sound, then the events of vv. 32-35 follow quite logically.[96] Weary from the long pursuit, and perhaps encouraged by Jonathan's example and especially by his words in v. 30,[97] the army pounces[98] upon the booty and, taking

---

93 Cf. Dozeman, "Troubler", 85; Gordon, *Samuel*, 56.

94 "Jonathan's Sacrilege", 440.

95 "Saul's Fall", 370.

96 On the coherence of these verses in their present context, see Blenkinsopp, "Jonathan's Sacrilege", 424.

97 Cf. McCarter, 249.

98 Reading the Qrê, ויעט; for a summary of attempts to defend the Kᵉthîbh, see Stoebe, 268. Among the versions ויעש is directly supported

animals and slaying them, begins to eat them "with the blood" (על־הדם). Although the preposition על carries various connotations,[99] in the present context it appears to suggest that the flesh is consumed with the blood still in it.[100] Thus, the offence involves a breach of the widespread prohibition in the Old Testament against eating blood.[101] Stoebe's contention that the sin has nothing to do with the prohibitions of Gen 9:4 and Deut 12:23 but revolves solely around the fact that "die Rechte Gottes an der Beute nicht gewährleistet sind" is interesting, placing the sin of ch. 14 in the same category as that of ch. 15, but it is unconvincing in the light of the prominence and antiquity of prohibitions against blood consumption in Israel and elsewhere in the ancient Near East.[102] Moreover, Saul's proscription of eating (v. 24) does not limit itself to food taken as booty.

When the army's action is reported to Saul, he intervenes immediately to regulate the slaughter of animals (vv. 33-34). As Smelik has observed, although at first glance Saul appears to be acting as "de ware konig Israëls", this impression is quickly diminished when we recall that a major share of responsibility for the army's loss of control belongs to Saul himself.[103] Moreover, the rarity of the verb עיט in the Old Testament[104] makes it unlikely that the proximity of the phrase ויעט העם אל־השלל in 14:32 to ותעט אל־השלל in 15:19 is merely coincidental. Rather, it would appear that the one is meant to provide oblique commentary on the other. Saul, who in ch. 14 seeks to prevent the people from sinning in regards to the spoils, will in ch. 15 be himself guilty of the same.[105]

The episode of the army's cultic infraction culminates in v. 35 with a reference to Saul's building of an altar. The general consensus of scholars is that v. 35 describes the *first* altar that Saul built and that he

---

only by LXX[L], but the other recensions of LXX as well as Targ. and Syr. seem to reflect נטה, which at least gives evidence of a ט in the root.

[99] See esp. Thompson, *Penitence*, 108-109.

[100] This sense is supported by LXX (σὺν τῷ αἵματι) and Vulg. (cum sanguine); and cf. also Exod 12:8; Num 9:11 (Driver, 115).

[101] E.g. Gen 9:4; Lev 3:17; 7:26, 27; 17:10, 12; 19:26; Deut 15:23; Ezek 33:25.

[102] Cf. Noth, *Das dritte Buch Mose*, 113; Bertholet, *Leviticus*, 59.

[103] *Saul*, 128.

[104] It occurs only in 1 Sam 14:32; 15:19; 25:14.

[105] Cf. Smelik, *Saul*, 128; Gordon, *Samuel*, 58.

later must have built others.[106] This interpretation, however, is problematic in several respects: 1) it would seem to require a plural מזבחות ('altars') in v. 35b instead of MT's מזבח; 2) the fact that no other altars built by Saul are ever mentioned is not easily dismissed; and 3) it is unclear whether the hiphil of חלל has in view the completion of something done for the first time or, as seems more likely, merely the commencement of an action. Compare, for example, Deut 2:31: "And Yahweh said to me, 'See, I have begun to deliver (הַחִלֹּתִי תֵּת) Sihon and his land over to you. Begin to occupy (הָחֵל רָשׁ), that you may possess his land'." In this and many other examples[107] the sense of חלל hi. is clearly 'to commence', and not 'to do for the first time'.[108] Had the narrator wished to express unequivocally that this was the first altar that Saul built, he might have done so in one of the following ways:

זה המזבח הראשון אשר בנה	This was the first altar that he built
(cf. המכה הראשונה	the first slaughter [1 Sam 14:14])

זה תחלת המזבחות אשר בנה	This was the first of the altars which he built[109]
(cf. תחלת דברי־פיהו	the first of the words of his mouth [Eccl 10:13])

or possibly even combining vv. 35a and 35b:

ויבן שאול בראשונה מזבח ליהוה	So Saul built for the first time an altar to Yahweh
(cf. ויסעו בראשונה	So they moved out for the first time [Num 10:13])

A more literal rendering of v. 35 as it stands might be: "So Saul built an altar to Yahweh, (that is)[110] he began to build it — an altar to

---

[106] It has even been suggested that this event places Saul in line with the patriarchs, whose piety was marked by altar-building; so, e.g., Smith (120), citing Gen 8:20; 12:7; 13:18; 26:25; 35:7.

[107] I.e. Deut 16:9; Judg 10:18; 16:19; 20:31, 39; Jonah 3:4; 1 Chr 27:24; 2 Chr 3:1, 2; 29:27.

[108] Possibly ambiguous cases are Gen 4:26; 11:6; 1 Sam 22:15; 2 Chr 31:21.

[109] Whether such an expression would have been used in a prose context is uncertain.

[110] The inverted word-order of v. 35b, אתו החל לבנות מזבח ליהוה, may indicate a circumstantial verbal clause, which according to GK §156d can be used "to particularize an action which has before been expressed generally" or even to express an antithesis.

Yahweh." Abrabanel[111] has suggested that Saul began to build an altar, utilizing the stone of v. 32 as a cornerstone, but failed to complete it at that time because of his desire to continue the pursuit of the Philistines (v. 36). The cryptic style of MT v. 35b makes it difficult to come to a firm conclusion regarding the significance of Saul's altar building, but as Jobling has argued, given the broader context of chs. 13-15, it is "hard to believe that the editors intend a favorable judgment here."[112]

14:36-46, The Troubler on Trial

The oath of abstinence having proved counter-productive, Saul reverses his approach in v. 36. Apparently capitalizing on the rapacity of his troops, he uses the prospect of further plunder to entice them to undertake a night raid. The troops are willing — "Do whatever seems good to you" (כל־הטוב בעיניך עשה [v. 36aδ]) — but the priest, presumably Ahijah (cf. 14:3, 18), intervenes: "Let us draw near here to God" (v. 36b). As Budde has observed, the priest's interference is unusual, for nowhere else does a priest take it upon himself to remind someone to consult the oracle, and, in point of fact, it should have been Saul who called for the oracle.[113] Budde's own approach to the problem was simply to rewrite the text, emending MT's ויאמר הכהן נקרבה הלם אל־האלהים to ויאמר לכהן הקרבה הלם את־האפוד ("And he [Saul] said to the priest, 'Bring the ephod here"). Such wholesale emendation, however, not only is methodologically dubious but also misses the significance of this notice as part of an overall pattern in chs. 13-14 of Saul's declining commitment to discovering the divine will.[114]

Though failing to take the initiative himself, Saul does not resist the priest's suggestion and in v. 37 inquires of Yahweh in words similar to those later used by David in 23:2-4 and 30:8. In contrast with those later situations, however, in the present one Yahweh remains silent: ולא ענהו ביום ההוא ("but he did not answer him on that day").[115] There is an implication of judgement in the divine silence; and we are

---

[111] Cited by Rosenberg, *Samuel I*, 114-115.

[112] "Saul's Fall", 373.

[113] Budde, 100-101; cf. Hertzberg, 92/ET 116.

[114] See especially our comments on 13:8-9; 14:18-19 and 14:36 in Ch. 1, p. 41.

[115] As testimony to the appropriateness of using the phrase "on that day" even after dark, see 1 Sam 3:2; cf. also BDB, 300; Jenni, "יום", 709, 711, 715.

reminded of Samuel's warning to the people in 1 Sam 8 that, as a result of their sinful request for a king, "Yahweh will not answer you in that day" (8:18).[116] Saul apparently understands the link between divine silence and divine displeasure, for he immediately sets about discovering the cause of the latter (vv. 38ff.).

Traditionally, Saul has been lauded for the piety that enabled him to subordinate even his own family-interests to the cause of justice:[117] "For as Yahweh, the deliverer of Israel, lives, even if it [the sin] is in Jonathan my son, he shall surely die" (v. 39). It is ironic, however, that Saul should specifically mention Jonathan's name. The reader has already learned that Jonathan did not hear Saul's adjuration and that he has unwittingly broken it (v. 27). Are we now to assume that Saul has at least an inkling of the same? But if this be the case, should we not expect Saul to seek to attenuate the consequences of Jonathan's inadvertence rather than to intensify them with repeated oaths (vv. 39, 44)? We have noted that evidence of discord between son and father appears already as early as 14:1b. In v. 29 this erupted into outright condemnation of Saul. Are we to infer from the latest events that Saul views Jonathan as a threat?[118] It is, at any rate, strange that there is never the slightest sign of regret or sorrow on Saul's part when the life of his son seems forfeit. The incongruity of Saul's reaction stands out in even bolder relief when compared with the reaction of Jephthah in Judg 11, where Jephthah's child also must die as a result of a vow made by her father.[119] Jephthah tears his clothes and cries out, "Alas, my daughter, you have brought me very low (הכרע הכרעתני), and you have become the supreme cause of my trouble (את היית בעכרי), because I have made a vow (lit. "opened my mouth") to Yahweh and cannot go back" (Judg 11:35).[120] Jephthah was 'troubled' (root עכר) by

---

[116] Apart from the present context, only in 28:6 is it recorded that Saul inquired of Yahweh, and there the correlation of silence and judgement is inescapable.

[117] E.g. Hertzberg, 92/ET 117.

[118] Cf. Whitelam, *Just King*, 78-81.

[119] The comparison of Jephthah and Saul has been noted by Miscall ("Literary Unity", 37 n. 6, 43; *idem*, "Jacob and Joseph", 30), but his judgement that "Saul and Jephthah stand as moral equals" (ibid.) may require revision in view of the divergent reactions of the two to the peril of their children. Contrast also Judg 17:1-2, where Micah's mother blesses him for confessing to a theft even after she had previously uttered a curse.

[120] On this rendering, see Burney, *Judges*, 321-22; Boling, *Judges*, 208-9.

his daughter's peril, whereas Saul, accused by Jonathan of 'troubling' the land, himself appears un-'troubled' when his son is about to die.

The progressive alienation of Saul, first from Samuel and then from his own son, takes on yet another dimension in v. 39. When Saul expresses his utter determination to discover and exterminate the culprit who has rendered further pursuit of the Philistines impossible, he is again (as in v. 37) met with silence, but this time from his troops (v. 39b). By their silence they not only register their depressed mood but also retain the option of later objecting to Saul's course of action.[121] And, in fact, a further hint of dissension is not long in coming. Apparently undeterred by the army's silence, Saul proceeds in v. 40 to define the first division in preparation for the lot-casting. This time the troops express consent in an almost verbatim repetition of v. 36aδ, though omitting the word "all": הטוב בעיניך עשה ("Do what seems good to you"; v. 40bβ). As subsequent events will confirm (vv. 44-45), the troops are, indeed, no longer willing to accede to *all* that may seem "good in the eyes of" Saul.

If we were to follow the longer readings offered by LXX for vv. 41-42, then we would have even more evidence of growing popular resistance to Saul's initiatives. LXX's longer version of v. 41 is generally preferred by commentators, while the opposite is true of LXX's plus in v. 42. The former preference is based on the apparent unintelligibility of the phrase הָבָה תָמִים in MT[122] and on the belief that homoioteleuton could account for MT's loss of everything between the first and last occurrences of "Israel" in v. 41 LXX. The LXX allows the following retroversion into Hebrew:[123]

---

[121] Cf. Budde, 102.

[122] But for a summary of attempts to maintain MT, see Toeg, "Note", 494-96.

[123] Cf. Toeg, "Note", 493-94; Driver, 117; McCarter, 247.

v. 41

ויאמר שאול יהוה אלהי ישראל	καὶ εἶπεν Σαοὺλ Κύριε ὁ θεὸς Ἰσραήλ,
למה לא ענית את עבדך היום	τί ὅτι οὐκ ἀπεκρίθης τῷ δούλῳ σου σήμερον;
אם יש בי או ביונתן בני העון הזה	ἢ ἐν ἐμοὶ ἢ ἐν Ἰωναθὰν τῷ υἱῷ μου ἡ ἀδικία;
יהוה אלהי ישראל הבה אורים	Κύριε ὁ θεὸς Ἰσραήλ, δὸς δήλους·
ואם ישנו בעמך ישראל הבה תמים	καὶ ἐὰν τάδε εἴπῃ, δὸς δὴ τῷ λαῷ σου Ἰσραήλ, δὸς δὴ ὁσιότητα.[124]

If MT represents a corruption of a longer reading such as this, then the unprecedented הָבָה תָמִים ("give a true decision")[125] must have originally read הָבָה תֻמִּים ("give Thummim"). E. Noort has defended the latter understanding on the basis of a citation of Deut 33:8 in 4Q 175, 14, which reads: וללוי אמר הבו ללוי תמיך ואורך לאיש חסידך ("And of Levi he said, 'Give to Levi your Thummim and your Urim, to your favoured man").[126] Driver (117) speaks for the majority of scholars when he states that the longer reading suggested by LXX for v. 41 "is both satisfactory in itself, and at once removes the obscurity and abruptness attaching to MT". Against the charge that the additional material in LXX is nothing more than midrashic elaboration, Toeg, citing 1 Sam 23:10f., argues that the formula יהוה אלהי ישראל demonstrates "conformity with a conventional liturgical formula in Israelite divination".[127] The cogency of Toeg's deduction that LXX preserves the more original reading has recently been challenged, however, by Pisano, who notes that the evidence cuts both ways: the presence of the formula in 23:10 "may be used either as the verification of

---

124 This last line of LXX[B] is problematic. For a defence of ישנו in the retroversion, see Wellhausen, *Text*, 94-95; cf. also McCarter, 247-48.

125 So Lindblom, "Lot-Casting", 176; but see Albrektson, "Some Observations", 6.

126 "Kurzbemerkung", 112-116. The phrase "Give to Levi" is lacking in MT Deut 33:8 and, though it is sometimes restored using the verb נתן, the Qumran evidence strongly suggests הבה (cf. now *BHS*). Noort concludes: "Die Imperativform הבו, ziemlich selten im AT, könnte also mit Urim und Tummim als Objekt im Bereich der Befragung dieses Orakels eine Anredeformel gebildet haben" (115).

127 "Note", 495-497.

its authenticity in 14:41, or as an indication that a later editor conceived of the idea of inserting it in 14:41 because of its use in 23:10".[128] In his extensive discussion of 14:41,[129] Pisano makes several observations which tend to place the shorter reading of MT in a more favourable light than heretofore. He notes, for example, that "the notion of 'giving <u>tammim</u>' is not entirely absent from the Bible",[130] while "the absence of <u>Urim</u> and <u>Tummim</u>, if they were original in the text, would surely have been noticed by anyone familiar with the text." He also recognizes the unlikelihood that "in two consecutive verses [i.e. 41-42] exactly the same type of error should have occurred."[131] We turn now to a consideration of v. 42.

Perhaps under the influence of Wellhausen's judgement that the addition in LXX v. 42 betrays "den Geist einer späteren Zeit" and arose under the influence of v. 45, scholars have been slower to accept the longer text of v. 42 than they have that of v. 41.[132] But in v. 42, even more so than in v. 41, MT's shorter reading might be explained by homoioteleuton, a scribe's eye having skipped from הפילו ביני ובין יונתן בני (MT) to ויפילו ביני ובין יונתן בנו (cf. LXX).[133] Driver reconstructs the omitted lines as follows: אשר ילכדנו יהוה ימות ויאמר העם אל שאול לא יהיה הדבר הזה ויחזק שאול מהעם ויפילו ביני ובין יונתן בנו. This longer reading is not without some notable supporters,[134] but again, as with v. 41, there is very little basis for deciding between MT and LXX, since MT makes reasonable sense as it stands. Gooding has argued that "Septuagint's plus in fact spoils the climax of the story by anticipating here the people's repudiation of Saul's stupidity when he finally tries to condemn Jonathan to death."[135] There is some force in this observation, but it is not sufficient by itself

---

[128] *Additions*, 198.

[129] *Additions*, 183-99.

[130] *Additions*, 194.

[131] *Additions*, 199.

[132] Wellhausen, *Text*, 95; cf. Driver, 118; Stoebe, 270.

[133] Cf. Pisano, *Additions*, 201. Notwithstanding, Pisano does not opt for the longer reading of v. 42, because he is of the opinion that the "LXX translators" sometimes would repeat at the end of an insertion the last few words of the text to which it was added, thus creating the "appearance that the shorter text had fallen victim to a textual accident" (204).

[134] E.g. Budde, 102-103; Smith, 122, 124; Dhorme, 124; McCarter, 244; Klein, 131-32.

[135] *Current Problems*, 11. Cf. Pisano, *Additions*, 202.

to prove that the LXX plus is secondary. It may, in fact, reflect a more Western than Hebrew viewpoint, for if the inference drawn from the omission of "all" in v. 36aδ above is valid, then there has already been a hint of reluctance in the people's response to Saul's initiatives. If v. 42 should contain a further sign of the people's hesitation to follow Saul, this would accord nicely with the pattern of increasing alienation which we have seen already in Saul's relationships with Samuel and with Jonathan. At any rate, since Saul prevails in LXX v. 42, the question of Jonathan's fate continues to press until v. 45. Thus, it is difficult to decide for or against the originality of the LXX plus in v. 42 simply on the basis of an estimation of what "would or would not have been right for the people to say on such an occasion."[136] Nevertheless, as Pisano argues, two other circumstances may tell against the LXX plus: the "apparent superfluousness of the material contained in the plus" and the "difficulty in providing a satisfying Hebrew retroversion".[137] In sum, neither in v. 41 or v. 42 are there sufficient grounds for preferring the longer readings of LXX over MT.[138]

When "Jonathan is taken" (v. 42b), Saul initiates the interrogation of the offender in words reminiscent of those addressed to him by Samuel in 13:11: מה עשית. In contrast to his father on that former occasion, however, Jonathan readily admits his guilt without excuse. He even refrains from explicitly criticizing his father for troubling the land (contrast v. 29), though the striking sense of disproportion achieved by his juxtaposition of the offence, טעם ... מעם דבש טעם טעמתי, and the punishment, הנני אמות, may have been a sufficient reminder of the foolish and arbitrary nature of Saul's adjuration. Perhaps in response to this implicit criticism, Saul in v. 44 reaffirms with yet another oath his determination that Jonathan shall die. The last word is not to be Saul's, however, for the people cannot abide the thought that Jonathan, who "brought about this great deliverance for Israel" and who "accomplished it with God this day", should now be put to death. So they interrupt Saul with an oath of their own: "as Yahweh lives, not a hair of his head shall fall to the ground" (v. 45). Saul must give way,

---

136 Pisano, *Additions*, 201.

137 *Additions*, 203.

138 It is occasionally argued that vv. 41-42 in MT seem truncated, but a terse, economical style is characteristic of 1 and 2 Samuel; cf. Pisano's observation that "such texts as 1 Sam 9:3f. and 13:9 show that, once an order is given, the action of its being carried out is not necessarily expressed" (*Additions*, 202).

and the army rescues Jonathan out of Saul's hand. Thus, the day that began with Jonathan placing his life in jeopardy by his daring attack against the Philistine outpost ends with him narrowly escaping death at the hands of his own father. And the day which held promise of a crushing victory over the Philistines ends rather meekly with Saul giving up the pursuit and the Philistines simply returning "to their own place" (v. 46). Rebuked by Yahweh, forsaken by Samuel, at odds with Jonathan, Saul ultimately finds himself completely isolated, alienated by his obduracy even from his own troops.

The Closing Frame
(1 Sam 14:47-51[52])

As we observed in the introduction to the preceding chapter, the summary of Saul's career which provides the closing frame for the account of his initial Philistine wars is similar to royal summaries found elsewhere in the DH. It displays the same basic components as are found, for example, in the more extensive summary of David's reign in 2 Sam 8, namely a synopsis of military accomplishments (14:47-48; 2 Sam 8:1-14) followed by a list of family and chief officers (14:49-51; 2 Sam 8:15-18). The closing frame in 1 Sam 14, however, raises two basic questions: why is it included here rather than later in the Saul traditions? and what is its significance?

Perhaps the best place to begin in seeking answers to these questions is to recall the centrality of the Philistine problem in Saul's original commission, discussed at length in Chapters 2 and 3. The implication that the viability and length of Saul's reign were somehow contingent upon his success in keeping his original charge found confirmation in Samuel's words in 13:13-14: "You have not kept the charge of Yahweh your God which he laid upon you; for then [i.e. had you kept it] Yahweh would have established your kingdom over Israel forever. But now your kingdom will not endure." The eventual doom of Saul's reign is sealed. Any dynastic hopes that he might have entertained (cf. 1 Sam 20:31) are dashed. Yahweh has sought out a new *nāgîd* (13:14). Thus, it is appropriate that the summary of Saul's reign should be placed at the end of the two chapters recounting his highly significant initial Philistine encounters. In addition, since according to Deut 25:17-19 Israel was to "blot out the memory of Amalek" at a time

when she would be established in the land and at rest from her enemies,
the summary of 1 Sam 14:47ff. provides the necessary backdrop to the
events of 1 Sam 15.

These observations help to explain the placing of the summary,
but they do not exhaust the question of its significance. In view of the
largely negative portrait of Saul in chs. 13-14, it seems remarkable that
our narrator has included records of Saul's military accomplishments
with such apparent objectivity. He acknowledges that wherever Saul
turned "he was victorious" (v. 47bβ),[139] and he "did valiantly" (v.
48aα).[140] Even apart from these comments (the interpretation of which
is debated[141]), the listing of Saul's various campaigns is sufficient to
dispel any notion that his failure stemmed from military ineptitude.
But despite its apparent objectivity, the concluding summary is not
without dark shadows — cast not so much by what is said as by what
is not said. Specifically, the lack of any mention of Yahweh or his involvement with Saul is disturbing, though not surprising in view of
the events of chs. 13-14. The apparent avoidance of the name Yahweh
becomes even more obvious when we compare the summary of David's
reign in 2 Sam 8. Twice it is said of David, וי(ו)שׁע יהוה את־דוד
בכל אשׁר הלך ("And Yahweh delivered David wherever he went"; 8:6,
14). Of Saul it is only said, ובכל אשׁר־יפנה[142] יִנָּשֵׁעַ ("And wherever
he turned he was victorious"; 14:47).

The final verse of the chapter returns to the problem that has
dominated the preceding narrative, namely the Philistine oppression:
ותהי המלחמה חזקה על־פלשׁתים כל ימי שׁאול (v. 52a). To be sure,
Israel is now in a better position militarily than at the beginning of ch.
13, but the Philistines have still not been dealt the decisive blow. Ultimately, it will fall to David to put an end to the Philistine threat (2
Sam 8:1). But as long as Saul is king, the war against the Philistines
will be severe. Indeed, it will be in battle against this foe that Saul

[139] So LXX: ἐσῴζετο = יִנָּשֵׁעַ. On the possibility that 14:47-48 may
have been adapted from the summary of David's victories in 2 Sam 8, and
that MT's יַרְשִׁיעַ ("make guilty, act wickedly"?) may therefore be original,
intending to diminish Saul's successes in the light of David's, see Stoebe,
"Zur Topographie", 270-71.

[140] So the most common rendering of MT's וַיַּעַשׂ חָיִל. For other possibilities, see Stoebe, 276 ("Er sammelte ein Heer"); McCarter, 253-55 ("and
acquired power"); Klein, 131 ("he acted with force").

[141] See the previous two notes.

[142] Following LXX; see above.

will finally take his own life (31:4). Thus, 14:52 concludes the account of Saul's first Philistine encounter by confirming Jonathan's earlier verdict that the victory could have been greater (14:30b). V. 52 also looks ahead, however, for the notice that "whenever Saul saw any mighty or valiant man he took him into his service (ויאספהו אליו)" (v. 52b) prepares the way for the one to whom that greater victory will belong.

Summary and Conclusions

Though our exegetical treatment has of necessity been less exhaustive at some points than at others, evidence has been adduced to support our theses 1) that 1 Sam 13-14 presents a connected, coherent and sequential narrative and 2) that a central function of the narrative is to describe (ch. 13) and to defend (ch. 14), largely through oblique modes of 'showing' rather than 'telling', the first rejection of Saul. Classical literary criticism has customarily included 1 Sam 13-14 in its putative pro-monarchical source and has viewed the portrait of Saul in these chapters as largely favourable. Our reading of the narrative, however, has attempted to show that the portrait of Saul in these chapters is predominantly negative. Two themes are especially evident in the unfavourable depiction of Saul in 1 Sam 13-14. The first is the contrastive characterization of Saul and Jonathan, the highlights of which were summarized already in Ch. 1, pp. 40-41. The second is the progressive alienation and isolation of Saul from those around him. In Ch. 2 of this thesis it was argued that the Gilgal episode (13:7b-15a) should be retained as integral to its present context. Reading 1 Sam 13-14 inclusive of the Gilgal episode makes it possible to see the deterioration of Saul's relationships with Jonathan and his troops as, in some sense, the outworkings of the more fundamental break in his relationship with Yahweh and his representative Samuel. It is Saul's foolishness in disregarding the stipulations of his first 'charge' (10:7-8; cf. 13:8) that elicites condemnation from Samuel. And though we are not explicitly told that knowledge of that former foolishness motivates Jonathan's decision to exclude his father from his plans in 14:1b, it is a subsequent foolish action, viz. the adjuration of the people in 14:24, that eventually elicites condemnation also from Jonathan (14:29). The width of the gulf that eventually developes between Saul and Jonathan is apparent from the ferocity of Saul's insistence, towards the end of ch. 14, that Jonathan must die for a mere inadvertence (14:39, 44). The people, however, will have none of it, so that by the end of the narrative Saul is totally isolated and alienated from all those around him. Yet none of the estrangements will prove to be final, for, as the story continues, the people will show signs of renewed loyalty to Saul (e.g. 23:19; 24:1), Jonathan will again become his confidant (20:2), and even Samuel will have further dealings with him (ch. 15).

As regards the nature of Saul's 'sin' in chs. 13-14, we have argued that it is not, at least in the first instance, a matter of cultic infraction but of disobedience to the 'charge' associated with his appointment as *nāgîd* . Saul's failure to recognize the necessity of strict obedience to the command of Yahweh as mediated by his spokesman is branded by Samuel as 'foolishness'. In acting independently, Saul disregards the prescribed authority structure and shows himself to be an unworthy vassal, thus necessitating the appointing ('charging') of another *nāgîd* (13:14). Yet there is nothing in Saul's early actions to suggest that they are malicious.[143] And, in fact, it is the sense that Saul is somehow acting in 'good faith' that has earned him the sympathy of readers. Nevertheless, the claim of 'good faith' is not sufficient to excuse Saul's 'foolishness', for, were it to use such terms, the prophetic perspective which informs these chapters would doubtless distinguish 'good faith' from 'true faith', the latter being characterized by insight and right action.[144] At any rate, the impression of 'good faith' begins to fade as we approach the end of ch. 14, and when the pursuit of the Philistines is forcibly halted by Yahweh's silence, we encounter the first signs of an obduracy in Saul which will become increasingly evident in ch. 15.

---

[143] See especially our interpretation of 13:12.

[144] Cf., in addition to our discussion of 14:1 at the beginning of this chapter, Ackroyd's brief study of the David-Jonathan narratives in which he draws attention to the successive recognition of David as legitimate monarch, first by Jonathan, then by Saul's officers, by all the people, and finally by Saul himself ("Verb Love", 213-14).

5

SAUL VERSUS THE AMALEKITES: THE FINAL REJECTION (1 SAM 15)

Literary- and historical-critical study of 1 Sam 15 has so far yielded little approaching the status of an assured result, excepting possibly the view that the section comprising vv. 24-29 (approx.) is intrusive. But even that view, discussed already in Chapter 1,[1] now seems seriously in doubt. As to the overall unity of the chapter, some challenge it,[2] while others are convinced that the story of Saul's Amalekite battle is basically unified.[3] Moreover, while some regard ch. 15 as an essentially independent tradition,[4] others discern numerous links with the surrounding chapters.[5] As to the literary tradition responsible for ch.

---

[1] See pp. 37-39.

[2] E.g. Seebass, "1 Sam 15", 148-54, 171-77; Grønbæk, *Geschichte*, 47-50; and, most recently, Foresti, *Rejection*. The latter contends that ch. 15 displays "classical signs, such as internal tensions and repetitions, of a text re-elaborated on successive occasions" (25). Noting, for example, that Samuel announces Saul's rejection twice (vv. 23b, 26b), Foresti asks how it can be that one author would repeat the same information twice in such close proximity (27). Similarly, Foresti asks how one can explain Samuel's opposing reactions to Saul's requests (vv. 25-26a, 30-31), when no change has occurred in Saul's disposition (28). Assuming that answers to these questions cannot be found, Foresti concludes in these and many other such cases that doublets are involved. In response, however, we need only recall the semantic potential of repetition in Hebrew narrative, in the light of which answers to Foresti's questions are readily forthcoming (see the exegesis below).

[3] Cf. Stoebe, 282 ("im wesentlichen einheitlich"); Smelik, 142 ("C. 15 is duidelijk een litteraire eenheid"); Birch, 96 ("no reason to challenge the literary unity of chapter 15").

[4] E.g. Weiser, "I Samuel 15", 3; Stoebe, 280. Veijola (*Ewige Dynastie*, 102 n. 156) postulates that ch. 15 and 28:17-19 were introduced by DtrP.

[5] E.g. Hertzberg, 98/ET 123-24; Smelik, *Saul*, 142; Donner, "Verwerfung", 244-46.

15, some draw attention to deuteronomistic features in the narrative,[6] while others deny these and assert a pre-deuteronomistic origin.[7] Not surprisingly in view of the lack of agreement on the preceding questions, there is also a wide diversity of opinion as regards the historicity of the chapter.[8] Finally, the role played by ch. 15 within the broader narrative of 1 Sam is also contested — does it mark the conclusion of Saul's reign, or serve as the introduction to "David's Rise",[9] or both? The last option seems to be the most likely, as Stoebe, who views ch. 15 in its present form as a transitional member ("verbindendes Glied"), explains:

> Obwohl es selbst noch uneingeschränkt der Saulüberlief-erung zugehört, bereitet es doch in seiner redaktionellen Verklammerung die eigentliche Davidgeschichte vor, insofern, als mit der hier geschilderten Verwerfung der Weg zum Königtum Davids eröffnet wird.[10]

As Stoebe goes on to observe, though ch. 13 already envisages the rise of David, there it is presented as a possibility ("mögliches Geschehen"), while in ch. 15 it is presented as an irrevocable fact ("unwiderrufliches Faktum").[11]

---

[6] E.g. Schunck, *Benjamin*, 82-84; Yonick, "Rejection", 40; Veijola, *Ewige Dynastie*, 102 n. 156.

[7] E.g. Budde, 107; Knierim, "Messianic Concept", 22; Grønbæk, *Geschichte*, 61; Stoebe, 279, 282; Mayes, "Period of the Judges", 296-97, 328; Foresti, 16. Proponents of a prophetic origin for ch. 15 include Weiser, "I Samuel 15", 17ff., 24; Birch, *Rise*, 103-04; Stolz, 99; McCarter, 20; Klein, 147.

[8] The historicity of the story is doubted or denied by, for example, Smith, 130; Smelik, *Saul*, 133-34, 142; Donner, "Verwerfung", 250; *idem*, "Historiography", 53; Foresti, *Rejection*, 181. Others allow that the chapter contains at least a historical kernel: e.g. Stoebe, 280-83; Budde, 107; Dhorme, 138-39; Schunck, *Benjamin*, 84; Grønbæk, *Geschichte*, 51. Ackroyd (122) remarks that the story "is theological rather than historical", but this should not imply that the two are mutually exclusive, for, as Driver (*Introduction*, 178) observes, "the fact that the history is told with a purpose does not invalidate its general truth" (cf. Weiser, "I Samuel 15", 16-18). Ishida (*Royal Dynasties*, 54) believes that both the rejection of Saul in ch. 13 and the whole of ch. 15 are "tendentious interpretations of the actual course of history from the viewpoint of the defence of David".

[9] So, e.g., Grønbæk, *Geschichte*, 64-65 and *passim*.

[10] Stoebe, 278.

[11] Stoebe, 278-79.

Ch. 15 can be divided into two scenes, the most natural division coming after v. 9, though vv. 10-11 serve a transitional function, voicing Yahweh's judgement upon Saul's performance in the first scene and, at the same time, preparing Samuel for his dialogue with Saul in the second. Our exegesis of the chapter will focus primarily on the inner workings of the narrative, though the results achieved occasionally bear upon questions of a historical- or literary-critical nature. As in the exegesis of chs. 13-14, questions pertaining to narrative coherence will be asked. Does the text in its present form display a logical storyline? Does the text display a consistent attitude towards Saul and the monarchy? Does a clear answer to the question of Saul's rejection emerge? And if so, is it compatible with the picture of Saul's failure in chs. 13-14?

Scene One: Saul's Flawed Victory
(1 Sam 15:1-9)

15:1-3, Samuel Issues Yahweh's Orders
Ch. 15 opens abruptly with Samuel already addressing Saul.[12] The emphatic word-order of Samuel's first sentence, "*Me* Yahweh sent to anoint you king over his people, over Israel",[13] affirms Samuel's mediatorial role in the founding of the monarchy (cf. 9:16; 10:1), and, along with the reminder that it was *Yahweh* who commissioned Saul's anointing over *his* (Yahweh's) people, sets the tone for the subsequent narrative. Saul is king by divine consent, and he must never lose sight

---

[12] Grønbæk (*Geschichte*, 45 n. 35) defends the use of an imperfect consecutive (ויאמר) to open his "Geschichte vom Aufstieg Davids" as nothing unusual ("nichts Absonderliches"). Gross, however, argues that when an imperfect consecutive from a verb other than היה stands "an größeren Erzähleinschnitten, so ist eine übergreifende literarische Bearbeitung und Komposition anzunehmen" ("Syntaktische Erscheinungen", 135); but cf. Num 1:1. On the general question, see Meyer, *Satzlehre*, §100.3.b; GK §49b n.1.

[13] The double expression על־עמו על־ישראל may be a conflation of variants; witness the inconsistent ordering of the elements in the MSS representing LXX[L]. LXX[B] omits על־עמו altogether and is preferred by McCarter, 260. Dhorme (130), on the other hand, retains על־עמו and dismisses על־ישראל as a gloss. In defence of MT, Kiel (140) compares 9:16 and suggests that the doubling of על in 15:1 serves to emphasize the importance of the matter.

of the fact that his sphere of authority is limited by the demand of obedience to prophetically-mediated divine commands.

"So now (ועתה)," says Samuel, moving on from the brief but important reminder of v. 1a to the injunction of v. 1b: "listen to the sound of the words of Yahweh (ועתה שמע לקול דברי יהוה)".[14] The combination ...קול דברי in MT (cf. LXX[L]) seems redundant and raises suspicion that a conflation of variant readings may be involved.[15] If this be the case, then the reading לקול יהוה[16] should be preferred to the more fanciful לדברי ("to my words") proposed by McCarter (260), since the expression קול יהוה is repeated several times later in the chapter (vv. 19, 20, 22). In fact, however, the expression קול דבר(ים) is not without biblical precedent,[17] and its use in 15:1 tends to add weight and urgency to Samuel's summons; Saul is required to listen with the utmost attention to what Samuel is about to say.[18] The significance of this emphasis will be seen better in the light of Saul's prevarications later in the chapter, where the keywords שמע and קול recur repeatedly.[19]

Samuel's delivery of the message in vv. 2-3 is prefaced, in typically prophetic style, by a messenger formula: כה אמר יהוה צבאות.[20] As in v. 1, so also in v. 3, the word עתה has hortative force before an imperative and marks a shift in Samuel's address. This time the shift

---

[14] The specific connotation of the expression ועתה, described by Laurentin ("Formule", 194) as "une expression très forte, avec des résonances émotives", must be determined in each case by the context; cf. Brongers' classification of eight possible senses, including the hortative ("Bemerkungen", 294-95). On שמע in the imperative governing an object and preceded by a particle of entreaty, and on its use in the delivery of a message, see Loewenstamm ("The Address 'Listen'", 126, 130).

[15] Cf. Stoebe, 283; McCarter, 260; etc.

[16] Reflected in LXX[B] and Vulg. and followed by the majority of commentators.

[17] Deut 1:34; 4:12; 5:25(2x); Dan 10:6(2x), 9(2x); Ps 103:20 (though the relevant phrase is lacking in Syr.). When joined to a form of שמע, the expression may suggest the physical act of hearing the *sounds* themselves.

[18] Cf. Stolz, 97: "Auf den Wortlaut der Worte Jahwes". Similarly, the "impression of heaviness" created by the juxtaposition of v. 1b with v. 2aα may serve an emphatic purpose, and so need not indicate that v. 1b is secondary, as Foresti (*Rejection*, 43) contends.

[19] See below, pp. 148, 151.

[20] Cf. Ch. 3, p. 86 n. 86. For a survey of research into the meaning of the highly debated formula יהוה צבאות, see van der Woude, "צבא", 503-507; see also, more recently, Emerton, "More Light".

is from the indicative statement of v. 2, viz. that Yahweh intends to punish[21] the Amalekites for what they did to Israel as it came up from Egypt, to the imperative of v. 3, viz. Saul is to attack the Amalekites and put them and everything they have under the ban. MT's reading of v. 3aβ, והחרמתם את־כל־אשר־לו ("and put [pl.] everything that belongs to them [lit. 'him', i.e. Amalek] under the ban"), should probably be emended on the basis of LXX to והחרמתו ואת־כל־אשר־לו ("and put [sg.] them and everything that belongs to them under the ban").[22] This reading has the advantage of retaining the 2 sg. throughout v. 3, in accordance with the chapter's emphasis upon Saul's personal responsibility to conduct the Amalekite battle as instructed.

The Hebrew in v. 2b alluding to Amalek's offence, אשר־שם לו בדרך בעלתו ממצרים, is difficult but perhaps not impossible.[23] The Amalekite treachery to which reference is made in v. 2b is mentioned briefly in Exod 17:8. Verses 9-13 of the same chapter describe a miraculous Israelite victory over the Amalekites, while in v. 14 Yahweh solemnizes his intention to "blot out utterly the memory of Amalek from under heaven", ordering that a declaration to that effect be written in a book and transmitted to Joshua. In Deut 25:17-19 the tradition of perpetual hostility against the Amalekites is recast in the form of a command. When once the people are established in the land and are experiencing rest from other enemies, they are to "blot out the memory of Amalek from under heaven". As we have already noted, the summary of Saul's reign (14:47ff.) may have been placed before ch. 15 to suggest that these necessary conditions had been met. In view of these considerations, the closest conceptual and stylistic affinities of 1 Sam 15:2 seem to be with the Deuteronomic tradition.[24]

---

[21] The verb פקד has in Hebrew, as Schottroff ("פקד", 470) observes, "eine beachtliche Bedeutungsbreite". Where the object of the verb is a crime previously committed, the connotation of פקד is that of retributive punishment or vengeance ("Ahndung"; ibid., 478). For a detailed discussion of this verb, see Scharbert, "Das Verbum PQD". On the use of the perfect tense to express determination, see Driver, 121-22.

[22] So Smith, 132; Budde, 108; McCarter, 261; Donner, "Verwerfung", 241 n. 33.

[23] The problematic phrase שם לו has been defended as a technical military expression by, for example, Driver (122) and Stoebe (284), who cite 1 Kgs 20:12 as a parallel example. McCarter's conjecture (260), based on LXX and Deut 25:18, that אשר קרהו בדרך ("when he confronted him") should be read, is undermined by the difficulty of explaining how an original קרהו could have been corrupted to שם לו.

[24] Cf. Grønbæk, *Geschichte*, 46; Stoebe, 284.

A sense of the absolute comprehensiveness of the annihilation to be wreaked upon the Amalekites is conveyed in v. 3b by a list of the several intended victims. Ironically, the closest parallel to this list, lacking only the reference to camels (which would have been inappropriate), is the list of Saul's victims at the priestly city of Nob (1 Sam 22:19).

15:3   מֵאִישׁ עַד־אִשָּׁה מֵעֹלֵל וְעַד־יוֹנֵק מִשּׁוֹר וְעַד־שֶׂה מִגָּמָל וְעַד־חֲמוֹר

22:19   מֵאִישׁ וְעַד־אִשָּׁה מֵעוֹלֵל וְעַד־יוֹנֵק וְשׁוֹר וַחֲמוֹר וָשֶׂה

15:4-9, Saul Executes the Battle — But Not Agag

In response to Samuel's exhortations to listen (שְׁמַע) to the words of Yahweh (v. 1b), Saul summons (וַיְשַׁמַּע)[25] the army and musters them at טְלָאִים, probably to be equated with טֶלֶם, listed in Josh 15:24 as one of the cities of Judah (v. 4).[26] Having assembled his forces, the size of which remains uncertain,[27] Saul "went to the city of Amalek and lay in wait[28] in the wadi" (v. 5). The reference in v. 6 to the Kenites dwelling amongst the Amalekites correlates well with the association of the two groups elsewhere in the Old Testament.[29] In view of the ḥesed which the Kenites had shown toward the Israelites on their way up from Egypt,[30] and perhaps also in accordance with an aspect of holy war ide-

---

[25] The piel of שמע occurs only one other time in the OT, viz. in 1 Sam 23:8, and it has been suggested that the piel should be repointed as a hiphil. Jenni (*Das hebräische Pi'el,* 220) retains the piel and tentatively suggests a meaning for it derived from the secondary connotation of שמע "gehorchen" — thus, "zur Heeresfolge verpflichtet machen = aufbieten".

[26] On the approximate location, see McCarter, 266. MT vocalizes טלאים as if it were the plural form of טלה, "lamb" (cf. 7:9); and this understanding is reflected also by Targ., באימרי פסחיא ("with paschal lambs"), and Vulg., *quasi agnos* ("like lambs"). Rashi maintains that since Gen 32:12 forbade the counting of Jews, lambs were used instead. Of more significance is LXX's ἐν Γαλγάλοις (cf. Josephus, *Ant.* 6.134). Dhorme (131) tries to explain this reading as a corruption of טלם, but Hertzberg (ET 125) speculates that the reference may reflect the location of Samuel's encounter with Saul prior to the muster.

[27] For a discussion of the problems involved in this verse, see esp. Grønbæk, *Geschichte,* 52-53.

[28] So McCarter, 261; for a survey of other options, see Stoebe, 284.

[29] E.g. Num 24:20-22; Judg 1:16, on which see Budde, 109.

[30] The object of this reference is obscure; but cf. Kiel, 143; Bach, *Aufforderung,* 50. On the biblical evidence for a relationship between the Kenites and the Israelites, see de Vaux, "Sur l'origine"; and on the possibility of an Israelite-Kenite treaty of alliance, see Gottwald, *Tribes,* 577-80.

ology described as the "Aufforderung zur Flucht",[31] Saul pauses, before crossing swords with the Amalekites, to allow the Kenites to depart, lest they too be "taken in"[32] or, perhaps, "swept away".[33] This warning to the Kenites is at least slightly reminiscent of the threat which, since 12:25, hangs over the heads of Saul and the people — if they "persist in doing evil" they too will be "swept away". The narrative significance of Saul's sparing of the Kenites, as Sternberg has recently observed, is that though it at first "looks like a divergence from the letter of the divine command", in fact "it manifests a remarkable grasp of the spirit informing that command."[34] Later in the narrative, this initial impression that Saul has rightly understood his instructions will recoil upon him, dispelling any suggestion that his divergence from the command issued by Samuel is the result of misunderstanding.[35]

The fighting begins in v. 7 and is described in the briefest possible terms; clearly the interest of the narrative lies elsewhere than in military tactics or strategy. Noting only that the victory was extensive, which seems to be the general import of MT's somewhat perplexing reading "from Havilah toward Shur, which is east of Egypt",[36] the narrative moves quickly to make its main point. Saul takes Agag king of Amalek alive, but he utterly destroys "all the people" with the edge of the sword (v. 8). "All the people" (כל־העם) may refer simply to the army or to all those, including civilians, who fell into the hands of Saul and his troops. The point is not that Saul was able to search out and destroy every living Amalekite, save Agag alone, but rather that of those whom he captured none was spared but Agag.

Not surprisingly in view of the reticence of the text, suggestions as to Saul's motivation for sparing Agag range widely.[37] V. 9 states simply that "Saul and the army spared (חמל) Agag and the best of the sheep, cattle," etc. The verb חמל encompasses notions of both emo-

---

[31] See Bach, *Aufforderung*, esp. 48-50; Stolz, 101.

[32] So MT, which vocalizes פן־אספך as a qal imperfect of אסף. MT is defended by Stoebe (284-85), who compares the German slang expression "jemanden einkassieren". Cf. also Hertzberg, ET 121; Driver, 123.

[33] Cf. Budde, 109; Dhorme, 131; McCarter, 261.

[34] "Bible's Art", 52.

[35] Cf. "Bible's Art", 52-53.

[36] For a brief summary of viewpoints regarding this phrase, see Klein, 150.

[37] Smith (134) summarizes various options: "pride, hope of ransom, an ill-timed emotion of pity, respect of persons".

tional reaction, 'have compassion upon', and active conduct, 'spare'.[38] The accent, however, generally falls on the latter aspect,[39] and thus in the present context reveals little about Saul's inner motivation. The appearance of the words חמל and חרם in v. 9, however, directly echoes v. 3 where Saul was unambiguously commanded to "destroy utterly" and not to "spare" either man or beast. In fact, however, Saul and the army spared "all that was good, and were not willing to destroy them utterly" (v. 9aβ). The explicit contrast between instruction and execution leaves little room, at least from the perspective of the authoritative narrator, for interpreting Saul's action as anything other than direct disobedience of the divine command.[40] Whether Saul himself views his actions in this way, however, depends on the sincerity of his protestations that the animals were spared only in order that they might be sacrificed to Yahweh at Gilgal (vv. 15, 21).[41] This question aside for the moment, the problem of Agag still remains. Does Saul's leniency toward Agag reflect a political motive?[42] Or does he wish to put Agag on public display as a trophy of war? The text leaves the question undetermined, though the erection of a victory stele (v. 12) may lend some support to the latter opinion.

---

[38] Cf. Tsevat, "חמל", 471.

[39] Stoebe, "רחם", 764.

[40] After offering a detailed analysis of the rhetoric of v. 9, Sternberg ("Bible's Art", 55-57) concludes: "By the end of verse 9, then, the case for the prosecution becomes so formidable that it is hard to believe that the narrator has put it together without uttering so much as a single word of overt condemnation" (57).

[41] See below under v. 15. Wénin ("Le discours", 4-6) has postulated a revocalization and redivision of MT of v. 9b to read: *wᵉkol-hammālēʾ kōhēn mabzeh* (TM *hammᵉlāʾkâ nᵉmibzâ) wᵉnāmēs ʾōtāh heheʾrîmû*, "Mais tout ce qui remplit un prêtre de mépris et de dépit, cela, ils le livrèrent à l'anathème" (4). This imaginative hypothesis would provide "un argument en faveur d'une certaine bonne foi chez Saül" (5), but there is little to commend it over MT, especially if Millard ("*Scriptio continua*") is correct in rejecting *scriptio continua* as a feature of early Hebrew writing.

[42] Cf. Ahab's sparing of Ben-Hadad in 1 Kgs 20:27ff.

Scene Two: Saul's Trial and Final Rejection
(1 Sam 15:10-35)

15:10-11, The Case for the Prosecution

Samuel, who in his capacity as Yahweh's spokesman opened the first scene, now reappears at the beginning of the second to receive Yahweh's evaluation of the intervening events. Yahweh announces, "I regret (נחמתי) that I have made Saul king" (v. 11). The same note will be sounded at the end of the scene (v. 35b), and an intervening, prima facie contradictory statement in v. 29 will provide added dimension and interest to the theme of Yahweh's repentance.[43] Yahweh's indictment of Saul comprises two parts — the more general charge that Saul has "turned away from me" (v. 11aβ),[44] followed by the specific complaint that he "has not carried out (לא הקים) my word" (v. 11aγ). This indictment recalls 12:14 where *listening (obeying)* and *following* are mentioned as prerequisites of a successful reign.

In view of Samuel's emphatic exhorting of Saul in v. 1b to listen to the words of Yahweh, his reaction to Yahweh's last statement is not surprising, even if not entirely transparent: ויחר לשמואל ויזעק אל־ יהוה כל־הלילה (v. 11b). Again the narrative leaves us to surmise. With whom or with what is Samuel angry? Yahweh? Saul? The situation as it has developed? E. M. Good's novel theory that "Samuel feels that he has already accomplished Saul's rejection (ch. 13) and is furious with Yahweh for not letting it go at that"[45] is inconsistent with the notice in v. 35 that Samuel mourned for Saul. A likelier theory is that Samuel's distress is over Saul's latest misdeeds, and thus he cries out in grief and anger, and perhaps even in intercession for him.[46] One thing, at least, is clear, and that is that Samuel takes no pleasure in Saul's failure, nor in the task that now confronts him.

---

[43] See the discussion at v. 29.

[44] When employed in a theological sense, the phrase שוב מאחרי parallels the notion of rebellion against Yahweh ("Abkehr von Gott"; so Soggin, "שוב", 888). The relatively few such occurrences include Num 14:43; 32:15; Josh 22:16, 18, 23, 29; 1 Kgs 9:6; Jer 3:19; 32:40.

[45] *Irony*, 70.

[46] Samuel's later rehearsal of "what Yahweh said to me last night" (vv. 16-19) may suggest that he was at first slow to accept Yahweh's final rejection of Saul.

15:12-14, Samuel Confronts Saul

Whatever Samuel's personal feelings about the matter, they do not deter him from the execution of his duty. Arising early in the morning, he goes to meet Saul. On the way he is informed that Saul came to Carmel,[47] erecting[48] to or for himself (לו) a monument (יד) there, but now has made his way to Gilgal.[49] It is widely agreed that Saul's monument should be understood as a victory stele of some sort,[50] but beyond this general consensus, opinions as to the precise nature of the monument differ considerably. Grønbæk, for example, maintains that it is highly unlikely ("ganz unwahrscheinlich") that Saul's monument would have been inscribed,[51] apparently basing this opinion upon his curious belief that the monument in question was a phallic symbol.[52] Victory stelae with inscriptions commemorating the valour of the king or the beneficence of his deity, or both, are well-known from the aNE, and as Weinfeld has observed, "there is no reason why an Israelite king might not engrave his thanks to his God on a monument he set up."[53] It is rather doubtful, however, that the import of Saul's monument, whether inscribed or not, can be understood as gratitude to Yahweh. Whereas Moses, after the defeat of the Amalekites in Exod 17, built an altar (מזבח) in honour of Yahweh (v. 15), Saul's monument was erected "to (or for) himself" (לו). The closest conceptual parallel is found in 2

---

[47] Modern ḥirbet el-kirmil, c. 12 km south of Hebron.

[48] MT's use of the participle מציב in the present context is unusual, and the text should perhaps be emended on the basis of LXX and Vulg. to read הציב, hi. perf. However, in view of the fact that a participle can express continuous action occurring not only in the present but in the past as well (e.g. 1 Kgs 3:3; cf. Williams, Syntax, §213), McCarter's contention (262) that והנה מציב in 15:12 "has the force of a parenthetical expression" is plausible.

[49] Transposition of the names Saul and Samuel has led to considerable confusion in LXX[B] of v. 12.

[50] E.g. Delcor, "Word יד", 139; Stoebe, 289; Mittmann, "Grabinschrift", 151 n. 63; Klein, 151; Schroer, "Deutung", 192 n. 8. Stolz's (103) tentative speculation that Saul's יד may have been erected *before* the battle and symbolized prayer seems highly improbable.

[51] Geschichte, 47 n. 42.

[52] Geschichte, 37 n. 1. On this he cites Delcor ("Word יד") but overlooks the fact that Delcor himself classifies the יד of 1 Sam 15:12 otherwise (139). In fact, Delcor's point regarding stelae in the form of a phallus is that they are too rare in the archaeological record to provide a convincing explanation of how the word יד came to mean phallus. He prefers rather to derive this usage from a second root יד with the meaning 'to love' (149).

[53] "Literary Creativity", 43-44.

Sam 18:18, where Absalom erects "to himself" (לוֹ) a monument
(מַצֶּבֶת) in the Valley of the Kings, the stated purpose being that his
name should be remembered. V. 18 concludes by noting that
Absalom's מצבת "is called Absalom's monument (יַד אַבְשָׁלֹם) to this
day." If, as this comparison suggests, a desire for personal recognition
motivated Saul's erection of a monument, this might provide indirect
evidence that Saul's sparing of Agag was similarly motivated — i. e. he
wished to put him on public display.

In v. 13, LXX again offers a longer text than MT, and various
scholars have suggested that MT may have lost a section through
homoioteleuton.[54] LXX[B] v. 13a reads: πρὸς Σαούλ, καὶ ἰδοὺ
αὐτὸς ἀνέφερεν ὁλοκαύτωσιν τῷ κυρίῳ, τὰ πρῶτα τῶν
σκύλων ὧν ἤνεγκεν ἐξ ᾿Αμαλήκ. καὶ παρεγένετο Σαμουὴλ
πρὸς Σαούλ, ... This implies a Hebrew retroversion such as the following: אֶל־שָׁאוּל וְהִנֵּה הוּא הֶעֱלָה עֹלוֹת לַיהוה אֶת רֵאשִׁית בַּשָּׁלָל
אֲשֶׁר הֵבִיא מֵעֲמָלֵק וַיָּבוֹא שְׁמוּאֵל אֶל־שָׁאוּל.[55] Formally, the shorter
reading of MT may look haplographic, but there are several factors in
the context which give MT the edge. First, Saul's requests in vv. 25
and 30 that Samuel return with him imply that he has not yet reached
Gilgal or, at least, that their conversation is not being held at the
sanctuary. Secondly, were Saul already in Gilgal, one might expect
him in v. 21 to say, "the army took from the spoil ... to sacrifice to
Yahweh your God *here* (בָּזֶה[56] or, less likely, פֹּה[57])", rather than "at
Gilgal". Since Gilgal was the intended site for the sacrifices (so v. 21),
these indications that Saul is not yet in Gilgal militate against the
longer reading of LXX. Finally, if, as LXX v. 13 states, Saul were
already in the process of sacrificing, Samuel's query in v. 14 regarding
the bleating of sheep and lowing of oxen would seem rather pointless.

---

[54] E.g. Dhorme, 133; McCarter, 262-63; Klein, 146.

[55] This reconstruction differs in two respects from that put forward by
McCarter, 262. First, although McCarter's reconstruction of לקח from
ἤνεγκεν is not impossible (we note that לקח is rendered by a form of φέρειν
in LXX of Gen 27:13 and possibly also in 2 Kgs 2:20 [though the relevant
phrase is lacking in LXX[AB]]), the Hebrew word which is most often rendered
by φέρειν in LXX is בוא hi. (140x). Secondly, McCarter's retroversion of
καὶ παρεγένετο as ויקרב seems even less likely. Unless this is the only
exception, παραγίνεσθαι is never employed in LXX to render קרב but in
most instances renders בוא qal. For a reconstruction similar to our own in these two respects, see Dhorme, 133.

[56] As in 1 Sam 1:26; 9:11; 21:10; 2 Sam 11:12.

[57] As in 1 Sam 16:11; 21:9; 23:3; etc.

The presence of sacrificial animals would hardly have been noteworthy at a cultic centre such as Gilgal, but would certainly have attracted attention if in the company of troops returning from a battle in which everyone and everything was to have been destroyed. The overall context, therefore, tends to favour the shorter reading of MT v. 13.[58]

As in ch. 13, so also in ch. 15, Saul's first words upon Samuel's arrival are a greeting. In ch. 15, however, Saul adds to his greeting a report of his own recent success: "I have carried out the word of Yahweh" (v. 13bβ). This report, a nearly verbatim reversal of Yahweh's indictment in v. 11aγ, "he has not carried out my word", adumbrates the radical conflict of perspectives that will characterize the dialogue between Saul and Samuel. For Samuel, who has just passed a sleepless night as a result of Saul's mishandling of the Amalekite affair, these words have an exceedingly hollow ring. But a question yet remains — is Saul sincerely unaware of wrongdoing, or is he merely feigning innocence?

Again as in ch. 13, Samuel's first words in ch. 15 take the form of an accusing question: "What [then] is the sound (קוֹל) of these sheep in my ears and the sound (קוֹל) of the cattle which I hear (שֹׁמֵעַ)?" (v. 14). The Targum supplies a protasis, וְאִלּוּ קִיּמְתָּא ("and if you have carried it out"), but this is unnecessary; the suppression of the protasis may simply reflect Samuel's agitation.[59]

15:15, Saul's Defence

In v. 15, Saul has an answer ready: "From Amalek they [the troops] brought them, that which the people spared ... in order to sacrifice to Yahweh, your god." Gunn has argued[60] that the unabashed readiness with which Saul volunteers the "pertinent 'facts'" both in this verse and in v. 20 provides strong support for his contention that Saul was completely unaware of wrongdoing in the Amalekite affair. He writes: "had they [the facts] been so patently in contravention of the instruction we might have expected the king to veil them in some way (by claiming, perhaps, that the livestock were captured elsewhere, and so on)."[61] We must not forget, however, that Samuel's question is not a straightforward interrogative requesting information but, as already

---

[58] Cf. also Pisano, *Additions*, 204-207.

[59] Cf. GK §154b; Stoebe, 290.

[60] *Fate*, 47-48; cf. *idem*, "A Man", 97-98.

[61] *Fate*, 48.

noted, an a*ccusing question* — that is, an accusation couched in the form of a question. This standard feature of judgement speeches to individuals[62] in no way implies that Samuel is ignorant of any of the "facts" — quite the contrary. Saul is in no position, therefore, to "veil them", but can only construe them as favourably as possible. This he does in v. 15, first by distancing himself from the questionable actions ("*they* brought them ... that which the *people* spared ..., but the rest *we* have utterly destroyed"), and secondly by claiming that the animals have been spared in order that they might be sacrificed to Yahweh "*your* [Samuel's] God".[63]

As regards the second point, it is difficult to be sure whether or not Saul actually intends to sacrifice some or even all of the animals. But, as Weiser has noted,[64] the passage makes the best sense if we allow that the sacrificial explanation enjoys at least a degree of validity in Saul's own mind. Gunn is quite willing to give Saul the benefit of the doubt, even implying that Saul intended all along to fulfil the ban order: "when the best of the livestock has been sacrificed the devotion to destruction of all Amalek will be complete."[65] But to insist on Saul's integrity at this point is to deny that of the narrator, for the narrator's description in v. 9 makes a clear distinction between "all that was good (כל הטוב)" and everything that was "despised and worthless". Saul and the army utterly destroyed (חרם) the latter, but the former they were *not willing to destroy* (ולא אבו החרימם). This is an odd way of expressing things, if Saul had in fact intended all along to fulfil the ban order. Any lingering doubt on this question will be removed in v. 19, where Samuel will accuse Saul of rushing upon the spoil and doing evil in the sight of Yahweh.

In the light of these considerations, the supposition that Saul was entirely unaware of wrongdoing or, to put it another way, that his error resulted simply from a technical misunderstanding of what was required must be judged, to borrow a phrase from Grønbæk, as "völlig abwegig".[66] More to the point is Grønbæk's own succinct appraisal:

---

[62] See above, Ch. 3, p. 86.

[63] On Saul's dual defence, cf. Weiser, "I Samuel 15", 9-10.

[64] "I Samuel 15", 8.

[65] *Fate*, 48.

[66] *Geschichte*, 58.

> Aus dem Gesamtzusammenhang geht hervor, daß das
> Volk trotz des Banngebotes begierig Kriegsbeute
> machte, und Saul, der dies nicht zu verhindern vermochte
> (oder durfte) hinterher vorzugaukeln versuchte, die Mo-
> tive seien doch sehr edel gewesen![67]

In short: Saul is bluffing. This is not to say that he might not *now*
intend to sacrifice the best of the livestock, as he claims, but only that
such an intention does not appear to have been the *original motivation*
for their exemption from destruction. Rather, finding himself embar-
rassingly impotent in the face of a conflict between the demands of the
army and the command of Samuel, Saul may have seized upon the idea
of sacrifice as a compromise,[68] or at least as an *ad hoc* explanation for
the presence of livestock in the camp. He now apparently entertains the
hope that this explanation will find acceptance with Samuel.

Should this line of defence fail, however, there is still the other,
namely the attempt to distance himself from the objectionable aspects
of the Amalekite affair by shifting the blame. As we have already seen,
v. 9 tends to invalidate this excuse. Gunn, however, has argued that the
syntax of v. 9 is ambiguous. He notes "a complexity of rhetorical
style: 'Saul and the people spared Agag and the livestock' may be read
as 'Saul spared Agag, and the people spared the livestock'".[69] But even
if it could be granted that v. 9 is ambiguous, which seems very doubtful,[70] the contrast between the supposed ambiguity of the first notice
and the unambiguity of Saul's own claims would still leave the
impression that Saul is attempting to exonerate himself. This is further suggested by his identification of the recipient of the sacrifices as
"Yahweh, *your* God". Indeed, there is even a sense of irritation in
Saul's protest — the *army* spared the animals to sacrifice to *your* God!
(So why am *I* now on trial?)

---

[67] *Geschichte*, 58.

[68] Even if all the animals were to be sacrificed, the army would have
enjoyed the prospect of a sacrificial meal; so Stoebe, 293; Gordon, *Samuel*,
58.

[69] "A Man", 98; cf. *idem, Fate*, 51-52. Grønbæk (*Geschichte*, 53)
attributes the ambiguity of v. 9, in contrast to vv. 20-21, simply to the
"vorbereitenden Charakter" of vv. 1-9.

[70] See the detailed discussion by Sternberg, "Bible's Art", 55-57.

15:16-19, Samuel's Response

Samuel is clearly unimpressed with Saul's brand of logic: "Stop it
(הרף), and I will tell you what Yahweh said to me last night" (v.
16aβ). Having made his defence, Saul allows Samuel to proceed. In
vv. 17-18 Samuel takes up and in turn refutes, though only indirectly,
each of Saul's defences. In response to his attempt to diminish his own
responsibility in the Amalekite affair, Samuel draws a contrast between
Saul's apparent minimalist view of his royal responsibilities and what
is actually required: "Though you (are/were) small in your own eyes,
you (are) head of the tribes of Israel" (v. 17a). Various scholars have
noted echoes of 9:21 in this verse and have suggested that Samuel is
here alluding to earlier expressions of humility by Saul.[71] But it is
difficult to see what significance an allusion to humility would have in
the present context. If, on the other hand, Samuel's intention were
merely to remind Saul of his objective lowliness prior to his elevation
by Yahweh, perhaps in order to stress Saul's obligation to the benefi-
cent deity, the qualifing "in your eyes (בעיניך)" would seem pointless.

What then is the point of calling Saul small in his own eyes? To
be sure, there is an ironic element in Samuel's words — the man distinguished for his great stature (9:2; 10:23) is yet small in his own
eyes. But this overtone does not exhaust the significance of the reference. As Weiser points out, the real point seems to be Saul's
"impotence" (*Ohnmacht*) in the face of popular pressure. Weiser writes:

> Samuel hat die Schwäche Sauls erkannt, die, wenn auch
> unausgesprochen, seine Worte verrieten, daß er, dem
> Willen des Volkes nachgebend, hat geschehn [*sic*]
> lassen, was er unbedingt hätte verhindern müssen; auf
> diese in seiner Nachgiebigkeit gegenüber dem Volks-
> willen zutage getretene Ohnmacht des Königs spielt das
> Wort Samuels an: Obwohl du klein bist, bist du doch das
> Haupt der Stämme Israels.[72]

Saul's tendency to give way before the will of the people is attested
also in ch. 14, but with an important difference. Whereas Saul's eventual capitulation in 14:45 involved rescission of his own words only

---

[71] E.g. McCarter, 267: "The reference is evidently to 9:21, where the
young Saul marvels that he, a humble Matrite of Benjamin, is being ac-
corded royal treatment."

[72] "I Samuel 15", 9; cf. Smith, 136 ("a rebuke of Saul's self-confessed
subservience to the people").

(i.e. 14:24, 39, 44), his acquiescence, if that is all it was,[73] in ch. 15 betrays an unpardonable nonchalance *vis-à-vis* the express command of Yahweh. In v. 17aγ Samuel stresses the absolute unacceptability of Saul's minimalist perspective. To be "head" implies leadership and the power to control the entity over which one is head. Saul's headship, moreover, is not one devoid of obligation to a higher authority. Repeating the name of Yahweh for emphasis, Samuel insists: "*Yahweh* anointed you king over Israel, and *Yahweh* sent you on a mission[74] and said,[75] 'Go and utterly destroy the sinners, the Amalekites, and fight against them until they are exterminated'" (vv. 17b-18).

Having thus dismantled Saul's first line of defence, Samuel turns to the second, but not without first posing another accusing question (v. 19a): "So why did you not listen (שׁמע) to the voice (קול) of Yahweh?" We may recall that in v. 1 Samuel exhorted Saul to listen carefully to the words of Yahweh (ועתה שׁמע לקול דברי יהוה); in v. 14 he couched his first probing question in terms of the sound (קול) of the livestock which he was hearing (שׁמע); now in v. 19 Samuel explicitly charges Saul with having failed in that most important responsibility to listen (שׁמע) to the voice (קול) of Yahweh. Sandwiched between this categorical denunciation in v. 19a and the similarly general charge at the end of the verse, "you did evil in the sight of Yahweh" (v. 19bβ), is a statement of Saul's specific offence, "you (sg.) pounced upon the spoil" (v. 19bα). That this charge is directed at Saul alone does not necessarily prove that he had initiated or even had actively participated in the taking of booty, though he may have done. It simply lays stress upon the fact that, contrary to Saul's minimalist perspective, he alone is finally responsible for the abuse — a conclusion which follows logically from Saul's position as "head of the tribes of Israel" (v. 17aγ). As for Saul's claim that the animals had been spared for sacrifice, Samuel offers no explicit comment, but the wording of his charge, "you pounced upon the spoil", amply indicates that he discounts it.

---

[73] We are not told in the narrative whether Saul's role was passive or active.

[74] Lit. דרך. On this rendering of the word, cf. 1 Sam 21:6; Sauer, "דרך", 457; McCarter, 259.

[75] LXX adds "to you", suggesting an original לך לך. MT may have lost a word by haplography.

15:20-21, Saul's Second Defence

Despite Samuel's obviously low opinion of Saul's excuses, Saul is not yet willing to drop them, and in vv. 20-21 he restates his double defence more adamantly than before, taking up each element of Samuel's accusation and reversing it: "I did listen to the voice of Yahweh (אשר שמעתי בקול יהוה)[76] and I went on the mission ...." As before, Saul lays the onus of responsibility for the sparing of banned goods on the army (v. 21a) and asserts that the animals are to be sacrificed "to Yahweh, your God" (v. 21b). In addition to these two familiar elements, Saul's reiteration of his defence introduces a surprising new element: in v. 20bα Saul mentions that he has brought back Agag, king of the Amalekites. But why should Saul volunteer this information at this point? Is it simply that he is here giving a full account of his handling of the Amalekite affair, whereas in v. 15 he was only responding to Samuel's specific query regarding the animals? Or is it that he is truly unaware of any wrongdoing in having spared Agag?

While all answers to these questions are, of necessity, conjectural, the following approach commends itself. Saul is doubtless aware that the presence of the Amalekite king in the Israelite camp is something which cannot long be hidden. In such a case, it is surely better to volunteer the information than to have it discovered. Moreover, by taking the initiative, Saul can present the facts in the best possible light. This he attempts to do by slipping in the reference to Agag between his twin claims to have obeyed the divine mandate (v. 20a) and to have utterly destroyed Amalek (v. 20bβ).[77] Avoiding the word חמל, since this might recall the original command in v. 3a not to "spare" Amalek, Saul states simply that he has "brought back" (בוא hi.) Agag. In contrast with Saul's own formulation, the narrator's earlier description of the offence placed the *sparing* of Agag immediately beside the *sparing* of booty (v. 9). Moreover, it stated only that Saul destroyed "all the army" (כל־העם) with the edge of the sword (v. 8b), whereas Saul now claims to have destroyed "Amalek" — a claim which echoes the more inclusive command of v. 3, "Go and smite Amalek", and is perhaps aimed at reinforcing his contention that he did indeed "obey the voice of Yahweh" (v. 20).

---

[76] On this use of אשר, see GK §157c; Driver, 127; Stoebe, 290.

[77] Cf. Sternberg, "Bible's Art", 77.

15:22-23, Samuel's Second Response and the Announcement of Judgement

Vv. 22-23, as Tosato has observed, represent the "punto culmi-nante" of 1 Sam 15.[78] The validity of this observation is evidenced not only by the elevated diction of the verses[79] but also by the delivery in v. 23b of the long-awaited announcement of judgement, without which the lengthy exchange between Samuel and Saul, described by Sternberg as "one of the Bible's most elaborate dialogues",[80] would be left hang-ing. Moreover, as Birch has pointed out, the two verses exhibit in succinct form the two basic elements of a judgement speech to an indi-vidual — accusation and announcement — and form a boundary be-tween the more extended presentation of the two elements in the prose narrative, viz., the accusation in vv. 14-21 and the announcement of judgement in vv. 24-31.[81]

Though most scholars recognize the important function of vv. 22-23, not all accept them as original to their present context in ch. 15. Grønbæk, for example, argues that vv. 22-23 in their entirety represent a later addition to the chapter. His basic argument is that the alterna-tives *ban or booty* constitute the original opposition in ch. 15, so that the alternatives *obedience or sacrifice* represent, with respect to the rea-son for Saul's rejection, a clear shift of accent ("Akzentverschiebung"):

> Die v. 22-23a bringen etwas völlig Neues und für den übrigen Bericht Belangloses. Die Alternative besteht nicht in Gehorsam oder Opfer, sondern in der Durch-führung des Banngebotes oder seiner Übertretung.[82]

By way of response to these assertions, we may note first of all that it is simply not true that vv. 22-23 bring something entirely new to ch. 15. As Foresti has recently observed, for example, there is a "logical interdependence" between vv. 22-23a, which "develop the theme of the opposition between sacrifice and obedience", and vv. 20-21. In particular, he draws attention to the linguistic links between the two: "v. 22aβ repeats word for word v. 20aα^2 and v. 22bα repeats both

---

[78] "La colpa", 251.

[79] See our discussion of poetry as heightened speech in Ch. 1, pp. 29-31.

[80] "Bible's Art", 67.

[81] See Birch, *Rise*, 99-101.

[82] *Geschichte*, 58.

v. 20aα² (*šāma'*) and v. 21b (*zābaḥ*)."[83] In fact, the logical interdependence of vv. 22-23a with other parts of ch. 15 is even more extensive than Foresti allows. As we have noted already, the phrase שְׁמַע לְקוֹל (or some variation upon it) recurs several times in ch. 15 (vv. 1, 14 [קוֹל only], 19, 20, 22, 24) and lends thematic continuity to the chapter.[84] Similarly, the issue of sacrifice does not arise for the first time in v. 21b but already in v. 15aβ.[85] Thus, far from introducing something entirely new and of little consequence for the rest of the chapter, vv. 22-23a weave together several important thematic threads already present in ch. 15.

But what of Grønbæk's other contention? Are the two sets of alternatives, ban vs booty and obedience vs sacrifice, sufficiently unrelated or even mutually exclusive to justify the conclusion that only one set can have been original? In view of the capacity of a speaker or writer to express issues and ideas on various levels of abstraction, the answer to this question must be in the negative. At the outset of ch. 15, for example, Samuel issues both an abstract, general command to *obey* the words of Yahweh (v. 1b) and a concrete, specific order to *destroy* Amalek (v. 3). This same expressive capacity is evident elsewhere in the chapter — in the description of Saul's response to his orders (abstract: v. 11aβγ; concrete: vv. 8-9), in Samuel's accusations (abstract: v. 19abβ; concrete: v. 19bα), and in Saul's self-defence (abstract: v. 20aα; concrete: vv. 20aβ-21). Thus, Samuel's reference in v. 22 to the general, overarching command to obey/listen rather than to the specific command to destroy Amalek is unobjectionable and makes good sense as a prelude to the formal announcement of judgement which comes in v. 23.

---

[83] *Rejection*, 34-35. Though Foresti is quite right in recognizing the interdependence of vv. 20-23a, his attempt to divorce this section from its broader context is unconvincing. Specifically, he compares v. 20 with v. 18 and v. 21 with v. 15 and asserts that the references to Agag in v. 20 and to Gilgal in v. 21 are "additions" to otherwise "parallel text[s]" (by which he seems to mean "doublets") and are "sufficiently artificial to reveal the secondary character of the two verses" (34). Having so dealt with vv. 20-21, Foresti simply deduces, on the basis of "linguistic connections" and "logical interdependence", that vv. 22-23a must also be secondary (35). The weakness in Foresti's position is that it tends to cite as arguments the very points it is trying to prove.

[84] Cf. pp. 27, 136, 148.

[85] Foresti's failure to recognize the broader thematic interdependence of vv. 22-23a with these earlier verses in ch. 15 reflects the restrictions imposed by his own particular theories regarding the redaction of ch. 15.

But what of the reference to sacrifice? Clearly there is no sense in which sacrifice can be viewed as the abstract, general counterpart to booty. A starting-point in resolving this tension is to recall that a major feature of Saul's self-defence in ch. 15 has been his attempt to divert attention from the idea of booty and to convince Samuel that the animals spared in the Amalekite encounter are to be sacrificed. Until v. 22, Samuel makes no explicit reference to the issue of sacrifice, though v. 19, as we have seen, indicates that he is more than sceptical of the sacrificial explanation. When Saul persists with this explanation, however, Samuel takes another tack, perhaps in a final attempt to convince Saul of his guilt. In v. 22 he tacitly acknowledges the sacrificial argument, and then proceeds to convict Saul even on his own terms. In other words, by meeting the sacrificial explanation head on, Samuel disarms Saul of his one remaining defensive weapon, reloads it and turns it back upon him.

In so doing, Samuel echoes the invectives against sterile ritual common not only among Israel's prophets[86] but also more broadly in the aNE from early times. Weinfeld has shown that an emphasis upon the primacy of morality over cult by no means found its first expression in Israel's eighth century prophets. He notes that in Egypt, as well as in Israel, "the problem of the religious value of sacrifices is dealt with in Wisdom literature, in texts of prophetic nature and in hymnic-thanksgiving literature." The point is not that sacrifices are totally rejected, but that "sacrifice has no value when accompanied by evil".[87] "It is clear then", writes Weinfeld, "that the prophets were not the first to undermine the value of sacrifice in worshipping God; this was already stressed hundreds of years before the prophets by the Egyptians and also by the Psalmists and wise men of Israel."[88]

In sum: we would contend that neither material considerations (the shift from ban vs booty to obedience vs sacrifice) nor chronological considerations (the notion, for example, that anti-cult polemic originated with the eighth century prophets) lend support to the view, espoused by Grønbæk, that vv. 22-23a are intrusive in ch. 15.

---

[86] E.g. Isa 1:10-17; Jer 6:19-20; 7:21-26; Hos 6:6; Amos 5:21-24; Mic 6:6-8.

[87] "Patterns", 192.

[88] "Patterns", 193. Cf. Thompson (*Penitence*, 110), who states with reference to 1 Sam 15:22, "it is now known that such sentiments were expressed in Egypt a thousand years before." Cf. also Stoebe, 294-95; Preß, "Prophet Samuel", 210-11; Weiser, "I Samuel 15", 18.

A more modest challenge to the originality of only v. 23a has been made by Tosato. In particular, he contests the common view that vv. 22-23a form a logical sequence comprising "domanda (v. 22ab)" [= v. 22a], "risposta (v. 22cd)" [= v. 22b] and "motivo della risposta (v. 23ab)" [= v. 23a]. He writes:

> Il fatto che la rebellione — o, se vogliamo, la disobbe-
> dienza — sia da considerare atto idolatrico (v. 23ab), non
> ha alcun rilievo per decidere la questione se valga più il
> sacrificio o l'obbedienza (v. 22ab).[89]

Contrary to this opinion, we would contend that v. 23a is indicative of the kind of reasoning behind Samuel's declaration in v. 22 that even the best of sacrifices[90] are worthless where obedience is lacking. In other words, in v. 23a Samuel explains the inner logic of the position that he has just taken. V. 23a*a* likens "rebellion" (מרי) to the "sin of divina-tion" (חטאת־קסם). The reference to "rebellion" ties in nicely with the fundamental and recurrent theme in ch. 15, namely the problem of Saul's not listening or obeying (לא שמע).[91] And, more specifically, it may link back to the statement in v. 9 that "Saul and the people ... were not willing [לא אבו] to destroy ...".[92] The sense of the analogy between rebellion and divination is explored by Weiser, who explains "das sündhafte Moment" common to both as follows:

> Das Wesen der Haltung, die sich beim קֶסֶם, auswirkt, ist
> die eigene Kraft und Technik, das Eigenmächtige des קֶסֶם
> gegenüber der Gottheit. Die Haltung, die Saul in seinem
> Ungehorsam bewiesen hat, daß der Bann nicht nach
> Jahwes Befehl durchführte, sondern mit der Opferung
> eines Teils des Banngutes einverstanden war, offenbart
> im Grunde die gleiche Eigenmächtigkeit des Menschen
> Gott gegenüber wie die des Zauberers.[93]

The second clause of v. 23a has been the subject of much debate, primarily as a result of difficulties in the Hebrew text. First, there is

---

[89] "La colpa", 254-55.

[90] Cf. Weiser, "I Samuel 15", 11.

[91] Cf. the paralleling of 'not listening' and 'rebellion' in 1 Sam 12:15: ואם־לא תשמעו בקול יהוה ומריתם את־פי יהוה.

[92] So Gordon (*Samuel*, 57), who notes the association of the root מרה and negated אבה ('to be [un]willing') in several Old Testament passages (e.g. Deut 1:26; Isa 30:9; Ezek 3:7ff.; 20:8).

[93] "I Samuel 15", 12.

the difficult phrase ואון ותרפים ("wickedness and teraphim").[94] It may
be possible to understand this phrase as a "hendiadys meaning evil
teraphim or worthless teraphim",[95] but most scholars prefer either to
delete the ו before תרפים (thus "wickedness of teraphim") or to emend
to עון תרפים ("guilt of teraphim"). The latter two options have the
advantage of establishing a closer syntactical parallel to the "sin of divination" in the first clause. But whichever option we prefer, the sense
of the expression remains pretty much the same.

Perhaps a more problematic element in v. 23a is the final word,
הַפְצַר, vocalized by the massoretes as an otherwise unattested hi. inf.
abs. of פצר, which in the qal means to "push" or "press". Scholars
who accept the massoretic pointing normally read the form as an
intransitive (or "inwardly transitive") hiphil,[96] meaning to "display
pushing", and interpret this to mean forwardness, arrogance, presumption and the like.[97] But again Weiser has offered an interesting alternative. Revocalizing הפצר as a niphal infinitive, meaning "sich drängen
lassen", Weiser takes this as a reference to Saul's "ängstlicher
Nachgiebigkeit gegen das Volk".[98] In his view, the point of the comparison between Saul's acquiescence in the people's demand and the
wickedness of teraphim, which he tentatively defines as "Schutzgötter
mit Abwehrfunktion",[99] is that both reveal "eine innere Unsicherheit,
ein Mißtrauen Gott gegenüber".[100] In many ways a viable alternative to
the more common view, the major weakness in Weiser's interpretation
is that it depends upon a particular, as yet unproven, understanding of

---

[94] As regards the nature and function of teraphim, the fifteen OT
references to teraphim do not yield a homogeneous picture. As Seybold
("תרפים", 1058) has remarked, however, "es ist davon auszugehen, daß sich
das (Fremd-)Wort in atl. Zeit nicht notwendig an allen Stellen auf dieselbe
Sache beziehen muß." Gen 31, for example, indicates that teraphim were
statuettes capable of being concealed in a camel's saddle, while 1 Sam
19:13ff. implies a larger object. Various passages associate teraphim with
divination — e.g. Ezek 21:26 (Eng. v. 21), which parallels teraphim with
three other methods of divination, including קסם; Zech 10:2, where the
teraphim *speak* iniquity (און); and possibly 2 Kgs 23:24.

[95] So Klein, 153.

[96] GK §53d.

[97] Cf. BDB, 823; Driver, 128, and most commentators.

[98] "I Samuel 15", 12.

[99] The etymology of teraphim preferred by Seybold ("תרפים", 1057)
may provide some support for this view. On the etymology, see further de
Ward, "Superstition", 4-6.

[100] "I Samuel 15", 14.

teraphim. On the positive side, it attempts to elucidate specifically the point of the relationship of הפצר to the wickedness of teraphim, and accords well both with the characterization of Saul in v. 17 as small in his own eyes, and with Saul's own admission in v. 24 that he feared and obeyed the people.

In sum, v. 23a suggests at least the following sense: Saul's disobedience (v. 22), likened in v. 23 to rebellion and presumption (?), involves "a kind of rejection of Yahweh" which places it on a level with idolatry and divination (and other forms of apostasy).[101] Thus, so long as the basic problem of disobedience remains unresolved, any attempt on Saul's part to make amends by ritual means is useless at best and at worst idolatrous.

Having neutralized each of Saul's defences (i.e. his minimalist perspective regarding his responsibilities and powers, and his claim that animals were spared only for the purpose of sacrifice), Samuel is at last ready to pronounce judgement. In a fine example of the correspondence motif often exhibited in prophetic judgement speeches,[102] Samuel announces: "Because you have *rejected* (מאס) the word of Yahweh, he has *rejected* you from being king" (v. 23b). The verb מאס, according to Andersen and Freedman, often refers to "disdainful rejection of God, his word, or his covenant", connoting a "perverse refusal to value a thing at its true worth".[103] Thus, Saul's failing in ch. 15 is not unlike his 'foolishness' in ch. 13, though in the present context the element of perverseness is more pronounced.

15:24-26, Saul's First Confession and Samuel's Response

The verdict having already been announced, Saul offers in v. 24 what appears to be a complete and proper confession. The effect of this cathartic moment, however, is not one of unqualified relief, for it cannot be forgotten that several thick defensive walls had to be breached before a proper confession could be wrested from the elusive, or perhaps deluded, defendant. Whatever favourable light now falls upon Saul for his candour is dimmed by the realization of how misguided, if not perjurious, his earlier asseverations had been. His earlier bold claim to have "carried out the word of Yahweh" (v. 13) must now be reversed: "I have sinned, for I have transgressed the command of Yahweh (עברתי

---

[101] McCarter, 268.

[102] See Ch. 3, pp. 85-86.

[103] *Hosea*, 353.

אֶת־פִּי־יהוה) and your word(s)" (v. 24a). His insistent claim, "I did listen to the voice of Yahweh" (v. 20), now yields to "I feared the people
and listened to their voice" (v. 24b).

These admissions strikingly recall Samuel's solemn exposition
(12:14-15) of the basis upon which the experiment of kingship must
succeed or fail: "If you *fear Yahweh* and serve him and *listen to his
voice* and do not *rebel* against *Yahweh's command* (אֶת־פִּי יהוה), both
you and the king who rules over you will be followers of Yahweh your
God.[104] But if you do not *listen* to *the voice of Yahweh* but *rebel*
against Yahweh's command (אֶת־פִּי יהוה), the hand of Yahweh will be
against you and your king to destroy you"[105] Against this background,
Saul's confession portends not so much the possibility of reconciliation
as the certainty of judgement. Saul is guilty as charged in v. 19. He
has "done evil in the sight of Yahweh", and for this crime, according to
12:25, he will be swept away.

But is the matter so simple? King David will later also be found
guilty, in the Uriah affair, of having done "evil in the sight of Yahweh"
(2 Sam 11:27; 12:9), and yet he will remain in office. Why then is
Saul rejected? Perhaps the answer lies not so much in the nature of
Saul's sin as in a qualitative difference between his repentance and that
of David. Commenting upon David's "total and immediate response of
repentance" in 2 Samuel 12:13, Brueggemann writes:

> There is no hint in the narrative that this is anything
> less than an authentic, rightly intentioned confession.
> It is presented without irony or suspicion.[106]

Can the same be said of Saul's repentance? It is certainly not immediate, as we have already seen. Nor is it necessarily total — Saul persists
in attributing the initiative for the breach of the ban to the people, even

---

[104] On this rendering of the last clause, cf. Klein, 111. Equally possible is the more common view which sees an aposiopesis at the end of the
verse; that is, the final clause continues the protasis, and an apodosis such
as "well and good" is only implied; cf. Driver, 94; Stoebe, 234; *NEB, NAB,
NIV*, etc. LXX[L] supplies an apodosis: "then he will rescue you".

[105] This rendering of the apodosis follows LXX[L]; cf. the conjoining
of people and king in 12:14, 25. LXX[B] omits "to destroy you", while MT
offers the difficult reading "and upon your fathers" (made comprehensible in
Targ. and Syr. by the insertion of "as it was [upon your fathers]"). For discussion, see McCarter, 212, who prefers LXX; so also Klein, 111. Stoebe
(234) retains MT but acknowledges its difficulty.

[106] "Trust and Freedom", 8.

though in the narrative account Saul's sparing of Agag is mentioned first. But is it at least authentic and rightly intentioned? Even on this point, the text does not allow a confident affirmative. First, we note that, in contrast to the straightforward simplicity of David's confession in 2 Sam 12:13, Saul's confession is coupled with two requests. The first of these seems unobjectionable enough, "But now, forgive my sin",[107] but this is not Saul's only request. "And return with me", he continues, "and I shall bow down before Yahweh" (v. 25).

Ignoring Saul's plea for forgiveness, Samuel in v. 26 responds only to the request to return. Though the text offers no commentary, we may perhaps infer from the focus and substance of Samuel's response 1) that he viewed the request to return as Saul's central concern, and 2) that he perceived in the request an attempt on Saul's part to mitigate his sentence. But this he rejects by reiterating the judgement delivered against Saul in v. 23b: "I will not return with you, for you have rejected the word of Yahweh, and Yahweh has rejected you from being king over Israel" (v. 26).

15:27-29, *The 'Significance' of the Torn Mantle*

Having finished his business with Saul, Samuel turns to go. But as he does so, *someone* grasps the edge (כְּנַף) of *someone's* mantle, and it tears (וַיִּקָּרַע). The most common understanding of this incident is that it is Saul who grabs and inadvertently tears Samuel's mantle. Strictly speaking, however, there are four possibilities, since, apart from the one just mentioned, Saul may have torn his own garment, or Samuel his own, or Samuel Saul's. All four options are discussed by Grønbæk,[108] who objects to the first two on the ground that they must assume an unannounced change of subject for וַיַּחֲזֵק.[109] The fourth option he rejects on the grounds that it is 1) inconsistent with the respect normally shown to the king and 2) subject to the syntactic objection that if Saul's mantle were indeed intended, one would expect an explicit genitive construction rather than an ambiguous pronominal suffix.[110] Grønbæk's own interpretation, however, that Samuel intentionally tore

---

[107] The confession is virtually identical with that of Pharaoh in Exod 10:17.

[108] *Geschichte*, 40-42.

[109] *Geschichte*, 41; but contrast Conrad ("Samuel", 275), who cites frequent change of subject, without nearer specification, as an attested stylistic feature of Hebrew prose.

[110] *Geschichte*, 42.

his own garment as a symbolic confirmation of Yahweh's decision to tear the kingdom from Saul, is itself not without difficulties. First, to make sense it must assume that Samuel grasped his mantle before turning to go,[111] whereas the text has the reverse order. Secondly, it regards the tearing of the garment as intentional,[112] which does not accord well with MT's niphal וַיִּקָּרַע, "and it tore" (v. 27b).[113] Thirdly, it leaves אֵלָיו in v. 28 without antecedent. All things considered, therefore, the first option, that Saul tore Samuel's robe, long considered to be the more obvious one in context,[114] retains its attraction.

Among the majority of scholars who share this basic understanding, recent debate has centred more upon the significance or implicit meaning of the incident. Conrad, for example, has suggested a reinterpretation of v. 27 in the light of several Mari texts in which a lock of hair and the fringe of a garment, taken from an ecstatic, a dreamer or other bearer of a prophetic message, are forwarded along with the message to the king of Mari. From his analysis of the Mari material, Conrad comes to the following conclusion:

> Das Abschneiden von Haar und Mantelsaum des Propheten drückt also ein Mißtrauen derer aus, die die Gottesbotschaft empfangen haben, äußert den Verdacht auf falsche Prophetie, die ja immer ein Problem darstellt, und gibt dem Staat Verfügungsgewalt über den Propheten.[115]

Applying this understanding to 1 Sam 15:27, Conrad argues that by tearing Samuel's garment Saul dishonoured him, divested him of the authority of his office, and brought him under the authority of the state. "Saul versucht — offensichtlich mit Erfolg —, den lästigen Mahner damit zum Schweigen zu bringen."[116]

---

[111] "Samuel wendet sich ... von Saul ab, ... , doch vorher faßt er so darb den Zipfel seines Gewandes an, daß es kaputt reißt" (*Geschichte*, 42).

[112] "Die in V. 27b vorgenommene Handlung geschieht also ganz bewußt" (*Geschichte*, 42).

[113] On attempts to circumvent this problem by revocalizing ויקרע as a qal, see p. 159 below.

[114] Rashi, e.g., labels this interpretation as the simple one (פשׁט). LXX and 4QSam[a] explicitly mention Saul as the one who grasps in v. 27.

[115] "Samuel", 279.

[116] "Samuel", 280.

Conrad's theory is interesting, but open to a number of objections. For example, in the light of vv. 28ff. it is unclear in what sense Saul can be said to have succeeded in silencing the prophet. Moreover, the theory requires that we regard the tearing of Samuel's garment, not just the grasping of the hem, as an *intentional* act. As noted above, such a view runs into trouble with MT's וַיִּקְרַע in v. 27b. To get round this problem, Conrad suggests revocalizing וַיִּקְרַע as a qal, and cites the last phrase of LXX v. 27b in support: καὶ διέρρηξεν αὐτό. But in this case the expected form in Hebrew would be וַיִּקְרָעֵהוּ.[117] Thus, it seems more likely that LXX is attempting to clarify an ambiguous text[118] than that MT has suffered corruption in several places.

A more general objection to Conrad's theory has to do with the narrow sampling of the evidence upon which it is based. Although Conrad notes the existence of six Mari texts in which hair and hem are mentioned, he arrives at his conclusions on the basis of only three of these, viz. *ARM*, VI.45, XIII.112, and a letter of Itur-Asdu to Zimri-Lim.[119] The other three texts mentioned are *ARM*, X.8.20ff., X.50.29ff., and X.81.16ff.[120] One other text, *ARM*, X.7, should also be classed with the above, although the relevant lines (23ff.) have been partially damaged. In the light of these further texts, several of Conrad's assertions regarding the meaning and purpose of the practice of taking hair and hem must be reconsidered.

As noted above, for example, Conrad argues that the confiscation of hair and hem implied mistrust and even suspicion of false prophecy. He apparently bases this judgement on the evidence of the Itur-Asdu text, in which the hair and hem of Malik-Dagan, a man from Shakka who in a dream had received a message for Zimri-Lim, are *not taken* (line 53). The reason for this departure from custom, according to Conrad, is that Malik-Dagan was an "official" of some sort (reading *awīlum šu kallu*) or, alternatively, a "trustworthy" person (reading

---

[117] So Segal in his Samuel commentary (cited by Brauner, "To Grasp the Hem", 36 n. 5).

[118] Cf. LXX's insertion of Σαούλ to remove ambiguity earlier in v. 27.

[119] Text and translation of the third text are available in Dossin, "Dagan", 128ff. Subsequent translations can be found in von Soden, "Verkündung", 398-99; *ANET*, 623a; *NERT*, 125-26.

[120] At the time Conrad wrote his article, these three texts had been published in cuneiform only. They appeared in the *ARM* series, transliterated and with French translation, in 1978.

awīlum šu ták-lu).[121] Von Soden, however, reads awīlum šu qal₄lu, "Mann geringer Herkunft",[122] which gives a quite different sense.

In addition to this uncertainty as to what exactly the attributive means, there is also ambiguity, occasioned by the preponderance of pronouns in line 53, as to whom the attributive describes.[123] In fact, Beyerlin conjectures that it applies not to Malik-Dagan at all but to the messenger whom Itur-Asdu is sending to Zimri-Lim with the report of Malik-Dagan's dream.[124]

In addition to these internal ambiguities in Conrad's proof-text, there is an even more damaging piece of external evidence. ARM, X.81, a letter from Inibšina to Zimri-Lim, contains a quotation from a certain prophetess named Innibana. Although several lines of the prophecy itself have been destroyed, the following excerpt is significant. Having delivered her prophecy, the prophetess continues: a-nu-um-ma ša-ar-ti ù si-si-ik-ti ad-di-na-ki-im li-za-ak-ku-ú ("Here then I have given you my hair and my hem, that one may [ritually] cleanse them").[125] It is apparent that in formulating his theory Conrad discounted the likelihood of such voluntary surrender of hair and hem by a prophet or prophetess,[126] and the fact that this did apparently take place considerably undermines the supposed negative connotations — mistrust, suspicion of false prophecy, etc. — which Conrad reads into the practice.

If, then, we are unable to accept Conrad's theory regarding the significance of hair and hem, especially as regards Saul's action in 1 Sam 15:27, what other possibilities are there? Conrad himself notes that in ARM, VI.26.3'f., 8'f. and XIII.148.8 the act of grasping the hem can connote political submission, but he rules out such an understanding for 1 Sam 15:27.[127] Brauner, on the other hand, takes up this notion

---

[121] "Samuel", 277.

[122] "Verkündung", 398-99.

[123] Cf. von Soden, "Verkündung", 399 n. 3.

[124] NERT, 126 nn. v and w.

[125] The second verb is a precative D-stem from zakû II. On the meaning "cleanse ritually" (Mari only), see CAD, 21:25, 32.

[126] Cf. Conrad, "Samuel", 278 n. 27.

[127] The two reasons which Conrad ("Samuel", 275) gives for this judgement are unconvincing: viz. 1) that it would be without parallel for a king to subordinate himself in this way to a prophet; and 2) that the tearing of Samuel's garment and its interpretation as merely a sign confirming the removal of Saul's kingdom would not do justice to the magical and symbolical significance of the hem.

and, in an article published in 1974, cites various examples in which the act of grasping the hem appears to signify "supplication, importuning, submission".[128] In addition to several Akkadian examples, he cites one in Old Aramaic (*KAI*, 221.11 = *SSI*, 2:14.11) and one from the OT (Zech 8:23). A further Akkadian example, not noted by Brauner, comes from a hymn of Ashurnasirpal I to Ishtar:

> I, Ashurnasirpal, the frightened, who fear you, who seize the fringe of your divinity, who pray to you as mistress — look upon me, lady, and then I will worship your decision (?)! You who are angry, have mercy on me, so that your countenance may be soothed![129]

Brauner points out that his examples, which refer only to grasping the hem, are more appropriate parallels to Saul's action in 15:27 than are the examples cited by Conrad, all of which mention both hair and hem.[130]

The texts assembled by Brauner serve as a helpful corrective to the rather one-sided picture presented by Conrad, but when it comes to interpreting 1 Sam 15:27, Brauner seems equally guilty of reading too much into Saul's action. He writes: "Clearly, Saul supplicates Samuel, importunes him not to abandon him and submits himself of [*sic*] Samuel's (and God's) authority — all, both in word and in the deed of taking hold of Samuel's cloak."[131] We would contend, however, that the question whether or not Saul is truly "penitent" (as Brauner also claims)[132] cannot be answered simply from the fact that he grasped Samuel's hem. It must be answered on the basis of the broader context. While the physical gesture of grasping the hem does seem to connote supplication of some sort,[133] it need not imply specific attitudes such as compliance, penitence or submission, etc. This point may be illustrated from the Ugaritic myth of Baal and Mot, in which Anat approaches Mot in order to make a request:

---

[128] "To Grasp the Hem", 36.

[129] *NERT*, 115.

[130] "To Grasp the Hem", 37 n. 9. Noth ("Remarks", 328) contends that "in the context of the magical conceptions of the world, hair *or* hem would suffice"; but contrast Malamat, "Prophetic Revelations", 225 n. 3.

[131] "To Grasp the Hem", 38.

[132] "To Grasp the Hem", 38.

[133] Cf. Greenstein, "Grasp the Hem", 217.

ủḫd.m[t] (10) *bsin.lpš.*	She seized Mot by the hem of (his) garment,
tšsq[nh] (11) *bqṣ.áll.*	she constrained [him] by the end of (his) robe;[134]

In this example it is clear that Anat's motivation for grasping Mot's garment is to *constrain* him in order to deliver her petition.[135] The idea of supplication is certainly present, but there is no notion either of penitence or of the darker significations suggested by Conrad. Indeed, as Greenstein has noted, when Anat again "seizes" Mot (lines 30b-31a), "she hacks him up, pulverizes him, and scatters his remains for the birds to eat".[136] The lesson to be drawn from all this is that the physical act of grasping the hem can mean various things, depending upon the context, so that it is a dubious procedure to import conclusions drawn in one context into the interpretation of a similar act in another.

In 1 Sam 15:27 we are told only that the physical action occurred. To discover what inferences can be drawn from it, we must look to its own context. In the debate between Saul and Samuel which leads up to v. 27, we saw repeated attempts by Saul to convince Samuel that his conduct in the Amalekite battle had been honourable. Samuel, however, consistently rejected Saul's rationalizations and concluded the debate with a formal announcement of Saul's own rejection. Perhaps in a final effort to turn the situation round, Saul reversed his earlier protestations of innocence and confessed to having heeded the people rather than Yahweh and his spokesman, adding to this confession a request that Samuel return with him to worship Yahweh. Now in v. 27, when even this request is refused, and Samuel turns to go, Saul, in a last desperate attempt to rescue the situation (or, at least, to receive a word of comfort from the intractable prophet), grasps the edge of Samuel's mantle and it tears.

This understanding of Saul's action finds confirmation in Samuel's reaction to it. Samuel shows no signs of recognizing Saul's clutching after him as a penitential gesture, but seizes upon the tearing of the robe as a fitting symbol by which to seal Saul's judgement: "Yahweh

---

[134] *CML*, 6.ii.9b-11a. For discussion of these lines, see Greenstein, "Grasp the Hem", 217-18.

[135] Cf. the succeeding lines: "she lifted up her voice and cried: 'Do you, Mot, give up my brother", etc. (*CML*, 6.ii.11bff.).

[136] "Grasp the Hem", 218.

has torn the kingdom of Israel from you this day and has given it to your neighbour, who is better than you" (v. 28aβ-b). Lest any doubt remain as to the finality of this judgement, Samuel follows in v. 29 with an averment reminiscent of Num 23:19. "Yes", he says, "the Glory of Israel[137] does not lie[138] nor change his mind, for he is not a man that he should change his mind."[139]

There is an apparent tension between the statement in v. 29 that Yahweh does not repent/change his mind (נחם) and vv. 11 and 35, where Yahweh states explicitly that he repents/is sorry (נחם) for having made Saul king. Accordingly, v. 29 is sometimes labelled a gloss. But, while there may be other reasons for regarding the verse as a gloss,[140] the assumption of logical or theological contradiction is not sufficient to decide the issue. Not only is the tension between v. 29 and vv. 11, 35 somewhat eased by the broad range of meaning enjoyed by the verb נחם,[141] but, as Moberly has observed,

> theological writing may involve the use of paradox and antinomy. Such is the inherently mysterious nature of God and his ways with man that it is often difficult to make a statement in a theologically reflective way without wishing to qualify it, sometimes by the assertion of an apparently opposite truth.[142]

According to Eichrodt, "the purpose of Num 23.19 and 1 Sam 15.29 ... is to combat the erroneous idea that it is easy to talk God

---

[137] On this rendering of the obscure epithet נצח ישראל, see Driver, 128-29. For other options, see, for example, Klein, 154.

[138] So MT, ישקר; LXX and 4QSamᵃ attest ישיב, "retract"; cf. McCarter, 264. While MT's ישקר comes closer in meaning to its counterpart (כזב) in Num 23:19, the alternative reading ישיב would provide a close parallel to נחם, "change his mind", in the subsequent phrase in 15:29 and might also suggest a word-play with Saul's pleas in vv. 26-30 that Samuel "return" (שוב).

[139] On the latter phrase, cf. Hos 11:9: "For I am God, and not man — the Holy One among you."

[140] Cf. Foresti, *Rejection*, 28-29 n. 8.

[141] In addition to the lexicons, see esp. Stoebe, "נחם", 64-65. Cf. de Ward's observation that "the literary device of using homonyms or words of one root in slightly different senses is common enough in the Old Testament: often it causes a deliberate ambivalence" ("Eli's Rhetorical Question", 119).

[142] *Mountain*, 33.

round, and that his threats and promises need not be taken seriously."[143]
Given this understanding, v. 29 makes very good sense in its present
context. Saul's efforts to mitigate his sentence, to manipulate the situation, are useless. The judgement is irrevocable, as is the decision to
transfer the kingdom to another.

15:30-35, *Saul's Second Confession and Samuel's Response*

Saul's last words in ch. 15 indicate that he has understood the message. Gone are the subterfuge and deception that marked his earlier ex-
postulations. In a second confession, which parallels in many respects
the first (vv. 24-25), Saul's true motives are laid bare. "I have sinned",
he says, "but now honour me before the elders of my people and before
Israel, and return with me that I may prostrate myself before Yahweh
your God" (v. 30). As is often the case in instances of near-verbatim
repetition, the numerous similarities between this confession and the
earlier one tend to cast the differences between them into even bolder
relief. The admission of guilt, which earlier filled a whole verse (v.
24), is now reduced to a single word, חטאתי (v. 30aα). No request for
forgiveness follows the pivotal עתה as in v. 25. There is instead a petition for honour before the elders of "*my* people" and before Israel (v.
30aβ). The request to return is very much the same as in the first confession (v. 25), though this time it is Yahweh "*your* God" to whom
Saul proposes to do obeisance.

Perhaps in recognition of the long-awaited candour of Saul's revised
'confession', or perhaps because he has unfinished business to attend to
in Gilgal, Samuel reverses his earlier decision (v. 26) and consents to
return with Saul (v. 30). After what has just transpired, there is at any
rate no longer any danger that Saul might misinterpret this action as a
relaxation of his sentence. Whether Samuel's willingness to return
with Saul also implies a willingness to honour him before the people
is left undetermined by the text; of Samuel's activities in Gilgal we are
told only that he called for Agag and slew him before Yahweh (vv. 32-
33). Yet this action itself may, in a certain sense, represent an answer
to Saul's request. Weiser explains:

> Es ist die Restituierung der göttlichen Autorität des
> Königtums vor den Ältesten und dem Volk im Blick auf
> die unbedingte Gehorsamspflicht dem göttlichen Gebot
> gegenüber, wenn Samuel durch die Tötung des Agag vor

---

[143] *Theology*, 1: 216.

Jahwe in Gilgal das Gewicht seiner Person mit eindrucksvoller Wucht in feierlicher Handlung einsetzt für
die Beachtung der Forderung Jahwes and damit die Seite
der königlichen Autorität stärkt, die durch Sauls
Nachgiebigkeit geschädigt war. So erfüllt Samuel in
gewissem Sinne die Bitte Sauls.[144]

So then, Samuel's public execution of Agag serves to restore royal authority in general *vis-à-vis* the elders and the people. At the same time,
however, it unavoidably represents a public rebuke of the one who
spared Agag in the first place. As Weiser succinctly puts it: "Das
Königtum wird gestützt, der König verworfen."[145]

The scene closes with a characteristic two-fold statement of departure:[146] Samuel goes to Ramah, and Saul goes up to his house in
Gibeah of Saul (v. 34). The final verse of the chapter is transitional;
its reference to Samuel's mourning for Saul links with a similar reference in 16:1. More importantly, v. 35 marks the definitive break between Samuel and Saul. The statement that "Samuel did not see Saul
again until the day of his death" is, as Gordon observes, "apparently the
narrator's way of emphasizing the irreconcilability of prophet and
king."[147] With the dissolution of that relationship through which divine initiatives were to be communicated to Saul, the basis of his
reign's theocratic legitimacy is destroyed, and thus, from the prophetic
perspective, Saul's reign has ended.

Summary and Conclusions

At the outset of this chapter we noted various debating points with
respect to 1 Sam 15 and set ourselves three primary questions to guide
our reading of the episode. The three questions were: 1) does 1 Sam 15
present a coherent and sequential story-line? 2) does it display a consistent attitude towards Saul and the monarchy? and 3) what does it indicate regarding the cause(s) of Saul's rejection? We are now in a position to draw some conclusions regarding these main questions and to

---

[144] "I Samuel 15", 15.
[145] "I Samuel 15", 16.
[146] On this narrative convention, see Ch. 3, p. 93 n. 122.
[147] *Samuel*, 53. Cf. also Jobling, "Jonathan", 10 n. 9.

offer provisional remarks on some other issues mentioned in the introduction to this chapter.

In the course of our analysis of 1 Sam 15, we discovered no elements that were intrusive or inappropriate or, for that matter, dispens-
able to the narrative — neither vv. 22-23 (nor parts thereof) nor the
section comprising approximately vv. 24-29 proved to be out of
place.[148] By attending closely to the intricate workings of the narrative,
we were able to recognize within 1 Sam 15, in its present form, a logically developed and credible story-line. We found it convenient to di-
vide the chapter into two scenes, the first of which (vv. 1-9) recounted
Samuel's (Yahweh's) commissioning of the Amalekite campaign and
Saul's faulty execution of it, and the second (vv. 10-35) traced the
lengthy debate between Samuel and Saul, which constituted the latter's
trial and which reached its climax in his definitive rejection.

To the question of the chapter's attitude towards Saul and the
monarchy, two separate answers must be given. First, nothing in 1
Sam 15 suggests an anti-monarchical perspective. V. 1 makes it clear
that the kingship has been instituted at Yahweh's command. The same
verse makes it equally clear that the form of monarchy thus created is
not to be autonomous, but is to remain strictly subordinate to Yahweh,
as his initiatives and instructions are made known by his prophetic
spokesman. Having brought Israel's monarchy into existence by acced-
ing to the people's request, Yahweh yet retains the right of control over
it (e.g., vv. 17-18, 23 and *passim*). Even Saul gives evidence of
understanding this arrangement (e.g., vv. 13, 24). Thus, monarchy *per
se* is no longer in question in 1 Sam 15. Saul's occupancy of the
throne, however, very much is. When in vv. 11 and 35 Yahweh expresses regret, it is not for having allowed Israel a king, but for having
made Saul king. And even when Saul's rejection has become an accomplished fact (vv. 23, 26), kingship itself is not thereby abolished.
It is simply transferred proleptically to another (v. 28). Thus, we conclude that 1 Sam 15 is neutral towards the monarchy but negative towards Saul.

How then is Saul's failure depicted? What light does 1 Sam 15
shed on the cause or causes of Saul's rejection? In our discussion of vv.
22-23, we argued that much of the confusion which has surrounded attempts to pinpoint Saul's offence in 1 Sam 15 can be resolved simply
by recognizing the narrator's ability to describe Saul's failings on

---

[148] Our main discussion of the latter was in Ch. 1, pp. 37-39.

different levels of abstraction. Saul's specific offence is his refusal to carry out the ban order against the Amalekites. But we saw that at a more general level this connotes disregard of the word of Yahweh and, thus, of the theocratic authority structure requisite to acceptable kingship in Israel. More generally still, Saul's 'not listening' is presented as the moral equivalent of rebellion, which in turn is likened to divination and idolatry. By means of this progressive generalizing of Saul's offence, the narrator is able to drive home his point that Saul's specific misdeed in ch. 15 is but a symptom of a more deep-seated ill.

If we compare these findings with the results of our investigation of 1 Sam 13-14, we discover some interesting correlations. As we argued at length in Chs. 2 and 3, recognition of the link between the 'charge' given to Saul at the time of his anointing (10:7-8) and the events of 13:3ff. is essential for a proper understanding of Saul's offence in ch. 13. At the time of his anointing, Saul is made heir to the military functions of Israel's charismatic tradition, but Samuel is to remain the conduit of divine initiative and instruction. Also at that time, Saul is given a two-part commission, which, as later events reveal, constitutes a test of his willingness to abide by the prescribed arrangement. Approaching ch. 13 with these things in mind, we were able to see that Saul's trespass in that chapter is not essentially cultic but, rather, religio-political in nature. By proceeding without Samuel, Saul either intentionally or unintentionally issues a challenge to the authority structure that Samuel has established in order that human kingship and theocracy might co-exist. In this light, it is apparent that Saul's basic offence is the same in both chs. 13 and 15. Attempts to trivialize it by reducing it to a cultic infraction in ch. 13 or to a transgression of some tenet of holy war ideology in ch. 15 are, therefore, fundamentally misguided — mistaking the symptoms for the disease.

Having drawn some conclusions on our three major questions, we may now offer a few tentative comments on other debated issues with respect to 1 Sam 15. As regards its relationship to the surrounding chapters in 1 Sam, we noted in the course of our reading a fair number of linkages with other sections.[149] By far the clearest links appear to be with ch. 12, and this is not surprising, of course, when we consider 1) that Samuel is the primary speaker in both contexts, and 2) that in ch. 12 he lays the ground rules for kingship, while in ch. 15 he rejects Saul

---

[149] For further cross-referencing with passages outside Samuel, see Donner, "Verwerfung", 241-48; *idem*, "Historiography", 48-50.

for failing to abide by these. The parenetic, deuteronomistic tone of both chapters would seem to hold promise for locating them historically, but the recent tendency to move away from Noth's view of 1 Sam 12 as a wholly deuteronomistic chapter,[150] along with a growing awareness of the difficulties of limiting 'deuteronomistic' style and terminology to a single period,[151] complicate the matter.

As to the role played by 1 Sam 15 in the overall structure of 1 Samuel, it is best described as pivotal or transitional. From the ideological perspective characteristic of the narrative, 1 Sam 15 marks the effective end of Saul's reign. *De facto* Saul will continue to occupy the throne for some time to come, but *de jure* his rejection is an accomplished fact. Having rejected Yahweh's word, he will no longer receive it (cf. 28:15). The vital link with Israel's Great King has been severed, and henceforth Yahweh's attention will fall upon another. In this sense, then, the chapter also serves as an introduction to the 'Rise of David'. After ch. 15, David will be the protagonist and Saul the antagonist.

In Part Three we shall test the results of our inquiry into the causes of Saul's rejection against the larger body of Saul material. Although we concluded that Saul's basic offence is essentially the same in chs. 13-14 and ch. 15, we were also able to discern a certain progression within the overall narrative. The sense that Saul is acting in 'good faith' is more pronounced in the earlier section, though in the latter parts of ch. 14 a darker side of Saul begins to show itself. In ch. 15 Saul gives evidence of having a clearer understanding of what is expected of him, but, after failing to meet these expectations, his defence before Samuel is characterized more by dissimulation than by 'good faith'. Thus, Saul's progressive increase in understanding is conjoined with a corresponding decrease in good will. There is little debate that this tendency towards an inverse relationship between knowledge and good will continues and intensifies in the account of Saul's decline in 1 Sam 16-31. Our focus in Part Three, therefore, will not be on chs. 16-

---

[150] Cf. Beuken's brief survey of opinion ("Twee visies", 350-52).

[151] Cf. Collier, "Problem of Deuteronomy"; Weippert, "Beurteilung"; Porter, "Historiograpy", 132-52; Willis, "Anti-Elide", 288-89 n. 3. Cf. also Weinfeld's brief discussion of "verbal resemblances" between Deuteronomy and Hosea, which Weinfeld describes as "particularly convincing" (*Deuteronomy*, 366-70). More recently, Rabin ("Discourse Analysis") has attempted to associate Deuteronomy with "Old Rhetoric" current in the early monarchy period prior to the major prophets.

31 but on the earlier chapters recounting Saul's rise, viz. 1 Sam 9-11. Because of the numerous literary difficulties raised by these chapters, we must preface our investigation of their portrayal of Saul with a consideration of the coherence, or lack thereof, of the section. Major issues relating to the issue of narrative coherence will be discussed in Ch. 6, while more minor ones will be taken up in Ch. 7 as they arise. In Ch. 7 we shall also seek to discover whether 1 Sam 9-11 present a consistent picture of Saul and, if so, how this picture correlates with his depiction elsewhere.

Part Three

Sense and Significance in the 'Rise of Saul'

6

ON THE ISSUE OF
NARRATIVE COHERENCE
IN 1 SAM 9-11

Introduction

Of the various phases of Saul's career as recounted in 1 Samuel, none has attracted more scholarly attention or spawned a more extensive literature than the initial phase which deals with his rise to power (chs. 8-12). Several observations may be offered in explanation of this intensity of interest in Saul's early career. First, the chapters under discussion purport to record a most significant transformation in the political and ideological life of ancient Israel, viz. the inception of the monarchy. Secondly, these chapters are often discussed in the context of early Israelite historiography and are thought to reveal something of its nature.[1] Thirdly, and perhaps most importantly, these chapters display a literary complexity that has posed an almost irresistible challenge to the ingenuity of scholars. Ishida speaks of the analysis and historical evaluation of the "Samuel-Saul complex" (chs. 7-15) as "among the most vexed questions in biblical studies".[2]

Commensurate with their literary complexity, the chapters dealing with Saul's rise have, in the words of A. D. H. Mayes, proved to be "a favourite hunting ground for source critics".[3] A survey of previous re-

---

[1] Witness, for example, the preoccupation with the Saul traditions in J. Licht's "Biblical Historicism" or in H. Donner's "Basic Elements of Old Testament Historiography Illustrated by the Saul Traditions". W. E. Evans ("Historical Reconstruction", 62) draws attention to a "general agreement" that the career of Saul marks "the threshold of actual historical events in the Bible." It is not our purpose here to debate the extent or validity of this "general agreement" but simply to note it as a stimulus of interest in the Saul material.

[2] *Royal Dynasties*, 26.

[3] *Story*, 9. Cf. Cooper's recent reference to 1 Sam 1-12 as "that *locus classicus* of source criticism" ("Act of Reading", 68).

search on the Saul traditions confirms Mayes's point but at the same time reveals considerable variation in the critical conclusions reached.[4] Characteristic of virtually all the major approaches is the assumption that "it is futile from the outset to attempt reconstruction of a harmonious history from all the narratives."[5] To be sure, dissenters have occasionally had their say, but none has yet succeeded in disfranchising this assumption from the almost *a priori* status which it has achieved.

The pessimism regarding the possibility of reconstructing a history of Saul's rise reflects two convictions of a literary nature about the section 1 Sam 8-12: 1) that it is not in any but the most artificial sense a literary unity, and 2) that even in its final redaction it does not present a very coherent sequence of events. Both these convictions are based upon perceived difficulties within the texts — tensions, contradictions, repetitions, and the like. The two most commonly cited inconcinnities are 1) the differing or even opposing attitudes toward the monarchy and 2) the 'multiple election' of Saul.[6] To these may be added a third, namely the wide narrative gap between 10:7-8 and 13:3ff.[7] The cumulative effect of these several difficulties has been a general lack of interest in the possibility of a holistic reading of Saul's rise. Witness, for example, the unselfconscious ease with which Halpern, on record as opposing "multiplying documentary sources unnecessarily",[8] speaks of "a division of sources in 1 Samuel 8ff." as the "*first step*" in investigating Saul's election" (italics mine).[9]

In his form-critical study of 1 Sam 8-12, D. J. McCarthy stressed the importance of "the internal articulation of the unit" and lamented the

---

[4] Summaries of critical research on Saul's rise abound, and it is unnecessary to repeat that information here. In addition to the histories and commentaries, see Langlamet, "Les récits"; Madl, *Untersuchungen*, 9-19 (focuses primarily on studies of 1 Sam 13-15 since 1943 but is of value also for the earlier chapters); Birch, *Rise*, 1-10; Fritz, "Deutungen des Königtums Sauls", 346-49; Ishida, *Royal Dynasties*, 27-28 (cf. also his bibliographic footnote, p. 26 n. 3); Kegler, *Politisches Geschehen*, 56-70 (deals with primarily German studies of 1 Sam 9-11); Veijola, *Königtum*, 5-14; Vannoy, *Covenant Renewal*, 197-225 (surveys literary criticism of 1 Sam 8-12 since Wellhausen); Childs, *Introduction*, 266-71, 277-78; Edelman, "Saul's Rescue", 196-97; Eslinger, *Kingship*, 11-40.

[5] Ishida, *Royal Dynasties*, 42.

[6] Ishida, *Royal Dynasties*, 28.

[7] Cf. Ch. 2, p. 65.

[8] "Uneasy Compromise", 64.

[9] "Uneasy Compromise", 63.

fact that concern for sources, as important as this concern is, "has drawn attention from the careful narrative construction of the unit as such."[10] Building on earlier insights by Tsevat,[11] McCarthy discerned within the unit a pattern of contrasts. On the formal level, this consists of an alternating pattern of "reports of assemblies" and "stories" recounting action. Anti-monarchical sentiments find their clearest expression in the assemblies, while the stories tend to be more positive — though, as McCarthy pointed out, "kingship as a problem" is the basic theme of the section, "and the reader is not allowed to lose sight of this even in the so-called pro-monarchical units."[12] McCarthy's analysis may be briefly summarized as follows:

B (-) 8:4-22   Report of an assembly: people request a king
A (+) 9:1-10:16   Story: the secret anointing of Saul
B (-) 10:17-27   Report of an assembly: public presentation
A (+) 11:1-13   Story: Saul's first exploit
B (-) 11:14-12:25 Report of an assembly: Samuel's speech[13]

Our aim in introducing McCarthy's work at this point is not to assess it (we shall have occasion to return to it below), but simply to echo his plea that the diachronic concerns of, for example, source and tradition criticism, legitimate as these concerns are, should not be allowed to blind us to meanings which a more synchronic reading of the unit might yield. But if by synchronic reading we mean an attempt to read off the account of Saul's rise as a coherent sequence of events, the objection might be raised that this has long since been shown to be impossible. Nevertheless, several points can be made in defence of such an attempt. First, it is never a good thing when a critical conclusion becomes so entrenched that it is no longer subject to scrutiny. B. W. Anderson has written:

> Biblical scholarship, insofar as it aims to be honest and "scientific," cannot remain satisfied with any hypothesis, even one that is supported by a consensus. If we are to escape the snares of subjectivism, however, a new be-

---

[10] "Inauguration", 403.

[11] "Biblical Account", 83-84

[12] "Inauguration", 403.

[13] A very similar scheme is proposed by B. Childs in his *Introduction*, 277-78. Cf. also Mayes, *Story*, 85-86.

> ginning must be guided by external controls over recon-
> struction of the prehistory of the text and must be an-
> chored firmly in the final form of the text which, after
> all, is the inescapable beginning and end of exegesis.[14]

Secondly, it seems quite clear that the form of the text before us, whatever its redactional history, now intends to present a coherent narrative
sequence of Saul's rise to power.[15] And finally, as we shall attempt to
show, the effect of much recent research has been to lessen the weight
of the most common objections to the unity of the account of Saul's
rise and thus to encourage a reappraisal of the possibility of a more
holistic reading of the narrative. Before embarking on such a reappraisal, however, we shall need to consider, in the light of recent research, those features of the section 1 Sam 8-12 most often thought to
demonstrate its disunity.

Opposing Attitudes Towards the Monarchy

It was Julius Wellhausen who first gave prominence to the notion
that the biblical account of Saul's rise may be divided into at least two
versions.[16] His delineation of a favourable version comprising 9:1-
10:16 and ch. 11 (excluding vss. 12-14) and an unfavourable version
comprising chs. 7, 8, and 10:17-12:25[17] has provided the starting-point
for virtually all subsequent source-critical work in this area.
Wellhausen saw reflected in the two versions with their differing attitudes toward monarchy "den geistigen Abstand zweier Zeitalter".[18] The
unfavourable version, in which kingship is regarded as "nur eine tiefere
Stufe des Abfalls",[19] he associated with the exilic or post-exilic period,
explaining that such sentiments were unthinkable in Judah "solange das

---

[14] The quote is from p. 103 of his review of R. Rendtorff's *Das überlieferungsgeschichtliche Problem des Pentateuchs*.

[15] See below, p. 184.

[16] *Prolegomena*, 257-66; *Composition*, 243-46.

[17] Wellhausen included ch. 11 also in his unfavourable version, but
argued that it had been secondarily introduced; *Prolegomena*, 260; *Composition*, 244-45.

[18] *Prolegomena*, 263.

[19] *Prolegomena*, 264.

Reich Davids bestand".[20] The favourable version he placed in the pre-exilic period when, in his view, kingship was still regarded as "der Höhepunkt der Geschichte und die grösste Segnung Jahves".[21]

As pervasive as Wellhausen's analysis has been, both its attempt at a neat division of the text according to pro- or anti-monarchical tendencies and its assumption that anti-monarchical sentiments arose late in Israel have, especially in recent years, been subjected to review and revision. In the following we shall reconsider these two tenets of the Wellhausen position in the light of more recent studies.

Redating the Origins of Anti-monarchism in Israel

Wellhausen's contention that the origins of anti-monarchical feelings, whether in Israel or in Judah, are to be sought in the wake of the fall of the respective kingdoms has been strongly challenged by several recent studies, but criticism or qualification of the view is by no means a new phenomenon.[22] M. Noth, for example, while agreeing with Wellhausen that the anti-monarchical passages in 1 Samuel are to be assigned to the deuteronomist,[23] nevertheless recognized in Israel's comparative tardiness in introducing kingship "bestimmte Hemmungen" as to the legitimacy of kingship in Israel. The roots of these inhibitions, according to Noth, are to be sought in the pre-monarchic period.[24] Marking a more radical departure from Wellhausen, A. Weiser, in his book entitled *Samuel: Seine geschichtliche Aufgabe und religiöse Bedeutung*, argued that the sections under discussion are not anti-monarchical *per se* but give evidence of a debate, probably going back to the time of Saul himself, about the form which Israelite kingship should take.[25]

---

[20] *Composition*, 246. Wellhausen admits that the prophet Hosea exhibited similar misgivings about the worth of a human king, but argues that Hosea was writing in the north and had the fall of Samaria in mind.

[21] *Prolegomena*, 263.

[22] On early signs of dissatisfaction and the progressive abandonment of Wellhausen's position", cf. Langlamet, "Les récits", 168ff.

[23] *ÜSt*, 54-55.

[24] *Geschichte*, 152-53. In particular, Noth cited the Gideon episode as reflecting pre-monarchic sentiments, even if the literary formulation of the text was much later.

[25] Cf. Thornton, "Davidic Propaganda", 417ff.

Following Weiser's lead, M. Tsevat has argued that anti-monarchism in Israel and Judah did not arise under Hoseanic or Deuteronomic influence, as Wellhausen had asserted, but that such sentiments as are expressed in the assemblies preceding Saul's inauguration accurately reflect the social and religious "agitation" which must have accompanied so radical a change in the life of Israel.[26] On the question of influence, he concludes: "There exists, then, in the literature of the periods of the declining kingdoms of Israel and Judah or of the Babylonian exile no statement of opposition to the monarchy."[27] While one may not wish to be quite as bold as this in banishing all anti-monarchical sentiments from the later period, Tsevat's discussion does at least raise serious doubts as to the legitimacy of Wellhausen's late dating of the anti-monarchical material.[28]

In their opinion that opposition to the monarchy goes back to the time of Saul, Weiser, Tsevat and others have found a recent ally in the person of T. Ishida. In his discussion of "the ideological problems in the establishment of the monarchy in Israel",[29] Ishida argues that "since the tribes of Israel had formed their fundamental traditions in the pre-monarchical period", resistance to the institution of monarchy at the time of its inception is only what one should expect.[30] He agrees basically with the source critics that "a distinction must be made between the pro-monarchical and the anti-monarchical narratives, or the pro-Saul and anti-Saul narratives", but he refuses to press these into a chronological or geographical scheme: "It seems more likely that the delicate shades of political opinion expressed in each narrative are a measure of the dynamic development of political and social conditions. We can hardly expect a static situation in an age of such momentous change as was the period of the formation of the early Israelite monar-

---

[26] "Biblical Account", 84.

[27] "Biblical Account", 78. Cf. Weiser, *Samuel*, 27 n. 1, 34; Thornton, "Davidic Propaganda", 417.

[28] Veijola (*Königtum*) represents a more recent attempt to order chronologically the pro- and anti-monarchical tendencies in the Deuteronomistic History; he assigns the favourable material to his early historian, DtrG, the unfavourable to a later editor, DtrN. Yet notwithstanding, Veijola recognizes that it is hardly likely "dass der späte Redaktor DtrN sich seine königtumskritische Betrachtungsweise aus den Fingern gesogen hätte" (120).

[29] *Royal Dynasties*, 26ff.

[30] *Royal Dynasties*, 30.

chies."[31] Like others before him, Ishida rejects "the view that the anti-monarchical arguments in the biblical sources either stemmed from or were revived by those who suffered from the monarchy in its late period, such as the prophet Hosea or the Deuteronomist." Instead, it was at the time of Saul's election that opposition to the monarchy had to be overcome and, according to Ishida, the "anti-monarchical argument had been silenced by the time of David and Solomon (cf. II Sam 7 11 I Chron 17 10), and was never resumed."[32]

A year after Ishida's book appeared, F. Crüsemann's *Der Widerstand gegen das Königtum* was published. Crüsemann begins his study with the observation that, in one way or another, most OT passages that touch upon the issue of kingship — "Jahwist und Josephgeschichte, Aufstiegsgeschichte und Nathanverheißung, Deuteronomistisches und Chronistisches Geschichtswerk, Weisheit und Psalmen, die gesamte vorexilische Prophetie mit Ausnahme Hosea" — see in it "mindestens eine positive Chance, oft sehr viel mehr, nämlich eine grundlegende, heilvolle Setzung Jahwes." In starkest contrast to this prevailing view, according to Crüsemann, stand the radically anti-monarchical documents — Judg 8:22; 9:8-15; passages in 1 Sam 8 (and 12). These texts belong to the "ungelösten Rätseln des Alten Testamentes", and it is concern with the question of when and under what circumstances these texts originated that motivates and forms the focal point of Crüsemann's study.[33]

In a general sense, Crüsemann's conclusions, though arrived at independently, agree with those of Ishida — viz. both scholars maintain that the origins of anti-monarchism in Israel are to be sought earlier rather than later. But beyond this broad agreement, the hypotheses are quite different. Taking as his starting-point Vatke's dictum "daß die Ablehnung des Königtums die Kenntnis desselben voraussetzt und daß Jahwe nur König sein kann, wenn man bereits Erfahrungen mit dieser hat",[34] Crüsemann eliminates from the outset the pre-monarchical period as a possible point of origin of the anti-monarchical texts.[35] Nor is it likely, says Crüsemann, that anti-monarchical feelings would have

---

[31] *Royal Dynasties*, 30-31.

[32] *Royal Dynasties*, 183.

[33] *Widerstand*, 1-2.

[34] Crüsemann's summary of Vatke's position (*Widerstand*, 3).

[35] *Widerstand*, 4. Against this view, see Weinfeld's comments below.

arisen during the period of Philistine pressure under Saul.[36] Thus, in Crüsemann's view, the anti-monarchism exhibited in the biblical texts could only have arisen in the Davidic-Solomonic period. The period of national security following David's extensive military victories proved conducive to rapid expansion of the royal administration and the increased burdens which such expansion placed upon society gave rise to anti-monarchical polemic.[37]

In his detailed review of Crüsemann's book, M. Weinfeld concurs with Crüsemann's "basic hypothesis that the anti-monarchic trend took shape in the days of the United Kingdom." But he objects to the *terminus a quo* chosen by Crüsemann and asks whether there is "any reason not to believe that the ideological struggle over the legitimacy of the monarchy began when the monarchic idea first appeared in Israel, i.e., in the days of Gideon?"[38] Weinfeld thinks not, and both the biblical and the extra-biblical evidence, such as the anti-monarchical sentiments expressed in the Amarna letters,[39] lead him to the conclusion that, although the pro- and anti-monarchical traditions received their "literary crystallization" in the tenth century, "the ideological struggle they reflect had been in process since the time of Gideon and Saul."[40]

It seems clear, even from this selective survey of opinion, that Wellhausen's designation of the exilic or post-exilic period as the *terminus a quo* for anti-monarchical sentiment in Israel can no longer be maintained. But recognition of the possible early origins of anti-monarchism is no more than a first step in solving the problem of the opposing attitudes towards kingship which appear in the Saul narratives. It continues to be common in studies of 1 Sam 8-12 to refer to pro- and anti-monarchical traditions as if the distinction between them were clear-cut. But is this the case? We would argue that to speak of the pericopes in 1 Sam 8-12 as simply pro- or anti-monarchic is greatly to over-simplify the issue. What is needed is a more careful definition of terms.

---

[36] *Widerstand*, 124.

[37] *Widerstand*, 125.

[38] Review of Crüsemann's *Widerstand*, 104.

[39] See the bibliographic footnote, ibid., 105 n. 22.

[40] Review of Crüsemann's *Widerstand*, 104-105.

Defining terms

It seems an obvious point, but one that is often overlooked in discussions of monarchical attitudes in the Saul traditions, that to describe a text simply as opposed to monarchy is to indulge in a rather vague assertion. What exactly is it that is being opposed? Is it monarchy *per se*, or is it monarchy 'as the nations'? Is it the people's *request* for a king that is condemned, or do the passages reflect a bias against Saul? All these questions must be asked of each passage, and the answers in each case may vary. Various scholars have exhibited sensitivity to these issues,[41] and there are hopeful signs in recent studies that a more nuanced approach to the monarchical issue is being taken.[42]

Moreover, one must ask not only *what* is being opposed but also *whose viewpoint* is being expressed and in *what context*. In his recent article entitled "Viewpoints and Points of View in 1 Samuel 8-12", L. Eslinger draws upon the insights of modern "comparative literary theory, especially narrative theory" (63) in order to reassess the validity of the pro- and anti-monarchical criterion as a basis for distinguishing blocks of material in 1 Sam 8-12. He shows that greater sensitivity to "the simple question of who says what to whom reveals some interesting correlations between evaluation stances and characters" (65). A brief survey of the five 'scenes' in 1 Sam 8-12 reveals that "in every scene both pro- and anti-monarchic attitudes are expressed or displayed by a variety of characters" (67). Neither Samuel nor Yahweh shows himself to be anti-monarchical in an absolute sense.[43] "Rather, what Yahweh and Samuel are critical of is the anti-covenantal sentiment they

---

[41] Boecker, for example, in his attempt to defend a unitary Deuteronomistic History, considered by many to be jeopardized by the conflicting attitudes towards kingship in 1 Samuel, argues that the deuteronomists were not anti-monarchic as such, but were against that form of monarchy which put the king in the place of Yahweh as guarantor of deliverance from Israel's enemies (*Beurteilung*, 98-99).

[42] Both J. H. Hayes and W. E. Evans, for example, distinguish between attitudes towards the monarchy as such and attitudes towards Saul in the various strands of tradition, though with differing conclusions. Hayes ("Unsung Hero", 38) argues that the primary deuteronomistic material in 1 Sam 7-12 is critical of the monarchy in general, while the anti-Saul tendency is of much earlier origin. W. E. Evans ("Historical Reconstruction", 63), on the other hand, argues that the prophetic and deuteronomistic strands in Samuel are anti-Saul but not necessarily anti-monarchic.

[43] Eslinger regards Samuel's absolute opposition to a human king, expressed in ch. 8, as but an initial reaction which is soon overcome (66).

hear in Israel's request" for a king "like the nations" (66). In fact, Yahweh exhibits a "particular brand of pro-monarchism" in his willingness to institute "a monarchy that will remain subordinate to the theocracy" (66-67). The "omniscient narrator", who stands outside the narrated events and serves as a guide to the reader (who also stands outside), reveals himself to be "anti-renegade" as regards "transgressions of law and covenant" (65, 68) but maintains "a steadfast neutrality towards the subject of monarchy" (68).

Eslinger's basic contention is helpful. Before we can speak responsibly about pro- and anti-monarchic tendencies in 1 Sam 8-12, we must clarify the question. What is the object of promotion or opposition? Whose viewpoint is being expressed to whom? What is the context in which a viewpoint is expressed? On the latter point, we may recall that Tsevat, McCarthy, Childs and others have described an alternating (BABAB) pattern of negative and positive sections in 1 Sam 8-12.[44] The most interesting feature of this arrangement, in my opinion, is not simply the alternation between negative and positive sections, but the fact that the more negative elements consistently occur in the context of the assemblies. Perhaps this fact, rather than the presence of disparate sources, may best account for the differences in tone between the various sections. As Tsevat has pointed out, "Assemblies are held to voice opinions and counteropinions."[45] It is only logical that evaluative statements occur predominantly in these contexts.

Summary

The above discussion is not intended to give an exhaustive account of the debate regarding attitudes towards the monarchy in 1 Sam 8ff. It is hoped, however, that sufficient has been said to indicate how far modern scholarship has moved away from Wellhausen's 'classic' view that the chapters recounting Saul's rise can be divided up into sources and the sources assigned to different eras on the basis of conflicting attitudes within them. It may be deemed curious that the increasing abandonment of this major tenet of Wellhausen's analysis of 1 Sam 8ff. has not led to a renewal of interest in reading the narrative of Saul's rise as an integral whole. But while this may be due in part to the simple tenacity of a 'Wellhausen conclusion', it also doubtless reflects other

---

[44] See above, pp. 174-75.

[45] "Biblical Account", 83-84; cf. Lind, *Yahweh is a Warrior,* 100ff.

difficulties in the text, not the least of which is the fact that Saul seems to have come to power by a number of different routes. It is to this problem that we now turn.

Multiple Accessions or Stages in a Process?

In his 1941 article investigating the circumstances of Saul's rise to power, W. A. Irwin embraced the then, as now, common view that 1 Sam 11 reflects the "real circumstances" of Saul's rise.[46] But Irwin was troubled by the presence in the so-called early source of another episode, 9:1-10:16, purporting to describe Saul's election. "We are embarrassed", he wrote, "by our very wealth! Either account would suffice as an explanation of this revolutionary change in Hebrew history, to be given both baffles credence."[47] If Irwin was embarrassed by the surfeit of material in the 'early source' alone, how much greater would his embarrassment have been had he considered the 'late source' as well.[48] Indeed, despite its limited focus, Irwin's comment gives apt expression to a general feeling about the biblical account of Saul's rise which has persisted to the present day, viz. that several disparate and mutually exclusive accession accounts have been woven together in 1 Sam 8-12 and that the end product of this process of compilation does not present a credible, unified narrative continuum. H. Donner summarizes the current consensus as follows: "It is well-known that there are at least two narrative accounts of Saul's rise to the throne of Israel in the first book of Samuel.... They contradict each other: Saul could not have become king in both these ways."[49] Putting the matter even more plainly, J. Licht writes, "The account of Saul's elevation to kingship is, to the

---

[46] For a listing of proponents and opponents of this view, see Edelman, "Saul's Rescue", 195 n. 1.

[47] "Samuel", 117.

[48] Irwin ("Samuel", 113-14) omitted the 'late source' from his discussion of the historical origins of monarchy, espousing the common view that "the account in 10:17f. of the official choice and proclamation of Saul as king is part of the late and theologically determined document interwoven in this section of the book".

[49] "Old Testament Historiography", 43.

critically minded, rather unconvincing as a statement of fact. Literary analysis reveals that it is a tangle of textual elements."[50]

That 1 Sam 8-12 is composed of "textual elements" is beyond dispute, but whether it is correct to describe the composition as a "tangle" is an open question. Licht himself admits that the pericope "combines several sources about a single event into a plausible reconstruction of a political process."[51] But can we even be sure that the various episodes in 1 Sam 8-12 represent divergent accounts of a *single* event, or might we not instead think of *successive stages* in Saul's progress towards the throne? The latter notion would seem to be the intention of the final redaction. Weiser regards it as unmistakable, "daß der Sammler bemüht war, die einzelnen Überlieferungen in eine erzählerische und zeitliche Abfolge einzuordnen".[52] To be sure, Weiser takes a rather dim view of the collector's success,[53] but it is our contention that recent advances in understanding the ideological background of the accession process in Israel suggest that the time has come to reconsider the possibility that 1 Sam 8-12 presents a more coherent narrative sequence than has commonly been allowed.[54]

---

[50] "Biblical Historicism", 107.

[51] "Biblical Historicism", 108.

[52] *Samuel*, 47. Cf. R. P. Gordon's observation (*Samuel*, 40) that "the story of Saul's emergence as Israel's first king proceeds by a number of stages which may be summarized as: (i) a request for a king by the tribal elders of Israel (8:1-22); (ii) the private anointing of Saul (9:1-10:16); (iii) divine nomination and public presentation (10:17-27); (iv) military successes and public acclamation (11:1-15); (v) final speech by Samuel (12:1-25). On stylistic and other grounds it seems likely that different sources or traditions have been combined to form the present neatly-structured narrative."

[53] He writes, "daß diese Zusammenordnung der Stoffe jedoch nur sehr äußerlich und notdürftig gelungen ist, hat man längst erkannt.... Das scheinbare Nacheinander der Erzählungsreihe löst sich bei kritischer Betrachtung auf in ein Nebeneinander der Erzählungsstücke, die z. T., ohne zur Deckung zu kommen, einander parallel laufen, z. T. sich zeitlich und sachlich überschneiden oder ausschließen und es somit dem Historiker verwehren, entweder die ganze Erzählungsreihe oder auch nur den einen oder anderen Traditionskomplex in ein lückenloses Bild der Ereignisfolge zu transponieren" (*Samuel*, 47-48).

[54] Our focus in what follows is upon narrative — not historical — plausibility, which is a broader question. Of course, the two issues are not unrelated, inasmuch as incoherent and contradictory narrative does not easily yield to historical reconstruction. On the other hand, it is obvious that internal coherence in a narrative is no guarantee of historicity.

Halpern and the Accession Process in Israel

The year 1981 saw the appearance of two works by B. Halpern, both of which took as their goal the elucidation of the ideological and socio-political environment in which the first monarchy in Israel was instituted. The shorter work, "The Uneasy Compromise: Israel between League and Monarchy", is, by the author's own admission,[55] a "far more accessible" version of arguments that he develops in his book *The Constitution of the Monarchy in Israel*. In his book, Halpern sets himself two ambitious objectives: "first, to isolate the structure of the accession process in Israel, and to coordinate it with the sacral concepts that informed it; second, to isolate from the sacral realm the actual political processes by which the monarchy was governed."[56] The ease with which Halpern moves from ideological and historiographical data to historical reconstruction is at times disconcerting,[57] but since the concern of our own study is with the degree of literary and logical coherence in the biblical account of the founding of the monarchy, and not primarily with its historicity, we may still profit from Halpern's exploration of ideological aspects of kingship in Israel.

Of particular significance for our own study is Halpern's delineation of two (or, rather, three) stages in the process of accession in Israel, at least as this is reflected in Israel's historiography. These may be summarized as 1) divine designation, 2) victory and 3) confirmation.[58] Halpern discerns this basic pattern not only in the book of Judges,[59] which he regards as the "sole clear literary deposit" reflecting "the ideo-

---

[55] *Constitution*, ix.

[56] *Constitution*, xvii.

[57] He writes, for example, "The implication of the testimony in 1 Samuel, however, is that the ritual expectations — the expectations derived from a conception of mundane leadership as replicative of the Divine Warrior's — were translated at least at the outset of the monarchy into very hard reality. This testimony is credible" (*Constitution*, 174). For other such assertions, see *Constitution*, 123, 179, 184; *idem*, "Uneasy Compromise", 72-73. Cf. also P. R. Davies' criticisms in his review of Halpern's book.

[58] Halpern generally speaks of only two stages, (divine) designation and confirmation (cf. *Constitution*, 125ff., 173-74), but it is clear from his discussion that a victory, real or ritual, normally followed the designation and led to the confirmation (cf. "Uneasy Compromise", 72; *Constitution*, 95, 173-74). On the validity of distinguishing three stages, see also Edelman, "Saul's Rescue", 198 n. 9.

[59] *Constitution*, 111-123; "Uneasy Compromise", 67-73.

logical and historiographical background of the monarchic era",[60] but also in ancient Mesopotamian myth and ritual. He argues that mythical patterns, as in, for example, the Babylonian creation epic *Enuma Eliš* — in which Marduk is chosen by the divine assembly to confront Tiamat and, upon his victorious return, is enthroned — are often reflected in the ideology and ritual of royal accession.[61] Presuming that a similar correspondence between myth and ritual existed in Israel, Halpern argues that the conception of Yahweh as Divine Warrior strongly influenced the ideology of Israelite kingship.[62]

Although we shall find it necessary to disagree with parts of Halpern's analysis,[63] there seems to be no reason to dispute his contention that an ideology of mundane leadership, in which the accession process comprises several stages, is reflected in both the book of Judges and the early chapters of 1 Samuel. The notion that there is conceptual continuity between the book of Judges and the chapters in 1 Samuel dealing with Saul's rise is a common one,[64] and one that remains empirically valid (on a literary and historiographical level) regardless of how the respective origins and development of the two books are conceived. Halpern summarizes the conceptual affinities as follows:

> In this respect, then, kingship arose in Israel in continuity with the traditions and theological conceptions of the pre-monarchic league. Like the savior-judge, the king-elect was designated by Yhwh. Like the savior-judge, he proved his "charisma" by defeating a

---

[60] "Uneasy Compromise", 67.

[61] *Constitution*, 51-61; "Uneasy Compromise", 68. On the broader issue of the impact of mythical and ideological paradigms upon history and historiography he writes, "such paradigms become powerful vehicles for historians and those who characterize contemporary event [*sic*] by them, and for directing actors themselves in the historical drama" (*Constitution*, xviii, cf. xxi).

[62] He writes, for example, "This [the Divine Warrior] pattern, attested as a type in cultures other than Israel's..., underlies much of Israelite historiography and theology. It is hardly the only ideological structure present; but it does inform, however deep the level, a vast variety of texts reflecting theological, religious, and cultural orientation, from the early (Ex 15) to the Exilic (Zech 1-6) eras. Together with the Mesopotamian parallels adduced above, and the intrinsic evidence of the texts themselves, the permeation of biblical literature by this pattern justifies the differentiation of the accession process into the stages of (divine) designation and confirmation" (*Constitution*, 125; cf. 61, 107-08, 147-48).

[63] See our discussion of his two-source theory below, pp. 190-93.

[64] See our discussion in Ch. 2, pp. 60-62.

foe. And, like the savior-judge as Israel's tradition recalled him, he assumed power thereafter permanently.
The narratives of Saul's rise represent historiographic
implementations of the pattern for a leader's accession.[65]

Having described the pattern of accession which seems to be operative in the literature pertaining to the inauguration of monarchy in
Israel, Halpern takes up the question of how this pattern is reflected in
the account of Saul's rise, 1 Sam 8-14.[66] His investigation leads him
to the conclusion that these chapters exhibit two exemplars of the
accession pattern described above. These in turn are indicative of two
sources — "A" (9:1-10:16; 13-14) and "B" (8; 10:17-27; 11; 12). We
shall return to Halpern's source theory below, but before doing so we
should mention a yet more recent study which offers a somewhat different analysis of the accession process in 1 Samuel.

Edelman and the Structure of 1 Sam 9-11

A simpler and in some respects more plausible analysis than
Halpern's source theory has been proposed recently by D. Edelman in
her article entitled "Saul's Rescue of Jabesh-Gilead (I Sam 11 1-11):
Sorting Story from History". Challenging the prevailing opinion that
1 Sam 11:1-11 preserves "the historical incident which led to Saul's elevation to kingship", Edelman contends that the Jabesh-Gileadite rescue
functions literarily[67] as a constituent element in the accession process.
In her view, "chs. 9-11 form a sort of core unit which has been framed
by discussions about kingship [chs. 8 and 12]". Within this core unit
"the three-part process of designation, battle, and confirmation" can be
identified.[68] 1 Sam 11:1-11 functions as the middle stage in this accession process. Edelman characterizes this as the "testing" stage — only
after Saul has stood the test can the "final coronation stage of the kingship process" take place (11:14-15).[69]

---

[65] "Uneasy Compromise", 72-73.

[66] *Composition*, 149-74; "Uneasy Compromise", 69-70.

[67] For an evaluation of Edelman's reasons for viewing ch. 11 as of
little historical value, see Ch. 7, pp. 230-31.

[68] "Saul's Rescue", 198. Cf. Knierim ("Messianic Concept", 40-41)
on the structure of "messianic theology" in which "sign" and "test" are not
identical.

[69] "Saul's Rescue", 199.

Thus, according to Edelman, 1 Sam 9-11 represents a carefully constructed narrative — a view which the author defends in part by pointing out the deficiencies of alternative hypotheses. Especially noteworthy are her comments regarding what we might term the 'local versions' hypothesis, as represented, for example, in the work of H. W. Hertzberg. According to Hertzberg's theory, three distinct versions of the founding of the monarchy, each exhibiting a two-fold pattern of designation and acclamation, "have been placed side by side to give a composite picture of this important event".[70] Edelman initiates her criticism of this theory with the general observation that it "fails to account for the way in which the person responsible for the sequence of chs. 9-11 carefully selected and arranged his material." But beyond this general objection, there are also specific failings.

Edelman notes, for example, that the section 10:17-27 seems an unlikely candidate for an independent tradition. It recounts only Saul's designation as "king-elect" but makes no reference to his coronation. Thus, it "appears to augment the discussion of the first stage of the process of installing the king" and to look forward to the coronation in 11:14-15.[71] A further difficulty has to do with the apparent traditio-historical complexity of the section. Edelman rightly recognizes that 10:7 implies some form of military accomplishment[72] which would function as "a 'testing' of Saul, after the designatory stages of anointing (10 1) and the reception of the divine spirit (10 6)." She perceives that, in fact, 10:7 points forward to the capture of "Gibeah" (Geba?) in ch. 13 and, following the lead of others before her,[73] she allows that there may have been an original connection between the two passages.[74] Of a possible relationship between 10:7 and 10:8 or of the obvious one between 10:8 and 13:8, Edelman has little to say; she notes only that "instead of 'testing' comes an order to assemble at Gilgal, which points forward to the site of the final coronation (10 7 [sic][75])." The point that

---

[70] Hertzberg links the three versions with three different centres — Ramah (9:1-10:16), Mizpah (10:17-27), and Gilgal (11:1-12:25).

[71] "Saul's Rescue", 200-02.

[72] Cf. Ch. 2, pp. 51-55.

[73] I.e. Miller, "Saul's Rise", 162; Mettinger, *King and Messiah,* 97; and we might add Stoebe, "Zur Topographie", esp. 277-80. All three recognize some connection between 1 Sam 10 and 1 Sam 13, and seek to explain it in traditio-historical terms.

[74] Cf. our discussions in Ch. 2 and below in this chapter.

[75] Read 10:8.

Edelman appears to be making in all this is that more seems to be involved in the section than a mere juxtaposition of self-contained narratives.

In this judgement, Edelman is doubtless correct, as a survey of the numerous links between the various episodes would confirm.[76] It is our contention, however, that the points she raises pose difficulties for her own interpretation as well. As far as the text before us is concerned, it is true that Saul's Ammonite victory functions as the "test" which, once completed, opens the door to Saul's final coronation. But it is equally true, as Edelman's own comments reveal, that the Ammonite threat is not that which is envisaged in the account of Saul's commission.[77] The author's attempt to get round this problem by postulating an earlier level of tradition in which chs. 10 and 13 were more closely connected does not ultimately alleviate the problem. For, given the freedom which she accords her hypothetical redactor to rearrange and modify the traditions,[78] it is indeed surprising that such an inconsistency should have been allowed to survive. Surely the anomaly could have been avoided either by relocating the Ammonite battle in the sequence[79] or by simply making the Ammonite threat the focus of Saul's commission.

Summary

The studies discussed above have gone a long way towards undermining the common view that 1 Sam 9ff. contains multiple accounts of Saul's accession and therefore cannot in any sense be read as a coherent and logical narrative sequence. Recognition of the existence of an accession process in Israelite ideology and historiography has shed new light on the story of Saul's rise and has opened the door to a greater appreciation of the interrelationship of the various episodes in 1 Sam 9-11

---

[76] Some of these will be highlighted below, pp. 190-91, 218-28.

[77] This point has already been made in Ch. 2, pp. 51-54.

[78] She contends, for example, that ch. 11 originally reported an incident which took place after Saul began to reign as king, but was reworked to portray Saul as a judge prior to his inauguration ("Saul's Rescue", 203).

[79] Cf. the historical reconstructions suggested by Seebass ("Vorgeschichte", 166-67), who places the Ammonite victory before the anointing, and Mettinger (*King and Messiah*, 97), who locates Saul's first Philistine encounter prior to the Ammonite affair.

within an overarching structure comprising designation, demonstration and confirmation. A major impediment to a synchronic reading of Saul's rise remains, however, and that is the wide narrative gap between Saul's commission in ch. 10, with its clear focus upon the Philistine menace, and its sequel in the Philistine battle of chs. 13-14. It is to this final difficulty that we now turn our attention.

The Problem of the Gap Between 10:5-8 and 13:3ff.

We have mentioned above several attempts to resolve, along traditio-historical lines, the difficulty of the awkward narrative gap between Saul's commission in ch. 10 and its qualified fulfilment in ch. 13. While there is little unanimity in matters of detail among scholars who adopt the traditio-historical approach, there is at least a broad consensus that the way to begin seeking a solution is to assume that Saul's commission was originally followed by an account of some act of defiance against the Philistines — either that which is now recorded in ch. 13 or some other. The difficulty of this approach, as we have suggested already, is that it must assume that a real tension in the tradition has gone unattended, despite the assumed freedom of tradents to alter the order or indeed the details of the tradition so as to make sense of it. The matter would be simpler, of course, if we were to assume that the redactors responsible for the final form of the text had freedom only to arrange their materials but not to alter them in any significant details. Such a premise is more characteristic of source-critical than of traditio-historical approaches, and it is not surprising that Halpern has recently attempted to resolve the difficulty in terms of a new theory of sources in 1 Sam 8ff.

Halpern's most significant innovation is his reallocation of ch. 11 in what is commonly, if mistakenly, regarded as the anti-monarchical source. In support of his contention that ch. 11 belongs with his "B" source, Halpern offers several arguments in addition to the obvious link between 10:27 and 11:12-13.[80] There is, for example, the fact that Saul is not properly introduced in ch. 11. Halpern looks to 10:20-21 to fulfil this need, though the obvious place to seek Saul's formal intro-

---

[80] *Constitution*, 155ff. On the extent of Halpern's "B" source, see the next paragraph.

duction, were it not for source theories such as Halpern's, is 9:1-2. He also notes that 11:4 assumes Gibeah to be Saul's home town, though this fact is explicitly stated only in 10:26. Finally, Halpern finds odd "the notion that any bucolic butcher could assemble the league army of Israel, then lead it into battle.... The savior-judges, by contrast, held their position through Yhwh's or the league's pleasure (Judg 3:15b; 4:4-6; 6:24/25, 34-40; 11:1-11)." Looking in the other direction, Halpern also seeks to establish a link between ch. 11 and ch. 12.[81] In addition to the explicit reference to the Ammonite affair in 12:12, there is the fact that "Samuel's address and pronouncement of the potential curse and blessing on the king and people presumes some such setting as that provided by the renewal, or confirmation, of the kingship of Saul in 11:14-15." Taken together, these arguments constitute a reasonably strong case for asserting an original link between ch. 11 and ch. 10, on the one hand, and between chs. 11 and 12, on the other — unless, of course, it can be demonstrated on empirical (and not simply presuppositional) grounds that the links are merely redactional.

Having established links between ch. 11 and the episodes which precede and succeed it, Halpern is in a position to distinguish two sources in the account of Saul's rise — an "A" source comprising 9:1-10:16 and chs. 13-14 and a "B" source comprising 8; 10:17-27; 11; 12. Halpern divides his sources not by appealing to the pro- and anti-monarchical argument, which he regards as circular, but solely on the basis of the presence of doublets in the account. In his putative "A" and "B" sources, he believes to have discovered two complete exemplars of the pattern of accession. The specifics of Halpern's analysis may be summarized in the following chart:

	"A"	"B"
Designation (and some form of acclamation)	9:22-24; 10:1	10:21-24
Victory	10:9-11; 13:2-4; chs. 13-14	11:1-11
Rule	14:47-52	11:14-15; ch. 12[82]

---

[81] *Constitution*, 157-58.
[82] Cf. "Uneasy Compromise", 70.

While in a very general sense, Halpern may have succeeded in describing certain points of comparison between his hypothetical sources, it is hardly correct to speak of "a thorough structural congruence" between them.[83] Is it legitimate, for example, to speak of an acclamation in the "A" source? Does Halpern regard 9:22-24 as fulfilling this role? Moreover, does it not seem that 13:2ff. presupposes some such event as that recorded in ch. 11?[84] By ch. 13 Saul already has at his disposal the beginnings of a standing army, and his son Jonathan is already installed as a subordinate commander. This situation is incongruous with the idea that ch. 13 recounts the immediate sequel to Saul's anointing and commission. By the same token, if we assume an "A" source in which ch. 13 followed immediately upon 9:1-10:16, the fact that Jonathan is credited with smiting the Philistine garrison becomes even more inexplicable.

It is questionable, in fact, whether Halpern would have arrived at his two-source theory, had he not regarded division of sources as the "first step in investigating Saul's election".[85] As we have noted above, Edelman's appraisal of 1 Sam 9-11 as a "core unit" within the account of Saul's rise demonstrates that other interpretations are possible — unless, of course, there are compelling reasons to separate 9:1-10:16 from its present context. In this latter regard, Halpern makes the following observations:

> In effect, 1 Sam 9:1-10:16 see Saul's appointment as standing in continuity with the history of the "judges." Saul arises to deal with a particular problem — the Philistine "oppression" (9:16; 10:1, reading with OG). By contrast, 1 Sam 8:7-8; 10:18-19 see this as a moment to recapitulate. It is the end of an era, the inception of a new relationship between Israel and her god. The very notion that kingship implies a rejection of god is incompatible with the idea (in 1 Sam 9:1-10:16) that Yhwh inspired the constitutional change.[86]

As regards Halpern's first point, it is difficult to see why Saul's appointment should not reflect elements of continuity with the judges tradition while at the same time marking the end of one era and the in-

---

83 "Uneasy Compromise", 70.
84 So Irwin, "Samuel", 114.
85 "Uneasy Compromise", 63.
86 "Uneasy Compromise", 65.

auguration of another. Clearly, ch. 11 — at the heart of Halpern's "B" source — also exhibits points of continuity with the judges tradition. As to his second point, Halpern himself suggests the answer; he rightly recognizes that in 9:1-10:16 "kingship is not the issue: it is, rather, a premise."[87] But in view of the magnitude of the change which the institution of monarchy represents, does not the fact that by ch. 9 kingship is already presupposed imply that deliberations and debate, such as are recorded in ch. 8, must have preceded?

On close inspection, Halpern's reasons for divorcing 9:1-10:16 from its narrative context prove unconvincing. What is more, the elimination of 9:1-10:16 from the narrative sequence 1 Sam 8ff. poses certain difficulties of its own. For instance, 8:22 records that after receiving Yahweh's instructions to appoint for the people a king, Samuel dismissed the men of Israel, each to his city. If Halpern is correct that ch. 8 links directly with 10:17ff., why did Samuel have to convene a "second convention" to select Saul by "sortition"?[88] Might not Samuel's delay be indicative that intermediate steps, such as designation (the anointing episode) and demonstration, were envisaged? There is, in fact, some evidence that 10:17ff. presupposes the anointing episode. Though our lack of knowledge regarding the lot-casting procedure precludes certainty, the fact that Saul is found hiding (10:22) suggests that he anticipated the outcome.

Conclusion

It should by now be clear that research into the biblical account of Saul's rise is in a period of ferment. There is widespread dissatisfaction with the two main criteria used in the past to distinguish sources. Various studies are adopting a more nuanced approach to the issue of differing monarchical attitudes in the traditions of Saul's rise. Recognition that the accession process, at least as it is represented in Hebrew historiography, comprised several stages is undermining the oft-repeated argument that "Saul could not have come to power in so many ways". The time has come to look afresh at the historiographical account of Saul's early phase, drawing upon the valid insights of earlier

---

[87] "Uneasy Compromise", 70.
[88] "Uneasy Compromise", 69.

generations, but untrammelled by foregone conclusions. The studies by Halpern and Edelman are indicative of such new approaches. Edelman's major contribution has been to demonstrate that 1 Sam 9-11 functions as a core unit within the larger context of Saul's rise. A major weakness of her approach, however, is that it does not adequately account for the fact that Saul's commission (10:5ff.) focuses upon the Philistines, not the Ammonites. Halpern recognizes the link between Saul's commission and its apparent fulfilment in ch. 13 and, like various others before him, assumes that an account of some act of hostility against the Philistines must originally have followed immediately upon his commission. There is a further possibility, however, which, to the best of the present writer's knowledge, has not yet been considered, viz., that the expectation aroused in the account of Saul's anointing and commission remains only that — an unfulfilled expectation. Might it not be that the long delay in fulfilling the reader's expectation and, indeed, the fact that it is Jonathan who at last takes the lead are significant for our understanding of the narrative portrayal of Saul in his early phase? In the following we shall attempt a reading of the account of Saul's rise in the light of this possibility.

7

TOWARD AN INTEGRATED READING OF SAUL'S RISE, WITH SPECIAL ATTENTION TO THE PORTRAYAL OF SAUL

Introduction

In the preceding chapter, we discussed several issues thought to constitute major obstacles to a coherent, sequential reading of the biblical account of Saul's rise. We saw how recent studies have tended to undermine the foundations of these obstacles and have opened the door to a more holistic or synchronic reading of 1 Sam 9-11.[1] We are encouraged by these results to look for a consistent and coherent portrait of Saul within the chapters recounting his early career. There yet remain, however, various tensions and difficulties of more limited scope and magnitude which if unresolved might, nevertheless, undermine an attempt at a holistic reading. Our aim in the following pages is, therefore, two-fold: 1) to evaluate those specific points of tension most frequently cited as evidence of disunity within or discontinuity between the various episodes which constitute Saul's rise; and 2) to test the conclusions drawn in Part Two, regarding the causes of Saul's rejection in 1 Sam 13-15, against the portrait of Saul which emerges in the earlier chapters recounting his rise. In keeping with these objectives, we shall focus upon those chapters in which Saul actually appears, viz. chs. 9-11, though this is not to deny the relationship that exists between these chapters and, on the one hand, ch. 8, in which the issue of kingship is introduced by the people's request, and, on the other, ch. 12, in which the monarchic era is introduced by Samuel's description of what kind of

---

[1] After the preceding chapter was completed and while the present chapter was in the final stages of preparation, there appeared L. Eslinger's *Kingship of God in Crisis*, in which the author attempts a synchronic reading of 1 Sam 1-12 in its entirety. For practical reasons, interaction with Eslinger's views will be largely limited to the footnotes.

kingship is acceptable in Israel. It is not our intention to attempt a 'close reading' *per se* of the entire section but rather to concentrate on those aspects of chs. 9-11 felt to be of significance either for the issue of narrative coherence and continuity or for the issue of Saul's rejection.

1 Samuel 9:1-10:16

Anonymous Seer or Samuel in 9:1-10:16?

A much discussed issue with respect to 1 Sam 9 concerns the fact that the "man of God" or "seer", who in the early verses of the chapter remains anonymous, is in the later verses (vv. 14ff.) explicitly identified as Samuel. The most common explanation of this state of affairs is that two originally independent sources or traditions have been combined. Hertzberg, for example, postulates "zwei Vorstufen" of the present narrative and associates these with two different localities. Though he admits that the two traditions have now been brought together in a "schönen und erfreuenden Weise" and can no longer be separated by literary critical means, he nevertheless continues to distinguish between a tradition in which Saul goes seeking the lost asses, encounters a village seer, and is promised a kingdom, and one in which Saul encounters Samuel and is anointed.[2] Recent scholarship, however, has increasingly drawn attention to the significance of the *process of discovery* in the narrative. Langlamet, for example, remarks, "L'auteur [of 1 Sam 9] sait ménager l'intérêt, préparer la surprise d'un dénouement inattendu."[3] More specifically, Birch writes,

> It would be in keeping with the dramatic flair of the tale if the author intended to give the impression that Saul was seeking out a local seer for advice when, much to the surprise and delight of the reader (or listener?), as Saul is entering the city it is Samuel who comes out to meet him. V. 18 shows that Saul does not recognize him, but he is only a youth.[4]

---

[2] Hertzberg, 59/ET 79. Cf. Seebass, "Vorgeschichte", 157-64; Mettinger, *King and Messiah*, 64-79, 88-89. For opposing views, see Wentz, *Monarchy*, 175-78; Willis, "Cultic Elements", 49.

[3] "Les récits", 173.

[4] Birch, *Rise*, 34-35 (=*idem*, "Development", 60), cf. 135.

Similarly, McCarter writes,

> Saul, the hero and the only figure with whom the account
> is really concerned is innocently blind to the reality be-
> hind the appearance. The process of discovery that he
> undergoes, his growth from simplicity to awareness, is
> shared by the audience, and thus the story finds its inter-
> est.[5]

A. D. H. Mayes has contested the notion that the masking of the
identity of the seer in the early part of the narrative is a "dramatic device
in which the naming of Samuel is a high point of the story". He states
two objections:

> ...in the first place, the climactic point of the story has
> not yet been reached; and, secondly, had Samuel been in-
> tended from the beginning, it is most unlikely that he
> would have been first described as a local seer from an
> anonymous village in the "land of Zuph" who was paid
> for his services.[6]

Taking Mayes' second point first, it should be observed that it is
by no means certain that the seer is depicted as a "local" seer — indeed,
there may be hints of a circuit[7] — or that Saul's concern with bringing
the seer a gift necessarily implies that the seer would have required
payment.[8] Moreover, the anonymity of the village might simply be a
necessary corollary to the anonymity of the seer. Of more weight is
Mayes' first point — that the climax of the story has not yet been
reached. The unveiling of Samuel in v. 14 may, of course, represent *a*
(not *the*) climactic moment, but we would suggest that Mayes'
observation nonetheless calls for the following modification of the
common understanding of the dramatic device.

While it is true that the narrative allows the reader or listener to
share *to some extent* in Saul's process of discovery, close attention to
the text suggests that it is *Saul's* ignorance, not that of the reader, that
is the real point at issue. In fact, the reader is explicitly informed of the

---

[5] McCarter, 185. Cf. also Gordon, *Samuel*, 45; Halpern, *Constitution*, 1 n. 1; *idem*, "Compromise", 65 n. 21.

[6] Mayes, "Rise", 13.

[7] See below, p. 198.

[8] See below, p. 201 and nn. 25, 26.

seer's identity (9:14) several verses *before* the climactic moment when Saul, standing before Samuel and asking him directions to the seer's house, is informed by Samuel that he is the seer (v. 18)![9] And even prior to the disclosure of v. 14, the attentive reader is provided with numerous hints that the anonymous man of God is, in fact, Samuel. First, the arrival of Saul and his servant in the "land of Zuph" (v. 5) recalls Samuel's genealogy in 1 Sam 1:1 ("There was a certain man from Ramathaim, a Zuphite...").[10]   Secondly, the servant's comment concerning the man of God — that "everything he says comes true" (v. 6) — may be compared with 1 Sam 3:19: "As Samuel grew, Yahweh was with him, and he let none of his words fall to the ground".[11]   Thirdly, the remark in v. 12 that the seer had just arrived in town for a sacrifice may suggest a circuit such as that described for Samuel in 7:16-17.[12] Finally, there may be evidence that "not just the explanatory note in 9:9 but the whole of 9:5-10 is concerned with the nomenclature of prophecy".[13] Curtis, for example, has suggested that Saul's question in 9:7, מַה־נָּבִיא לָאִישׁ, reflects a folk etymology of the word "prophet", נָבִיא.[14] More recently, Shaviv has contested this notion of a folk etymology in 9:7 and has argued rather that what is involved is a "word-play developed in many different directions".[15] Despite their differences, both Curtis and Shaviv would probably agree that even before the unmasking in 9:14, the בא/נביא resonances provide a veiled reference to Samuel, who was confirmed as a prophet in 3:20.

Thus, the anonymity of the "man of God" or "seer" in the early verses of 1 Sam 9 and his later unveiling as Samuel need not indicate distinct traditions but can satisfactorily be explained as a dramatic literary device whereby the reader is allowed to share Saul's process of dis-

---

[9] In contrast to vv. 11-14, where third person plural pronouns dominate, the servant finds no mention in v. 18, and the focus at the climactic moment is entirely upon Saul.

[10] צוּפִים of MT should probably read צוּפִי, the ם having arisen through dittography of the following מ; so Driver, 1; Stoebe, 89; McCarter, 51.

[11] On this point, see Gordon (*Samuel*, 45) who compares בּוֹא יָבוֹא of 9:6 with Deut 18:22 where the test of genuine prophecy is that it "comes true".

[12] As Smelik (*Saul*, 104) observes, this insight neatly resolves the apparent discrepancy between vv. 6 and 12.

[13] So Gordon (*Samuel*, 45).

[14] "Etymology", 491-93.

[15] "*nābî'* and *nāgîd* ", 110.

covery, or, more properly, to *observe* it. We shall have more to say on this point below.

The Portrait of Saul in 9:1-10:16

Saul's Introduction

In its present context, 1 Samuel 9 opens with an air of expectancy. The words of divine concession which brought the Ramah assembly to a close are still ringing in the ears: "Listen to their voice, and appoint them a king" (8:22a). Samuel's initial response to Yahweh's order had been simply to dismiss the men of Israel, each to his city (8:22b). Apparently there was no question of electing a king on the spot, by sortition or otherwise.[16] Thus, the pressing questions as ch. 9 opens are: Who will be king? And how and when will he be chosen? With the introduction of Saul in 9:1-2 as a "choice[17] and handsome [man]" (בחור וטוב), a man of incomparable stature and the son of a גבור חיל, there would seem to be little doubt about the direction the narrative is taking.

The traditional assessment of the portrayal of Saul in this first episode is well represented by the following words of P. K. McCarter:

> Saul makes his first appearance in the Bible as an agreeable young man, motivated only by a sense of family duty, unassuming, deferential, and, as far as we can see, without high ambition.[18]

Birch rightly observes that the focus of the section "seems to be more on God's calling of Saul than on Saul himself", but he nonetheless continues to view the section as positive towards Saul.[19]

---

[16] For a possible explanation of this delay, see Ch. 6, p. 193. Most recently, Eslinger (*Kingship*, 282) has interpreted Samuel's dismissal of the people as an "inability to follow orders" — "Samuel does not immediately make the king because he does not know what kind of king Yahweh has in mind, and he refuses to make the kind of king that the people have in mind". One weakness in this interpretation is the fact that no time-scale for the king-making is specified in the text (in contrast, for example, to 10:7 where Saul is charged to do what his hand finds to do "when these signs have come upon you").

[17] For a defence of this rendering of בחור, see p. 204 below.

[18] McCarter, 184.

[19] "Development", 68.

Although there is a degree of truth in the view espoused by Mc-
Carter and others, the section is not "so frankly pro-Saulist"[20] as is often assumed. From the very beginning of the account of Saul's rise,
the narrative contains hints of deficiencies in Saul which will ultimately lead to his undoing. Not even the introductory verses are free of
a "discordant subtone", as W. L. Humphreys has observed. He writes:

> ...while it is similar to notes about David and Joseph (1
> Sam 16:18; Gen 39), 1 Sam 9:1-2 corresponds most
> closely to words about another doomed potential king,
> namely Absalom (2 Sam 14:25-6). Attention is called to
> the striking physical appearance of Saul and Absalom,
> but, unlike the notes of David and Joseph, their other
> abilities are not detailed, and of neither Saul nor Absa-
> lom is it said that "Yahweh was with him" (cf. 1 Sam
> 16:18; Gen 39:2, 3, etc.). Thus in the introductory no-
> tice Saul appears as a figure of heroic potential, but a
> subtone of uncertainty as to the direction this potential
> will take resonates in the background.[21]

Saul and His Servant

Apart from the allusions to Saul's heroic proportions, the episode
begins inauspiciously. Kish's she-asses have strayed, and Saul is instructed to take a servant and go find them (v. 3). Several days[22] of
searching prove fruitless (v. 4), and when Saul and his servant come to
the land of Zuph (צוּף), Saul proposes to abandon the search, "lest my
father stop [worrying] about the asses and become worried about us" (v.
5). Saul's concern for his father is not unfounded (cf. 10:2), but the
servant, apparently less ready to accept defeat than his master, entreats

---

20 So Irwin, "Samuel", 127.

21 "Tragedy", 20. Humphreys is not the first to have noted the correspondence between Saul and Absalom and their exclusively outward descriptions; Ginzberg (*Legends*, 6:238 n. 80) cites the view in early Jewish tradition "that Saul and Absalom possessed beauty of body but not of soul".
Josephus (*Ant.* VI.45) seeks to redress the balance in Saul's description by
adding a reference to gifts of spirit and mind surpassing his outward qualities, but this addition merely emphasizes the lack of such reference in the
original text.

22 Cf. 9:20, where Samuel refers to the loss of the asses three days
before.

Saul to try one more thing: "Look (הִנֵּה־נָא)![23] There is a man of God in this city, and the man is held in honour. All that he says surely comes to pass. So let us go there! Perhaps he will advise us about our journey which we have undertaken" (v. 6). At first, Saul has misgivings: "Look (וְהִנֵּה), if we do go,[24] what shall we bring the man? For the bread in our sacks is gone, and there is no gift[25] to bring the man of God. What do we have?" (v. 7).[26] Again the servant persists, as the Hebrew seems to stress (וַיֹּסֶף הַנַּעַר לַעֲנוֹת), and offers a solution: "Look, I find in my hand[27] a quarter shekel of silver, and I will give it to the man of God that he may advise us about our journey" (v. 8).

---

[23] For the use of this expression to introduce entreaties or requests, cf. Gen 12:11; 16:2; 18:27; 1 Sam 15:15-16; 2 Sam 13:24; 1 Kgs 20:31; etc. A dynamic equivalent in English might be "Listen!"

[24] On the use of וְהִנֵּה to introduce a protasis carrying the approximate force of "an emphatic conditional clause" (so McCarter, 176), cf. GK §159w[1] and the cross-references cited by Stoebe, 194.

[25] The derivation and meaning of the *hapax legomenon* תְּשׁוּרָה, here translated "gift", has been a matter of considerable discussion. S. M. Paul ("Interview Fee", 542-43) has revived the view of medieval commentator Menahem ben Saruq that תְּשׁוּרָה is derived from the root שׁר (or, more properly, שׁוּר) "to see" and thus connotes "the fee of seeing [i.e., having an interview]". Paul finds support for this explanation in what appears to be an Akkadian semantic equivalent, *namurtu/tamartu* "gift", which is derived from *amaru* "to see", and which J. N. Postgate has defined as "an 'audience fee' — a payment made by the king's subjects whenever they came to him for a favor or some kind of help" (quoted by Paul, "Interview Fee", 543).

[26] Josephus (*Ant.* VI.48) assumes that Saul's question exhibits ignorance of the fact that the prophet would accept no reward. Our text, however, is silent on this matter, for there is no mention of payment when Saul meets Samuel. It is clear that the literary prophets disdained those who prophesied for payment: Amos denies being such a prophet (Amos 7: 12; cf. Curtis, "Etymology", 492); and Micah explicitly condemns prophets who divine for money (Mic 3:5, 11; cf. also Ezek 22:25; Jer 6:13; 8:10; 14:18). The attitude of pre-literary Yahwistic prophecy, however, is less clear. There are a number of references to goods being sent or offered in return for prophetic favours (1 Kgs 13:7-9; 14:3; 2 Kgs 4:42; 5:15ff.; 8:8), but the only indication of tribute actually being accepted is in 2 Kgs 4:42, where Elisha does not benefit personally but, to the apparent consternation of his 'attendant' (מְשָׁרְתוֹ), orders that the twenty loaves of barley and ears of grain be set before the people to eat. In 1 Kgs 14:3 and in 2 Kgs 8:8 the prophecy given is decidedly negative, or indeed misleading, while in 1 Kgs 13:7-9 and 2 Kgs 5:15ff. payment is explicitly refused. Thus, we would conclude that there is no firm biblical evidence that pre-literary, Yahwistic prophetic attitudes towards payment for services differed from those of the literary prophets (contra Curtis, "Etymology", 492).

[27] Lit. נִמְצָא בְיָדִי, "there is found in my hand".

This answer seems to satisfy Saul, and he responds, "What you say is good. Come, let's go" (v. 10).

The quarter shekel of silver is not mentioned again in the narrative, and, in view of the general sparsity of extraneous descriptive detail in Hebrew narrative, the reader is encouraged to inquire as to the possible significance of the brief dialogue between Saul and his servant. McCarter has noted how adventitiously the money simply turns up in the servant's hand,[28] and has seen in this "a clue to the providential direction of the entire adventure."[29] A further significance of the incident may be implied by the fact that it is in the *servant's* hand that the money is found. This point of detail reinforces a growing impression throughout these early verses that it is the servant who is taking the lead. It is he who first mentions the existence of the man of God, it is he who persists when Saul raises a practical objection, and it is he who not only suggests a solution but offers to execute it as well: "There is found in *my* hand a quarter shekel of silver, and *I* will give it[30] to the man of God" (v. 8). In short, it is the servant who initiates and facilitates movement towards Samuel. By contrast, Saul appears hesitant, passive, tending even to impede rather than further the action. At the same time, there is nothing to suggest that Saul is somehow acting in bad faith — he does eventually concede the wisdom of the servant's suggestion — but there is a certain misguidedness about Saul's actions when compared with those of the servant. It is the latter's initiative and persistence that keep the action moving in the providentially appointed direction.

The contrast between the activity of the servant and the passivity of Saul is suggestive of the similar contrast between Saul and Jonathan found in 1 Sam 13-14. In our investigation of those chapters, we noted

---

[28] He notes (176) the use of the expression נמצא ביד in preference to the more common יש לי.

[29] McCarter, 185; cf. 176.

[30] MT ונתתי. Since Thenius' description of the reading attested in LXX, και δωσεις (= ונתתה), as "unstreitig am Passendsten..., indem der Herr und nicht der Diener in dieser Angelegenheit zu handeln hat" (42), most commentators have preferred LXX (cf. Budde, 61; Driver, 71; McCarter, 168-69; Klein, 81-82). It seems likely, however, that the reading in LXX, as indeed the variant readings of other versions (e.g., Vulg. and some Targ. witnesses attest 1st pers. pl. ונתן), represent modifications "aus inhaltlicher Bedenklichkeit" (so Stoebe, 194). Moreover, we shall argue below that the initiative of the servant, as indicated in MT, is a significant feature in the scene.

that Jonathan characteristically takes the initiative and is the primary agent of deliverance, while Saul remains largely passive, his few interventions tending only to diminish the success of the campaign. It is noteworthy that even in the earliest episode of Saul's rise, there is a hint of a deficiency in Saul which becomes increasingly apparent as the narrative progresses.

Saul's Encounter with Samuel

Perhaps the most disconcerting aspect of the portrayal of Saul in this first episode is his rather conspicuous ignorance of the "man of God". In this regard, Saul again stands in contrast to his servant, who not only knows of the man of God's existence and whereabouts but also regards him as a respected individual whose every word comes true (9:6). As we learn later in the narrative, Saul's uncle also seems to know of Samuel and is eager to hear what he has said (10:15). Saul's ignorance of Samuel and his failure to recognize him even in a face to face encounter (v. 18) is disturbing, especially when we recall the conversation which Saul has just had with the maidens at the well (9:11-13). Alter has described the scene at the well as a betrothal type-scene, and has argued that the fact that the type-scene is aborted

> ...is probably a deliberate strategy of foreshadowing. The sense of completion implicit in the betrothal of the hero is withheld from this protagonist; the deflection of the anticipated type-scene somehow isolates Saul, sounds a faintly ominous note that begins to prepare us for the story of the king who loses his kingship, who will not be a conduit for the future rulers of Israel, and who ends skewered on his own sword. If this interpretation seems to exert too much pressure on half a dozen words of the Hebrew text, one must keep in mind the rigorous economy of biblical narrative. For the particular encounter on unfamiliar territory with maidens by a well would otherwise be gratuitous.[31]

We would concur with Alter's observation that, in view the economy of Hebrew narrative, the conversation with the maidens must somehow be significant. But perhaps a less subtle explanation of its significance may be possible. In response to Saul's inquiry about the seer, the young girls stress that he should find him *immediately* upon entering the city: "*As soon as* you enter (כבאכם) the city, you will

---

[31] *Art*, 60-61.

surely (כן) find him, before he goes up to the high place to eat.... So go up right away, for him[32] — just now (כהיום) — you will find him!" (v. 13). The sense of urgency is underscored by the preceding statement that the seer is "ahead of you" and by the order to "hurry!" (v. 12). In the light of this rather elaborate briefing by the maidens, it is disquieting that Saul not only fails to recognize Samuel in the gate — who, after all, is in the predicted place at the predicted time — but even inquires about the location of the seer's house. Did Saul even listen to what the maidens were saying? Again the reader has an uneasy sense of a certain incomprehension and ineptitude in Saul's actions. (It is interesting to recall that 'not listening' is one of Saul's major failings in ch. 15.)

Many, like Birch, have sought to explain Saul's remarkable failure to recognize Samuel on the basis of his supposed youthfulness.[33] Presumably the assumption that Saul is but "a diffident youth"[34] in 1 Sam 9 is based upon observations such as the following: 1) Saul is described as בחור וטוב (9:2); 2) he is sent by his father to perform a supposedly menial task (9:3); 3) he is accompanied by a servant (9:3); and 4) his father becomes worried about him (9:5; 10:2). None of these factors, however, compels one to conclude that Saul is a youth at the time of his first encounter with Samuel. We learn from 9:2 that Saul has already attained his full adult stature — or so it would seem, at least, for he is already a head taller than all the people! Moreover, in keeping with this emphasis upon Saul's commanding physique, and in view of its coupling with the adjective טוב, בחור should probably be rendered as a passive participle (verbal adjective) meaning 'chosen (choice)',[35] rather than as a substantive meaning 'young man' — though the two ideas are not mutually exclusive.[36] At any rate, the emphasis in Saul's

---

[32] Retaining MT's כי-אתו, lacking in LXX, but defended by Stoebe (195; following Buber) as characterizing "die aufgeregte Sprechweise der Mädchen". MT is also defended by Driver, 72-73.

[33] *Rise*, 35; cf. Irwin, "Samuel", 121; Seebass, "Vorgeschichte", 159; Ishida, *Royal Dynasties*, 44-45.

[34] So Irwin, "Samuel", 121.

[35] For possible examples of this use of the participle, cf. Ps. 89:20; Jer 49:19 (=50:44); Cant 5:15 ("choice as cedars"); Exod 14:7 ("select chariots"). For numerous occurrences of בחור in this sense in military contexts, see BDB, 104 (7).

[36] Some lexicographers (e.g.*HAL*, 115) posit two roots, but it is not impossible that the meaning 'young man' is related to the fact that in mili-

introduction seems to be upon physical stature and comeliness, not age. As to the second point, the assumption that Saul must have been but a youth to have still been under his father's authority appears to reflect a modern western rather than an ancient Hebrew sociological perspective. De Vaux has observed that the Hebrew household often comprised several generations and that "the father had absolute authority over his children, even over his married sons if they lived with him, and over their wives."[37] As regards the fact that Saul was accompanied by a servant, it may be observed that Kish, in making the assignment, addresses himself directly to Saul (9:3) rather than to the servant, as might have been expected if the servant were being sent, so to speak, to 'watch after' the young Saul. And as for the fourth point, it is difficult to imagine at what age a son would cease to be the object of his father's concern. In short: there is nothing in 1 Sam 9 to confirm the notion that Saul is but a youth when he first encounters Samuel. The problem of his failure to recognize Samuel remains.

The awkward moment passes quickly, however, for Samuel, after informing Saul that he is the seer (9:19aα), immediately invites Saul and his servant to attend the sacrifice: "Go up (sg.) before me to the high place, and eat (pl.) with me today, and I shall send you (sg.) [on your way] in the morning. And all that is on your (sg.) mind I shall tell you (sg.)" (9:19aβb). It is not possible to determine from the syntax of this verse[38] whether "in the morning" (v. 19b) refers only to the sending away[39] or also to the promised disclosure of all that is on Saul's mind. If Saul's concern was with both "the lost asses and the lack of provisions", then, strictly speaking, Samuel's promises are fulfilled the next day (10:2-4).[40] Nevertheless, Samuel does not hesitate to demonstrate his abilities as a seer by anticipating Saul's concern:[41] "The asses lost to you these three days — don't be concerned about them;

---

tary contexts the 'select' or 'choice' men would be fairly young, that is, in the prime of manhood.

[37] *Ancient Israel*, 1:20. Gen 42:37 provides an example of a married son with children who was nonetheless still under his father's authority and susceptible to tasks and duties which his father might impose (cf. 42:1-2).

[38] But N.B. the disjunctive object-verb word order of v. 19bβ.

[39] So Schulz, mentioned by Stoebe, 196.

[40] Cf. Birch, *Rise*, 34.

[41] As the servant had testified, "dieser Seher versteht sein Geschäft" (so Hertzberg, 61/ET 83). Budde (63) compares Samuel's accomplishment to that by which Daniel proved his superiority over the dream interpreters of Nebuchadnezzar in Dan 2.

they have been found. And for whom is all the desire (כל־חמדת) of
Israel?[42] Is it not for you and all your father's house?" (9:20). In
response to this unanticipated expression of favour, Saul stresses his
humble origins and asks, "So why have you spoken to me in this
way?" (9:21).[43]

For the time being, Samuel responds only with actions rather than
words. Escorting Saul and his servant into the banquet hall (v. 22a),[44]
Samuel places them in seats of honour at the head of the thirty or so
invited guests. He then presents Saul with a special portion of meat
which had been reserved for him in anticipation of his arrival. There is
a clear sense of divine guidance in the unusual course taken by Saul's
quest for the lost asses,[45] but the full significance of Samuel's dealings
with Saul will not be made known until the following day.

Saul's Anointing and Commission

Next morning, as Samuel prepares to send Saul away, he first has
the servant sent ahead and then taking a flask of oil he anoints Saul,
kisses him and proclaims his appointment as *nāgîd* over the people of
Yahweh (9:26-10:1). In the longer reading of 10:1 attested by LXX,
there is a close parallel, in terms of content, between Saul's commis-

---

[42] Cf. Stoebe, 191 ("auf wen richtet sich (jetzt) das ganze Sehnen
Israels?"); Ehrlich, 3:199 ("Gemeint ist das Königtum, wonach das gesamte
Volk verlangt hatte; vgl. 8,5"); *NIV*. Others follow LXX and Vulg. in rendering ...כל־חמדת concretely, "all that is desirable"; cf. Driver, 74 (who
cites Hag 2:7 as a parallel example but admits that both should possibly be
repunctuated as passive participles). Stoebe (196) conjectures that the
"Doppelsinnigkeit" may be intentional.

[43] The objection, or *Einwand des Berufenen*, is a standard feature of
call narratives (cf. Gideon's similar expressions of inadequacy in Judg
6:15). The anomaly in Saul's case is that his commission has not yet been
given (cf. 10:1ff.). We are not told how much Saul understands of what is in
store for him, but the preferential treatment may have been sufficient to
elicit his response.

[44] Some see a contradiction between this notice and Samuel's earlier
instruction to Saul to "go up before me" (v. 19aβ). Birch (*Rise*, 34) attempts to resolve the discrepancy by distinguishing between passage to the
high place and entry into the hall. Greßmann (25), on the other hand, assumes that the conversation between Samuel and Saul took place as they as-
cended the hill. This latter understanding is possible if we assume that "go
up ahead of me" in 9:19 signifies deference and not temporal or spatial distance. The latter interpretation finds support in 1 Sam 14:12, where
Jonathan's injunction, "go up after me" (עלה אחרי), clearly means "follow
immediately behind me (and not at some great distance!)".

[45] Cf. Gunn, *Fate*, 61; Eslinger, *Kingship*, 314.

sion in 10:1 and the divine words to Samuel in 9:16-17. Birch has charted the correspondences as follows:

10:1 משחך לנגיד על־עמו על־ישראל	9:16 ומשחתי לנגיד על־עמו ישראל
10:1 ואתה תעצר בעם יהוה	9:17 זה יעצר בעמי
10:1 ואתה הושיענו מיד איביו מסביב	[46]והושיע את־עמי מיד פלשתים 9:16

The parallels are not at all surprising when we recall Samuel's intermediary role in issuing Saul's call and commission.[47] This same factor may account for the apparent absence of an 'appearance' (*Erscheinung*), according to Richter one of the standard elements of call narratives.[48] In a modified sense, there is an *Erscheinung* or, as Birch terms it, a "divine confrontation",[49] but the recipient is Samuel (9:15),[50] who thus becomes the mediator of Saul's call.

The main difference between 9:16-17 and 10:1 is that the latter, by generalizing Saul's task to encompass Israel's *enemies round about*, might seem to lessen the urgency of Saul's dealing specifically with the Philistine problem. We would recall, however, that the general mandate of 10:1 is augmented in 10:7 by a specific assignment: "When these signs come to you, do what your hand finds to do, for God is with you." This injunction, with its assurance of divine accompaniment, strongly suggests that Saul is to initiate active opposition as soon as the signs are fulfilled. The bestowal of the divine spirit upon Saul as part of the third sign (cf. 10:6, 10), moreover, seems to point in the same direction. Finally, reference in v. 5aβ to a Philistine נציב at the site of the third sign offers a strong hint as to what Saul's "hand should find to do".[51]

When Saul arrives at Gibeath-elohim (v. 10) and meets a band of prophets (as Samuel had predicted in v. 5), he is overcome by the רוח אלהים (Samuel had predicted the רוח יהוה)[52] and joins with the band in prophesying. The stage is now set for Saul to act. But he does

---

[46] Birch, *Rise*, 37. הושיענו in Birch's rendering of 10:1 should probably read תושיענו (cf. Driver, 78).

[47] See Ch. 2, pp. 60-62.

[48] Richter ("*nāgîd* -Formel", 78-79)

[49] *Rise*, 35-36, following Habel's schema.

[50] So Birch, *Rise*, 36.

[51] For a full discussion of all these issues, see Ch. 2 above.

[52] On the significance of this variation, see below, p. 228.

nothing. Before considering the implications of Saul's inaction, we should digress briefly to consider how Saul's prophesying contributes to his characterization. If the first to comment on the event — viz. "all who knew him previously" (v. 11) — "were not unnaturally astounded at his action of which they had had no previous hint",[53] subsequent commentators have been similarly exercised by the onlookers' proverbial response: "Is Saul also among the prophets?"[54] It is not necessary in this context to review the extensive literature which this saying has generated, but any investigation of its significance must take into account the fact that it is repeated in 1 Sam 19:24. What are we to make of this? Is the presence of two passages reciting the same proverb merely the result of competing etiologies, as Alter[55] and many others assume? Or should we regard the second passage as a "satirical recapitulation" of the first?[56] The specific locations of the two passages in 1 Samuel suggests the latter alternative.[57] But if this is the case, wherein lies the satire? Gunn poses the right question when he remarks that "at issue <u>in context</u> is whether the saying indicates a positive or negative attitude towards Saul".[58] In order to answer this question, we must make a careful distinction. While it is apparent that 'prophesying' *per se* would be viewed positively in 1 Sam 10, as in the Books of Samuel generally,[59] this does not mean that Saul is favourably portrayed simply because he is allowed to prophesy. Indeed, the reaction of Saul's acquaintances, who apparently regarded 'religious' activity as completely out of character for Saul, suggests a different evaluation. In a narrative context in which prophecy is approved, does not their aston-

---

[53] So Philips, "Ecstatics' Father", 183 (in reference to 10:11).

[54] Perhaps a better rendering would be "Is even Saul among the prophets?" or "Is Saul really among the prophets?" Of the five passages in the Old Testament in which הֲגַם occurs (besides the three occurrences in 1 Samuel) four favour the rendering of גַם as "even" (or "really", "indeed") rather than "also" — i.e. Gen 16:13; 1 Kgs 17:20; Job 41:1 (Eng. 41:9); Esth 7:8. The fifth, Ps 78:20, is ambiguous.

[55] *Art*, 89.

[56] So Jobling, "Jonathan", 10.

[57] Humphreys ("Hero", 116 n. 41) notes that "the use of the proverb in 19:24 as well as in 10:11 sets a pair of brackets about the narrative, presenting Saul's first and last encounter with the spirit. The first comes just before he attains kingship, the last just before his full descent from kingship into madness and death".

[58] *Fate*, 63.

[59] Cf. Gunn, *Fate*, 63; Phillips, "Ecstatics' Father", 191.

ishment at Saul's involvement with prophets reflect negatively on Saul? If some ambiguity at this point remains — perhaps Saul really is among the prophets — the ironic repetition of the saying in 19:24 would seem to remove all doubt.

Returning to the issue of Saul's inaction, the question that arises is why it is that Saul simply "stopped prophesying and went home."[60] Has he failed to understand his charge, or is he simply reluctant to accept it? In our analysis of 1 Sam 9, we observed various hints of both hesitancy and incomprehension in Saul. We noted, for example, the servant's primary role in bringing Saul into contact with the seer, and Saul's failure to recognize Samuel as the seer, in spite of his rather elaborate briefing by the young girls at the well. In the light of these earlier signals, it may be that Saul's inaction is due to a simple failure to grasp the full significance of Samuel's instructions in 10:5-7. There is evidence elsewhere, however, that Saul did understand his assignment, for his immediate response to Jonathan's overthrow of the Philistine נציב in 13:3 is to repair to Gilgal to wait for Samuel, according to the pattern established in 10:7-8. But whether through reluctance or incomprehension, or a combination of the two, Saul's failure in ch. 10 to "do what your hand finds to do" does not bode well for his success.

If this interpretation is basically correct, it may shed new light on the problematic section 1 Sam 10:14-16. Saul's conversation with his דוד (uncle?) has always seemed a rather curious conclusion to the momentous events of the day.[61] D. R. Ap-Thomas sketches the problem as follows:

> From the fact that Abner later became the commander of Saul's army and even maintained the Israelite cause against the Philistines after Saul's death (2 Sam. ii 8), it

---

[60] MT's הבמה, "to the high place", is difficult and would require ויעל instead of ויבא. Many modern commentators prefer to read הביתה, as attested by Josephus (*Ant.* VI.58); cf. Smith, 71; McCarter, 172; Klein, 83. The sense may be "not so much *his* house, as *the* house, as opposed to the street" (Driver, 83). For a summary of other suggestions, see Stoebe, 199.

[61] Both the proper understanding of the Hebrew word דוד in this context — whether 'uncle' (cf. J. J. Stamm, "Name"), 'kinsman' (cf. Josephus, *Ant.* VI.58; BDB, 187), 'loved one' (BDB, 187), or 'deputy ruler, governor' (Ap-Thomas, "Saul's 'Uncle'", 245) — as well as the identity of the person involved — whether Ner (cf. 1 Sam 9:1; 14:50-51) or Abner (cf. 1 Chr 8:33 [=9:39]; Josephus, *Ant.* VI.58) — remain obscure, but these questions do not materially affect the interpretation suggested below.

> might be suggested that if he were the uncle here, and if
> some inkling of what had happened at Ramah (?) during
> Saul's visit to Samuel (x 1) had reached Abner's ears, then
> he might well have been anxious to begin active
> opposition to the hated Philistine oppressor. But if this
> indeed lies behind our passage, why does Saul conceal
> the true facts from his strongest and most faithful sup-
> porter?[62]

Why indeed? McCarter senses the difficulty of Saul's silence at this point and confesses that this "secrecy motif...has never been fully explained." McCarter would somehow relate Saul's behaviour to that of Samson (Judg 14:9), "who hides his inspired feats of strength from his parents",[63] but the differences between the two should not be overlooked. In the case of Samson, several motivations may underlie his silence: a desire to safe-guard his riddle (14:12ff.); reticence to admit that he, a Nazirite (13:5), has approached a dead body (cf. the prohibition in Num 6:6); or perhaps simply the fact that he, unlike Saul, was not interrogated. A more instructive parallel to Saul's silence is found in the account of Jehu's secret anointing in 2 Kgs 9:6ff. Though hesitant at first to disclose what the "madman" (v. 11) had told him, when urged Jehu complies (v. 12) and is immediately thrust into the path of action leading to his kingship (v. 13ff.).

Ap-Thomas himself offers a rather different explanation. He argues that the דּוֹד mentioned in 10:14-16 is not Saul's uncle but rather the Philistine prefect himself.[64] This highly speculative interpretation has found little acceptance,[65] but even if it were to prove correct, it would not suggest a positive evaluation of Saul's actions. After all, the implication of 10:5-7 was that Saul's first act of deliverance should have been an attack upon the Philistine prefect! Most commentators, both ancient and modern, have lauded Saul's silence (10:16) as an admirable mark of humility[66] or of sensible caution[67] or as a matter of military

---

[62] "Saul's 'Uncle'", 241-42.

[63] McCarter, 187-88 and n. 5.

[64] "Saul's 'Uncle'", 242-45.

[65] See Birch, *Rise*, 41 n. 72; Stoebe, 199.

[66] McCarter (184, q.v. for references) notes that Jewish tradition has consistently taken this view. Among modern commentators, cf. Goslinga, 135.

[67] Josephus, *Ant.* VI.59.

expediency.[68] But given the interpretation that we have put forward, Saul's silence appears not as that of a man whose hour has not yet come, but as that of a man who has failed, or is about to fail, in his first assignment and would just as soon keep quiet about it. Perhaps Saul feared that his 'uncle' would censure him for his inaction or, worse still, by some precipitate action, force his hand. Whatever may be said on points of detail, the narrative is certainly more suggestive of timidity than of humility.

1 Sam 10:17-27

Some Reflections on the Unity/Disunity of 10:17-27

The major challenge to the internal unity of 10:17-27 was issued by O. Eissfeldt in 1931.[69] He argued that there is evidence within the section that two originally distinct traditions regarding Saul's public election have been intertwined in the text as we have it. In the one (10:17-21bα), Saul is selected by lot, and in the other (10:21bβ-27), the height of the candidate seems to have been the determining factor. In support of his theory, Eissfeldt offered four arguments. First, the apparently favourable judgement upon kingship in 10:24-27 conflicts with the more anti-monarchical tone of Eissfeldt's postulated strand III, which comprises ch. 8; 10:17ff.; ch. 12; ch. 15.[70] Secondly, in 10:24-27 the king is not, as in ch. 8, demanded by the people (there is even a contingent that treats the new king with contempt) but is provided by Yahweh and Samuel. Thirdly, the content of the divine inquiry of 10:22a MT, "*Ist noch einer hierher gekommen?*" (הבא עוד הלם איש), makes little sense as a follow-on to the selection of Saul by lot in v. 21 but seems to presuppose some other context, viz. one in which the superior stature of the candidate is the criterion by which Yahweh's

---

[68] Cf. Demsky, "Geba", 28.

[69] *Komposition*, 7-8, 10.

[70] The centrality to Eissfeldt's theory of this 'monarchical argument' has been emphasized by Boecker: "Es ist bezeichnend, daß auch bei Eissfeldt die Beurteilung des Königtums als erstes und wichtigstes Argument für die Behauptung der literarischen Uneinheitlichkeit des Abschnittes genannt wird" (*Beurteilung*, 44).

choice is to be recognized.[71]   Fourthly, on the assumption that "Samuels Abschiedsrede (Kap. 12)" is directed to the people still gathered in Mizpah (10:17ff.), the dismissal of the people and of Saul in 10:25f. is "undenkbar".[72]

Eissfeldt's first, second and fourth arguments can be dealt with quite briefly. As regards the first, we have already discussed the inadequacy of 'monarchical sentiments' as a criterion for distinguishing sources.[73] And, in any case, it is not at all clear that 10:24ff. is pro-monarchic (see below). As regards the second, 10:18-19 makes it clear that kingship is instituted by *divine* concession to the *people's* request and through the agency of *Samuel*. The dissent expressed in v. 27, moreover, is not directed towards the idea of having a king but rather towards *Saul's suitability* for the task — "How can *this one* save us?" (מה־יֹשִׁעֵנוּ זֶה). As for Eissfeldt's fourth argument, there is nothing in the text of ch. 12 to suggest that the setting is Mizpah. In view of 11:14, which Eissfeldt does *not* regard as a redactional insertion,[74] the most likely setting for ch. 12 is Gilgal.

Eissfeldt's third argument fares somewhat better than the other three, and it is not surprising that it is this argument that is most often cited in discussions of 10:17-27. Though few scholars have been willing to adopt Eissfeldt's theory without modification, a fair number have accepted his basic conclusion that the section is not a unity.[75] There have been others, however, who have strongly contested this conclusion,[76] and the trend in more recent studies seems to be away from it. Ishida, for example, argues that "both the source theory [of Eissfeldt]

---

[71] Eissfeldt (*Komposition*, 7) also cites the change from Samuel as subject in 10:17-21bα to "eine[r] nicht näher bezeichnete[n] Menge (3. pers. plur.)" in vv. 21bβ, 22 as evidence of two sources. But this argument has little force, for as Halpern (*Constitution*, 154 n. 45) has observed, "the switch to third pl. (the assembly) in 10:21bβ is occasioned by the content (who, after all, 'sought' Saul? The people). This may have led to the pl. of v 22a."

[72] *Komposition*, 7.

[73] See esp. Ch. 6, pp. 176-82.

[74] *Komposition*, 10.

[75] Cf., e.g., Hylander, *Samuel-Saul Komplex*, 126f.; Hertzberg, 66/ET 88; Seebass, "Traditionsgeschichte", 288 n. 9; Birch, *Rise*, 43ff. Boecker (*Beurteilung*, 44-48; following Noth, *ÜSt*, 58) attributes the modification of the more primitive account by the introduction of the lot-casting motif to the Deuteronomist, who wished to stress the divine initiative in selecting a king.

[76] For a summary of the debate, see Boecker, *Beurteilung*, 44-47.

and the modification theory [of Noth and Boecker] are untenable". He explains:

> On the one hand, if we try to divide the narrative into sources, they become too fragmentary to be considered independent sources. On the other, if the Deuteronomistic invention of the story of Saul's election by lot stemmed from the Deuteronomist's theological point of view, he could have completely deleted the old tradition of choice by oracle instead of making a clumsy halfway modification. It seems that the narrative was composed from the beginning as a literary unit.[77]

Before we can accept this conclusion, however, the tension created by v. 22aβ must be resolved. The most straightforward solution is suggested by LXX — *El ἔρχεται ὁ ἀνὴρ ἐνταῦθα*; ("Has the man come here?") — which may reflect a Hebrew text, הבא עד הלם האיש.[78] Yahweh's answer in the subsequent clause, "Behold, <u>he</u> is hiding..." (v. 22b), seems to presuppose a definite antecedent and thus, as Driver has observed, "agrees better with the question, 'Is *the* man come hither...?' than with 'Is there still *a* man come hither?'".[79] An original עד in v. 22aβ may have been corrupted to עוד under the influence of עוד in the preceding clause, וישאל־עוד ביהוה (v. 22aα).[80]

Eissfeldt himself admits that it is just such a question — *"Ist der Mann hierher gekommen?"* — that one would expect after v. 21.[81] Some have objected to this understanding on the grounds that the lot-

---

[77] *Royal Dynasties*, 45. Other proponents of the essential unity of the present recension include Mettinger, *King and Messiah*, 179-82; Halpern, *Constitution*, 153-54.

[78] This reading is preferable to the more speculative reconstruction suggested by Mettinger (*King and Messiah*, 180-81): הבה עוד הלם האיש ("Oh, bring the man here again!"). Albrektson ("Some Observations", 1-5) has subjected Mettinger's emendation to close scrutiny and has convincingly demonstrated that "the traditional *hᵃba'* found in the MT and attested by ancient versions ought to be preferred to the suggested emendation *habā'* (5).

[79] Driver, 84; following Wellhausen.

[80] So McCarter, 190. But if עוד "yet" is comparable in usage to English "yet", which in a negative or interrogative sentence may mean "so soon as now or then, by this or by that time, so far, in the immediate future" (*OED*, 1354), then we could read, "Has the man come here yet?" The only necessary modification of MT would be to read האיש (following LXX) instead of איש.

[81] *Komposition*, 7.

casting procedure must have required the physical presence of the candidates. Birch, for example, argues that since "the lot could answer only yes or no or give no answer at all",[82] "it is highly unlikely that one who was not present could be chosen by the lot as the present text seems to indicate". The logic of this deduction is difficult to trace, however, for there is nothing in the data available to us to preclude the possibility that one could be selected by lot *in absentia*.[83] Schulz, for example, writes,

> Wahrscheinlich müssen wir uns den Schluß der Wahl so denken: Der Vorsteher der letzten Gruppe gab an, welche Männer zu ihr gehörten, und sodann wurde das Los geworfen, ohne daß die einzelnen zugegen zu sein brauchten.[84]

Smith offers a similar speculation:

> Kish would represent the household now chosen. Among his sons the name of Saul finally came out, but the man himself was not to be found.[85]

We are not told at what point in the proceedings Saul went into hiding. Budde and Mettinger assume that he remained among the crowd until the lot fell, then immediately slipped away to conceal himself.[86] More conceivable, however, is the suggestion that Saul's hiding simply assumes the events of 9:1-10:16. Smelik, for example, writes,

---

[82] *Rise*, 44; cf. Lindblom, "Lot-Casting", 171-72.

[83] Cf. Halpern, *Constitution*, 154 n. 45.

[84] Schulz, 155.   Contra Boecker, *Beurteilung*, 45.

[85] Smith, 73.   Boecker (*Beurteilung*, 45 n. 4) dismisses all such interpretations as mere "Verlegenheitsauskunft", but, given the limitations of our knowledge of the Israelite practice of lot-casting, this criticism seems unfounded.   At any rate, these interpretations require far less speculative imagination than Eissfeldt's source theory or Boecker's own modification theory.

[86] Budde (71) writes, "Saul hat sich wohl aus Bescheidenheit zuerst hintangehalten, dann, sofort als das Los gefallen war, versteckt."   Cf. Mettinger (*King and Messiah*, 181): "When Saul, who was present *in figura* at this procedure, was taken by lot he immediately disappeared and hid himself among the baggage."

> Het feit, dat Saul kennelijk op de hoogte van de uitslag
> is, toont overigens aan, dat de auteurs 9-10:16 bij de
> lezer bekend veronderstellen.[87]

In conclusion, although we have disagreed with Mettinger's specific analysis at several points, we would concur with his general contention that 1 Sam 10:17-27 contains but "a single tradition of Saul's divine election. There is no reason to assume an echo of a tradition of a divine oracle referring to the height of the chosen one."[88]

The Portrait of Saul in 10:17-27

Whereas the section 9:1-10:16 has customarily been assigned to the so-called pro-monarchical source, 10:17-27 is generally included with chs. 8 and 12 in the anti-monarchical source. We have seen, however, that these labels are simplistic and at times quite inaccurate.[89] Nevertheless, 10:17-27 does exhibit a certain negativity in tone. The most explicit criticism is levelled not against kingship but against the *people's request* for a king, which is regarded as tantamount to rejection of Yahweh (vv. 18-19).[90] It is the attitude of the narrative towards Saul, however, that chiefly concerns us here.

In terms of its formal structure, the section opens like a prophetic oracle of judgement.[91] Birch identifies the following elements: call to assembly (v. 17), messenger formula (v. 18aα), recitation of saving acts (v. 18aβb), accusation (v. 19a), and announcement (v. 19b).[92] The last-mentioned element is especially noteworthy, for though it exhibits the characteristic form of an announcement of judgement,[93] it lacks any explicit reference to the *judgement* but contains rather Samuel's order that the people assemble themselves for the lot-casting which is to identify the king.[94] Birch's attempt to resolve the difficulty by pointing

---

[87] Smelik, *Saul*, 110-111.

[88] *King and Messiah*, 182.

[89] Cf. Ch. 6, pp. 176-83.

[90] Birch (*Rise*, 51) observes, "There is indeed a judgement implied in v. 19a, but it is against the people and not the kingship."

[91] On this genre, see Ch. 3, pp. 85-86.

[92] "Choosing", 452-54; *idem, Rise*, 48-51.

[93] E.g., it begins with the deictic particle ועתה.

[94] Judg 6:7-10, which exhibits striking parallels to 1 Sam 10:17-19 (cf. Birch, "Choosing", 451; *idem, Rise*, 47), also appears at first glance to lack a proper announcement of judgement. In fact, however, the order of the

to the reassertion of the divine will as the "divine response to the people's rejection"[95] is not entirely satisfactory. More plausible is McCarter's observation that the king is, in some sense, himself presented as a judgement upon the people. He writes, "It would be overstating the case only slightly to say that this arrangement implies that the gift of a king is a kind of punishment".[96]

As regards the selection process itself, Soggin has noted that, apart from the P material, there are only three instances in the Old Testament of the use of lots to designate individuals — the present passage, the Achan episode in Joshua 7, and the Jonathan episode in 1 Sam 14.[97] Of these, the Achan episode and the selection of Saul exhibit the closest parallels.[98] The numerous correspondences between these two accounts have been adequately described elsewhere[99] and need not detain us here, but, as Blenkinsopp has observed, this casting of the material tends to portray Saul in a less than favourable light.[100] McCarter again offers a helpful comment:

> While it is certainly true that lot casting was used for other purposes than the exposure of a criminal (including, indeed, the designation of individuals for office), the combination of features that appears here — an oracle of judgement followed by the injunction to cast the lots — casts a shadow over Saul's election. Again it would be overstating the case to say that all of this means Saul is guilty of something — that will come later — but there is a clear if subtle implication that he is an offending party by virtue of the election itself.[101]

McCarter's observation that the shaping of the material casts a shadow over Saul's election is apposite, but is he correct in disavowing

---

elements has simply been modified by the context — the accusation (vv. 7-10) comes in answer to the cry of the people concerning the judgements already announced in vv. 1-6.

[95] "Choosing", 454; *idem, Rise*, 51.

[96] McCarter, 195.

[97] *Königtum*, 38. Cf. Gordon, *Samuel*, 46-47.

[98] Regarding the latter, Budde ("Saul's Königswahl", 233) observes that it is the "Achan-Geschichte...die allein in allen Stücken damit überein-stimmt." Cf. Birch, "Choosing", 449.

[99] See esp. Blenkinsopp, "Jonathan's Sacrilege", 428-29; *idem*, "Quest", 76 n. 2.

[100] "Quest", 76.

[101] McCarter, 196.

any actual guilt on Saul's part? If our interpretation of Saul's response, or rather lack of response, to his commission in the preceding episode is basically correct, then McCarter perhaps goes too far in absolving Saul from any responsibility for the rather negative tone given to the proceedings at Mizpah.

On the surface, Samuel's exclamation in v. 24 might appear to express a very positive attitude towards Saul: "Do you see the man whom Yahweh has chosen? There is no one like him among all the people." But again, as in 9:2, the emphasis is exclusively upon Saul's external qualities (v. 23). Samuel's words are either intended ironically, or they simply reflect the popular tendency to assess a leader according to his external qualities[102] — a tendency which Yahweh will explicitly reject in 16:7. To be sure, Samuel's exclamation must have expressed the feelings of the people as Saul stood before them, a commanding figure (v. 23b), but it must not be forgotten that the king-designate had just been dragged from behind the baggage where he had been hiding (v. 23a). The ironic incongruity of the hiding giant is obvious.

The above interpretation assumes a negative stance towards Saul's hiding, but there is considerable disagreement on this point. Many scholars follow Josephus[103] in regarding Saul's hiding as an indication of "restraint and modesty".[104] Stoebe, on the other hand, sees in it "eine Ausformung des Niedrigkeitsmotivs" which underscores the incomprehensibility of Yahweh's actions.[105] McCarter poses the dilemma very simply — is Saul's motive modesty or timidity?[106] As he goes on to point out, we are not explicitly told *why* he hides. This fact should not prevent us from asking the question, however,[107] for

---

[102] I.e. to assess a king 'like all the nations'. Gordon (*Samuel*, 46) notes that in the popular imagination of the ancient Near East the king "could fail to measure up to his task — literally!" He cites an interesting example in the Ugaritic epic "Baal and Mot", where Athtar, aspiring to the throne of Baal, is judged unworthy "because his legs were too short to reach the footstool and his head did not reach the top!"

[103] *Ant.* VI.63.

[104] Cf., for example, Kirkpatrick, 111; Smith, 73; Goslinga, 138.

[105] Stoebe, 218.

[106] McCarter, 196.

[107] Nor should the matter of a possible word-play on the name Saul in v. 22. The verb שאל occurs only once in v. 22, and McCarter's assertion that "the purpose for which this little incident is told is word-play, and its chief interest is Saul's name" (196) places too great a weight of importance on a single stylistic feature.

much of the message of 1 Samuel is conveyed indirectly by implication and oblique reference.[108]

In our analysis of 9:1-10:16, we saw several indications of ineptitude and timidity in Saul and of a reluctance to assume the office conferred upon him by Yahweh. Saul's hiding seems to fit this picture exactly and to reflect badly on Saul. This is not to suggest, of course, that a spontaneous expression of personal inadequacy was not considered entirely appropriate in the face of the divine call; the so-called *Einwand des Berufenen* is a constant feature in call narratives. But when the designee continues to falter and resist even after a sign has been given and an assurance of divine accompaniment issued (cf. 10:7),[109] then such persistent reluctance can become reprehensible.[110]

1 Samuel 11

1 Sam 11 in Context

Though commonly included in the so-called pro-monarchical source,[111] the rather high historical assessment of ch. 11[112] (excluding possibly vv. 7, 12-14) has nevertheless tended to set it apart from traditions considered to be historically more suspect.[113] As regards its immediate textual environment, belief in ch. 11's essential independence is based primarily on perceived tensions and contradictions between this chapter and the surrounding materials. It is argued, for example, that, contrary to what might be expected after 10:17-27, ch. 11 shows no awareness of Saul's election to the kingship: he is not introduced as

---

[108] Cf. Ch. 1, pp. 31-34.

[109] On these and other elements of call narratives, see esp. Richter, *Berufungsberichte*, 142-69. A brief survey of research into call narratives is provided by W. E. March, "Prophecy", 170-72. For analyses of 1 Sam 9:1-10:16 in terms of the call narrative schema, see Schmidt, *Menschlicher Erfolg*, 88-89; Birch, *Rise*, 35-41.

[110] Cf. Exod 4:1-14, where Moses' continued hesitation eventually arouses Yahweh's anger.

[111] Cf. Ch. 6, pp. 176ff.

[112] "The historical value of c 11 has been taken for granted by most scholars" (so McCarter, 207 n. 7). Cf. Langlamet, "Les récits", 167; Ishida, *Royal Dynasties*, 48; Birch, *Rise*, 55.

[113] Cf. Birch, *Rise*, 54 n. 98.

king but appears rather as an agriculturalist; the message of distress brought from Jabesh-gilead to the inhabitants of Gibeah is not addressed in the first instance to Saul, nor is there any hint that the messengers intended that he in particular hear it; there is no hint in the reaction of the inhabitants of Gibeah that they viewed Saul in any special sense as a possible source of deliverance.[114]

Convinced by these arguments that ch. 11 is an essentially independent tradition (and buttressing this view by eliminating as redactional any elements, such as references to Samuel, which might suggest otherwise), scholars have tended to interpret the chapter in isolation from its broader context. This tendency, perhaps more than any other factor, has led to the conclusion that the chapter is strongly pro-Saulide — i.e. Saul appears as a successful hero-deliverer in the Judges tradition. Before we can address the question of the *Tendenz* of the chapter *vis-à-vis* Saul, therefore, it is first necessary to evaluate the specific arguments raised in support of ch. 11's essential independence from its present textual environment. The issue is not, in fact, whether the traditions recorded in ch. 11 once existed independently, for, assuming the basic historicity of an Ammonite victory, this would likely have been the case; it stands to reason that such an event would have been recounted orally and possibly even committed to writing prior to its incorporation into a larger literary context. The issue, rather, is whether it can adequately be demonstrated from the available evidence that at some earlier stage the tradition differed significantly from the extant version. Can it be demonstrated, for example, that references to Samuel are secondary, or that vv. 12-14 are redactional insertions? Depending on the answers to these questions, there may be grounds for reassessing the attitude of the narrative towards Saul.

Does 1 Sam 11 Presuppose Saul's Election?

In MT, 1 Samuel 11 begins rather abruptly with the statement that Nahash the Ammonite went up and besieged Jabesh-gilead.[115] Unwill-

---

[114] Cf. Wellhausen, *Prolegomena*, 260; idem, Composition, 243-44.

[115] In all probability, however, the longer reading attested in 4QSam[a] (and reflected in Josephus) is to be preferred. Advocates of the originality of 4QSam[a] include Ulrich, *Qumran Text*, 166-67; Cross, "Ammonite Oppression" (the content of this article was disseminated in one form or another in 1979, 1980 and 1983); McCarter, 199; Eves, "Ammonite Invasion", 318-24. For an opposing view, see Rofé, "Acts of Nahash", 129-33.

ing to accept Nahash's cruel conditions, the elders of Jabesh-gilead request a seven-day reprieve in order that they might "send messengers throughout the territory of Israel" (v. 3a*β*). The elders propose that if in the allotted time no deliverer (מוֹשִׁיעַ) can be found, "we will come out to you" (v. 3). In the present context, the implication of this phrase appears to be "we will come out to you *without a fight*" — or so, it would seem, the elders wish Nahash to understand. But the polysemy of the verb יצא, often used in military contexts of troops going out to fight,[116] hints at an irony which finds fuller expression as the narrative progresses. In v. 10, after the men of Jabesh have received news of their impending rescue by Saul (v. 9), they report to the Ammonites, "Tomorrow we will come out to you, that you may do to us whatever is good in your eyes". The ironic use of יצא in this context has not gone unnoticed; Hertzberg, for example, observes: "Der verborgene Doppelsinn des Satzes 'Morgen kommen wir zu euch heraus' ist dabei eine besondere, von den alten Hörern sicherlich mit hohem Beifall aufgenommene Feinheit".[117] It is obvious to the reader, if not to Nahash, that the purpose of the Jabesh-gileadites' report is deception. But what else would one expect between sworn enemies?

Recognition of the Jabesh-gileadites' deceptiveness in v. 10 sheds new light on another feature of ch. 11. As already noted, the plea of the elders in v. 3 was that they might be given time to send messengers "throughout the territory of Israel" in search of a deliverer (v. 3). Are we to assume that this proves their ignorance of Saul's appointment? If deception is the *modus operandi* of the Jabeshites in dealing with the Ammonites, it is at least a fair question whether this request is sincere or simply a first clever deception. As has often been observed, the narrative records no actual dispersal of messengers throughout the territory of Israel. We may not simply assume, of course, given the economy of Hebrew narrative, that this necessarily rules out the possibility that messengers were sent to other villages.[118] Nevertheless, the assumption of a general dispersal raises other problems, as Stoebe notes:

---

[116] E.g., Gen 14:8; Deut 23:10; 1 Sam 8:20; 18:30; 2 Sam 18:2-4, 6; Amos 5:3, etc. Cf. Jenni, "יצא", 757; BDB, 424. For יצא in the sense of going out in surrender, see 2 Kgs 24:12; Isa 36:16; Jer 38:17.

[117] Hertzberg, 71/ET 93; cf. Lasine, "Guest", 43.

[118] Various scholars postulate that an original account did include a report of a general dispersal. Budde (74), for example, writes, "Jetzt liest sich v. 4 immerhin, als wenn sie sich sofort nach Gib'a begeben hätten, weil sie dort den neuerwählten König von Israel wussten. Es ist ganz

Der zur Verfügung stehende Zeitraum wäre dann sehr knapp bemessen, außerdem wäre nicht einzusehen, warum die Etappen des Weges nicht mehr genannt, der Mißerfolg nicht beschrieben wurde. Das hätte jedenfalls die Spannung in eindrucksvoller Weise gesteigert.... Geschichtlich geurteilt werden die Jabeschiten sich direkt nach Gibea gewendet haben.[119]

There is considerable force in these observations. It is somewhat surprising, therefore, that Stoebe nevertheless assumes that MT now wishes to give the appearance that, before arriving in Gibeah, the messengers had traversed the entire Israelite territory.[120] In fact, MT implies nothing of the kind but reports only that the messengers went to Gibeah of Saul: ויבאו המלאכים גבעת שאול (v. 4). To be sure, by rendering the waw-imperfect in a temporal sense, "*When* the messengers came to Gibeah of Saul...", we could give the impression that they had already visited other villages. But apart from the dubious assumption that the elders of Jabesh have spoken candidly to Nahash, there is no reason to prefer the temporal rendering here. All that can be said with certainty from the waw-imperfect in the present context is that, subsequent to or as a logical consequence of the elders' request, "the messengers came to Gibeah of Saul". According to v. 7, it was after their arrival in Gibeah (v. 4) that the messengers were sent "throughout the territory of Israel" to deliver Saul's summons. "Then the dread of Yahweh fell on the people, and they came out as one man" (v. 7b). If seven days seems a short, though not impossible,[121] amount of time for

---

wahrscheinlich, dass die Redaktion einen Absatz gestrichen hat, um dieses Verständnis zu ermöglichen." For a similar view, cf. Hertzberg, 69/ET 92-93. Josephus (*Ant.* VI.73) actually records a dispersal of messengers to each Israelite city, but this can only be regarded as an interpretative paraphrase — for other alterations of the tradition in the immediate context, cf. the order of events in *Ant.* VI.76-77.

[119] Stoebe, 226.

[120] Stoebe, 226.

[121] In his discussion of the logistics of military campaigns in the ancient Near East, Eph'al ("On Warfare", 99) sets the average rate of march for armies at 25-30 km per day. Messengers on an urgent mission could be expected to travel much more quickly — 50 km or more per day. The distance between Jabesh-gilead and Gibeah is c. 75 km as the crow flies or 90-100 km via Beth-shan and Shechem (cf. *SMM*, 7-1). By this reckoning, the Jabeshite messengers could reasonably have reached Gibeah of Saul within two days, if not less. By the same token, they would not likely have required more than two days or so to disperse "throughout the territory of

all these events to take place, how much greater the difficulty if we were to assume two dispersals of the messengers throughout the Israelite territory.[122]

A further indication that the messengers came directly to Gibeah is the fact that it is not "a messenger" or even simply "messengers"[123] that arrive in Saul's town but "the messengers" — as if the entire contingent is in view. While it would be unwise to press this point too far, in view of the occasional use of the Hebrew definite article where English (or German) usage would require an indefinite,[124] the suggested interpretation finds some confirmation in v. 7. There it appears that the messengers who had arrived in Gibeah were sufficient in number to execute Saul's order to deliver the bovine remains throughout the territory of Israel: ויקח צמד בקר וינתחהו וישלח בכל גבול ישראל ביד המלאכים, "And he took a yoke of oxen and cut them into pieces and sent [them] throughout the territory of Israel *by the hand of the messengers*" (v. 7).[125] If we assume, as the verisimilitude of the account would seem to require, that Nahash would have limited the number of

---

Israel" with the ox parts (v. 7a). This would leave three days for the assembling of the people in Bezek (vv. 7b-8).

[122] Cf. Stoebe, 226; Möhlenbrink, "Sauls Ammoniterfeldzug", 63.

[123] Cf. Judg 6:35.

[124] Cf. GK §126q, but notice that this paragraph describes "the employment of the article to denote a *single* person or thing (primarily one which is *as yet unknown,* and therefore not capable of being defined) as being present to the mind under given circumstances" (italics mine).

[125] Attempts to distinguish the messengers commissioned in v. 7 from those mentioned in v. 4 are unconvincing. McCarter (200), for example, argues that the messengers dispersed in v. 7 cannot have been from Jabesh-gilead, since "the Jabeshite messengers are sent on a different errand in v 9". This argument is without value, however, inasmuch as v. 9 records events that took place during the general muster in Bezek (v. 8), at which time the Jabeshite messengers would have regathered along with all Israel, who "came out as one man" (v. 7). Stoebe's (221) arguments are even less compelling. His first point is that "the messengers" (v. 7), despite the article, should be regarded as indefinite. But in view of the fact that "the messengers" have already been introduced in v. 4, the burden of proof lies with those who would distinguish "the messengers" mentioned in v. 7 (if an indefinite group of messengers had been in view, the article could have been omitted as in v. 3). In support of his second point — "auch mit dem überlieferten Text sind nicht die Boten von Jabesch gemeint" — Stoebe cites only Ehrlich. But, in fact, Ehrlich (Randglossen 3:205) argues precisely the opposite: "Somit standen Saul zur Zeit noch keine Boten zur Verfügung, und er war deshalb gezwungen, sich für den dringenden Zweck der Männer zu bedienen, welche die Botschaft der Jabesiter nach Gibea gebracht hatten. Daher המלאכים = die oben genannten Boten."

messengers allowed to leave Jabesh to approximately those required to cover the territory, the logical implication of v. 7 is that virtually the entire contingent must have come together to Gibeah. This conclusion alone does not, of course, prove that ch. 11 presupposes knowledge of Saul's appointment as king.[126] It does, however, invalidate the argument that the opposite, viz. the chapter's ignorance of Saul's appointment, is evidenced by a general dispersal "throughout the territory of Israel".

If we assume, then, that the messengers were sent to Gibeah to find Saul, we are faced with another problem. How can we explain the fact that they do not deliver the message specifically to Saul but convey it to the people generally? Saul learns the news only by inquiring of those around him about the weeping of the people. The difficulty here raised is more apparent than real, for, as the text indicates, Saul was not present when the messengers arrived in Gibeah. There is no reason to assume that in Saul's absence the messengers would have withheld the nature of their mission from the inhabitants of Gibeah. And while the distress of the people upon hearing the news does suggest a sense of unpreparedness to deal with the crisis, this does not necessarily imply ignorance of the events at Mizpah in the previous chapter. Their distress may simply betray scepticism such as was expressed in 10:27, viz. how can this one save us who has yet done nothing to prove himself?[127] As the people are weeping, "just at that time (וְהִנֵּה) Saul is coming in behind the oxen from the field" (v. 5).[128] While still on his way,[129] Saul

---

[126] Various scholars have argued that the convergence of the Jabeshite messengers on Gibeah was motivated not by Saul's presence there at all but by some special relationship that existed between Jabesh and Benjamin. Cf. Möhlenbrink, "Saul's Ammoniterfeldzug", 57-64; Stoebe, 226-27. It is worth noting, however, that in ch. 11 only Gibeah is mentioned — and not the tribe of Benjamin, as might be expected. Schunck (*Benjamin*, 118 note 42) recognizes that ch. 11 gives the impression that the messengers came directly to Gibeah, but, assuming that Saul "noch nicht genauer bekannt gewesen sein kann", he concludes that the explanation must lie in "alten verwandtschaftlichen Beziehungen" between the inhabitants of Jabesh and Gibeah.

[127] Cf. Eslinger, *Kingship*, 364: "Even the inhabitants of Saul's own home town do not consider Saul, their elected king, as a possible deliverer. ...they seem to agree with the doubts of the 'renegades' about the ability of Saul's monarchy to serve as Israel's delivering agency."

[128] McCarter's translation (198); cf. Stoebe: "Doch da in dem Augenblick kam Saul hinter seinen Pflugrindern vom Felde her" (219).

[129] Indicated by the qal participle בָא.

hears the weeping of the people and asks, presumably at the first opportunity, what it means. Under such circumstances, it is dubious, at best, to argue that Saul is not the intended recipient of the message simply because he does not receive it at first hand from the Jabeshite emissaries. In sum: the arguments used to support the view that ch. 11 knows nothing of Saul's election have been found wanting.

Are References to Samuel in 1 Sam 11 Secondary?

In support of the prevailing opinion that 1 Samuel 11 represents an essentially independent tradition, it is customary to regard elements in the text which would establish links between ch. 11 and the preceding episodes as redactional. The reference to Samuel in v. 7, for example, is labelled a gloss, while later references to the prophet in vv. 12 and 14 are also discounted on the assumption that the section comprising vv. 12-14 is a harmonizing insertion.[130] How are we to evaluate these judgements?

So entrenched is the notion that Samuel does not belong in v. 7 that the reasoning behind it is seldom explicitly stated. When reasons are given, the major observation is simply that Samuel plays an uncharacteristically secondary role in the chapter — indeed, he appears to be almost superfluous. He is not mentioned in the episode prior to v. 7, nor is he said to play a significant role in the subsequent victory over Nahash.[131] Also sometimes cited as evidence is the orthographic disparity between אַחֲרֵי שָׁאוּל and אַחַר שְׁמוּאֵל (v. 7a), which is taken to suggest that the latter phrase is a gloss.

In response to these arguments, we would observe, first of all, that the last-mentioned piece of evidence is open to various explanations and is far too ambiguous to carry much weight. It is possible, for instance, that the text may have suffered slight corruption, the loss or addition of a י after a ר being quite conceivable. But assuming the soundness of the text, it may simply be that alternative forms of the preposition have been used in the interest of stylistic balance — the longer form coming first and accompanying the shorter name and vice versa. At any rate, it

---

130 Cf. Mettinger, *King and Messiah*, 84-85.

131 Cf. Mettinger, *King and Messiah*, 84-85; Birch, *Rise*, 55. Budde (75) adds yet another reason: "Samuel selbst hält sich hier laut 10 7 für völlig überflüssig." This observation apparently rests on the assumption that the Ammonite episode represents an unqualified fulfilment of 10:7, but it is now fairly widely recognized that the proper fulfilment of 10:7 is found in 13:3ff (see Chs. 2, 6 and *passim*).

seems just as likely that an original narrator might introduce stylistic variation as that an interpolator would do so.

Secondly, as regards Samuel's role in the episode, while it is certainly true that the focus of ch. 11 is upon *Saul's* dramatic rescue of Jabesh-gilead, this need not suggest that Samuel had no part to play. As we noted in Ch. 2, it is widely recognized that prophets and priests played significant roles in warfare, not only in Israel but throughout the ancient Near East. Moreover, the fact that Samuel is not mentioned in the episode prior to v. 7 implies nothing about Samuel that could not also be said of Saul, who likewise appears (v. 5) without prior introduction in the episode.[132] There appears, then, to be no compelling reason to drop the reference to Samuel in v. 7, and, indeed, all along some scholars have kept open the possibility of its originality.[133]

But what of the references to Samuel in vv. 12 and 14? Since it is unmistakable that the dissenters to Saul's rulership previously mentioned in 10:27 are again in view in 11:12-13, and since the former verse is often regarded as secondary, the latter verses have come under suspicion by association. Moreover, the "clearest evidence of redactional activity" in ch. 11, according to Birch,[134] is the contradiction between "the exhortation of Samuel [in v. 14] 'to renew the kingdom' נחדש שם המלוכה at Gilgal" and the statement of v. 15 "that it was on this occasion at Gilgal that Saul was actually 'made king' וימלכו שם את־שאול by the people".[135]

The gravity of this problem has been elaborated by Vannoy in his book *Covenant Renewal in Gilgal*. His main points are the following. First, he argues that attempts to explain חדש pi. as meaning simply 'inaugurate', 'confirm', or 'celebrate' must be regarded as dubious.[136] Rather, it appears from the biblical evidence "that in all of its occurrences חדש speaks of the restoration or repair of something that already exists, be that a material or immaterial entity, but which in some sense

---

[132] The only previous allusion to Saul is in the name of the village גבעת שאול in v. 4, but this reference presupposes that Saul is already known. The specific information that Saul was a resident of Gibeah is first introduced in 10:26 (cf. Halpern, *Constitution*, 155), though already in 9:1-2 Saul is identified as a Benjaminite.

[133] Cf. Kirkpatrick, 115; Kittel, *Geschichte*, 81 n. 4, 82; Hertzberg, 70 n. 2/ET 90 n. b; Ishida, *Royal Dynasties*, 47-48.

[134] *Rise*, 60.

[135] *Rise*, 56.

[136] *Covenant Renewal*, 62-64; 126.

is in a condition of deterioration."[137] Secondly, he refutes the view that מלך hi. in v. 15 may refer simply to Saul's public anointing[138] and insists, rather, that מלך hi. "is consistently utilized to designate the official inauguration of someone's rule as king". Thirdly, he observes that there is not "any indication that he [Saul] assumed the responsibilities and prerogatives of a newly installed king" at the time of 10:17-27.[139] Adding these points together, Vannoy concludes that the 'renewal' of which 11:14 speaks *cannot* refer to Saul's kingship, but must refer to the kingship of Yahweh.[140]

While the overall thesis of Vannoy's book — viz. that 1 Sam 12 represents a covenant renewal ceremony subsequent to the Ammonite defeat — has much to commend it, we would concur with the judgement of P. J. M. Southwell that "the case for seeing המלוכה in xi. 14 as a reference to the kingship of Yahweh is not really made out".[141] As Vannoy himself recognizes, the focus in the immediate context is upon the kingship of Saul (11:12, 15; 12:1, 2).[142] Moreover, even if we grant Vannoy's main points about the meanings of חדש and מלך hi., a better solution to the apparent tension between 11:14 and 11:15 may be possible in the light of the three-part accession process discussed in the previous chapter. According to this pattern, the initial designation of the chosen individual was to be followed by a real or ritual victory,

---

[137] *Covenant Renewal*, 64.

[138] He regards LXX's καὶ ἔχρισεν Σαμουήλ as an interpretation of וימלכו rather than as evidence that a phrase has dropped out of MT (*Covenant Renewal*, 85-86).

[139] *Covenant Renewal*, 86-87.

[140] *Covenant Renewal*, 67-68; 81-82; 126-27.

[141] Review of *Covenant Renewal*, 119.

[142] *Covenant Renewal*, 68. This is not to deny Vannoy's observation (ibid.) that the kingship of Yahweh is also at issue in the broader context — he notes מלך terminology applied to Yahweh in 8:7; 12:12 (cf. 10:19). On the antiquity of the concept of Yahweh's kingship, see Vannoy's extensive discussion (*Covenant Renewal*, 69-80). Cf. also Ishida's summary of various opinions on this important question (*Royal Dynasties*, 37-39). Ishida's view is that the origin of the concept of Yahweh as king is to be sought in the pre-monarchical Shilonite tradition. He notes that "the two epithets by which Yahweh was called at Shiloh — Yahweh $ṣ^eba'ôt$ (I Sam $1_{3.11}$ 4_4) and Yahweh who sits above the Cherubim (4_4)...are perfectly fit for Yahweh as king" (37-38). He suggests that Samuel's position as inheritor of this Shilonite tradition explains not only his constant reference to "Yahweh as king (12_{12}) and deliverer of Israel (7_3 10_{18-19} 11_{13} $12_{7.11}$; cf. 7_8 9_{16} 10_1 LXX)" but his adverse reaction to the Israelite elders' demand for a king as well (39).

which in turn would lead to confirmation of that individual's leadership. The "official inauguration"[143] would not take place until after the victory — in Saul's case, as it turned out, after the defeat of Ammon.[144] To suggest, however, that we cannot speak of Saul's kingship in any sense until after the third stage of the process seems unjustified. This does not appear to be the perspective of the narrative elsewhere. In 10:25, for example, which describes the proclamation, inscription and deposition of the המלוכה משפט, human kingship is clearly in view.[145] And even as early as the account of Saul's secret anointing, the narrator regards Saul's kingship as at issue: "but of the matter of the kingdom (המלוכה) he told him nothing" (10:16). In the light of these observations, it would appear that, while Saul's kingship was "officially inaugurated" (the sense of מלך hi. in 11:15)[146] only after the demonstration of his ability to deliver, it is nonetheless admissible to speak of Saul's "kingship" from the very beginning of the accession process.

How then are we to understand the "renewal" of the kingdom? In what sense is it possible to speak of Saul's kingship as in a state of deterioration[147] and in need of renewal? Again, we must recall our discussion of the anointing episode. There we argued that Saul's anointing and its confirmation by three signs should have been followed by an act of provocation against the Philistines.[148] Such an action would have brought Saul to public attention by demonstrating his abilities as a deliverer. In a manner not inconsistent with his character as depicted elsewhere, however, Saul hesitated to 'do what his hand found to do' (cf. 10:7), and the accession process was, temporarily at least, arrested. In the absence of any demonstration of his saving abilities, even Saul's selection by lot and his commanding physique were insufficient to gain him the unanimous support of the people (cf. 10:27). Finally, the Ammonite victory, though not *the* demonstration envisaged at the time of Saul's anointing and commissioning, was sufficient to silence the dissenters and set the accession process back on

---

[143] Which is the connotation of מלך hi. in 11:15, according to Vannoy (see the preceding paragraph).

[144] We note that the regnal formula marking the *official* beginning of Saul's reign is introduced in 13:1.

[145] Cf. Southwell, Review of Vannoy's *Covenant Renewal*, 119.

[146] See above, pp. 225-26.

[147] Cf. Vannoy's formulation quoted above.

[148] See above, p. 207, and for full discussion, see Ch. 2.

track. It seems likely that the 'renewing of the kingdom' served as a public recognition of this change in the situation.

In the light of these considerations, we would conclude that there is no essential contradiction between vv. 14 and 15, and the case for regarding 11:12-14 as a harmonizing insertion is not compelling. There is therefore no reason to regard references to Samuel in these verses or, as we have already seen, in v. 7 as secondary, and our contention that ch. 11 is integral to its present textual context is strengthened.[149]

The Portrait of Saul in 1 Samuel 11

If there is any episode in Saul's career in which he is depicted positively, it must be ch. 11. When the messengers arrive from Jabesh-gilead, it is Saul who is propelled into action by the divine spirit (רוח אלהים; v. 6).[150] It is Saul who leads the dramatic rescue of the Jabesh-gileadites. And in the aftermath of the battle it is Saul who intervenes on behalf of those who had earlier questioned his ability to deliver Israel (v. 13). It is easy to see how 1 Sam 11 has come to be regarded as a high point in Saul's career, for this it undoubtedly is.

Yet even this most positive episode does not qualify as a purely pro-Saulide account. In the first place, MT's רוח אלהים (v. 6) rather than רוח יהוה may imply an intentional avoidance of linking the name Yahweh with Saul.[151] Secondly, the Ammonite victory is, as we have suggested, a substitute demonstration, not the one envisaged in Saul's initial commissioning. Israel's major problem, the Philistines, is left unresolved.[152] Thirdly, there may also be a negative side to Saul's portrayal in the style of a pre-monarchic hero-deliverer. Edelman, for example, has recently challenged the prevalent notion that Saul's appearance in the role of a "šopeṭ deliverer of Israel" in 1 Sam 11:1-11 is to

---

[149] For further arguments in support of this view, see Ch. 6, pp. 190-91.

[150] LXX attests רוח יהוה and is followed by, for example, Budde (75) and Smith (78).

[151] On the possibility that this avoidance contains an implicit criticism, see Wentz, Monarchy, 216-17. We have already noted this same feature in our discussions of 10:5, 10; 14:47-48. Cf. also Beuken ("1 Samuel 28", 5). A similar instance may be found in Num 22 (esp. vv. 7-20) where Balaam consistently refers to the deity as Yahweh, while the narrator very deliberately uses the more generic "God" in relation to Balaam.

[152] Cf. Ch. 2, pp. 51-55; Ch. 6, pp. 188-89, 193-94.

be positively assessed.[153] She argues that this depiction, in fact, represents a demotion of Saul from his status as king to that of "a humble farmer upon whom the 'spirit of Yahweh'[154] descended". Reasons for this demotion, according to Edelman, include a desire to provide an adequate fulfilment of the intermediate, testing stage of the "three-part structure of kingship elevation" and a desire to bring Saul "into the historical scheme developed in the Book of Judges as a continuation of the tradition of the temporary military 'savior' of Israel". In addition to these two motivations, Edelman cites approvingly G. W. Ahlström's suggestion, conveyed in private conversation, that the depiction of Saul as behaving like a judge "may reflect the desire to detract from Saul's status as first king of Israel, hoping to imply that David filled this role".[155]

While Ahlström's suggestion is problematic,[156] we would concur in a general way with several of Edelman's observations — viz. that Saul is depicted in 1 Sam 11 as standing in the 'judges tradition', that the events of the chapter represent the testing stage in Saul's ascent to the throne, and that the portrayal of Saul in the chapter is perhaps not as favourable as has generally been assumed. It is doubtful, however, that Saul's depiction in ch. 11 represents a *demotion* in the sense envisaged by Edelman. In her view, at the time of the Ammonite siege of Jabesh, Saul was already an "established king of known repute in Cisjordan, with a strong military force."[157] On the basis of this historical judgement, she argues,

> ...the writer of the story...seems to have taken a battle fought by king Saul, removed it from its historical context, and used this event as the core of his portrayal of Saul as a *šopeṭ* deliverer of Israel. In so doing, Saul was demoted from king to a humble farmer....[158]

---

[153] "Saul's Rescue", 207-208.

[154] Edelman apparently follows LXX here; MT reads רוח־אלהים.

[155] "Saul's Rescue", 207-208.

[156] It not only must ignore the other Saul traditions in which Saul appears as Israel's first king, but it also overlooks the fact that one of the major purposes of the episode before us is to show how the opposition to Saul's kingship was silenced.

[157] "Saul's Rescue", 203.

[158] "Saul's Rescue", 207.

The thread of argument whereby Edelman arrives at this historical reconstruction, as distinct from the literary "depiction of history",[159] seems thin at several points. Her argument runs as follows. The terms of David's overture to the Jabesh-gileadites in 2 Sam 2:4b-7 — i.e. "the phrase *'aśâ haṭṭôbâ*, 'make a friendship treaty', together with the title 'lord' (*'adôn*) to designate Saul's status *vis-à-vis* Jabesh-gilead"[160] — indicate that the relationship of Saul to the city of Jabesh-gilead had not been that of king to subject but of suzerain to vassal. If this is so, she argues, "Jabesh-gilead was not a corporate, constituent member of the Israelite state in the time of Saul", and "the people's appeal to Saul could not have been based on 'tribal' ties as member of an entity called 'Israel' as the story now claims."[161] By this line of reasoning Edelman arrives at the following historical conjecture:

> The Jabesh-gileadites would have recognized him [Saul] as an equal or rival to Nahash, who would have been ca-pable of defending their city from the present Ammonite attack and other future foreign incursions. This tradition thus seems to presume a historical situation in which Saul already was an established, successful king, even though it is being used to illustrate Saul's suitability to become king in its present form and location.[162]

Having adopted the above hypothesis, Edelman is led to draw some far-reaching conclusions about "the traditio-historical development of 1 Sam 11 1-11":

> Since Jabesh-gilead was not Israelite, all references which suggest that it was a member of Israel, appealing to its brethren for help, must be later additions (2b, 3-4). Since the historical situation behind the narrative pre-supposes Saul's kingship, his characterization as a farmer in V. 5 cannot be original, nor can the related portrayal of him as a *śopeṭ* receiving divine charisma in V. 6.[163]

When all is said and done, Edelman is left with only "VV. 1-2a or b, 4a, 8a, and 9-11" as reflecting the "original form of the story in 1

---

[159] "Saul's Rescue", 195.
[160] "Saul's Rescue", 202.
[161] "Saul's Rescue", 203.
[162] "Saul's Rescue", 203.
[163] "Saul's Rescue", 205.

Sam 11 1-11", though even these verses do not necessarily "stem directly from an 'original account'".[164] She concludes: "The present form of the tradition in 1 Sam 11 1-11, which depicts Saul's charismatic rescue of his beleagered [*sic*] Israelite brethren, therefore can be exposed as a literary fiction."[165]

Edelman's traditio-historical theory is open to objection at several points. As regards the phrase *'aśâ haṭṭôbâ*, for example, Edelman admits that it "was not limited to a specific form of treaty",[166] and she offers no reason why such a phrase might not be used in royal covenants. Mettinger, in fact, comes to that very conclusion: "this term refers to a royal covenant in 2 S 2,6."[167] If Mettinger is correct, the sole foundation of Edelman's historical reconstruction is destroyed.[168] Further incongruities in her argument include her somewhat conflicting observations regarding the advantages or disadvantages of vassalage versus annexation[169] and her failure to explain why, if Saul were already an established king of known repute and "an equal or rival to Nahash",[170] Nahash would have allowed the Jabeshites time to seek help from Israel in the first place. Thus, while showing keen insight in her discussion of the Ammonite episode as the 'testing stage' in Saul's rise to power (see Ch. 6 above), Edelman is less convincing in her explanation of the motivation behind Saul's depiction in ch. 11.

Perhaps the negative elements in the portrait of Saul in ch. 11 are to be seen differently. In our analysis of chs. 9 and 10, we noted that in various ways Saul is portrayed as the reluctant monarch, a hesitant ap-

---

[164] "Saul's Rescue", 206.

[165] "Saul's Rescue", 208-209.

[166] "Saul's Rescue", 202.

[167] *King and Messiah*, 149; cf. 147-48. For further literature on this treaty terminology, see ibid., 147 nn. 32, 33; Edelman, "Saul's Rescue", 202 nn. 29, 30.

[168] It is perhaps not inconsequential that David mentions his kingship over Judah in the same breath with his appeal to Jabesh-gilead (2 Sam 2:7).

[169] She observes ("Saul's Rescue", 203) that as a vassal, Jabesh-gilead would not only serve as a "valuable buffer city-state in Transjordan" but would also "supply the state of Israel with tribute and troops when needed; as an annexed territory, it would have cost the state much money to protect and maintain." But on p. 205 she argues that, had Saul wished to utilize the region in "power politics", "he would have annexed the territory of Jabesh-Gilead into his state and made it part of Israel rather than allowing it to remain an independent vassal region."

[170] "Saul's Rescue", 203.

pointee who not only fails to accomplish his first assignment but is
reticent even to speak of the kingship (10:16) or to show himself at his
public election (10:22-23). In ch. 11, Saul's appearance in the style of
a pre-monarchic judge tends to underscore this aspect of his portrait.
Saul has apparently done little, if anything, to realize his kingship. He
may even have returned to farming (11:5). It is perhaps not insignifi-
cant that when Saul finally begins to act, he does so in ways strongly
reminiscent of Judg 19:29. It is widely recognized that Judg 19 and 1
Sam 11 are analogous at numerous points.[171] The significance(s) of the
correspondences and the issue of possible dependence, however, continue to be debated,[172] so that few conclusions can be drawn. It is at
least interesting to note that the gruesome action of the Levite in Judg
19 took place at a time when "there was *no king* in Israel".[173] Is there
perhaps an insinuation in 1 Sam 11 that, due to Saul's inaction since
his appointment to 'save Israel',[174] the situation has not yet much im-
proved?[175]

Conclusion

In keeping with our stated objectives, this chapter has focused on
two main issues: 1) the question of narrative coherence and continuity
among the constituent episodes in chs. 9-11 and 2) the portrayal of Saul
in these chapters. The first issue required discussion of various diachronic questions which are frequently raised with respect to the several

---

[171] See, e.g., Hertzberg, 72-73/ET 93; Ackroyd, 91; Smelik, 113;
McCarter, 203; Kiel, 101; Jüngling, *Richter 19*, 36, esp. 236-37; Klein,
107; Lasine, "Guest", 41-43.

[172] The common view that Judg 19 is dependent upon 1 Sam 11 has
recently been challenged by Jüngling (*Richter 19*, 237; for literature sup-
porting the common view, see Jüngling's listing, ibid., 36, n. 155).

[173] Judg 19:1; cf. 17:6; 18:1; 21:25.

[174] 1 Sam 9:16; 10:1 (LXX). Cf. also the taunting question which
immediately precedes ch. 11, "How can this one save us?" (10:27).

[175] As our focus is upon the portrait of Saul in 1 Sam 11, we have considered the significance of the Judg 19 parallel only as it relates to this issue. But there may well be other implications. It may, for example, contain
an implicit criticism of the people's earlier request for a king — the old system could have sufficed (cf. 1 Sam 12:11-12) — or perhaps a hint that even
after the introduction of kingship, "deliverance may still come in the old
way" (Gordon, *Samuel*, 48).

episodes comprising 'Saul's Rise' — for example, the seer-Samuel identification in 9:1ff., the two-source theory in 10:17ff., the question of the independence of ch. 11 from its present context, etc. The conclusion was reached that those features most often cited as evidence of disunity within the individual sections, or of their mutual independence, can be explained satisfactorily in literary, narrative terms. This conclusion does not deny, of course, the very logical assumption that antecedent traditions underlie the present form of the narrative in 1 Sam 9-11, but it does call in question our ability to reconstruct these traditions in the kinds of ways often advocated by Old Testament scholars.

As regards the second issue: while it is true that, if Saul's career is to be allowed a positive phase at all, it must be the period of his election and ascent to the throne, our investigation has uncovered even in these earlier episodes various negative elements in Saul's portrayal. These negative elements, to borrow Alter's words from another context, are no more than "subliminal intimation[s] of things to come", but this is not surprising in the text of Samuel where, as in other Old Testament narratives, "terse understatement remains the norm, and future turns of events are adumbrated by the slight, disturbing dissonance produced when [for example] in a pattern of repetition some ambiguous phrase is substituted for a more reassuring one",[176] or when in a pattern of expectation such as the accession process events do not unfold as anticipated. It should be observed that none of the subtle dissonances in Saul's depiction in chs. 9-11 were found to suggest ill-will on Saul's part. But the hints of passivity and imperception, hesitancy and inability to listen, along with the emphasis on external, to the exclusion of internal, qualities, do suggest to the attentive reader that Saul may well be ill-suited to the role of king. In these respects, the conclusions of our investigation of Saul's early career accord well with our findings regarding chs. 13-15.

---

[176] Alter, *Art*, 101.

Concluding Reflections

This study began with the observation that King Saul and the biblical traditions describing his career pose difficult interpretive questions on several different levels, including the literary, theological and historical. One of the most vexing issues, and the one with which we have been chiefly exercised in the foregoing pages, is the matter of Saul's rejection. As it would have been impracticable within the limits of this study to attempt to do justice to all three areas mentioned above, we have chosen to concentrate our efforts on what Tsevat has described as the "main business" of "commentators on the historical books of the Old Testament", namely "the elucidation of what the books mean to convey",[1] insofar as such intentionality exists and is accessible to the modern reader. Our approach, accordingly, has been primarily literary and theological (or ideological). Historical questions have on occasion been considered, but these have been mostly of the "generalizing" variety.[2] No attempt has been made to reconstruct a history of Saul's reign. Much more groundwork remains to be done before a historical reconstruction (if indeed such is possible on the basis of the available evidence) can be attempted. Nevertheless, since historical reconstructions of the period depend heavily for their data on literary judgements regarding the sources, our results may well have an eventual contribution to make in that area.

Summaries of the results of our study are included at the end of each chapter, making full description unnecessary here. A brief overview, however, is in order. Ch. 1 laid the theoretical foundations for the synthetic literary method that we would pursue in our investigation of the Saul traditions. Ch. 2 introduced the very important matter

---

[1] "Israelite History", 177. For this task, as Tsevat goes on to say, "it makes no difference whether one assumes or denies historical ascertainability of the primary event" (181).

[2] Tsevat ("Israelite History", 185) describes "generalizing history" as that which concerns itself with the "social, economic, cultural, and religious background" of texts, as opposed to "individualizing history" which concerns itself with "particular circumstances, special events, specific individuals", etc.

of the relationship between Saul's 'first charge' at the time of his anointing in 1 Sam 10 and the events surrounding his first Philistine encounters in 1 Sam 13-14. We discovered that the widespread opinion, since Wellhausen, that the Gilgal episode in 13:7b-15a along with its obvious anticipation in 10:8 are out of place in their respective contexts is based on insubstantial evidence. With the Gilgal episode reinstated in ch. 13, we were able to recognize (Chs. 3 and 4) that the business of 1 Sam 13-14 is the description and defence of the rejection of Saul, the latter accomplished largely through modes of indirect characterization. Neither in these chapters nor in 1 Sam 15 (discussed in Ch. 5) were Saul's offences found to be 'trivial'. Recognition of the relationship between the charge given Saul at the time of his *nāgîd* anointing and the events of 1 Sam 13 led to a perception of Saul's disobedience as a (witting or unwitting) failure to accept the authority structure by which human kingship was to be made acceptable within the theocratic *Weltanschauung* of Hebrew historiography. Having gained a perspective on the internal and external factors contributing to Saul's failure, we turned in Chs. 6 and 7 to test our results in the light of the much-debated traditions recounting Saul's early career, viz. 1 Sam 9-11. Recognition of a 'pattern of accession' within Israel's historiographical traditions was but one of several factors which seemed to call for a re-assessment of the reputation of 1 Sam 9-11 as a *locus classicus* for source criticism in Samuel.

A major result of our synthetic literary investigations of 1 Sam 9-15 was the discovery within these chapters of a higher degree of narrative coherence and ideological consistency than has commonly been recognized. This in turn opened the door to a clearer perception of the (largely unfavourable) portrayal of Saul in these chapters. Even those sections commonly assigned to an assumed pro-monarchical source were found to contain numerous hints of deficiencies in Saul. As regards attitudes to the monarchy, we recognized the necessity of distinguishing clearly between attitudes towards 1) monarchy in general, 2) Saul's kingship in particular, and 3) the people's request for a king. The narratives were found to be predominantly ambivalent regarding the first, (sometimes implicitly) unfavourable regarding the second, and explicitly negative regarding the third.

We may now consider the significance of these findings for a theological assessment of Saul's failure. As noted at the beginning of this study, the specific nature of Saul's sin or sins in chs. 13 and 15 has long been a matter of debate. The comments of H. Donner, writing in 1981, are not atypical:

> There seem to be too many rather than too few answers, especially since the explanatory accounts [i.e., according to Donner, 13:7b-15a; 14:23b-46; ch. 15; and ch. 28] are not in agreement — in fact they contradict each other and have in common only that Saul's rejection was a result of his religious lapses.[3]

In recognizing a common element underlying all of Saul's offences, viz. religious inadequacy, Donner is perhaps closer to resolving the apparent contradiction than he realizes. We argued at some length in Ch. 5 that much confusion has arisen from a failure by many commentators to observe that Saul's offences are described in the narratives on different levels. In 1 Sam 13, for example, Saul's specific offence is his failure to await Samuel's arrival before beginning to 'consecrate battle'. On a more general level, this connotes disobedience to Yahweh's previous instructions as issued through the prophet (cf. the explicit indictment in 13:13). And at a deeper level still, it indicates a disregard on Saul's part for the structure of authority established at the time of his *nāgîd* appointment (cf. 13:14). In the same way, while Saul's specific offence in 1 Sam 15 is his failure to execute the ban completely, again the more basic wrong is his disobedience to the word of Yahweh through the prophet and, ultimately, his disregard for the aforementioned authority structure. Thus, in both instances the surface-level offences are distinct, while the failure at a deeper level is one and the same. These observations go some way towards elucidating the matter of Saul's rejection, at least in terms of his own share in the responsibility. But there is more that can be said.

Gunn in his book *The Fate of King Saul* poses a more fundamental and more provocative question. He asks, "Does Saul fail as king because of his own inner inadequacy as a human being, or because he is brought low essentially by external forces or circumstances?" (115). Gunn's answer embraces both options, but not in equal measure. To be sure, "it would be simplistic to claim that Saul makes no contribution to his own fate" (116). But it is not Saul, in Gunn's view, who is primarily responsible. "Saul, one may say, is culpable, but ... ; and the 'but' sends us back to look again closely at the announcement of re-

---

[3] Donner, "Historiography", 44.

jection, its author, and its motivation" (120). After all, Saul "is not God's enemy through his own choosing. His role as king is thrust upon him by Yahweh" (124). His rejection, moreover, when it comes, seems "calculated and contrived" (115). "Saul's culpability is more technical than of moral substance. His condemnation (rejection) is radically out of balance with the nature of his 'crimes'" (124). In short, according to Gunn, "Saul's rejection is not intrinsically and inevitably the outcome of his actions" (124). Saul appears, rather, as "essentially an innocent victim of God" (123) to whom "the judgements of Yahweh must have appeared as outbreaks of irrationality" (128). All of this, Gunn concludes, makes questions about the "moral basis of Yahweh's action" inescapable:

> If we are to condemn Saul for his jealous persecution of David, how much more is Yahweh to be condemned for his jealous persecution of Saul! ... He is insulted, feels jealous, is anxious to justify himself. It is tempting to say that this is the human face of God — but to say that is perhaps to denigrate man, and that is not something this Old Testament story does; rather we might say that here we see the dark side of God. (129)

While Gunn shows keen insight at numerous points and argues his case with considerable skill, our own analysis of the traditions recounting Saul's rise and rejection yields several points of major disagreement. We agree with Gunn that both "inner inadequacy" and "external forces or circumstances" play a part in Saul's failure. We agree that kingship was not something that Saul sought but something that was thrust upon him. We agree that, in the early stages at least (chs. 13-14), the judgements of Yahweh appear to baffle Saul. And we agree that Saul appears in some sense to be a "victim". We do not agree, however, that Saul's rejection was "calculated and contrived" or that it was "radically out of balance with the nature of his 'crimes'". As we have already seen, Saul's concrete misdeeds, whether the result of misunderstanding (possibly, though not necessarily, in ch. 13) or disregard (clearly in ch. 15), are but symptomatic of a far more fundamental problem, namely an unreadiness or inability on Saul's part to conform himself to the 'bifurcated' authority structure established by Samuel at the time of his anointing (10:7-8) and reiterated just prior to the Amalekite campaign (15:1). Since, according to the theocratic perspective of the narratives as we have them, compliance in this regard is essential to the success of Israelite kingship, Saul's rejection is clearly based on more than a mere technicality. There is a direct relationship between Saul's misdeeds and the failure of his kingship, and there is, therefore, no cause to question the "moral basis of Yahweh's action".

But we have already agreed with Gunn that Saul in some sense appears as a victim — he neither grasped the kingship for himself nor does he seem to grasp the full import of his offences. How are we to understand these features? Gunn maintains that we must look again closely at the *announcement of rejection* to find answers. We would suggest, however, that we should look first at the *circumstances of Saul's election*. And, in fact, Gunn pursues this idea up to a point. He observes that "the story of Saul is about kings and kingship: the people want a king, their God grants them their wish and chooses one" (123). Saul, then, is in a very real sense the "people's king" (125). They take the initiative, and Yahweh, after warning them, accedes to their request (1 Sam 8). That this initiative-taking by the people is viewed as 'sinful' is made quite clear in each of Samuel's speeches in 1 Sam 8; 10:17ff.; 12. It has been observed by McCarthy[4] and others that the people's sin is expiated through their repentance in ch. 12. While there is a sense in which McCarthy is right in saying that the events of ch. 12 resolve the conflict between Yahweh and the people with respect to human kingship, Gunn is quite correct in insisting that "the people's repentance is only part of the quid pro quo demanded by Yahweh" (127). Our point of disagreement with Gunn is in his contention that the "other part", in his view a function of the "repentance" or "expiation" of Yahweh, is the mandatory rejection of Saul (127). We would maintain, rather, that "the other part" demanded by Yahweh, before Saul's kingship can be confirmed, is a clear demonstration of Saul's willingness to accept a circumscribed royal authority — to rule, in other words, as a vassal of Yahweh. Compliance with the procedure set forth in Saul's first charge (10:7-8) would have served admirably as such a demonstration. But Saul failed, as we have seen, in precisely this matter, and it is this failure, and not some necessity on Yahweh's part to "expiate" his own involvement in the institution of human kingship, that accounts for Saul's rejection.

But why did Saul fail? Throughout our investigations of 1 Sam 9-11 we observed numerous dissonances in the portrayal of Saul. We saw that the effect of these is to suggest that Saul may well be ill-suited to the throne of Israel. Among the more obvious is the consistent avoid-

---

[4] Cited by Gunn, *Fate*, 126f.

ance of references to Saul's internal qualities or to Yahweh's being with him. But if Saul is not suited to the task and is thus destined to fail, why is kingship thrust upon him? It is our contention that everything in the narrative points to the people, and not Yahweh and Samuel (*pace* Gunn), as those *ultimately* responsible for the situation. It might be objected, of course, that Yahweh could have appointed someone else who would have been better suited to the task. And, indeed, this is precisely what he does when he appoints a *nāgîd* "of his own choosing" (13:14) — a king "for myself" (16:1), as opposed to a king "for them" (8:22). In the light of these considerations, we may not discount the possibility of a punitive element in the appointment of Saul. We are reminded of 10:17ff. where, as we saw, the selection of Saul comes at just that point in Samuel's speech where an announcement of judgement is expected. Perhaps there is justification for discerning an allusion to Saul and a similar viewpoint in Hosea 13:11: "I gave you a king in my anger, and took him away in my wrath". The implication of this verse, according to Andersen and Freedman, is that "even the original concession [to the people's request for a king] was an act of divine wrath".[5]

Whether and to what extent 1 Samuel's depiction of Saul and of the failure of his reign corresponds to historical reality is a question beyond the scope of the present study. In view of the paucity of extra-biblical evidence, moreover, an answer to this question might prove very difficult to obtain. While a clearer understanding of the coherence of the Saul material as part of a continuous narrative tends to undermine some negative historical judgements, it remains, to a degree at least, a matter of predisposition or, as Tsevat puts it, "personal decision"[6] whether one perceives literary history or literary fiction (or some combination of the two) in the books of Samuel. Perhaps a way forward is indicated by the comparative generic studies which have appeared with increasing frequency in recent years.[7] Whitelam, for example, in his article entitled "The Defence of David", argues that "the narrative complex 1 Sam 9-2 Kgs 2" [*sic*, read 1 Kgs] is best understood as "royal propaganda".[8]

---

[5] *Hosea*, 636.

[6] "Israelite History", 184.

[7] E.g., Whitelam, "Defence"; Perdue, "Testament of David"; Tadmor, "Autobiographical Apology"; McCarter, "Apology"; Humphreys, "Rise and Fall".

[8] "Defence", 75-76.

Given the "consistently anti-Saul and pro-David"[9] slant of the material, this seems a reasonable suggestion, so long as we bear in mind that propaganda is a neutral term.[10] As to the provenance of this material, Whitelam writes:

> It is by no means unreasonable to believe that the Judean royal bureaucracy was capable of producing written propaganda or apologetic aimed at an élite audience when the literary output of neighbouring bureaucracies is taken into consideration. Written propaganda emanating from the Near Eastern royal chancelleries is well attested over a considerable period of time.[11]

The results of Whitelam's and other similar studies tend to call in question, for example, Smelik's contention that the lack of comparative historiographical literature in the archaeological record rules out the possibility that the Saul narratives could stem from the early first millennium.[12] This having been said, however, questions still remain. How, for example, is the notion of propaganda to be reconciled with the apparently prophetic tone and theological point of view so evident in the narratives? And how do these features affect our understanding of the historicity of the material? Such questions require to be studied at greater length than is possible here. But in parting, we can perhaps do no better than to quote Soggin, whose comments regarding the dominance of "theological" over "economic and political" concerns in the Deuteronomistic History seem equally applicable to the Saul narratives that have formed the focus of our study:

> In this sense, then, Dtr is a history, but the criteria for the choice and collection of its material are substantially different from those that a modern historian would consider suitable for corroborating his theories. We must therefore accept without regret the accusation of tendentiousness, remembering at the same time that every history is tendentious in that it presupposes certain conditioning factors in history writing (no

---

[9] So Evans, "Historical Reconstruction", 64.

[10] So also Whitelam, "Defence", 65.

[11] "Defence", 71. Whitelam mentions in particular the "apology of Hattusili III" and the "prophecy of Neferti".

[12] Smelik argues, for instance, that "de schrijvers ten tijde van David (en ook nog Salomo) weinig inspirerende voorbeelden uit die *Umwelt* gekend kunnen hebben" (*Saul*, 76; cf. his other conclusions on the same page).

historian starts from an ideological void) and also certain features which it seeks to prove and certain aims which it seeks to achieve.[13]

---

[13] *Introduction*, 163.

Bibliography

Included in this listing are only works cited above. Short titles are indicated in parentheses at the end of each entry.

Abrabanel, I. (יצחק אברבנאל)
 פירוש על נביאים ראשים [*Commentary on the Major Prophets*].
 Jerusalem: הוצאת ספרים תורה ודעת,1955. .... (פירוש)

Abrams, M. H.
 A Glossary of Literary Terms. 4th ed. New York: Holt, Rinehart and
 Winston, 1981. .... (*Glossary*)

Ackroyd, P. R.
 "The Hebrew Root באש". *JTS* n.s. 2 (1951) 31-36. .... ("Root באש")

 1 Samuel. CBC. Cambridge: University Press, 1971. .... (Ackroyd)

 "The Verb Love — '*āhēb* in the David Jonathan Narratives. A Footnote". *VT* 25 (1975) 213-14. .... ("Verb Love")

Ahlström, G. W.
 "Der Prophet Nathan und der Tempelbau". *VT* 11 (1961) 113-27. ....
 .... ("Prophet Nathan")

 "The Travels of the Ark: A Religio-Political Composition". *JNES* 43
 (1984) 141-49. .... ("Travels of the Ark")

Albrektson, B.
 "Some Observations on Two Oracular Passages in 1 Sam." *ASTI* 11
 (1977/78) 1-10. .... ("Some Observations")

Alonso Schökel, L.
 "Of Methods and Models". SVT 36 (1985) 3-13. .... ("Of Methods")

Alter, R.
 The Art of Biblical Narrative. New York: Basic Books, 1982. .....(*Art*)

 "How Convention Helps Us Read: The Case of the Bible's Annunciation Type-Scene". *Proof* 3 (1983) 115-30. ....
 .... ("How Convention Helps")

 "A Literary Approach to the Bible". *Commentary* 60 (1975) 70-77. ....
 .... ("Literary Approach")

"Sacred History and Prose Fiction". In *The Creation of Sacred Literature*, 7-24. Ed. by R. E. Friedman. NES 22. Berkeley: University of California, 1981. ....("Sacred History")

Althann, R.
"1 Sam 13,1: A Poetic Couplet". *Bib* 62 (1981) 241-46. ....
....("1 Sam 13,1")

Andersen, F. I. and Freedman, D. N.
Hosea: A New Translation with Introduction and Commentary. AB 24. Garden City: Doubleday, 1980. .... (*Hosea*)

Anderson, B. W.
Review of R. Rendtorff's *Das überlieferungsgeschichtliche Problem des Pentateuchs.* *CBQ* 40 (1978) 100-103. ....
....(Review of Rendtorff's *Problem*)

Ap-Thomas, D. R.
"Notes on Some Terms Relating to Prayer". *VT* 6 (1956) 225-41. ......
....("Notes")

"Saul's 'Uncle'". *VT* 11 (1961) 241-45. .... ("Saul's 'Uncle'")

Arnold, W. R.
"The Word פרש in the Old Testament". *JBL* 24 (1905) 45-53. ....
....("Word פרש")

Bach, R.
Die Aufforderungen zur Flucht und zum Kampf im alttestamentlichen Prophetenspruch. WMANT 9. Neukirchen: Neukirchener Verlag, 1962. ....(*Aufforderungen*)

Bacon, W. A.
The Art of Interpretation. 2nd ed. New York: Holt, Rinehart and Winston, 1972. .... (*Art of Interpretation*)

Bar-Efrat, S.
העיצוב האמנותי של הסיפור במקרא (*The Art of the Biblical Story*). Tel Aviv: Sifriat Poalim, 1979. ....(העיצוב האמנותי)

"Literary Modes and Methods in the Biblical Narrative: In View of 2 Samuel 10-20 and 1 Kings 1-2". *Imm* 8 (1978) 19-31. ....
....("Literary Modes")

"Some Observations on the Analysis of Structure in Biblical Narrative". *VT* 30 (1980) 154-73. ....("Some Observations")

Barr, J.
The Bible in the Modern World. New York: Harper & Row, 1973. ......
....*(Bible in the Modern World)*

"Childs' *Introduction to the Old Testament as Scripture*". *JSOT* 16
(1980) 12-23. ....("Childs' *Introduction* ")

"Story and History in Biblical Theology". In *The Scope and Authority
of the Bible*, 1-17. Explorations in Theology 7. London: SCM,
1980. ....("Story and History")

Barton, J.
Reading the Old Testament: Method in Biblical Study. London:
Darton, Longman and Todd, 1984. ....*(Reading)*

Berlin, A.
"Characterization in Biblical Narrative: David's Wives". *JSOT* 23
(1982) 69-85. ....("Characterization")

"On the Bible as Literature". *Proof* 2 (1982) 323-27. ....
....("Bible as Literature")

Poetics and Interpretation of Biblical Narrative. Sheffield: Almond,
1983. ....*(Poetics)*

Bertholet, A.
Leviticus. KHC. Tübingen und Leipzig: J. C. B. Mohr, 1901. ....
....*(Leviticus)*

Beuken, W. A. M.
"1 Samuel 28: The Prophet as 'Hammer of Witches'". *JSOT* 6 (1978) 3-
17. ....("1 Samuel 28")

"Twee visies op de laatste rechter. Opmerkingen bij 1 Samuël 12".
Bijdr 37 (1976) 350-60. ....("Twee visies")

Beyerlin, W.
"Das Königscharisma bei Saul". *ZAW* 73 (1961) 186-201. ....
....("Königscharisma")

Near Eastern Religious Texts relating to the Old Testament. Trans. by
J. Bowden. London: SCM, 1978. [Original: *Religionsgeschicht-
liche Textbuch zum Alten Testament*. Göttingen: Vandenhoeck &
Ruprecht, 1975]. ....*(NERT)*

Birch, B. C.
"The Choosing of Saul at Mizpah". *CBQ* 37 (1975) 447-57. ....
....("Choosing")

"The Development of the Tradition on the Anointing of Saul in 1 Sam 9:1-10:16". *JBL* 90 (1971) 55-68. ....("Development")

The Rise of the Israelite Monarchy: The Growth and Development of 1 Samuel 7-15. SBLDS 27. Missoula: Scholars Press, 1976. *(Rise)*

Blaikie, W. G.
The First Book of Samuel. Expositor's Bible. London: Hodder and Stoughton, 1892. ....(Blaikie)

Blenkinsopp, J.
A History of Prophecy in Israel: From the Settlement in the Land to the Hellenistic Period. London: SPCK, 1984. ...(*History of Prophecy*)

"Jonathan's Sacrilege. 1 Sam 14,1-46: A Study in Literary History". *CBQ* 26 (1964) 423-49. ....("Jonathan's Sacrilege")

"The Quest of the Historical Saul". In *No Famine in the Land: Studies in Honor of John L. McKenzie*, 75-99. Ed. by J. W. Flanagan and A. W. Robinson. Missoula: Scholars, 1975. ....("Quest")

Boecker, H. J.
Die Beurteilung der Anfänge des Königtums in den deuteronomistischen Abschnitten des 1. Samuelbuches: Ein Beitrag zum Problem des "Deuteronomistischen Geschichtswerks". WMANT 31. Neukirchen-Vluyn: Neukirchener Verlag, 1969. ....(*Beurteilung*)

Boer, P. A. H. de
Research into the Text of 1 Samuel I-XVI. Amsterdam: H. J. Paris, 1938. ....(*Research*)

Boling, R. G.
Judges: A New Translation with Introduction and Commentary. AB 6A. Garden City: Doubleday, 1975. ....(*Judges*)

Botterweck, G. J. and Ringren, H., eds.
Theological Dictionary of the Old Testament. Trans. by J. T. Willis et al. Grand Rapids: Eerdmans, 1974-. [Original: *Theologisches Wörterbuch zum Alten Testament*. Stuttgart: W. Kohlhammer, 1970-.] ....(*TDOT*)

Brauner, R. A.
"'To Grasp the Hem' and 1 Samuel 15:27". *JANES* 6 (1974) 35-38. .....
....("To Grasp the Hem")

Bright, J.
   A History of Israel. 3rd ed. London: SCM, 1981. ....*(History)*

Brinkman, J. A.
   A Political History of Post-Kassite Babylonia 1158-722 B.C. AnOr
   43. Rome: Pontificum Institutum Biblicum, 1968. ....
   ....*(Political History)*

Brongers, H. A.
   "Bemerkungen zum Gebrauch des adverbialen We'ATTAH im AT". *VT*
   15 (1965) 289-299. ....("Bemerkungen")

Brown, F., Driver, S. R., and Briggs, C. A., eds.
   A Hebrew and English Lexicon of the Old Testament. Oxford:
   Clarendon, 1907. ....(BDB)

Brueggemann, W.
   "On Trust and Freedom. A Study of Faith in the Succession Narrative".
   Int 26 (1972) 3-19. ....("On Trust")

Buber, M.
   "Die Erzählung von Sauls Königswahl". *VT* 6 (1956) 113-173.
   Republished under the title "Wie Saul König wurde" in Buber's
   Werke, 2: 743-811............................... ("Sauls Königswahl")

   "Leitworstil in der Erzählung des Pentateuchs". In *Die Schrift und ihre
   Verdeutschung,* 211-38. By M. Buber and F. Rosenzweig. Berlin:
   Schoken, 1936. Republished in Buber's *Werke,* 2: 1131-49. ....
   ....("Leitworstil")

   Werke. 2 vols. München: Kösel-Verlag, 1964. ....*(Werke)*

Buccellati, G.
   "1 Sam 13:1". *BeO* 5 (1963) 29. ....("1 Sam 13:1")

Budde, K. D.
   "Saul's Königswahl und Verwerfung". *ZAW* 8 (1888) 223-48. ....
   ....("Saul's Königswahl")

   Die Bücher Samuel. KHC VIII. Tübingen: J. C. B. Mohr, 1902. ....
   .... (Budde)

Burney, C. F.
   The Book of Judges with Introduction and Notes. 2nd ed. London:
   Rivingtons, 1930. .... *(Judges)*

Buss, M. J.
  "Prophecy in Ancient Israel". *IDBSup*: 694-97. ....("Prophecy")

Buttrick, G. A. et al., eds.
  The Interpreter's Dictionary of the Bible. 4 vols. Nashville: Abingdon, 1962. ....*(IDB)*

Caird, G. B.
  The Language and Imagery of the Bible. London: Duckworth, 1980.
  ....*(Language and Imagery)*

Cannon, W. W.
  "The Reign of Saul". *Theology* 25 (1932) 326-35. ..("Reign of Saul")

Charles, R. H.
  The Apocrypha and Pseudepigrapha of the Old Testament. 3rd ed.
  Princeton: Princeton University Press, 1969. ....*(APOT)*

Childs, B. S.
  Introduction to the Old Testament as Scripture. Philadelphia: Fortress,
  1979. ....*(Introduction)*

Clines, D. J. A.
  "Story and Poem: The Old Testament as Literature and as Scripture". *Int*
  34 (1980) 115-27. ....("Story and Poem")

  "X, X ben Y, ben Y: Personal Names in Hebrew Narrative Style". *VT* 22
  (1972) 266-87. ....("X, X ben Y")

Coats, G. W.
  "On Narrative Criticism". *Semeia* 3 (1975) 137-41. ..("On Narrative")

Collier, G. D.
  "The Problem of Deuteronomy: In Search of a Perspective". *RQ* 26
  (1983) 215-33. ....("Problem of Deuteronomy")

Conrad, D.
  "Samuel und die Mari-'Propheten'. Bemerkungen zu I Sam. 15:27".
  ZDMG Sup. 1 (1969) 273-80. ....("Samuel")

Conroy, C.
  "A Literary Analysis of 1 Kings I 41-53, with Methodological Reflections". *SVT* 36 (1985) 54-66. ....("Literary Analysis")

Cooper, A.
  "The Act of Reading the Bible". In *Proceedings of the Eighth World
  Congress of Jewish Studies (1981),* 61-68. Jerusalem: Magnes,
  1983. ....("Act of Reading")

Corney, R. W.
"Eli". *IDB* 2: 85. .... ("Eli")

Crenshaw, J. L.
Samson: A Secret Betrayed, A Vow Ignored. London: SPCK, 1979
(Atlanta: John Knox, 1978). ....(*Samson*)

Crim, K. et al., eds.
The Interpreter's Dictionary of the Bible, Supplementary Volume.
Nashville: Abingdon, 1976. ....(*IDBSup*)

Cross, F. M.
"The Ammonite Oppression of the Tribes of Gad and Reuben: Missing
Verses from 1 Sam 11 Found in 4QSam^a". In *History, Historio-
graphy and Interpretation: Studies in Biblical and Cuneiform
Literature*, 148-58. Edited by H. Tadmor and M. Weinfeld.
Jerusalem: Magnes, 1983. .... ("Ammonite Oppression")

Canaanite Myth and Hebrew Epic. Cambridge, MA: Harvard University
Press, 1973. .... (*CMHE*)

Crüsemann, F.
*Der Widerstand gegen das Königtum: die antiköniglichen Texte des
Alten Testamentes und der Kampf um den frühen israelitischen
Staat.* WMANT 49. Neukirchen-Vluyn: Neukirchener Verlag,
1978. ....(*Widerstand*)

Culley, R. C., ed.
Perspectives on Old Testament Hebrew Narrative. Semeia 15 (1979)....
....(*Perspectives*)

Curtis, J. B.
"A Folk Etymology of *nābî'* ". *VT* 29 (1979) 491-93. .("Etymology")

Dalman, D. G.
"Der Paß von Michmas". *ZDPV* 27 (1904) 161-73. .... ("Paß")

"Das Wādi eṣ-ṣwēnīt". *ZDPV* 28 (1905) 161-75. ....("Wādi")

Davidson, A. B.
Hebrew Syntax. 3rd ed. Edinburgh: T. & T. Clark, 1902. ......(*Syntax*)

Davies, P. R.
"Ark or Ephod in 1 Sam. XIV. 18?" *JTS* 26 (1975) 82-87. ...... ("Ark")

250   *REIGN AND REJECTION OF KING SAUL*

"The History of the Ark in the Books of Samuel". *JNSL* 5 (1977) 9-18.
....("History of the Ark")

Review of B. Halpern's *The Constitution of the Monarchy in Israel*. *JTS* n.s. 34 (1983) 203-07. ... (Review of Halpern's *Constitution*)

Delcor, M.
"Two Special Meanings of the Word יד in Biblical Hebrew". In *Religion D'Israël et Proche Orient Ancien: Des Phéniciens aux Esséniens*, 139-49. Leiden: E. J. Brill, 1976. .... ("Word יד")

Demsky, A.
"Geba, Gibeah, and Gibeon — An Historico-Geographic Riddle". *BASOR* 212 (1973) 26-31. ....("Geba")

Dietrich, W.
"David in Überlieferung und Geschichte". *VF* 22 (1977) 44-64. ....
....("David in Überlieferung")

Dhorme, E. P.
Les livres de Samuel. EB. Paris: J. Gabalda, 1910. ....(Dhorme)

Donner, H.
"Basic Elements of Old Testament Historiography Illustrated by the Saul Traditions". *OTWSA* 24 (1981) 40-54. ... ("Historiography")

"Die Verwerfung des Königs Saul". *SWGGU* 19 (1983) 229-260. ....
....("Verwerfung")

_____, and Röllig, W.
Kanaanäische und Aramäische Inschriften. 3 vols. Wiesbaden: Otto Harrassowitz, 1973-79. ....(*KAI*)

Dossin, G.
"Une révélation du dieu Dagan à Terqa". *RA* 42 (1948) 125-34. ....
....("Dagan")

Dothan, T.
The Philistines and Their Material Culture. New Haven and London: Yale, 1982. ....(*Philistines*)

Dozeman, T. B.
"The 'Troubler' of Israel: 'KR in 1 Kings 18:17-18". *StudBT* 9 (1979) 81-93. ....("Troubler")

Driver, S. R.
An Introduction to the Literature of the Old Testament. 9th ed. Edinburgh: T. & T. Clark, 1913. ....(*Introduction*)

Notes on the Hebrew Text and the Topography of the Books of Samuel.
2nd ed. Oxford: Clarendon, 1913. ....(Driver)

Edelman, D.
"Saul's Rescue of Jabesh-Gilead (1 Sam 11 1-11): Sorting Story from
History". *ZAW* 96 (1984) 195-209. ....("Saul's Rescue")

Ehrlich, A. B.
*Randglossen zur Hebräischen Bibel: Textkritisches, Sprachliches und
Sachliches.* 7 vols. Leipzig: J. C. Hinrichs, 1908-18. ....
.... *(Randglossen)*

Eichrodt, W.
Theology of the Old Testament. 2 vols. Trans. by J. A. Baker. OTL.
Philadelphia: Westminster, 1975. [Original: *Theologie des Alten
Testaments.* 3 vols. Leipzig: Hinrichs, 1933, 1935, 1939. Rev.
ed. (2 vols.) Stuttgart: Ehrenfried Klotz, 1959 (vol. 1, 6th ed.),
1964 (vol. 2, 5th ed.).] .... *(Theology)*

Eissfeldt, O.
Die Komposition der Samuelisbücher. Leipzig: J. C. Hinrichs, 1931...
....*(Komposition)*

Emerton, J. A.
"New Light on Israelite Religion: The Implications of the Inscription
from Kuntillet 'Ajrud". *ZAW* 94 (1982) 2-20. ....("New Light")

Eph'al, I.
"On Warfare and Military Control in the Ancient Near Eastern Empires:
A Research Outline". In *History, Historiography and Interpreta-
tion: Studies in Biblical and Cuneiform Literature,* 88-106. Ed. by
H. Tadmor and M. Weinfeld. Jerusalem: Magnes, 1983. ....
....("On Warfare")

Eslinger, L.
Kingship of God in Crisis: A Close Reading of 1 Samuel 1-12.
Sheffield: Almond, 1985. ....*(Kingship)*

"Viewpoints and Point of View in 1 Samuel 8-12". *JSOT* 26 (1983) 61-
76. ....("Viewpoints")

Evans, W. E.
"An Historical Reconstruction of the Emergence of the Israelite King-
ship and the Reign of Saul". In *Scripture in Context II: More
Essays on the Comparative Method*, 61-77. Ed. by W. W. Hallo,
J. C. Moyer and L. G. Perdue. Winona Lake, IN: Eisenbrauns,
1983. .... ("Historical Reconstruction")

Eves, T. L.
"One Ammonite Invasion or Two? 1 Sam 10:27-11:2 in the Light of
4QSamᵃ". *WTJ* 44 (1982) 308-26. ....("Ammonite Invasion")

Fackre, G.
"Narrative Theology: An Overview". *Int* 37 (1983) 340-52. ....
.... ("Narrative Theology")

Ficker, R.
"רכב *rkb* reiten, fahren". *THAT* 2: 777-781. .... ("רכב")

Fishbane, M.
"Recent Work on Biblical Narrative". *Proof* 1 (1981) 99-104. ....
.... ("Recent Work")

Fokkelmann, J. P.
King David (II Sam 9-20 & I Kings 1-2). Vol. 1 of *Narrative Art and
Poetry in the Books of Samuel*. Assen: Van Gorcum, 1981. ....
.... (*King David*)

Foresti, F.
*The Rejection of Saul in the Perspective of the Deuteronomistic
School: A Study of 1 Sm 15 and Related Texts*. Studia Theologica-
Teresianum 5. Roma: Edizione del Teresianum, 1984. (*Rejection*)

Fritz, V.
"Die Deutungen des Königtums Sauls in den Überlieferungen von seiner
Entstehung". *ZAW* 88 (1976) 346-62. ....
.... ("Deutungen des Königtums Sauls")

Galling, K.
Biblisches Reallexikon. HAT 1. Tübingen: J. C. B. Mohr, 1937. .....
....(*Reallexikon*)

Garsiel, M. (laysrg hvm)
"(י"ג-י"ד א"שמ) עיון היסטורי־ספרותי — קרב מכמש" ["The Battle of
Michmash: An Historical-Literary Study (1 Sam 13-14)"]. In
Studies in Bible and Exegesis: Arie Toeg in Memoriam, 15-50.
Ed. by M. Goshen-Gottstein and U. Simon. Ramat-Gan: Bar-Ilan
University Press, 1980. ....("קרב מכמש")

Gelb, I. J.
"Two Assyrian King Lists". *JNES* 13 (1954) 209-300. ..("King Lists")

_____, et al., eds.
The Assyrian Dictionary of the Oriental Institute of the University of Chicago. Chicago: Oriental Institute, 1964-. ....(*CAD*)

Gibson, J. C. L.
Canaanite Myths and Legends. Edinburgh: T. & T. Clark, 1977. ....
.... (*CML*)

Textbook of Syrian Semitic Inscriptions. 3 vols. Oxford: Clarendon, 1971-82. .... (*SSI*)

Ginzberg, L.
The Legends of the Jews. Trans. by H. Szold and P. Radin. Index by B. Cohen. 7 vols. Philapdelphia: The Jewish Publication Society of America, 1909-38.. (*Legends*)

Glück, J. J.
"Paronomasia in Biblical Literature". *Semitics* 1 (1970) 50-78. ....
....("Paronomasia")

Good, E. M.
Irony in the Old Testament. London: SPCK, 1965. ....(*Irony*)

Gooding, D. W.
Current Problems and Methods in the Textual Criticism of the Old Testament. An Inaugural Lecture delivered before the Queen's University of Belfast on 10 May 1978. Belfast: Mayne, Boyd & Son, 1979. ....(*Current Problems*)

Gordon, R. P.
"David's Rise and Saul's Demise: Narrative Analogy in 1 Samuel 24-26". *TynB* 31 (1980) 37-64. .... ("David's Rise")

1 & 2 Samuel. Old Testament Guides. Sheffield: JSOT, 1984. (*Samuel*)

Goslinga, C. J.
Het eerste boek Samuël. COT. Kampen: J. H. Kok, 1968. ..(Goslinga)

Het tweede boek Samuël. COT. Kampen: J. H. Kok, 1962. ....
....(*Tweede boek Samuël*)

I Samuël. KV. Kampen: J. H. Kok, 1948. ....(*I Samuël*)

Gottwald, N. K.
"Holy War". *IDBSup*: 942-44.   ....("Holy War")

The Tribes of Yahweh: A Sociology of the Religion of Liberated Israel, 1250-1050 B.C.E. London: SCM, 1979. ....(*Tribes*)

Gnuse, R. K.
The Dream Theophany of Samuel: Its Structure in Relation to Ancient Near Eastern Dreams and Its Theological Significance. Lanham, MD: University Press of America, 1984. ....(*Dream Theophany*)

Graetz, H.
Geshichte der Israeliten. Leipzig: Oskar Leiner, 1874. ....(*Geschichte*)

Grayson, A. K.
Assyrian and Babylonian Chronicles. Texts from Cuneiform Studies 5. Locust Valley, NY: J. J. Augustin, 1977. ....(*ABC*)

Assyrian Royal Inscriptions. 2 vols. Wiesbaden: Otto Harrassowitz, 1972-76. ....(*ARI*)

"1 Sam 13:1". *BeO* 5 (1963) 86, 110. ....("1 Sam 13:1")

Greenstein, E. L.
"Biblical Narratology". *Proof* 1 (1981) 201-08. ....("Narratology")

"'To Grasp the Hem' in Ugaritic Litertature". *VT* 32 (1982) 217-18. ....
....("Grasp the Hem")

Greßmann, H.
Die älteste Geschichtsschreibung und Prophetie Israels. SAT II, 1. Göttingen: Vandenhoeck & Ruprecht, 1910. ....(Greßmann)

Grønbæk, J. H.
Die Geschichte vom Aufstieg Davids (1. Sam. 15-2. Sam. 5): Tradition und Komposition. Acta theologica danica 10. Copenhaghen: Munksgaard, 1971. ....(*Geschichte*)

Gunn, D. M.
The Fate of King Saul: An Interpretation of a Biblical Story. JSOTSS 14. Sheffield: JSOT, 1981. ....(*Fate*)

"A Man Given Over to Trouble: The Story of King Saul". In *Images of Man and God: Old Testament Short Stories in Literary Focus*, 89-112. Ed. by B. O. Long. Sheffield: Almond, 1981. .....("A Man")

Gunneweg, A. H. J.
"Anmerkungen und Anfragen zur neueren Pentateuchforschung". *TRu* 48 (1983), 227-53. .... ("Anmerkungen")

Gutbrod, K.
Das Buch vom König: Das erste Buch Samuel. BAT XI, 1. Stuttgart: Calwer, 1956. ....(Gutbrod)

Habel, N.
"The Form and Significance of the Call Narrative". *ZAW* 77 (1965) 297-323. .... ("Call Narrative")

Halpern, B.
The Constitution of the Monarchy in Israel. HSM 25. Chico, CA: Scholars, 1981. .... (*Constitution*)

"The Uneasy Compromise: Israel between League and Monarchy". In *Traditions in Transformation: Turning Points in Biblical Faith*, 59-96. Festschrift F. M. Cross, 60th birthday. Ed. by B. Halpern and J. D. Levenson. Winona Lake, IN: Eisenbrauns, 1981. ....
....("Uneasy Compromise")

Hauer, C. E.
"Does 1 Sam 9_1-11_{15} Reflect the Extension of Saul's Dominions?" *JBL* 86 (1967) 306-10. ....("Saul's Dominions")

"The Shape of Saulide Strategy". *CBQ* 31 (1969) 153-67. ... ("Shape")

Hayes, J. H.
"Saul: The Unsung Hero of Israelite History". *TUSR* 10 (1975) 37-47.
....("Unsung Hero")

_____, ed.
Old Testament Form Criticism. San Antonio: Trinity University Press, 1974. ....(*Form Criticism*)

Hertzberg, H. W.
Die Samuelbücher. ATD 10. 2nd ed. Göttingen: Vandenhoeck & Ruprecht, 1960. [ET: *I & II Samuel.* Trans. by J. S. Bowden. OTL. Philadelphia: Westminster, 1964.] .... (Hertzberg)

Houtsma, M. T.
"Textkritisches". *ZAW* 27 (1907) 57-59. ....("Textkritisches")

Humphreys, W. L.
"From Tragic Hero to Villain: A Study of the Figure of Saul and the Development of 1 Samuel". *JSOT* 22 (1982) 95-117. .....("Hero")

"The Rise and Rall of King Saul: A Study of an Ancient Narrative Stratum in 1 Samuel". *JSOT* 18 (1980) 74-90......("Rise and Fall")

"The Tragedy of King Saul: A Study of the Structure of 1 Samuel 9-31". *JSOT* 6 (1978) 18-27. ....("Tragedy")

Hylander, I.
Der literarische Samuel-Saul Komplex (1 Sam. 1-15) traditions-geschichtlich untersucht. Uppsala: Almquist & Wiksell, 1932. ...
....(*Samuel-Saul Komplex*)

Irwin, W. A.
"Samuel and the Rise of the Monarchy". *AJSL* 58 (1941) 113-134. ....
....("Samuel")

Ishida, T.
"נגיד: A Term for the Legitimization of the Kingship". *AJBI* 3 (1977) 35-51. ....("נגיד")

The Royal Dynasties in Ancient Israel: A Study on the Formation and Development of Royal-Dynastic Ideology. Berlin: Walter de Gruyter, 1977. ....(*Royal Dynasties*)

Jenni, E.
Das hebräische Pi'el: Syntaktisch-semasiologische Untersuchung einer Verbalform im Alten Testament. Zürich: EVZ-Verlag, 1968. ....
....(*Das hebräische Pi'el*)

"יום *jōm* Tag". *THAT* 1: 707-26. ....("יום")

"יצא *js'* hinausgehen". *THAT* 1: 755-61. ....("יצא")

_____, and Westermann, C., eds.
Theologisches Handwörterbuch zum Alten Testament. 2 vols. München: Chr. Kaiser Verlag, 1971-76. ....(*THAT*)

Jobling, D.
"Jonathan: A Structural Study in 1 Sam." In *The Sense of Biblical Narrative,* 4-25. JSOTSS 7. Sheffield: JSOT, 1978. [Originally published in SBLSP (1976) 15-32. Page numbers cited refer to the 1978 publication.] ....("Jonathan")

"Saul's Fall and Jonathan's Rise: Tradition and Redaction in 1 Sam 14:1-46". *JBL* 95 (1976) 367-76. ....("Saul's Fall")

"Structuralism, Hermeneutics, and Exegesis: Three Recent Contributions to the Debate". *USQR* 34 (1979) 135-47. ("Structuralism")

Jones, G. H.
"'Holy War' or 'Yahweh War'?" *VT* 25 (1975) 642-58. ....("Holy War")

Joüon, P.
"Notes de Lexicographie Hébraïque: II. VII נציב = *poste, garnison* ".
MUSJ 5 (1911/12) 414-15. ....("Notes")

Jüngling, H.-W.
Richter 19—Ein Plädoyer für das Königtum: Stilistische Analyse der Tendenzerzählung Ri 19,1-30a; 21,25. AnBib 84. Rome: Biblical Institute, 1981. ....(*Richter 19*)

Kautsch, E., ed.
Gesenius' Hebrew Grammar. Trans. by A. E. Cowley. 2nd English ed. Oxford: Clarendon, 1910. ....(GK)

Kegler, J.
Politisches Geschehen und theologisches Verstehen: Zum Geschichtsverständnis in der frühen israelitischen Königszeit. CTM 8. Stuttgart: Calwer, 1977. ....(*Politisches Geschehen*)

Keil, C. F.
The Books of Samuel. Trans. by J. Martin. Grand Rapids: Eerdmans, 1973 reprint. ....(Keil)

Kessler, M.
"An Introduction to Rhetorical Criticism of the Bible: Prolegomena".
Semitics 7 (1980) 1-27. ....("Introduction")

Kiel, Y. (יהודה קיל)
(שמואל א) ספר שמואל). Jerusalem: Mosad Harav Kook, 1981. ......(Kiel)

Kikawada, I. M.
"Some Proposals for the Definition of Rhetorical Criticism". *Semitics* 5 (1977) 67-91. ....("Some Proposals")

Kirkpatrick, A. F.
The First Book of Samuel. CB. Cambridge: Cambridge University Press, 1881. ....(Kirkpatrick)

Kittel, R.
Geschichte des Volkes Israel. Vol. 2: *Das Volk in Kanaan: Geschichte der Zeit bis zum babylonischen Exil.* 7th ed. Gotha: Leopold Klotz, 1925. ....(*Geschichte*)

Klein, R. W.
1 Samuel. WBC 10. Waco, TX: Word, 1983. ....(Klein)

Klostermann, D. A.
Die Bücher Samuelis und der Könige. KK. Nördlingen: C. H. Beck,
1887. ....(Klostermann)

Knierim, R.
"The Messianic Concept in the First Book of Samuel". In *Jesus and the
Historian*, 20-51. In Honour of E. C. Colwell. Ed. by F. T.
Trotter. Philadelphia: Westminster, 1968. ....
....("Messianic Concept")

Koch, K.
Was ist Formgeschichte? Methoden der Bibelexegese. 3rd ed.
Neukirchen-Vluyn: Neukirchener Verlag, 1974. [ET: *The Growth
of the Biblical Tradition: The Form-Critical Method.* Trans. from
2nd German ed. by S. M. Cupitt. London: A & C Black, 1969.] ....
....(*Formgeschichte*)

"Die Hebräer vom Auszug Ägypten bis zum Grossreich Davids". *VT* 19
(1969) 37-81. ....("Hebräer")

Koehler, L. and Baumgartner, W.
Hebräisches und Aramäisches Lexikon zum Alten Testament. 3rd ed.
Leiden: E. J. Brill, 1967-83. ....(*HAL*)

König, E.
Historisch-kritisches Lehrgebäude der hebräischen Sprache. 3 vols.
Leipzig: Hinrichs, 1881, 1895, 1897. ....(*Lehrgebäude*)

Kugel, J.
The Idea of Biblical Poetry: Parallelism and Its History. New Haven:
Yale, 1981. ....(*Idea*)

"James Kugel Responds". *Proof* 2 (1982) 328-32. ("Kugel Responds")

"On the Bible and Literary Criticism". *Proof* 1 (1981) 217-36. ....
....("Bible and Literary Criticism")

Kuhl, C.
"Die 'Wiederaufnahme' — ein literarkritisches Prinzip?" *ZAW* 64
(1952) 1-11. ....("Wiederaufnahme")

Langlamet, F.
"Les récits de l'institution de la royauté (I Sam, VII-XII). De
Wellhausen aux travaux récents". *RB* 77 (1970) 161-200. ....
....("Les récits")

Lasine, S.
"Fiction, Falsehood, and Reality in Hebrew Scripture". *HS* 25 (1984) 24-40. ....("Fiction")

"Guest and Host in Judges 19: Lot's Hospitality in an Inverted World". *JSOT* 29 (1984) 37-59. ....("Guest")

Laurentin, A.
"We'attah-Kai nun. Formule caractéristique des textes juridiques et liturgique". *Bib* 45 (1964) 168-97. ....("Formule")

Levenson, J. D.
"1 Samuel 25 as Literature and as History". *CBQ* 40 (1978) 11-28. .....
....("1 Samuel 25")

Licht, J.
"Biblical Historicism". In *History, Historiography and Interpretation: Studies in Biblical and Cuneiform Literature*, 107-20. Edited by H. Tadmor and M. Weinfeld. Jerusalem: Magnes, 1983.................
....("Historicism")

Storytelling in the Bible. Jerusalem: Magnes, 1978. ...*(Storytelling)*

Lind, M. C.
Yahweh is a Warrior: The Theology of Warfare in Ancient Israel. Scottsdale, PN: Herald, 1980. ....*(Yahweh is a Warrior)*

Lindblom, J.
"Lot-Casting in the Old Testament". *VT* 12 (1962) 164-78. ....
....("Lot-Casting")

Loader, J. A.
Polar Structures in the Book of Qohelet. Berlin: Walter de Gruyter, 1979. ....*(Polar Structures)*

Lods, A.
Israel from its Beginnings to the Middle of the Eighth Century. Trans. by S. H. Hooke. London: Kegan Paul, Trench, Trubner, 1932. .....
....*(Israel)*

Loewenstamm, S. E.
"The Address 'Listen' in the Ugaritic Epic and the Bible". In *The Bible World: Essays in Honor of Cyrus H. Gordon*, 123-31. New York: KTAV, 1980. ....("Address 'Listen'")

Lohse, E.
Die Texte aus Qumran. Darmstadt: Wissenschaftliche Buchgesellschaft, 1971. ....(*Texte aus Qumran*)

Lombardi, G.
"Alcune questioni di topographia in 1 Sam 13,1-14,15". *SBFLA* 9
(1959) 251-82. ....("Alcune questioni")

Long, B. O.
"Some Recent Trends in the Form Criticism of Old Testament
Narratives". In *Proceedings of the Seventh World Congress of
Jewish Studies (1977),* 63-72. Jerusalem: Magnes, 1981. ....
....("Trends")

Madl, H.
Literarkritische und formanalytische Untersuchungen zu 1 Sam 14.
Bonn: Rheinische Friedrich-Wilhelms-Universität, 1974. ....
.... (*Untersuchungen*)

Malamat, A.
Early Israelite Warfare and the Conquest of Canaan. The Fourth Sacks
Lecture delivered on 21st June 1977. Oxford: The Oxford Center
for Postgraduate Hebrew Studies, 1978. ....(*Early Israelite Warfare*)

"How Inferior Israelite Forces Conquered Fortified Canaanite Cities".
BAR 8/2 (1982) 24-35. .... ("Inferior Israelite Forces")

"Prophetic Revelations in New Documents from Mari and the Bible".
SVT 15 (1965) 207-27. ....("Prophetic Revelations")

March, W. E.
"Prophecy". In *Old Testament Form Criticism,* 141-77. Ed. by J. H.
Hayes. San Antonio: Trinity University Press, 1974. ....
....("Prophecy")

Mauchline, J.
1 and 2 Samuel. NCB. London: Oliphants, 1971. ....(Mauchline)

Mayes, A. D. H.
"The Period of the Judges and the Rise of the Monarchy". In *Israelite
and Judean History,* 285-331. Ed. by J. H. Hayes and J. M. Miller.
OTL. London: SCM, 1977. ....("Period of the Judges")

"The Rise of the Israelite Monarchy". *ZAW* 90 (1978) 1-19. .. ("Rise")

*The Story of Israel between Settlement and Exile: A Redactional Study
of the Deuteronomistic History.* London: SCM, 1983. .....(Story)

McCarter, P. K.
"The Apology of David". *JBL* 99 (1980) 489-504. ....("Apology")

I Samuel: A New Translation with Introduction, Notes & Commentary.
AB 8. Garden City: Doubleday, 1980. ....(McCarter)

II Samuel: A New Translation with Introduction, Notes & Commentary.
AB 9. Garden City: Doubleday, 1984. ....(*II Samuel*)

McCarthy, D. J.
"The Inauguration of Monarchy in Israel: A Form-Critical Study of 1
Samuel 8-12". *Int* 27 (1973) 401-12. ....("Inauguration")

McKane, W.
I & II Samuel. TBC. London: SCM, 1963. .... (McKane)

Melugin, R. F.
"Muilenburg, Form Criticism, and Theological Exegesis". In *En-
counter with the Text*, 91-100. Ed. by M. J. Buss. Philadelphia:
Fortress, 1979. ....("Muilenburg")

Mendenhall, G. E.
"The Census Lists of Numbers 1 and 26". *JBL* 77 (1958) 52-66. ....
....("Census Lists")

Mettinger, T. N. D.
*King and Messiah: The Civil and Sacral Legitimation of the Israelite
Kings.* CBOTS 8. Lund: CWK Gleerup, 1976. (*King and Messiah*)

Meyer, D. R.
Hebräische Grammatik III: Satzlehre. 3rd ed. Berlin: Walter de Gruyter,
1972. ....(*Satzlehre*)

Milgrom, J.
"The Cultic שגגה and Its Influences in Psalms and Job". *JQR* 58 (1967)
115-25. ....("Cultic שגגה")

Millard, A. R.
"*Scriptio continua* in Early Hebrew: Ancient Practice or Modern
Surmise?" *JSS* 15 (1970) 2-15. ....(*"Scriptio continua* ")

Miller, J. M.
"Geba/Gibeah of Benjamin". *VT* 25 (1975) 145-66. ..("Geba/Gibeah")

"Saul's Rise to Power: Some Observations Concerning 1 Sam 9:1-
10:16; 10:26-11:15 and 13:2-14:46". *CBQ* 36 (1974) 157-74. ...
....("Saul's Rise")

Miscall, P. D.
"The Jacob and Joseph Stories as Analogies". *JSOT* 6 (1978) 28-40. ..
....("Jacob and Joseph")

"Literary Unity in Old Testament Narrative". In *Perspectives on Old Testament Narrative*, 27-44. Ed. by R. C. Culley. *Semeia* 15. Missoula: Scholars, 1979. ....("Literary Unity")

The Workings of Old Testament Narrative. Philadelphia: Fortress, 1983. ....(*Workings of Old Testament Narrative*)

Mittmann, S.
"Die Grabinschrift des Sängers Uriahu". *ZDPV* 97 (1981) 139-52. ......
....("Grabinschrift")

Moberly, R. W. L.
At the Mountain of God: Story and Theology in Exodus 32-34. JSOTSS 22. Sheffield: JSOT, 1983. .... (*Mountain*)

Möhlenbrink, K.
"Sauls Ammoniterfeldzug und Samuels Beitrag zum Königtum des Sauls". *ZAW* 58 (1940/41) 57-70. ... ("Sauls Ammoniterfeldzug")

Momigliano, A.
"Biblical Studies and Classical Studies: Simple Reflections about Historical Method". *BA* 45 (1982) 224-28. ...("Biblical Studies")

Montgomery, J. A. and Gehman, H. S.
The Books of Kings. ICC. Edinburgh: T. & T. Clark, 1951. ...(*Kings*)

Mowinckel, S.
"Drive and/or Ride in O. T." *VT* 12 (1962) 278-99. ....("Drive")

Muilenburg, J.
"Form Criticism and Beyond". *JBL* 88 (1969) 1-18. ....
....("Form Criticism")

"A Study in Hebrew Rhetoric: Repetition and Style". SVT 1 (1953) 97-111. ....("Rhetoric")

Münderlein, G.
"גֹּרֶן *gōren* ". *TDOT* 3:62-65. ....("גֹּרֶן")

Nassouki, E.
"Grande liste des rois d'Assyrie". *AfO* 4 (1927) 1-11. ...("Grande liste")

Nicholson, E. W.
  Deuteronomy and Tradition. Oxford: Basil Blackwell, 1967. ....
  ....*(Deuteronomy)*

  Interpreting the Old Testament: A Century of the Oriel Professorship.
  Oxford: Clarendon, 1981. ....*(Interpreting the Old Testament)*

Noort, E.
  "Eine weitere Kurzbemerkung zu I Samuel XIV 41". *VT* 21 (1971) 112-
  116. .... ("Kurzbemerkung")

Noth, M.
  Das dritte Buch Mose. ATD. Göttingen: Vandenhoeck & Ruprecht,
  1962. ....*(Das dritte Buch Mose)*

  Geschichte Israels. 2nd ed. Göttingen: Vandenhoeck & Ruprecht,
  1969 [7th printing]. ....*(Geschichte)*

  "Remarks on the Sixth Volume of the Mari Texts". *JSS* 1 (1956) 322-
  33. ....("Remarks")

  *Überlieferungsgeschichtliche Studien: Die sammelnden und bearbeit-
    enden Geschichtswerke im Alten Testament*. 2nd, unaltered ed.
  Tübingen: Max Niemeyer, 1957. [ET: *The Deuteronomistic
  History*. JSOTSS 15. Sheffield: JSOT, 1981.] ....*(ÜSt)*

Oeming, M.
  "Bedeutung und Funktionen von 'Fiktionen' in der altestamentlichen
  Geschichtsschreibung". *EvT* 44 (1984) 254-66. .... ("Fiktionen")

Paul, S. M.
  "1 Samuel 9,7: An Interview Fee". *Bib* 59 (1978) 542-44. ....
  ....("Interview Fee")

Perdue, L. G.
  "The Testament of David and Egyptian Royal Inscriptions". In
  Scripture in Context II: More Essays on the Comparative Method,
  79-96. Ed. by W. W. Hallo, J. C. Moyer and L. G. Perdue. Winona
  Lake, IN: Eisenbrauns, 1983. ....("Testament of David")

Philips, A.
  "The Ecstatics' Father". In *Words and Meanings: Essays Presented to
  David Winton Thomas*, 183-94. Ed. by P. R. Ackroyd and B.
  Lindars. Cambridge: Cambridge University Press, 1968. ....
  ....("Ecstatics' Father")

Piper, O. A.
"Knowledge". *IDB* 3: 42-48. ....("Knowledge")

Pisano, S.
Additions or Omissions in the Book of Samuel: The Significant Pluses and Minuses in the Massoretic, LXX and Qumran Texts. OBO 57. Göttingen: Vandenhoeck & Ruprecht, 1984. ....(*Additions*)

Porter, J. R.
"Ancient Israel". In *Divination and Oracles*, 191-214. Ed. by M. Loewe and C. Blacker. London: George Allen & Unwin, 1981. ....
....("Israel")

"Old Testament Historiography". In *Tradition and Interpretation*, 125-62. Ed. by G. W. Anderson. Oxford: Clarendon, 1979. ....
....("Historiography")

Preß, R.
"Der Prophet Samuel". *ZAW* 56 (1938) 177-225. ...("Prophet Samuel")

Pritchard, J. B., ed.
Ancient Near Eastern Texts Relating to the Old Testament. 3rd ed. Princeton: Princeton University Press, 1969. ....(*ANET*)

Pury, A. de
"La guerre sainte israélite: réalité historique ou fiction littéraire?" *ETR* 56 (1981) 5-38. ....("La guerre sainte")

Rabin, C.
"Discourse Analysis and the Dating of Deuteronomy". In *Interpreting the Hebrew Bible: Essays in Honour of E. I. J. Rosenthal*, 171-77. Ed. by J. A. Emerton and S. C. Reif. Cambridge: Cambridge University Press, 1982. ....("Discourse Analysis")

Rad, G. von
"Das formgeschichtliche Problem des Hexateuch". In *Gesammelte Studien zum Alten Testament*, 9-86. München: Chr. Kaiser Verlag, 1958. ....("Problem des Hexateuch")

"Gerhard von Rad über Gerhard von Rad". In *Probleme biblischer Theologie*, 659-61. Ed. by H. W. Wolff. München: Chr. Kaiser Verlag, 1971. ....("Gerhard von Rad")

Der heilige Krieg im alten Israel. Zürich: Zwingli, 1951. ....(*Krieg*)

Theologie des Alten Testaments. 2 vols. München: Chr. Kaiser Verlag, 1957-60. ....(*Theologie*)

"Zwei Überlieferungen von König Saul". In *Gesammelte Studien zum Alten Testament*, vol. 2: 199-211. Ed. by R. Smend. München: Chr. Kaiser Verlag, 1973. ....("Zwei Überlieferungen")

Richter, W.
"Die *nāgīd*-Formel: Ein Beitrag zur Erhellung des *nāgīd*-Problems". *BZ* n.s. 9 (1965) 71-84. ....("Die *nāgīd*-Formel")

Die sogenanten vorprophetischen Berufungsberichte. Eine literaturwissenschaftliche Studie zu 1 Sam 9,1-10, 16, Ex 3f. und Ri 6, 11b-7. FRLANT 101. Göttingen: Vandenhoeck & Ruprecht, 1970. ....(*Berufungsberichte*)

Traditionsgeschichtliche Untersuchungen zum Richterbuch. BBB 18. Bonn: Peter Hanstein, 1963. .... (*Untersuchungen*)

Robbins, V. K. and Patton, J. H.
"Rhetoric and Biblical Criticism". *QJS* 66 (1980) 327-37. ....
....("Rhetoric")

Robertson, D.
The Old Testament and the Literary Critic. Philadelphia: Fortress, 1977. ....(*Literary Critic*)

Rofé, A.
"The Acts of Nahash according to 4QSamᵃ". *IEJ* 32 (1982) 129-33. ....
....("Acts of Nahash")

Rosenberg, A. J.
Samuel I: A New English Translation of the Text and Rashi, With a Commentary Digest. New York: Judaica Press, 1980. ...(*Samuel I*)

Rost, L.
Die Vorstufen von Kirche und Synagoge im Alten Testament. Eine Wortgeschichtliche Untersuchung. 2nd ed. Darmstadt: Wissenschaftliche Buchgesellschaft, 1967. .... (*Vorstufen*)

Roth, W. M. W.
"A Study of the Classical Hebrew Verb *skl* ". *VT* 18 (1968) 69-78. .....
....("Study")

Ryken, L.
The Literature of the Bible. Grand Rapids: Zondervan, 1974. ....
....(*Literature*)

Saggs, H. W. F.
"Assyrian Warfare in the Sargonid Period". *IRAQ* 25 (1963) 145-54.
.... ("Assyrian Warfare")

Sandars, N. K.
The Sea Peoples: Warriors of the Ancient Mediterranean, 1250-1150 BC. London: Thames and Hudson, 1978. ....(*Sea Peoples*)

Sasson, J. M.
"Wordplay in the OT". *IDBSup*: 968-70. ....("Wordplay")

Sauer, G.
"דֶּרֶךְ *dæræk* Weg". *THAT* 1: 456-60. ....("דרך")

Scharbert, J.
"Das Verbum PQD in der Theologie des Alten Testaments". *BZ* n.f. 4 (1960) 209-26. [Republished in *Um das Prinzip der Vergeltung in Religion und Recht des Alten Testaments*, 278-99. Ed. by K. Koch. Darmstadt: Wissenschaftliche Buchgesellschaft, 1972.] ...
....("Verbum PQD")

Schicklberger, F.
"Jonathans Heldentat: Textlinguistische Beobachtungen zu I Sam XIV 1-23a". *VT* 24 (1974) 324-33. .... ("Jonathans Heldentat")

Schmidt, L.
Menschlicher Erfolg und Jahwes Initiative: Studien zu Tradition, Interpretation und Historie in Überlieferungen von Gideon, Saul und David. WMANT 38. Neukirchen-Vluyn: Neukirchener Verlag, 1970. ....(*Menschlicher Erfolg*)

Schneider, W.
Grammatik des biblischen Hebräisch. München: Claudius Verlag, 1974. ....(*Grammatik*)

Schottroff, W.
"פקד *pqd* heimsuchen". *THAT* 2: 466-486. ....("פקד")

Schroer, S.
"Zur Deutung der Hand unter der Grabinschrift von Chirbet el Qôm". *UF* 15 (1983) 191-99. ....("Deutung")

Schultz, A.
Die Bücher Samuel. EH 8, 1. Münster: Aschendorff, 1919 [First Samuel]. ....(Schultz)

Schunck, K.-D.
Benjamin: Untersuchungen zur Entstehung und Geschichte eines israelitischen Stammes. BZAW 86. Berlin: Alfred Töpelmann, 1963. .... (*Benjamin*)

Schwally, F.
Semitische Kriegsaltertümer. Leipzig: Dieterich'sche Verlagsbuchhandlung, 1901. .... (*Kriegsaltertümer*)

Seebass, H.
David, Saul und das Wesen des biblischen Glaubens. Neukirchen-Vluyn: Neukirchener Verlag, 1980. .... (*David*)

"I Sam 15 als Schlüssel für das Verständnis der sogenannten königsfreundlichen Reihe I Sam 9 1 — 10 16 11 1-15 und 13 2 — 15 52". *ZAW* 78 (1966) 148-79. .... ("I Sam 15")

"Traditionsgeschichte von I Sam 8, 10$_{17}$ff. und 12". *ZAW* 77 (1965) 286-96. .... ("Traditionsgeschichte")

"Die Vorgeschichte der Königserhebung Sauls". *ZAW* 79 (1967) 155-71. .... ("Vorgeschichte")

"Zum Text von I Sam XIV 23b-25a und II 29,31-33". *VT* 16 (1966) 74-82. .... ("Zum Text")

Segert. S.
"Paronomasia in the Samson Narrative in Judges XII-XVI". *VT* 34 (1984) 454-61. .... ("Paronomasia")

Seybold, K.
"Reverenz und Gebet: Erwägungen zu der Wendung *ḥillā panîm* ". *ZAW* 88 (1976) 2-16. .... ("Reverenz und Gebet")

"תְּרָפִים *t^erāfîm* Idol(e)". *THAT* 2: 1057-60. .... ("תרפים")

Shaviv, S.
"*nābî'* and *nāgîd* in I Samuel ix 1- x 16". *VT* 34 (1984) 108-112. ....
.... ("*nābî'* and *nāgîd*")

Smelik, K. A. D.
Saul, de voorstelling van Israels eerste Konig in de Masoretische tekst van het Oude Testament. Amsterdam: Drukkerij en Uitgeverij P. E. T., 1977. .... (*Saul*)

Smith, G. A.
    The Historical Geography of the Holy Land. 25th ed. London: Hodder
    and Stoughton, 1931. .... (*Historical Geography*)

Smith, H. P.
    A Critical and Exegetical Commentary on the Books of Samuel. ICC.
    Edinburgh: T. & T. Clark, 1899. .... (Smith)

Soden, W. von
    Akkadisches Handwörterbuch. 3 vols. Wiesbaden: Harrassowitz,
    1965-81. ....(*AHw*)

    "Verkündung des Gotteswillens durch prophetisches Wort in den
    altbabylonischen Briefen aus Mâri". *WO* 1 (1952) 397-403. ....
    ....("Verkündung")

Soggin, J. A.
    *Introduction to the Old Testament From Its Origins to the Closing of
    the Alexandrian Canon.* Trans. and rev. by R. J. Coggins. OTL.
    Philadelphia: Westminster, 1976. .... (*Introduction*)

    Das Königtum in Israel. BZAW 104. Berlin: Alfred Töpelman, 1967.
    ....(*Königtum*)

    "שוב *šūb* zurückkehren". *THAT* 2:884-91. .... ("שוב")

Southwell, P. J. M.
    Review of J. R. Vannoy's *Covenant Renewal at Gilgal.* *JTS* 31 (1980)
    117-119. ....(Review of Vannoy's *Covenant Renewal*)

Spanuth, J.
    *Die Philister, das unbekannte Volk: Lehrmeister und Widersacher der
    Israeliten.* Osnabrück: Otto Zeller, 1980. ....(*Philister*)

Stacy, W. D.
    "A Pre-Battle Rite in Ancient Israel?". In *Studia Evangelica* 7: 471-73.
    Ed. by E. A. Livingstone. Berlin: Akademie-Verlag, 1982. ....
    ....("Pre-Battle Rite")

Stamm, J. J.
    "Der Name des Königs David". SVT 7 (1960) 165-183. ....("Name")

Sternberg, M.
    "The Bible's Art of Persuasion: Ideology, Rhetoric, and Poetics in
    Saul's Fall". *HUCA* 54 (1983) 45-82. .... ("Bible's Art")

Stoebe, H. J.
   Das erste Buch Samuelis. KAT VIII, 1. Gütersloh: Gerd Mohn, 1973. . .
   ....(Stoebe)

   "נחם *nḥm* pi. trösten". *THAT* 2: 59-66. ....("נחם")

   "רחם *rḥm* pi. sich erbarmen". *THAT* 2: 761-68. ....("רחם")

   "Tenne". *BHH* 3: 1952. ....("Tenne")

   "Zur Topographie und Überlieferung der Schlacht von Mikmas, 1 Sam
   13 und 14". *TZ* 21 (1965) 269-80. ....("Zur Topographie")

Stolz, F.
   Das erste und zweite Buch Samuel. ZBK, AT 9. Zürich: Theologischer
   Verlag, 1981. ....(Stolz)

Tadmor, H.
   "Autobiographical Apology in the Royal Assyrian Literature". In
   *History, Historiography and Interpretation: Studies in Biblical
   and Cuneiform Literatures*, 36-57. Ed. by H. Tadmor and M. Weinfeld. Jerusalem: Magnes, 1983. ....("Autobiographical Apology")

Talmon, S.
   "The Biblical Idea of Statehood". In *The Bible World: Essays in Honor
   of Cyrus H. Gordon*, 239-48. Ed. by G. Rendsburg et al. New
   York: KTAV, 1980. ....("Statehood")

Thenius, O.
   Die Bücher Samuelis. KeH 4. 3rd ed. Revised by M. Löhr. Leipzig: S.
   Hirzel, 1898. ....(Thenius-Löhr)

Thompson, R. J.
   Penitence and Sacrifice in Early Israel outside the Levitical Law.
   Leiden: E. J. Brill, 1963. ....(*Penitence*)

Thornton, T. C. G.
   "Studies in Samuel. I. Davidic Propaganda in the Books of Samuel".
   CQR 168 (1967) 413-23. ....("Davidic Propaganda")

Toeg, A.
   "A Textual Note on I Sam XIV 41". *VT* 19 (1969) 493-98. ....("Note")

Toombs, L. E.
   "War, Ideas of". *IDB* 4: 796-801. ....("War")

Tosato, A.

"La colpa di Saul (1 Sam 15, 22-23)". *Bib* 59 (1978) 251-59. ....
.... ("La colpa")

Tsevat, M.

"The Biblical Account of the Foundation of the Monarchy in Israel". In *The Meaning of the Book of Job and Other Biblical Studies: Essays on the Literature and Religion of the Hebrew Bible,* 77-99. New York: KTAV, 1980. ....("Biblical Account")

"חָמַל *chāmal;* חֶמְלָה *chemlāh* ". *TDOT* 4: 470-72. ....("חמל")

"Israelite History and the Historical Books of the Old Testament". In *The Meaning of the Book of Job and Other Biblical Studies: Essays on the Literature and Religion of the Hebrew Bible,* 177-87. New York: KTAV, 1980. ....("Israelite History")

"Marriage and Monarchical Legitimacy in Ugarit and Israel". *JSS* 3 (1958) 237-43. ....("Marriage")

"Samuel, I & II". *IDBSup*: 777-81. ....("Samuel")

"Studies in the Books of Samuel: I Interpretation of I. Sam. 2:27-36. The Narrative of <u>Kareth</u>". *HUCA* 32 (1961) 191-216. ....
.... ("I. Sam. 2:27-36")

Tsumura, D. T.

"Literary Insertion (AXB Pattern) in Biblical Hebrew". *VT* 33 (1983) 468-82. ....("Literary Insertion")

Tucker, G. M.

Form Criticism of the Old Testament. Philadelphia: Fortress, 1971. ...
.... (*Form Criticism*)

Ulrich, E. C.

The Qumran Text of Samuel and Josephus. HSM 19. Missoula: Scholars, 1978. ....(*Qumran Text*)

Vannoy, J. R.

Covenant Renewal at Gilgal: A Study of I Samuel 11:14-12:25. Cherry Hill, NJ: Mack, 1978. ....(*Covenant Renewal*)

Vaux, R. de

Ancient Israel. 2 vols. New York: McGraw-Hill, 1965. [Original: *Les Institution de L'Ancien Testament.*] ....(*Ancient Israel*)

"Sur l'origine kénite ou madianite du Yahvisme". In Eretz Israel 9, 28-32. Ed. by A. Malamat. Jerusalem: Israel Exploration Society, 1969. ....("Sur l'origine kénite")

Veijola, T.
Die Ewige Dynastie: David und die Entstehung seiner Dynastie nach der deuteronomistischen Darstellung. AASF Series B 193. Helsinki: Suomalainen Tiedeakatemia, 1975. ....(*Ewige Dynastie*)

Das Königtum in der Beurteilung der deuteronomistischen Historiographie: Eine redaktionsgeschichtliche Untersuchung. AASF Series B 198. Helsinki: Suomalainen Tiedeakatemia, 1977. (*Königtum*)

Vries, S. J. de
"Temporal Terms as Structural Elements in the Holy-War Tradition". *VT* 25 (1975) 80-105. ....("Temporal Terms")

Ward, E. F. de
"Eli's Rhetorical Question: 1 Sam. 2:25". *JJS* 27 (1976) 117-37. ......
....("Eli's Rhetorical Question")

"Superstition and Judgment: Archaic Methods of Finding a Verdict". *ZAW* 89 (1977) 1-19. ....("Superstition")

Watson, W. G. E.
Classical Hebrew Poetry: A Guide to its Technique. JSOTSS 26. Sheffield: JSOT, 1984. ....(*Classical Hebrew Poetry*)

Weinfeld, M.
"Ancient Near Eastern Patterns in Prophetic Literature". *VT* 27 (1977) 178-95. ....("ANE Patterns")

Deuteronomy and the Deuteronomic School. Oxford: Clarendon, 1972. ....(*Deuteronomy*)

"Literary Creativity". In *The Age of the Monarchies: Culture and Society,* 27-70. Vol. 4/2 of *The World History of the Jewish People.* Ed. by B. Mazar and A. Peli. Jerusalem: Massada, 1979. .... ("Literary Creativity")

Review of F. Crüsemann's *Der Widerstand gegen das Königtum. VT* 31 (1981) 99-108. ....(Review of Crüsemann's *Widerstand*)

Weippert, H.
"Die 'deuteronomistische' Beurteilung der Könige von Israel und Juda und das Problem der Redaktion der Königsbücher". *Bib* 53 (1972) 301-39. ....("Beurteilung")

Weiser, A.
"I Samuel 15".   ZAW 54 (1936) 1-28.   .... ("I Samuel 15")

Samuel: Seine geschichtliche Aufgabe und religiöse Bedeutung.
Göttingen: Vandenhoeck & Ruprecht, 1962.   ....(Samuel)

Weisman, Z.
"Anointing as a Motif in the Making of the Charismatic King".   Bib 57
(1976) 378-98.   ....("Anointing")

Wellhausen, J.
Die Composition des Hexateuchs und der historischen Bücher des Alten
Testaments. 2nd printing with Nachträge. Berlin: Georg Reimer,
1889.   ....(Composition)

Prolegomena zur Geschichte Israels. 3rd ed. Berlin: Georg Reimer,
1886.   ....(Prolegomena)

Der Text der Bücher Samuelis.   Göttingen: Vandenhock & Ruprecht,
1871.   ....(Text)

Wénin, A.
"Le discours de Jonathan à David (1 S 20,12-16) et autres notes (2,20;
9,24; 15,9)".   Bib 64 (1983) 1-19.   ....("Le discours")

Wensinck, A. J.
"Some Semitic Rites of Mourning and Religion".   VAWA n.r. 18/1
(1917) 1-12.   ....("Semitic Rites")

Wentz, H. S.
The Monarchy of Saul: antecedents, 'Deuteronomic' interpretations and
ideology.   Exeter PhD, 1970/71.   ....(Monarchy)

Westermann, C.
Grundformen prophetischer Rede. BEvT 31. München: Chr. Kaiser
Verlag, 1960. [ET: Basic Forms of Prophetic Speech. Trans. by
H. C. White. London: Lutterworth, 1967.] ....(Grundformen)

"נגד ngd hi. mitteilen".   THAT 2: 31-37.   ....("נגד")

Whitelam, K. W.
"The Defence of David".   JSOT 29 (1984) 61-87.   ....("Defence")

The Just King.   Monarchial Judicial Authority in Ancient Israel.
JSOTSS 12.   Sheffield: JSOT, 1979.   ....(Just King)

Wiesner, J.
   Fahren und Reiten in Alteuropa und im alten Orient. AO 38/2-4.
   Leipzig: Hinrichs, 1939. ....(*Fahren und Reiten*)

Wilcoxen, J. A.
   "Narrative". In *Old Testament Form Criticism*, 57-98. Ed. by J. H.
   Hayes. San Antonio: Trinity University Press, 1974. ....
   .... ("Narrative")

Williams, R. J.
   Hebrew Syntax: An Outline. 2nd ed. Toronto: University of Toronto
   Press, 1976. ....(*Hebrew Syntax*)

Williamson, H. G. M.
   1 & 2 Chronicles. NCB. Grand Rapids: Eerdmans, 1982. (*Chronicles*)

Willis, J. T.
   "An Anti-Elide Narrative Tradition from a Prophetic Circle at the
   Ramah Sanctuary". *JBL* 90 (1971) 288-308. ....("Anti-Elide")

   "Cultic Elements in the Story of Samuel's Birth and Dedication". *ST* 26
   (1972) 33-61. ....("Cultic Elements")

Wilson, R. R.
   "Form-critical Investigation of the Prophetic Literature: The Present
   Situation". In SBLSP 1973, 1:100-127. ....
   ....("Form-critical Investigation")

   Prophecy and Society in Ancient Israel. Philadelphia: Fortress, 1980.
   ....(*Prophecy*)

Woude, A. S. van der
   "צבא *ṣābāʾ* Heer". *THAT* 2: 498-507. ....("צבא")

Würthwein, E.
   Der Text des Alten Testaments: Eine Einführung in die Biblia Hebraica.
   4th ed. Stuttgart: Württembergische Bibelanstalt, 1973. ....(*Text*)

Yadin, Y.
   *The Art of Warfare in Biblical Lands: in the Light of Archaeological
   Discovery.* Trans. by M. Pearlman. London: Weidenfeld and
   Nicolson, 1963. ....(*Art of Warfare*)

Yonick, S.
   "The Rejection of Saul: A Study of Sources". *AJBA* 1.4 (1971) 29-50.
   ....("Rejection")

Zakovitch, Y.
"Story Versus History". In *Proceedings of the Eighth World Congress of Jewish Studies (1981)*, 47-60. Jerusalem: Magnes, 1983. ......
....("Story")

Bibliographic Addendum

The following is a brief selection of works that appeared after the essential completion of the foregoing dissertation and that touch upon its general topic in one way or another.

Bettenzoli, G.
"Samuel und das Problem des Königtums: Die Tradition von Gilgal".
BZ 30 (1986) 222-36.

"Samuel und Saul in geschichtlicher und theologischer Auffassung".
ZAW 98 (1986) 338-51.

Cook, A.
"'Fiction' and History in Samuel and Kings". *JSOT* 36 (1986) 27-48.

Dietrich, W.
David, Saul und die Propheten: Das Verhältnis von Religion und Politik nach den prophetischen Überlieferungen vom frühesten Königtum in Israel. Beiträge zur Wissenschaft vom Alten und Neuen Testament 122. Stuttgart: W. Kohlhammer, 1987.

Edelman, D.
"Saul's Battle Against Amaleq (1 Sam. 15)". *JSOT* 35 (1986) 71-83.

Eron Brown, M. H.
The One Whom the Lord Has Chosen: Monarchy in Theocracy, I Samuel 8:1-16:13. Ph.D., Marquette University, 1986.

Gordon, R. P.
1 & 2 Samuel: A Commentary. Exeter: Paternoster, 1986. Grand Rapids: Zondervan, 1988.

"Simplicity of the Highest Cunning: Narrative Art in the Old Testament". *Scottish Bulletin of Evangelical Theology* 6 (1988) 69-80.

Jobling, D. *The Sense of Biblical Narrative II: Structural Analyses in the Hebrew Bible.* JSOTSS 39. Sheffield: JSOT, 1986.

Miscall, P. D.
1 Samuel: A Literary Reading. Bloomington: Indiana University Press; 1986.

Polzin, R.
   "The Monarchy Begins: 1 Samuel 8-10". In *SBL 1987 Seminar Papers*, 120-43. Atlanta: Scholars, 1987.

   Samuel and the Deuteronomist: A Literary Study of the Deuteronomic History. Part 2: 1 Samuel. San Francisco: Harper & Row, 1989.

Praag, H. M. van
   "The Downfall of King Saul: The Neurobiological Consequences of Losing Hope". *Judaism* 35 (1986) 414-28.

Seidl, T.
   "David statt Saul: Göttliche Legitimation und menschliche Kompetenz des Königs als Motive der Redaktion von I Sam 16-18". *ZAW* (1986) 39-55.